MAP INSIDE
BACK COVER

CALIFORNIA

TOP SIGHTS, AUTHENTIC EXPERIENCES

Amy C Balfour, Brett Atkinson, Andrew Bender, Alison Bing,
Cristian Bonetto, Celeste Brash, Jade Bremner, Michael
Grosberg, Ashley Harrell, Mark Johanson,
Andrea Schulte-Peevers, Wendy Yanagihara

Contents

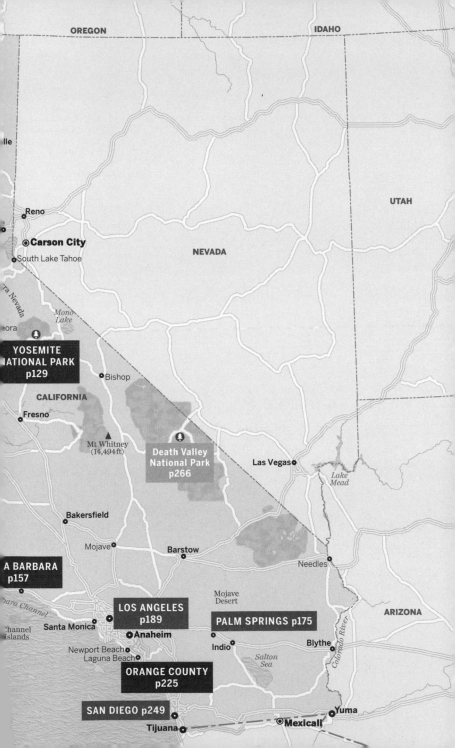

OREGON

IDAHO

UTAH

Reno

◎ **Carson City**
South Lake Tahoe

NEVADA

Sierra Nevada

Mono Lake

ora

**YOSEMITE
NATIONAL PARK
p129**

Bishop

CALIFORNIA

Fresno

▲ Mt Whitney
(14,494ft)

🌲 **Death Valley
National Park
p266**

Las Vegas

*Lake
Mead*

Bakersfield

Mojave

Barstow

Needles

Colorado River

**A BARBARA
p157**

*Mojave
Desert*

ARIZONA

bara Channel

**LOS ANGELES
p189**

PALM SPRINGS p175

*Channel
Islands*

Santa Monica

Anaheim

Indio

Blythe

Newport Beach
Laguna Beach

*Salton
Sea*

**ORANGE COUNTY
p225**

SAN DIEGO p249

Tijuana

◎ **Mexicali**

Yuma

Welcome to California

From misty Northern California redwood forests to sun-kissed Southern California beaches, the Golden State seduces travelers with its striking beauty – not to mention its vastly diverse cultures, fabulous cities and mouth-watering food.

California's natural beauty is instantly captivating. It's no wonder that the Golden State is the home of Hollywood; the state's natural features are wildly dramatic, shaped by tectonic upheavals that threaten to shake it right off the western edge of the continent. Today, old-growth trees, reclaimed rivers and clean beaches are highlights, made possible by passionate environmentalists after 19th-century mining, logging and oil-drilling threatened the state's natural splendors. Eco-pioneers also created the national and state parks that continue to astound visitors today.

California's vibrant cities are showstoppers too, taking on a twinkling magic as the sun sets over the Pacific and lights begin to sparkle across golden hillsides. Lamps illuminate San Diego's Gaslamp Quarter, the Hollywood sign glows as bright as the moon over LA, and Bay Bridge lights welcome San Francisco arrivals with a wink and a shimmy. Consider this your invitation to come out and play, and join the crowds at LA's star-studded nightclubs and movie palaces, San Francisco's historic LGBTIQ+ hot spots and San Diego's brewpubs. It will be a night on the town like no other.

> *Consider this your invitation to come out and play*

Tuolumne Meadows (p139), Yosemite National Park
ADONISVILLANUEVA/GETTY IMAGES ©

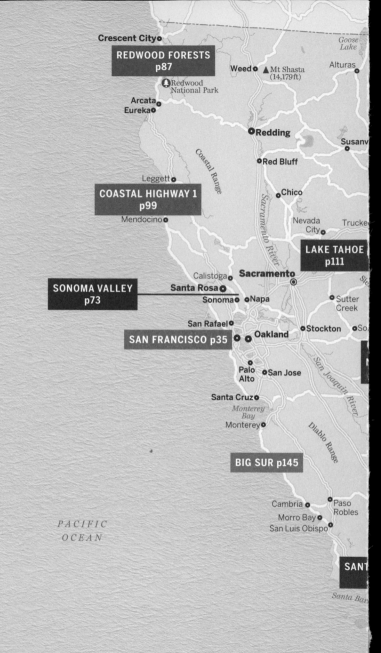

Crescent City

REDWOOD FORESTS p87

Weed ▲ Mt Shasta (14,179ft)

Goose Lake

Alturas

🏛 Redwood National Park

Arcata
Eureka

Redding

Susanv

Red Bluff

Coastal Range

Chico

Leggett

COASTAL HIGHWAY 1 p99

Mendocino

Sacramento River

Nevada City

Trucke

LAKE TAHOE p111

Calistoga **Sacramento**

Santa Rosa

SONOMA VALLEY p73

Sonoma Napa

Sutter Creek

San Rafael

SAN FRANCISCO p35 Oakland

Stockton So

Palo Alto San Jose

San Joaquin River

Santa Cruz

Monterey Bay

Monterey

Diablo Range

BIG SUR p145

Cambria Paso Robles

Morro Bay

San Luis Obispo

*PACIFIC
OCEAN*

SAN

Santa Bar

N 0
0

200 km
100 miles

In Focus

Survival Guide

Wine barrels, Santa Ynez
Valley (p164), Santa Barbara
Wine Country
MCCAIG/GETTY IMAGES ©

We have re-checked every business in this book before publication to ensure that it is still open after 2020's COVID-19 outbreak. However, the economic and social impacts of COVID-19 will continue to be felt long after the outbreak has been contained, and many businesses, services and events referenced in this guide may experience ongoing restrictions. Some businesses may be temporarily closed, have changed their opening hours and services, or require bookings; some unfortunately could have closed permanently. We suggest you check with venues before visiting for the latest information.

Plan Your Trip
California's Top 12

San Francisco

A wonder of food, culture and beauty

As anyone who has ever clung to the side of a cable car can tell you, this city (p35) gives you a heck of a ride, from the Marina's chic waterfront to the edgy Mission District. And just when you think you have a grasp on its charms, you turn another corner to find a brightly painted alleyway mural, a filigreed Victorian roofline or a hidden stairway climbing to bay-view panoramas that will entirely change your outlook. Left: Painted Ladies (p290); Right: Cable car (p40)

1

Sonoma Valley

Sun-drenched hills and vast vineyard landscapes

Locals call it 'Slow-noma,' for unlike fancy Napa, nobody in folksy Sonoma (p73) cares if you drive a clunker and vote Green. Rolling grass-covered hills rise alongside pastoral Hwy 12, peppered by vineyards, family farms and gardens. Amid this bucolic ideal, charming towns lie in the folds of the valley, waiting to host you for a meal or overnight on your jumps between wineries.

2

Redwood Forests

Wander among awe-inspiring giants

Hugging a tree never came so naturally as it does in California's sun-dappled groves of ancient redwoods (p87), the world's tallest trees. These gentle giants are quintessentially Californian: their roots may be shallow, but they hold each other up and reach dizzying heights. Even a short stroll on the soft forest floor beneath these ancient wonders puts the day-to-day troubles of the rest of the world into perspective.

3

Coastal Highway 1

An epic drive into California's wild north

Coastal Highway 1 (p99) is a legendary road trip, twisting and turning a thousand feet above the vast blue Pacific, hugging the skirts of mile-high sea cliffs. Along the route you'll pass picture-perfect little towns and eventually come to salt-washed Mendocino. This legendary bohemian outpost is lined with bookstores, natural food shops and fascinating galleries, all swirled in mists carrying fragrant bursts of lavender, jasmine and weed.

Lake Tahoe

A mountain playground for any season

High in the Sierra Nevada Mountains, this all-seasons adventure base camp centers on the USA's second-deepest lake (p111). In summer, startlingly blue waters invite splashing, kayaking and even scuba diving. Meanwhile, mountain bikers career down single-track runs and hikers climb trails through thick forests to secluded alpine lakes. After dark, retreat to cozy lakefront cottages and toast s'mores in fire pits. When the lake turns into a winter wonderland, gold-medal ski resorts come alive. Stand-up paddleboarding

ENRIQUE AGUIRRE AVES/GETTY IMAGES ©

Yosemite National Park

Feeling so small has never felt so grand

Everything is monumental at Yosemite National Park (p129): thunderous waterfalls tumble over sheer cliffs, granite domes tower overhead and the world's biggest trees cluster in mighty groves. Conservationist John Muir, who lobbied for the creation of the national park, considered Yosemite a great temple, and awe is the natural reaction to these vast wildflower-strewn meadows and valleys carved over millennia. Half Dome (p134)

Big Sur

Explore the dramatic edge of the continent

Waterfalls splash down bluffs in rainbow mists and yurt retreats perch at the edge of redwood forests (p145). Beyond purple-sand beaches and coves lined with California jade, pods of migrating whales dot the sparkling Pacific. But don't forget to turn around: hiding behind these coastal bluffs are hot springs and literary retreats, with California condors circling over the cliffs. Bixby Bridge (p148)

7

Santa Barbara

Seaside elegance and culinary decadence

Waving palm trees, powdery beaches, fishing boats clanking in the harbor – it'd be a travel cliché if it wasn't the plain truth. But Santa Barbara (p157) worked hard to stay so idyllic: downtown was rebuilt in signature Spanish Colonial Revival style after a 1925 earthquake and environmentalists lobbied to clean up the beaches in the '60s and '70s. California's 'Queen of the Missions' is a rare beauty, with its signature red-roofed, whitewashed adobe buildings.

Palm Springs

High-class oasis in the desert

A star-studded oasis in the Mojave since the heyday of old Blue Eyes and his Rat Pack, Palm Springs (p175) draws LA urbanites seeking retro-chic R&R. Follow the lead of A-list stars and hipsters: lounge by the pool at your mid-century-modern hotel, hit the galleries and vintage stores, then refresh with post-sunset cocktails. Too passive? Then explore desert canyons across Native American tribal lands or scramble to a summit in the San Jacinto Mountains, accessed via aerial tramway. Left: Coachella Valley (p180), Joshua Tree National Park; Right: Vintage truck, Palm Springs

/GETTY IMAGES ©

Los Angeles

Glitz, grit and endless sunshine

When you're ready for your close-up, there's only one place to go. The stars come out at night for red-carpet premieres at restored movie palaces, and you too can have your Hollywood moment on the pink-starred Walk of Fame. But beyond the streets of Hollywood, Los Angeles (p189) is flourishing, with a thriving art scene, a newfound vibrancy downtown and ultra-hip beach communities.

Clockwise from top: Hollywood Blvd; Hollywood Walk of Fame (p195); Los Angeles skyline

10

NATALIA MACHEDA/SHUTTERSTOCK ©

Orange County

Classic beaches and a Magic Kingdom

Where orange groves and walnut trees once grew, Walt Disney built his dream world. Since his 'Magic Kingdom' opened in 1955, Disneyland has expanded to neighboring Disney California Adventure to become SoCal's most-visited tourist attraction. For more OC (p225) adventures, hit the world-class beaches; while surfers hang loose in Huntington Beach and yachties mingle in Newport Beach, Laguna Beach (pictured) lures them all with its natural beauty.

PNG STUDIO PHOTOGRAPHY/SHUTTERSTOCK ©

San Diego

Beaches, craft beer and an incredible zoo

San Diego (p249) is known for its golden beaches, but there's another side to this seaside town. Beautiful Balboa Park is the pride of San Diego, with Spanish Colonial and Mission Revival–style architecture along El Prado promenade and more than a dozen art, cultural and science museums. Glimpse exotic wildlife and ride the 'Skyfari' aerial tram at San Diego's world-famous zoo, or wander the streets of its historic old town. Flamingoes, San Diego Zoo (p253)

Need to Know

When to Go

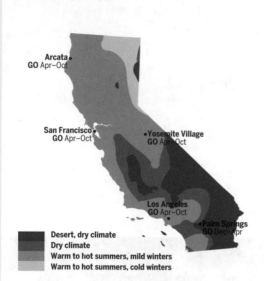

Arcata
GO Apr–Oct

San Francisco
GO Apr–Oct

Yosemite Village
GO Apr–Oct

Los Angeles
GO Apr–Oct

Palm Springs
GO Dec–Apr

Desert, dry climate
Dry climate
Warm to hot summers, mild winters
Warm to hot summers, cold winters

High Season (Jun–Aug)

○ Accommodations prices rise 50% to 100% on average; major holidays are even busier and more expensive.

○ Summer is low season in the desert, where temperatures exceed 100°F (38°C).

Shoulder (Apr–May & Sep–Oct)

○ Crowds and prices drop, especially on the coast and in the mountains.

○ Mild temperatures and sunny, cloudless days; typically wetter in spring, drier in autumn.

Low Season (Nov–Mar)

○ Accommodations rates lowest along the coast.

○ Chilly temperatures, frequent rainstorms and heavy snow in the mountains.

○ Winter is peak season in SoCal's desert regions.

Currency
US dollar ($)

Language
English

Visas
Generally not required for stays of 90 days or less for citizens of Visa Waiver Program (VWP) countries with ESTA approval (https://esta.cbp.dhs.gov) – apply online at least 72 hours in advance.

Money
ATMs widely available. Credit cards required for car and hotel reservations. Checks are rarely accepted. Tipping is customary, not optional.

Cell Phones
Foreign GSM multiband phones will work in the USA. Prepaid cell phones are widely available. Coverage can be spotty in remote areas.

Time
Pacific Standard Time (UTC minus eight hours). Clocks are set one hour ahead during Daylight Saving Time (DST), from the second Sunday in March until the first Sunday in November.

Daily Costs

Budget: Less than $100

- Hostel dorm beds: $30–70
- Takeout meal: $7–12

Midrange: $100–200

- Motel or hotel double room: $100–150
- Sit-down restaurant meal: $20–40

Top End: More than $300

- Upscale hotel or beach resort room: from $250
- Three-course meal in top restaurant excluding drinks: $80–120

Useful Websites

Visit California (www.visitcalifornia.com) Multilingual trip-planning guides.

Lonely Planet (www.lonelyplanet.com/usa/california) Destination information, hotel bookings, traveler forum and more.

LA Times Travel (www.latimes.com/travel) Travel news, deals and blogs.

California State Parks (www.parks.ca.gov) Outdoor activities and camping.

CalTrans (www.dot.ca.gov) Current highway conditions.

Opening Hours

Shops and restaurants may close earlier and on additional days during the winter off-season (November to March). Otherwise, standard opening hours are as follows:

Banks 9am–6pm Monday to Friday, some 9am–1pm or later Saturday

Bars 5pm–2am daily

Clubs 10pm–4am Thursday to Saturday

Restaurants 7:30am–10am, 11:30am–2pm and 5pm–9pm daily, some open later Friday and Saturday

Shops 10am–6pm Monday to Saturday, noon–5pm Sunday (malls open later)

Supermarkets 8am–9pm or 10pm daily, some 24 hours

Arriving in California

Los Angeles International Airport (p310) Taxis to most destinations ($30 to $50) take 30 minutes to one hour; fares for ride-hailing companies are cheaper. Door-to-door shuttles ($15 to $20) operate 24 hours. FlyAway bus ($9.75) runs to Downtown LA. Free shuttles connect with LAX City Bus Center and Metro Rail station.

San Francisco International Airport (p310) Taxis into the city ($45 to $65) take 25 to 50 minutes; fares for ride-hailing companies are cheaper. Door-to-door shuttles (from $19) operate 24 hours. BART trains ($9.65, 30 minutes) serve the airport, running from 5:30am (later on weekends) to midnight daily.

Getting Around

Most people drive themselves around California. You can also fly (it's expensive) or take cheaper long-distance buses or scenic trains. In cities, when distances are too far to walk, hop aboard buses, trains, streetcars, cable cars or trolleys, or grab a taxi or a rideshare.

Car Metro-area traffic can be nightmarish, especially during weekday commuter rush hours (roughly 6am to 10am and 3pm to 7pm). City parking is often an expensive hassle.

Train The fastest way to get around the San Francisco Bay Area and LA, but lines don't go everywhere. Pricier regional and long-distance Amtrak trains scenically connect some destinations.

Bus Usually the cheapest and slowest option, but with extensive metro-area networks. Inter-city, regional and long-distance Greyhound routes are limited and more expensive.

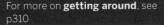

For more on **getting around**, see p310

Plan Your Trip
Hot Spots for...

RONNIE CHUA/SHUTTERSTOCK ©

Incredible Food

New cravings have been invented at California's cultural crossroads for 200 years, so get set for the latest trends, from Peking duck empanadas to vegan soul food.

San Francisco
Global inspirations and culinary trends make San Francisco a foodie heaven.

Ferry Building
Sustainable food and a farmers market (p47; pictured).

Sonoma Valley
Global acclaim in the 1970s bolstered local cheesemakers and restaurateurs.

Cafe La Haye
All produce sourced from within 60 miles (p83).

Los Angeles
Within LA's famous sprawl is a melting pot of food from around the world.

Mariscos 4 Vientos
Spectacular fried shrimp tacos in East LA (p216).

ROBERT HARDING/500PX ©

National & State Parks

Jagged mountain peaks, high-country meadows, desert sand dunes and wind-tossed offshore islands – California's wild diversity is astonishing.

Yosemite National Park
Ascend the Sierra Nevada, where waterfalls tumble into glacier-carved valleys and wildflowers bloom.

Glacier Point
Hike or drive up to this lookout (p132) for sunset.

Redwood Forests
Get lost ambling among ancient groves of the world's tallest trees on the foggy North Coast (pictured).

Avenue of the Giants
Drive beneath the boughs of old-growth redwoods (p92).

Death Valley National Park
Uncover secret pockets of life in this austere desert landscape, peppered with geological oddities.

Artists Drive
A one-way scenic loop drive (p267).

Beaches

If your dream vacation involves bronzing on the beach, digging in the sand and paddling in the Pacific, head to Southern California (SoCal).

KESTERHU/SHUTTERSTOCK ©

Orange County
When it comes to beautiful beaches (and some excellent surf), OC enjoys a burden of riches.

Huntington City Beach
Some of the best swimming (p241; pictured) on the coast.

Santa Barbara
This classy beach town is the perfect destination for beachcombers, sunbathers and surfers alike.

Arroyo Burro Beach
Sandy gem known locally as Hendry's Beach (p163).

San Diego
California's southernmost beach town has an excellent surf scene and good weather year-round.

Mission & Pacific Beaches
Crowded, but the people-watching is great (p256).

Museums & Galleries

Who says California only has pop culture? Break up your beach days with top-notch art galleries, science exhibits, planetariums, museums and more.

CORY WOODRUFF/SHUTTERSTOCK ©

San Francisco
Home to a collection of world-class destinations that make for an excellent week of museum hopping.

SFMOMA
New media and photography shine at SFMOMA (p53).

Los Angeles
A thriving art and architecture scene has brought tourists and culture back to downtown LA.

LA County Museum of Art
The largest art musuem (p208) in the western US.

San Diego
San Diego has a lot of culture on offer, including San Diego Museum of Art (pictured).

Balboa Park Museums
First-rate art, history and science museums (p253).

Plan Your Trip
Essential California

Activities

California is an all-seasons outdoor playground. Hike among desert wildflowers in spring, dive into the Pacific in summer, mountain bike through fall foliage and ski down wintry mountain slopes. Once California gets your adrenaline pumping, you'll also be ready to hang glide off ocean bluffs, scuba past coastal shipwrecks, scale sheer granite cliffs or white-water raft the rapids. You'll also find that every seaside town has a number of excursions to get you out on and in the water, from guided whale-watching to extended surf tours.

Shopping

It doesn't matter where you go in California, especially along the coast: there's a rack of haute couture, an outlet-mall bargain or a vintage find begging to be stashed in your suitcase. Los Angeles has more star-worthy boutiques than any other place in the state, while San Francisco is more about eclectic indie flavor. If you want incredible vintage gear, head to Palm Springs, where thrift-store shoppers seek retro 20th-century gems, and there's outlet shopping, too.

Eating

As you graze the Golden State, you'll often want to compliment the chef – and that chef will pass it on to the local farmers, fishers, ranchers, winemakers and artisan food producers who make their menu possible. California cuisine is a team effort that changes with every season – and it's changed the way the world eats. Every region will have its specialty, but the secret to so many of California's mind-blowing menus is that big swath of green in the middle of the state, the Central Valley. This incredibly fertile area feeds the nation, and brings a constant supply of fresh ingredients to the table.

JUANMONINO/GETTY IMAGES ©

Drinking & Nightlife

Go VIP all the way at California's chic city nightclubs – or skip the velvet ropes and dress codes, and hit the state's come-as-you-are watering holes. LA has glam Hollywood clubs and a thriving scene in WeHo, while San Francisco is all about eclectic lounges, fancy mixology and the chance to party in the famous LGBTIQ+ enclave of the Castro. If you're out on the town in San Diego, put on your best flip-flops for surfer bars, or your walking shoes for pub crawls through the Gaslamp Quarter, downtown's historic red-light district.

Entertainment

California – perhaps LA specifically – may be the entertainment capital of the world, but that's only the opening act. Aside from world-class venues in thriving music capitals such as San Francisco and LA, every little town you pass is likely to have a regional playhouse or little indie movie theater. California's great year-round

★ Best California Cuisine

Al's Place (p66)

Gjusta (p220)

Juniper & Ivy (p262)

Rich Table (p67)

Bouchon (p172)

weather also makes it home to some of the nation's most incredible festivals, from whale-watching celebrations to Coachella Valley Music & Arts Festival. Then there's live sports: California has more professional sports teams than any other state, and loyalties to NBA basketball, NFL football and major-league baseball teams run deep.

From left: Kitesurfing, Arroyo Burro Beach County Park (p163); Clam chowder, Fisherman's Wharf (p52), San Francisco

Plan Your Trip
Month by Month

January

January is the wettest month in California and a slow time for coastal travel. Mountain ski resorts and Southern California deserts hit their stride.

❧ Rose Bowl & Parade

The famous New Year's parade held before the Tournament of Roses college football game draws more than 700,000 spectators to the LA suburb of Pasadena.

❧ Lunar New Year

Firecrackers, parades, lion dances and Chinatown night markets usher in the lunar new year, falling in late January or early February. California's biggest parade happens in San Francisco.

February

As California sunshine breaks through the drizzle, skiers hit the slopes in T-shirts and wildflowers bloom.

☬ Wildlife-Watching

February is prime time for spotting whales offshore, monarch butterflies wintering in California groves, and elephant seals nursing pups in Central Coast dunes.

☆ Academy Awards

Hollywood rolls out the red carpet for movie-star entrances on Oscar night at the Dolby Theatre.

March

As ski season winds down, the beaches warm up – just in time for spring break.

❧ Mendocino Coast Whale Festivals

Mendocino, Fort Bragg and nearby towns toast the whale migration with wining and dining, art shows and naturalist-guided walks and talks.

Above: Penn State Blue Band, Rose Bowl & Parade

FREDERICK M. BROWN/GETTY IMAGES ©

CHRISTOPHER POLK/GETTY IMAGES FOR COACHELLA ©

✿ Festival of the Swallows

After wintering in South America, the swallows return to Mission San Juan Capistrano in Orange County around March 19 – and the historic mission town celebrates its Spanish and Mexican heritage.

April

Wildflower season peaks in the high desert.

☆ Coachella Valley Music & Arts Festival

Headliners, indie rockers, rappers and cult DJs converge outside Palm Springs for a three-day musical extravaganza held over two weekends in mid-April.

☆ San Francisco International Film Festival

The nation's oldest film festival lights up San Francisco nights with star-studded US premieres of hundreds of films from around the globe.

★ Best Festivals

Rose Bowl & Parade, January

Coachella Music & Arts Festival, April

Pride Month, June

Comic-Con International, July

Monterey Jazz Festival, September

May

Weather starts to heat up statewide. Memorial Day holiday weekend marks the official start of summer.

⚐ Bay to Breakers

On the third Sunday in May, costumed joggers, inebriated idlers and renegade streakers dash from San Francisco's Embarcadero to Ocean Beach.

Above: Coachella Valley Music & Arts Festival

🏃 Kinetic Grand Championship

Artists spend months preparing for this 'triathlon of the art world,' inventing outlandish human-powered and self-propelled sculptural contraptions to cover 42 miles from Arcata to Ferndale.

June

Once school lets out for the summer, everyone heads to California beaches. Mountain resorts offer cool escapes, but the deserts are just too darn hot.

🎊 Pride Month

California celebrates LGBT pride with costumed parades, film fests, marches and street parties. SF Pride sets the global standard, with more than a million people.

July

California's campgrounds, beaches and theme parks hit peak popularity, especially on the July 4 holiday.

☆ Comic-Con International

The nation's biggest annual convention of comic-book fans, pop-culture collectors, and sci-fi and anime devotees brings costumed madness to San Diego.

August

School summer vacations may be over, but beaches and parks are still packed.

🎊 Old Spanish Days Fiesta

Santa Barbara shows off its early Spanish, Mexican and American *rancho* roots with parades, rodeo events, arts-and-crafts, live music and dance.

September

Summer's last hurrah is Labor Day holiday weekend, which is busy almost everywhere in California (except hot SoCal deserts).

☆ Monterey Jazz Festival

Old-school jazz cats, cross-cultural sensations and fusion rebels all line up to play the West Coast's legendary jazz festival, held on the Central Coast.

🎊 Tall Ships Festival

The West Coast's biggest gathering of historical tall ships happens at Dana Point in Orange County.

October

Fog season concludes in Northern California and coastal weather is warm and sunny.

☆ Hardly Strictly Bluegrass

More than half a million people converge for free outdoor concerts in Golden Gate Park during the first weekend in October.

🍷 Vineyard Festivals

All month long, wine countries celebrate bringing in the vineyard harvest with food-and-wine events, harvest fairs, barrel tastings and grape-stomping 'crush' parties.

🎊 Halloween

Hauntings and fright-fests take place all month at theme parks. On the 31st, hundreds of thousands of revelers descend on West Hollywood for all-day partying and over-the-top costumes.

November

Temperatures drop statewide, the first raindrops fall along the coast and, with any luck, ski season begins in the mountains.

🎊 Día de los Muertos

Mexican communities, especially in San Francisco, LA and San Diego, honor deceased relatives on November 2 with costumed parades, sugar skulls, graveyard picnics, candlelight processions and fabulous altars.

December

As winter rains reach coastal areas, SoCal's sunny, dry deserts draw travelers.

☉ Parade of Lights

Deck the decks with boughs of holly: boats dressed with holiday cheer and twinkling lights float through coastal California harbors, including Orange County's Newport Beach and San Diego.

Plan Your Trip
Plan Your Trip
Get Inspired

Read

On the Road (Jack Kerouac; 1957) The epic road trip that inspired free spirits everywhere to come to California.

My California: Journeys by Great Writers (Angel City Press; 2004) Insightful stories by California chroniclers.

Where I Was From (Joan Didion; 2003) California-born essayist shatters palm-fringed fantasies.

If They Come in the Morning (Angela Davis; 1971) Chronicles the Black Power movement, collected by one of its leaders.

Hollywood Babylon (Kenneth Anger; 1959) The tell-all book that exposed the scandals of Hollywood.

Watch

Maltese Falcon (1941) Humphrey Bogart as a San Francisco private eye.

Sunset Boulevard (1950) The classic bonfire of Hollywood vanities.

Blade Runner (1982) Ridley Scott's futuristic cyberpunk vision of LA.

LA Confidential (1997) Neo-noir tale of corruption and murder in 1950s LA.

Dogtown and Z-Boys (2001) Story of the teenage SoCal misfits who made skateboarding cool.

Milk (2008) Spotlights first openly gay man to hold a major US political office.

Once Upon a Time... in Hollywood (2019) Quentin Tarantino's ode to late 1960s Hollywood.

Listen

California Girls (Beach Boys; 1965) Early California surf sounds.

California Dreaming (The Mamas & the Papas; 1966) Counterculture folk rock hit.

California (Joni Mitchell; 1971) Haunting ballad.

California Sun (Ramones; 1977) The definitive cover version.

California Love (2Pac; 1996) Comeback single featuring Dr Dre.

Californication (Red Hot Chili Peppers; 1999) Pop-punk portmanteau.

California (Phantom Planet; 2002) Theme song from *The OC*.

California Gurls (Katy Perry; 2010) Pop diva meets rapper Snoop Dogg.

Above: Death Valley National Park (p266)

Plan Your Trip
Five-Day Itineraries

Bay Area Escape

Explore the best of Northern California with a romp through San Francisco, a Sonoma Valley stopover and a quick escape up the coast. This is all about great museums and incredible drives, electric nightlife and world-class food and wine.

② Sonoma Valley (p73) Enjoy laid-back wineries and the Sonoma town plaza, a hotspot for food, art and shopping.
🚗 1 hr to Bodega Bay

Bodega Bay (p106) Follow Hwy 12 northwest through Sonoma Valley to coastal hiking, tide-pooling and views of harbor seals. ③

San Francisco (p35) Savor international fare at the Ferry Building, ride a cable car, and explore Golden Gate Park. 🚗 1 hr to Sonoma Valley ①

Huntington Beach
(p240) Watch daredevils barreling through tubes, hit the surfing museum, soak up rays and build a beach bonfire.
🚗 30 mins to Laguna Beach

① ②

Laguna Beach (p236)
In dreamy Laguna the coast holds public art, a divers' cove and sunbathing spots.
🚗 1 hr 30 mins to Mission Beach

SoCal Beaches

All-star attractions, bodacious beaches and fresh seafood are yours to discover on this Southern California sojourn, covering 100 miles of sun, sand and surf. Start here if you've always wanted to live in a Beach Boys song.

Mission Beach & Pacific Beach (p256)
Home to an ocean walk, amusement park and sun worshippers galore, San Diego's most vibrant beaches are a blast.
③

①

②

Plan Your Trip
10-Day Itinerary

SF to LA

You've got 10 days to settle California's longest-running debate: which is California's better half, north or south? Try not to be distracted by the dazzling ocean views as you navigate the glorious 450-mile coastal drive stretching from the spectacular north to the sunny south.

San Francisco (p35) One-of-a-kind attractions include Alcatraz, the Golden Gate Bridge, Coit Tower and Lombard Street. 🚗 2 hrs to Monterey

1

Monterey (p150) Hwy 1 leads to Monterey and its mesmerizing aquarium, housed in a converted sardine cannery. 🚗 30 mins to Big Sur

2

3

Hearst Castle (p154) Architect Julia Morgan designed Hearst Castle for early-20th-century newspaper magnate William Randolph Hearst. 🚗 2½ hrs to Santa Barbara

Big Sur (p145) Continue south on Hwy 1 to photogenic Bixby Bridge then stop for clifftop views, waterfalls, redwoods and purple sand. 🚗 30 mins to Hearst Castle

4

Malibu (p211) Beach-y fun and chic style collide in celeb friendly Malibu, home to the Getty Villa museum and gardens. 🚗 30 mins to Santa Monica

5

Santa Babara (p157) A Spanish Colonial-style downtown, a historic mission, great seafood plus scenic wineries nearby. 🚗 1¼ hrs to Malibu

6 **7**

Los Angeles (p189) Sit back for the final 18 miles to Santa Monica, where a Ferris wheel awaits on the pier. Fun bike path too.

Plan Your Trip
Two-Week Itinerary

California Classics

Cover the Golden State's greatest hits on this grand tour. Start amid giant redwoods, seek out the bridge in foggy San Francisco, take in the grand views of Yosemite and get up close and personal with some exotic friends in San Diego.

San Francisco (p35) Enjoy museums, foodie spots, Golden Gate Bridge attractions and the buzzy energy of the city.
🚗 4 hrs to Yosemite Valley

Yosemite National Park (p129) Half Dome, El Capitan and Yosemite Falls are showstoppers in Yosemite Valley.
🚗 5½ hrs to Los Angeles

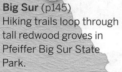

❶ Big Sur (p145) Hiking trails loop through tall redwood groves in Pfeiffer Big Sur State Park.
🚗 2¾ hrs to San Francisco

Palm Springs & Joshua Tree National Park (p175) Explore the mid-century modern charms of Palm Springs then check out desert flora in the national park.
🚗 2¼ hrs to Disneyland

Los Angeles (p189) Take a studio tour, appreciate art at the Broad and Getty Museums and relax at the beach. 🚗 1¾ hrs to Palm Springs

Disneyland (p228) Space Mountain is a highlight along with twirling in teacups and watching nightly fireworks. 🚗 1½ hrs to San Diego

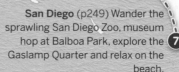

San Diego (p249) Wander the sprawling San Diego Zoo, museum hop at Balboa Park, explore the Gaslamp Quarter and relax on the beach.

Plan Your Trip
Family Travel

The Lowdown

California is a tailor-made destination for family travel. The kids will be begging to go to theme parks, and teens to celebrity hot spots. And, of course, there's the great outdoors – from sunny beaches shaded by palm trees to misty redwood forests to four-seasons mountain playgrounds. Really, there's not too much to worry about when traveling in California with your kids...as long as you keep them covered in sunblock.

Theme Parks

California is theme park heaven, with Disneyland Resort (p228) topping almost every family's must-do list.

Note that some theme park rides may have minimum-height requirements, so let younger kids know about this in advance to avoid disappointment and tears.

National & State Parks

Ask at national and state park visitor centers about family-friendly, ranger-led activities and self-guided 'Junior Ranger' programs, in which kids earn themselves a badge after completing an activity booklet.

Accommodations

Rule one: if you're traveling with kids, always mention it when making reservations. At a few places, notably B&Bs, you may have a hard time if you show up with little ones. When booking, be sure to request the specific room type you want, although requests often aren't guaranteed.

Motels and hotels typically have rooms with two beds or an extra sofa bed. They also may have rollaway beds or cots, usually available for a surcharge (request these when making reservations). Some offer 'kids stay free' promotions, which may apply only if no extra bedding is required.

KEN WOLTER/SHUTTERSTOCK ©

Dining Out

It's fine to bring kids along to most restaurants, except top-end places. Casual restaurants usually have high chairs and children's menus and break out paper place mats and crayons for drawing. At theme parks, pack a cooler in the car and have a picnic in the parking lot to save money. On the road many supermarkets have wholesome, ready-to-eat takeout dishes.

Need to Know

Baby supplies Baby food, infant formula, disposable diapers and other necessities are widely sold at supermarkets and pharmacies.

Car seats Any child under the age of six or weighing less than 60lb must be buckled up in the car's back seat in a child or infant safety seat – book ahead when renting a car. Bring in-car distractions for inevitable traffic delays.

Discounts Children's discounts are available for everything from museum admission and movie

★ Best Museums

Exploratorium (p52)
New Children's Museum (p257)
La Brea Tar Pits & Museum (p209)
California Academy of Sciences (p61)
Griffith Observatory (p196)

tickets to bus fares. The definition of a 'child' varies – from 'under 18' to age six.

Toilets Many public toilets have a baby-changing table, while private gender-neutral 'family' bathrooms may be available at airports, museums etc.

From left: California Academy of Sciences (p61); Griffith Observatory (p196), designed by architect John C. Austin

Bay Bridge

SAN FRANCISCO

Rincon Park

Financial District

Nob Hill (p87)

Chinatown (p48)

San Francisco

Grab your coat and a handful of glitter, and enter the land of fog and fabulousness. So long, inhibitions; hello, San Francisco. Consider permission permanently granted to be outlandish: other towns may surprise you, but in San Francisco you will surprise yourself. Good times and social revolutions tend to start here, from manic gold rushes to blissful hippie be-ins. If there's a skateboard move yet to be busted, a technology still unimagined, a poem left unspoken or a green scheme untested, chances are it's about to happen here. Yes, right now. This town has lost almost everything in earthquakes and dot-com gambles, but never its nerve.

San Francisco in Two Days

On day one, hop aboard the Powell-Mason cable car and hold on for hills and thrills. Have lunch in the **Ferry Building** (p47), then catch your prebooked ferry to spooky **Alcatraz** (p113). On day two, get the camera ready for **Golden Gate Bridge** (p107) vistas. Make a trip across the spanner, or visit Golden Gate Park for views from **de Young Museum** (p61).

San Francisco in Four Days

Start day three in **Chinatown** (p48). Hit **Fisherman's Wharf** (p52) in the afternoon and take the **Powell-Hyde cable car** past zigzagging **Lombard Street** (p57) to **Maritime National Historical Park** (p52). Begin day four ogling **Balmy Alley** (p62) in the Mission. Explore the hippie-historic **Haight** (p59), and end the evening with live music at **Bottom of the Hill** (p71) or drinks at **Trick Dog** (p69).

Previous page: The Golden Gate Bridge at sunset (p38)
BLUEJAYPHOTO/GETTY IMAGES ©

MAP IMAGES CLOCKWISE FROM TOP: JAVEN/SHUTTERSTOCK ©, MICHAEL URMANN/SHUTTERSTOCK ©, LUCIANO MORTULA - LGM/SHUTTERSTOCK ©, JEJIM/GETTY IMAGES ©, JU.HROZIAN/SHUTTERSTOCK ©, I AND S WALKER/SHUTTERSTOCK ©, WONDERLUSTPICSTRAVEL/SHUTTERSTOCK ©, KARLA A DESART/SHUTTERSTOCK ©

Map

Nob Hill, Russian Hill & Fillmore
These hills are the stomping grounds of millionaires and urban hikers.

North Beach & Chinatown
Wild parrots circle over Italian cafes and bohemian bars, and historic back alleys are filled with temple incense.

Alcatraz

Oakland International ✈ (14mi)

Golden Gate National Recreation Area

Ferry Building

The Marina, Fisherman's Wharf & the Piers
The waterfront is a major attraction for sea-lion antics and getaways to and from Alcatraz.

PACIFIC OCEAN

San Francisco Bay

Golden Gate Bridge

Downtown, Civic Center & SoMa
All the urban amenities are here: art galleries, swanky hotels, first-run theaters, malls and XXX cinemas.

Chinatown

Presidio National Park

The Haight, NoPa & Hayes Valley
Hippie idealism lives in the Haight, with street musicians, anarchist comic books and psychedelic murals galore.

Cable Cars

CalTrain Depot

The Mission & Potrero Hill
With a book in one hand and a burrito in the other, laze amid murals, sunshine and the usual crowd of filmmakers, techies, grocers, skaters and novelists.

Golden Gate Park & the Avenues
Hardcore surfers and gourmet adventurers meet in this totally chill global village.

Golden Gate Park

The Castro & Noe Valley
Rainbow flags wave their welcome in the Castro, while megastrollers brake for bakeries and boutiques in Noe Valley.

San Francisco International ✈ (9mi)

San Francisco Map (p54)
The Mission & Potrero Hill Map (p58)
The Haight & Golden Gate Park Map (p60)

0   2   4 km
0   2 mile

Haight & Ashbury (p59)

Arriving in San Francisco

San Francisco Airport (SFO) Fast rides to downtown San Francisco on Bay Area Rapid Transit (BART) cost $9.65; door-to-door shuttle vans cost $19 to $23, plus tip; express bus fare to Temporary Transbay Terminal is $2.50 via SamTrans; taxis cost $45 to $60, plus tip.

Oakland International Airport (OAK) Catch BART from the airport to downtown SF ($10.95); take a shared van to downtown San Francisco for $35 to $45; or pay $40 to $80 for a rideshare or taxi to San Francisco destinations.

Sleeping

San Francisco hotel rates are among the world's highest. Plan ahead – well ahead – and grab bargains when you see them. Given the choice, San Francisco's boutique properties beat chains for a sense of place – but take what you can get at a price you can afford.

The Golden Gate Bridge at dusk

SETH K. HUGHES/GETTY IMAGES ©

Golden Gate Bridge

The city's most spectacular icon towers 80 stories above the roiling waters of the Golden Gate, the narrow entrance to San Francisco Bay. When the fog clears it reveals magnificent views.

Great For...

☑ Don't Miss

The steel-model 'Test Tower', a 1933 scale model at Golden Gate Bridge Pavilion Visitor Center.

Other suspension bridges boast impressive engineering, but none can touch the Golden Gate Bridge for showmanship. On sunny days, it transfixes crowds with its radiant glow – thanks to 25 daredevil painters, who reapply 1000 gallons of International Orange paint weekly.

Construction

Nobody thought it could happen. Not until the early 1920s did the City of San Francisco seriously investigate building a bridge over the treacherous, windblown strait. The War Department owned the land on both sides and didn't want to take chances with ships: safety and solidity were its goals, and naval officials preferred a hulking concrete span, painted with caution-yellow stripes, over the soaring art deco design of architects Gertrude and Irving Murrow and engineer Joseph B Strauss.

The Golden Gate Bridge at night

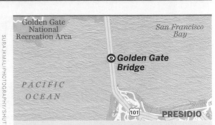

❶ Need to Know

📠toll information 877-229-8655; www.
goldengatebridge.org/visitors; Hwy 101;
northbound free, southbound $5-8; 🚌28, all
Golden Gate Transit buses

✕ Take a Break

Off the Grid (📞415-339-5888; www.
offthegridsf.com; 2 Marina Blvd, Fort Mason
Center; items $6-15; ⏱5-10pm Fri Mar-Oct;
🚻; 🚌22, 28) food trucks and pop-up
cubes circle their wagons Friday nights
at Fort Mason Center, and 11am to 4pm
Sunday for Picnic at the Presidio on the
Main Post lawn.

★ Top Tip

Stop at the **Golden Gate Bridge
Pavilion Visitor Center** (www.ggnpc.org;
Golden Gate Bridge toll plaza; ⏱9am-6pm).

Luckily, however, the green light was giv-
en to the counter-proposal by Strauss and
the Murrows for a subtler suspension span,
which was economic in form and harmo-
nized with the natural environment. Before
the War Department could insist on an
eyesore, laborers dove into the treacherous
riptides of the bay and got the bridge under
way in 1933. Just four years later workers
balancing atop swaying cables completed
what was then the world's longest suspension bridge – nearly 2 miles long, with
746ft suspension towers, higher than any
construction west of New York.

Views of the Bridge

As far as best views go, cinema buffs
believe Hitchcock had it right: seen from
below at Fort Point, the 1937 bridge induces
a thrilling case of *Vertigo*. Fog aficionados
prefer the north-end lookout at Marin's
Vista Point, to watch gusts billow through
bridge cables like dry ice at a Kiss concert.

To see both sides of the debate, hike or
bike the 1.7-mile span. Muni bus 28 runs
to the parking lot, and pedestrians and
cyclists can cross the bridge on sidewalks.

Crossing the Bridge

Pedestrians take the eastern sidewalk.
Dress warmly! From the parking area and
bus stop (off Lincoln Blvd), a pathway leads
past the toll plaza, then it's 1.7 miles across.
If the 3.4-mile round-trip seems too much,
take a bus to the north side via Golden Gate
Transit, then walk back.

By bicycle, from the toll-plaza parking area
ride toward the Roundhouse, then follow
signs to the western sidewalk, reserved for
bikes only.

Powell-Mason Cable Car

Cable Cars

Offering million-dollar vistas and the promise of adventure, cable cars are one of the finest ways to explore San Francisco. These ratcheting wonders bring you lurching into the heart of the city's best neighborhoods.

Today the cable car seems more like a steampunk carnival ride than modern transport, but Andrew Hallidie's 1873 contraptions have held up miraculously well on San Francisco's giddy slopes, and they remain a reliable, low-impact way to conquer San Francisco's highest hills.

Powell-Hyde Cable Car

The ascent up Nob Hill feels like the world's longest roller-coaster climb – but on the Powell-Hyde cable car, the biggest thrills are still ahead. This cable car bobs up and down hills, with the Golden Gate Bridge popping in and out of view on Russian Hill. Hop off the cable car at Lombard St to walk the zigzagging route to North Beach. Otherwise, stop and smell the roses along stairway walks to shady Macondray Lane and blooming Ina Coolbrith Park.

Great For...

☑ **Don't Miss**

The view of twisty Lombard St on the Powell-Hyde line.

California Street Cable Car

LUCIANO MORTULA - LGM/SHUTTERSTOCK ©

erators leaping out, gripping the chassis of each trolley and slowly turning the car atop a revolving wooden platform. Cable cars can't reverse, so they need to be turned around by hand here at the **terminus** (Map p54; www.sfmta.com; cnr Powell & Market Sts; 🚠Powell-Mason, Mason-Hyde, Ⓜ Powell, Ⓑ Powell) of the Powell St lines. Riders queue up midmorning to early evening here to secure a seat, with raucous street performers and doomsday preachers on the sidelines as entertainment.

Powell-Mason Cable Car

The Powell-Hyde line may have multimillion-dollar vistas, but the Powell-Mason line has more culture. The route cuts through North Beach at Washington Sq, where you're surrounded by alleyways named after Beat poets. Near Washington Sq, jump off early for delicious focaccia bread from **Liguria Bakery** (Map p54; ☏415-421-3786; 1700 Stockton St; focaccia $4-6; ⊗8am-2pm Tue-Fri, from 7am Sat, 7am-noon Sun; 🚼🚻; 🚌8, 30, 39, 41, 45 ⓂT). The terminus at Bay and Taylor Sts is handy for visiting two truly riveting attractions: the USS *Pampanito* and the Musée Mécanique.

Powell Street Cable Car Turnaround

Peek through the passenger queue at Powell and Market Sts to spot cable-car op-

California Street Cable Car

History buffs and crowd-shy visitors prefer San Francisco's oldest cable-car line: the California St cable car, in operation since 1878. This divine ride west heads through Chinatown past Old St Mary's Cathedral and climbs Nob Hill to Grace Cathedral. Hop off at Polk St for Swan Oyster Depot (p65), tempting boutiques and cocktail bars. The Van Ness Ave terminus is a few blocks west of Alta Plaza and Lafayette Parks, which are both ringed by stately Victorians.

Alcatraz

Over the decades Alcatraz has been the nation's first military prison, a forbidding maximum-security penitentiary and disputed territory between Native American activists and the FBI.

Early History

It all started innocently enough back in 1775, when Spanish lieutenant Juan Manuel de Ayala sailed the *San Carlos* past the 22-acre island that he called Isla de Alcatraces (Isle of the Pelicans). In 1859 a new post on Alcatraz became the first US West Coast fort and it soon proved handy as a holding pen for Civil War deserters, insubordinates and the court-martialed.

By 1902 the four cell blocks of wooden cages were rotting, unsanitary and ill-equipped for the influx of US soldiers convicted of war crimes in the Philippines that arrived that year. The army began building a new concrete military prison in 1909, but upkeep was expensive and the US soon had other things to worry about: WWI, financial ruin and flappers.

Great For...

☑ **Don't Miss**

The feeling of isolation in the chilling D-Block solitary-confinement cells.

ⓘ Need to Know

Alcatraz Cruises 415-981-7625; www.
alcatrazcruises.com; tours adult/child 5-11yr
day $39.90/24.40, night $47.30/28, behind the
scenes $92.30 (over 12yr only); call center
8am-7pm, ferries depart Pier 33 half-hourly
8:45am-3:50pm, night tours 5:55pm & 6:30pm

✕ Take a Break

Most people spend three to four hours;
bring lunch to linger longer. Note: eating
is allowed only at the ferry dock. There's
limited food on the island.

★ Top Tip

Find out if there's a site-specific art
installation during your visit, and plan
to see it.

Inmates, Escape & Abandonment

In 1934 the Federal Bureau of Prisons took
over Alcatraz as a prominent showcase for
its crime-fighting efforts. The Rock aver-
aged only 264 inmates, but its roster read
like a list of America's Most Wanted. A-list
criminals doing time on Alcatraz included
Chicago crime boss Al 'Scarface' Capone,
dapper kidnapper George 'Machine Gun'
Kelly and hot-headed Harlem mafioso and
sometime poet 'Bumpy' Johnson.

Although Alcatraz was considered
escape-proof, in 1962 the Anglin brothers
and Frank Morris stuffed their beds with
dummies, floated away on a makeshift raft
and were never seen again.

Security and upkeep proved prohibitively
expensive and finally the island prison was
abandoned to the birds in 1963.

Native American Occupation

Native Americans claimed sovereignty over
the island in the 1960s, noting that Alcatraz
had long been used by the Ohlone people
as a spiritual retreat. In 1969, 79 Native
American activists swam to the island and
took it over. During the next 19 months,
some 5600 Native Americans would visit
the occupied island. Public support eventually pressured President Richard Nixon
in 1970 to restore Native territory and
strengthen self-rule for Native nations.

Visiting Alcatraz

The weather changes fast. It's often windy
and colder on Alcatraz, so wear extra layers.

Visiting Alcatraz means walking – a lot.
The ferry drops you off at the bottom of a
130ft-high hill, which you'll have to ascend
to reach the cell block. For people with
mobility impairment, there's a twice-hourly
tram from dock to cell house.

Alcatraz

A HALF-DAY TOUR

Book a ferry from Pier 33 and ride 1.5 miles across the bay to explore America's most notorious former prison. The trip itself is worth the money, providing stunning views of the city skyline. Once you've landed at the ❶ **Ferry Dock & Pier**, you begin the 580yd walk to the top of the island and prison; if you need assistance to reach the top, there's a twice-hourly tram.

As you climb toward the ❷ **Guardhouse**, notice the island's steep slope; before it was a prison, Alcatraz was a fort. In the 1850s, the military quarried the rocky shores into near-vertical cliffs. Ships could then only dock at a single port, separated from the main buildings by a sally port (a drawbridge and moat in what became the guardhouse). Inside, peer through floor grates to see Alcatraz' original prison.

Volunteers tend the brilliant ❸ **Officers' Row Gardens**, an orderly counterpoint to the overgrown rose bushes surrounding the burned-out shell of the ❹ **Warden's House**. At the top of the hill, by the front door of the ❺ **Main Cellhouse**, beautiful shots unfurl all around, including a view of the ❻ **Golden Gate Bridge**. Above the main door of the administration building, notice the ❼ **historic signs & graffiti**, before you step inside the dank, cold prison to find the ❽ **Frank Morris cell**, former home to Alcatraz' most notorious jail-breaker.

Historic Signs & Graffiti
During their 1969–71 occupation, Native Americans graffitied the water tower: 'Home of the Free Indian Land.' Above the cellhouse door, examine the eagle-and-flag crest to see how the red-and-white stripes were changed to spell 'Free.'

Warden's House
Fires destroyed the warden's house and other structures during the Native American Occupation. The government blamed the Native Americans; the Native Americans blamed agents provocateurs acting on behalf of the Nixon administration to undermine public sympathy.

Parade Grounds

Officers' Row Gardens
In the 19th century soldiers imported topsoil to beautify the island with gardens. Well-trusted prisoners later gardened – Elliott Michener said it kept him sane. Historians, ornithologists and archaeologists choose today's plants.

TOP TIPS

➡ Book at least one month prior for self-guided daytime visits, longer for ranger-led night tours. For info on garden tours, see www.alcatraz gardens.org.

➡ Be prepared to hike; a steep path ascends from the ferry landing to the cell block. Most people spend two to three hours on the island. You need only reserve for the outbound ferry; take any ferry back.

➡ There's no food (just water) but you can bring your own; picnicking is allowed at the ferry dock only. Dress in layers as weather changes fast and it's usually windy.

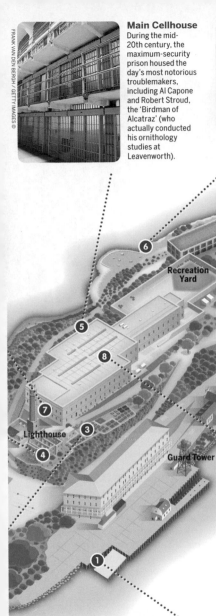

Main Cellhouse
During the mid-20th century, the maximum-security prison housed the day's most notorious troublemakers, including Al Capone and Robert Stroud, the 'Birdman of Alcatraz' (who actually conducted his ornithology studies at Leavenworth).

View of the Golden Gate Bridge
The Golden Gate Bridge stretches wide on the horizon. Best views are from atop the island at Eagle Plaza, near the cellhouse entrance, and at water level along the Agave Trail (September to January only).

Power House

Recreation Yard

Water Tower

Officers' Club

Guard Tower

Lighthouse

Guardhouse
Alcatraz' oldest building dates to 1857 and retains remnants of the original drawbridge and moat. During the Civil War the basement was transformed into a military dungeon – the genesis of Alcatraz as a prison.

Frank Morris Cell

Peer into cell 138 on B-Block to see a recreation of the dummy's head that Frank Morris left in his bed as a decoy to aid his notorious – and successful – 1962 escape from Alcatraz.

Ferry Dock & Pier
A giant wall map helps you get your bearings. Inside nearby Building 64, short films and exhibits provide historical perspective on the prison and details about the Native American Occupation.

Tacro (combination of a taco and a croissant), Ferry Building

BRANNON_NAITO/SHUTTERSTOCK ©

Ferry Building

Global food trends start in San Francisco. To sample tomorrow's menu today, wander through the city's monument to trailblazing, sustainable food. The Ferry Building has the best bites from Northern California.

Other towns have gourmet ghettos, but San Francisco puts its love of food front and center at the Ferry Building. The once-grand port was overshadowed by a 1950s elevated freeway – until the overpass collapsed in 1989's Loma Prieta earthquake. The Ferry Building survived and became a symbol of San Francisco's reinvention, marking your arrival at America's forward-thinking food frontier.

History

The trademark 240ft tower greeted dozens of ferries daily after its 1898 inauguration. But with the opening of the Bay and Golden Gate Bridges, ferry traffic subsided in the 1930s. An overhead freeway was built, obscuring the building's stately facade and turning it black with exhaust fumes. Only after the 1989 earthquake did city planners

Great For...

☑ Don't Miss

Heading out along the Embarcadero waterfront promenade for Bay Bridge views.

Ferry Building at night

NICKOLAY STANEV/SHUTTERSTOCK ©

❶ Need to Know

Map p54; ☎415-983-8000; www.ferry
buildingmarketplace.com; cnr Market St & the
Embarcadero; ⊙10am-7pm Mon-Fri, 8am-
6pm Sat, 11am-5pm Sun; ♿; ☐2, 6, 9, 14, 21,
31, Ⓜ️Embarcadero, ⒷEmbarcadero)

✕ Take a Break

Slurp the bounty of the North Bay at **Hog
Island Oyster Company** (Map p54; ☎415-
391-7117; www.hogislandoysters.com; 1 Ferry
Bldg; 6 oysters $19-21; ⊙11am-9pm) ✿.

★ Top Tip

You can still catch ferries at the Ferry
Building and, on sunny days, crossing
the sparkling bay is a great escape.

realize what they'd been missing: with its
grand halls and bay views, this was the
perfect place for a new public commons.

Foodie Hot Spot

Today the grand arrivals hall tempts com-
muters to miss the boat and get on board
with San Francisco's latest culinary trends
instead. Indoor kiosks sell locally roasted
espresso, artisan cheese and cured meats,
plus organic ice-cream flavors to match –
that's right, Vietnamese coffee, cheese
and prosciutto. People-watching wine bars
and award-winning restaurants are further
enticements to stick around, and raise a
toast to San Francisco.

Ferry Plaza Farmers Market

Even before Ferry Building renovations
were completed in 2003, the **Ferry Plaza**

Farmers Market (Map p54; ☎415-291-3276;
www.cuesa.org; street food $3-12; ⊙10am-2pm
Tue & Thu, from 8am Sat; ♿👪) ✿ began operating out front on the sidewalk. Soon the
foodie action spread to the bayfront plaza,
with more than 100 local food purveyors
now catering to hometown crowds three
times a week. While locals sometimes
grumble that the prices are higher here
than at other markets, there's no denying
that the Ferry Plaza market offers seasonal,
sustainable, handmade gourmet treats and
specialty produce not found elsewhere.

Join San Francisco's legions of professional chefs and semiprofessional eaters,
and taste-test the artisan goat cheese,
fresh-pressed California olive oil, wild boar
and organic pluots for yourself. The Saturday morning farmers market offers the
best people-watching – it's not uncommon
to spot celebrities – but arrive early if
you're shopping.

Chinatown

The 41 historic alleyways packed into Chinatown's 22 blocks have seen it all since 1849: gold rushes and revolution, incense and opium, fire and icy receptions.

In clinker-brick buildings lining Chinatown's narrow backstreets, temple balconies jut out over bakeries, laundries and barbers – there was nowhere to go but up in Chinatown after 1870, when laws limited Chinese immigration, employment and housing.

Grant Avenue

Enter Chinatown through the Dragon's Gate, donated by Taiwan in 1970, and you'll find yourself on the street formerly known as Dupont in its notorious red-light heyday. The pagoda-topped 'Chinatown deco' architecture beyond this gate was innovated by Chinatown merchants, led by Look Tin Ely, in the 1920s – a pioneering initiative to lure tourists with a distinctive modern look.

It's hard to believe this souvenir-shopping strip was once notorious and brothel-lined. The **Chinese Historical**

Great For...

🚶 🍴 💬

☑ **Don't Miss**

Hearing mah-jongg tiles, temple gongs and Chinese orchestras as you wander Chinatown's alleyways.

MICHAEL URMANN/SHUTTERSTOCK ©

ⓘ Need to Know

Map p54; btwn Grant Ave, Stockton St, California St & Broadway; 🚋1, 30, 45, 🚠Powell-Hyde, Powell-Mason, California

✕ Take a Break

Ingenious Chinese–Californian signatures in Mister Jiu's (p65) include quail and Mission-fig sticky rice, hot-and-sour Dungeness crab soup and Wagyu sirloin. Don't skip dessert.

★ Top Tip

Parking is tough. There's public parking underneath Portsmouth Sq and the Good Luck Parking Garage,

Society of America (CHSA; Map p54; ☎415-391-1188; www.chsa.org; 965 Clay St; ⊙11am-4pm Wed-Sun; 🚹; 🚋1, 8, 30, 45, 🚠California, Powell-Mason, Powell-Hyde, Ⓜ🚈) FREE has information about the neighborhood in the past.

Waverly Place

Grant Ave may be the economic heart of Chinatown, but its soul is Waverly Pl, lined with flag-festooned temple balconies. Due to the 19th-century race-based restrictions, family associations and temples were built right on top of the barber shops, laundries and restaurants lining these two city blocks. Through good times and bad, Waverly Pl stood its ground, and temple services have been held here since 1852 – even after San Francisco's 1906 earthquake and fire, when altars were still smoldering.

Spofford Alley

Sun Yat-sen once plotted the overthrow of China's Manchu dynasty here at No 36, and, during Prohibition, this was the site of turf battles over local bootlegging and protection rackets. Spofford has mellowed with age: it's now lined with seniors community centers. But the action still starts around sundown, when a Chinese orchestra strikes up a tune and the clicking of a mah-jongg game begins.

Jack Kerouac Alley

'The air was soft, the stars so fine, the promise of every cobbled alley so great...' This ode by the *On the Road* and *Dharma Bums* author is embedded in his namesake alley, a fittingly poetic, streetwise shortcut between Chinatown and North Beach via his favorite haunts City Lights (p57), Vesuvio (p68) and a stool near the golden Buddha statue at Li Po – Kerouac was a true believer in literature, Buddhism and beer.

Walking Tour: North Beach Beat

Hit North Beach literary hot spots and walk in the footsteps of San Francisco's Beat poets.

Start City Lights Books
Distance 1.5 miles
Duration Two hours

4 Peaceful **Bob Kaufman Alley** is named after the legendary street-corner poet who endured a 12-year vow of silence.

3 Look for parrots in the treetops and octogenarians in tai chi stances on the lawn of **Washington Sq**.

Classic Photo Browsing the shelves at City Lights

1 Pick up a copy of Ferlinghetti's *San Francisco Poems* from **City Lights Books** (p57), home of Beat poetry and free speech.

2 With opera on the jukebox and potent espresso, **Caffe Trieste** (p68) is where Coppola allegedly drafted screenplay of *The Godfather*.

5 The **Beat Museum** is the closest you can get to the complete Beat experience without breaking the law.

6 Finish your tour, but start your evening, at memorabilia-heavy **Specs** (p68), the perfect jumping-off point for a literary bar crawl.

Take a Break Pop into **Vesuvio** (p68) for a beer.

Filbert St

Union St

Kearny St

Green St

Grant Ave

Vallejo St

Broadway

START

FINISH

Pacific Ave

Columbus Ave

Washington St

Grant Ave

0 400 m
0 0.2 miles

1 ROBERT MULLAN/SHUTTERSTOCK © 3 MARK ZHU/GETTY IMAGES © 5 KRIS DAVIDSON/LONELY PLANET ©

◎ SIGHTS

Most major museums are downtown, though Golden Gate Park is home to the de Young Museum and the California Academy of Sciences. The city's most historic districts are the Mission, Chinatown, North Beach and the Haight. Galleries are clustered downtown and in North Beach, the Mission, Potrero Flats and Dogpatch. You'll find hilltop parks citywide, but Russian, Nob and Telegraph Hills are the highest and most panoramic.

◎ The Marina, Fisherman's Wharf & the Piers

Sights along **Fisherman's Wharf** (Map p54; www.fishermanswharf.org; 🚻; 🚌19, 30, 47, 49, 🚋Powell-Mason, Powell-Hyde, MF) FREE – the Embarcadero and Jefferson St waterfront running from Pier 29 to Van Ness Ave – are geared entirely to tourists, particularly families, and it's easy to get stuck with so much vying for your attention. Stick to the waterside and keep moving.

Maritime National Historical Park   Historic Site

(Map p54; ☑415-447-5000; www.nps.gov/safr; 499 Jefferson St, Hyde St Pier; 7-day ticket adult/child under 16yr $15/free; ⊙9:30am-5pm Oct-May, to 5:30pm Jun-Sep; 🚻; 🚌19, 30, 47, 🚋Powell-Hyde, MF) Five historic ships are floating museums at Fisherman's Wharf's most enduring attraction. Moored along Hyde St Pier, the three-star attractions are the 1891 schooner *Alma*, which hosts guided sailing trips in summer; 1890 steamboat *Eureka*; and iron-hulled 1886 *Balclutha*, which brought coal to San Francisco. It's free to walk the pier; pay only to board ships. The park includes the 1939 **Aquatic Park Bathhouse** (10am to 4pm), featuring Maritime Museum exhibits and fabulous art-deco friezes by African American sculptor Sargent Johnson.

Exploratorium   Museum

(Map p54; ☑415-528-4444; www.exploratorium.edu; Pier 15/17; adult/child $29.95/19.95, 6-10pm Thu $19.95, Tactile Dome 30/60min $8/15; ⊙10am-5pm Tue-Sun, over 18yr only 6-10pm Thu; P🚻; ME, F) ✏ Can you stop time, sculpt

Maritime National Historical Park

fog or make sand sing? At San Francisco's hands-on, living laboratory of science and human perception, you'll discover super-human abilities you never knew you had. But the Exploratorium's not just for kids: After Dark Thursdays offer mad-scientist cocktails, technology-assisted sing-alongs and themed exhibits for 18-plus crowds. Book ahead to slide, climb and feel your way in total darkness through the labyrinthine Tactile Dome, and emerge with a renewed sense of wonder (reservations required).

⊚ Downtown & Civic Center

Asian Art Museum   Museum
(Map p54; ☑415-581-3500; www.asianart.org; 200 Larkin St; adult/student/child $15/10/free, 1st Sun of month free; ☺10am-5pm Tue, Wed & Fri-Sun, to 9pm Thu; ﹠; MCivic Center, BCivic Center) Imaginations stretch across three floors spanning 6000 years of Asian art, from med-itative Tibetan mandalas to palace-intrigue Mughal miniatures, with stops to admire intricate Islamic geometric tilework, giddy arrays of Chinese snuff bottles, and an entire Japanese minimalist teahouse. Besides the largest collection of Asian art outside Asia – 18,000-plus works – the museum offers excellent all-ages programs, from shadow-puppet shows to DJ mixers. Expanded ground-floor galleries host groundbreaking contemporary installations, from Jean Shin's melted cell-phone towers to teamLAB's immersive Tokyo dreamscapes.

Contemporary Jewish Museum   Museum
(Map p54; ☑415-655-7856; www.thecjm.org; 736 Mission St; adult/student/child $14/12/free, after 5pm Thu $8; ☺11am-5pm Fri-Tue, to 8pm Thu; ﹠; ☐14, 30, 45, BMontgomery, MMontgomery) That upended blue-steel box miraculously balancing on one corner atop the Contem-porary Jewish Museum perfectly suits an institution that upends conventional ideas about art and religion. Architect Daniel Libeskind designed this museum to be rational, mystical and powerful: building onto a 1907 brick power station, he added blue-steel elements to form the Hebrew word *l'chaim* (life). Original shows and

👪 San Francisco for Children

San Francisco is packed with family-friendly attractions, including the California Academy of Sciences (p61) in Golden Gate Park and the waterfront Exploratorium (p52).

Prison tours of Alcatraz (p113) fasci-nate kids and give them an interesting, safe place to run around, while in SoMa the **Children's Creativity Museum** (Map p54; ☑415-820-3320; http://creativity. org/; 221 4th St; $12.95; ☺10am-4pm Tue-Sun summer, Wed-Sun rest of year; ﹠; ☐14, MPowell, BPowell) has technology that's too cool for school: robots, live-ac-tion video games and 3D animation workshops.

Plus there's always an old-school cable-car ride – a joy for the whole family.

California Academy of Sciences (p61)
ANTON_IVANOV/SHUTTERSTOCK ©

contemporary-art commissions truly bring this museum to life, from Rube Goldberg's mysterious machines to Annabeth Rosen's psychedelic ceramic totems.

San Francisco Museum of Modern Art   Museum
(SFMOMA; Map p54; ☑415-357-4000; www. sfmoma.org; 151 3rd St; adult/ages 19-24yr/under 18yr $25/19/free; ☺10am-5pm Fri-Tue, to 9pm Thu, atrium from 8am Mon-Fri; ﹠; ☐5, 6, 7, 14, 19, 21, 31, 38, MMontgomery, BMontgomery) The mind boggles at SFMOMA, where boundary-pushing modern and contemporary masterworks sprawl over seven floors of galleries. Start with the world-class 3rd-floor photography collection, meditate in Agnes

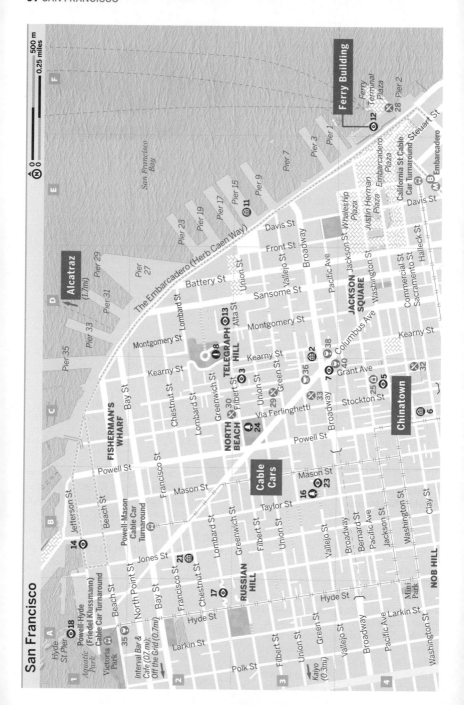

San Francisco

Alcatraz (1.7m)

Ferry Building

Cable Cars

Chinatown

FISHERMAN'S WHARF

NORTH BEACH

TELEGRAPH HILL

RUSSIAN HILL

NOB HILL

JACKSON SQUARE

San Francisco Bay

The Embarcadero (Herb Caen Way)

Aquatic Park

Victoria Park

Mini Park

500 m
0.25 miles

San Francisco

Martin's secluded shrine behind 4th-floor abstract paintings, get an eyeful of Warhol's pop art on the 5th floor, and immerse yourself in 7th-floor cutting-edge contemporary installations. Head to the 2nd floor to see how SFMOMA began, with colorful characters worthy of SF by Frida Kahlo, Diego Rivera, Paul Klee and Henri Matisse.

Museum of the
African Diaspora   Museum

(MoAD; Map p54; ☎415-358-7200; www.moadsf.org; 685 Mission St; adult/student/child $10/5/free; ☉11am-6pm Wed-Sat, noon-5pm Sun; P❋; ☐14, 30, 45, ⓜMontgomery, ⓑMontgomery) MoAD assembles an international cast of characters to tell epic stories of diaspora, starting with a moving video of slave narratives featuring Maya Angelou. Standouts among quarterly changing exhibits have included homages to Harlem's queer ballroom scene, Kwame Brathwaite's uplifting 1960s Black Is Beautiful photography, and Angela Hennessey's altarpieces made

entirely of woven hair. Public events include poetry slams, artist talks, film screenings, concerts with SFJAZZ, and Third Thursday nights, when the museum is free and open until 8pm.

Compton's Transgender
Cultural District   Area

(Map p54) The world's first official transgender district was created to commemorate historical sites and preserve existing nonprofits, businesses and nightlife venues that center and support the community. Boundaries include Market St between Taylor St and Jones St, to the south side of Ellis St between Mason St and Taylor St, and the north side of Ellis St between Taylor St and Jones St, as well as the 6th St corridor between Market St and Howard St.

◎ North Beach & Chinatown

Coit Tower   Public Art

(Map p54; ☎415-249-0995; www.sfrecpark.org; Telegraph Hill Blvd; nonresident elevator fee adult/child $9/6, mural tour full/2nd fl only $8/5; ⊗10am-6pm Apr-Oct, to 5pm Nov-Mar; 🚍39) The exclamation mark atop Telegraph Hill is Coit Tower, dedicated to SF first responders by firefighting millionaire Lillie Hitchcock Coit. The lobby is lined with 1930s murals celebrating SF workers – initially denounced as communist, but now landmarked. For a parrot's-eye panoramic view of San Francisco 210ft above the city, take the elevator to the tower's open-air platform. Book docent-led, 30- to 40-minute mural tours online – tour all murals or just the seven recently restored hidden stairwell murals.

City Lights Books   Cultural Center

(Map p54; 📞415-362-8193; www.citylights.com; 261 Columbus Ave; ⊗10am-midnight; 📖; 🚍8, 10, 12, 30, 41, 45, 🚋Powell-Mason, Powell-Hyde, MT) FREE Free speech and free spirits have rejoiced here since 1957, when City Lights founder and poet Lawrence Ferlinghetti and manager Shigeyoshi Murao won a landmark ruling defending their right to publish Allen Ginsberg's magnificent epic poem *Howl*. Celebrate your freedom to read freely in the designated Poet's Chair upstairs overlooking Jack Kerouac Alley, load up on zines on the mezzanine and entertain radical ideas downstairs in the new Pedagogies of Resistance section.

Filbert Street Steps   Architecture

(Map p54; 🚍39) Halfway through the steep climb up the Filbert St Steps to Coit Tower, you might wonder if it's all worth the trouble. Take a breather and notice the scenery you're passing: sweeping Bay Bridge vistas, hidden cottages along Napier Lane's wooden boardwalk, and sculpture-dotted gardens in bloom year-round. If you need further encouragement, the wild parrots in the trees have been known to interject a few choice words your gym trainer would probably get sued for using.

◎ Nob Hill & Russian Hill

Diego Rivera Gallery   Gallery

(Map p54; 📞415-771-7020; www.sfai.edu; 800 Chestnut St; ⊗9am-7pm; 🚍30, 🚋Powell-Mason)

FREE Diego Rivera's 1931 *The Making of a Fresco Showing the Building of a City* is a *trompe l'oeil* fresco within a fresco, showing Diego pausing to admire his own work and the efforts of fellow workers building the modern city of San Francisco. The fresco covers an entire wall of the Diego Rivera Gallery in the **San Francisco Art Institute** (SFAI; Map p54; ⊗Walter & McBean Galleries 11am-7pm Tue, to 6pm Wed-Sat, Diego Rivera Gallery 9am-7pm) FREE. For sweeping views of the city Diego admired, head to the terrace cafe for espresso and panoramic bay vistas.

Lombard Street   Street

(Map p54; 🚋Powell-Hyde) You've seen its eight switchbacks in movies, but Lombard St doesn't deserve its nickname as 'San Francisco's crookedest street' – Vermont St in Potrero Hill has that honor. Lombard is more scenic, with flowerbeds lining its brick-paved 900 block. It wasn't always so bent: it plunged straight downhill until too many joyriders crashed in the 1920s. Today traffic is slow and skating is banned – so Lombard St thrills featured in Tony Hawk's Pro Skater video game are strictly virtual.

Vallejo Street Steps   Architecture

(Map p54; Vallejo St, btwn Mason & Jones Sts; 🚋Powell-Mason, Powell-Hyde) Reach staggering heights with spectacular views along this staircase connecting North Beach with Russian Hill. Ascend Vallejo toward Mason St, where stairs rise toward Jones St, passing poetic **Ina Coolbrith Park** (Map p54; www.sfparksalliance.org/our-parks/parks/ina-coolbrith-park; cnr Vallejo & Taylor Sts; 🚍41, 45, 🚋Powell-Mason). Pause at the top for nighttime views of the shimmering Bay Bridge lights, then continue west to Polk St for nightlife.

Grace Cathedral   Church

(Map p54; 📞415-749-6300; www.gracecathedral.org; 1100 California St; suggested donation adult/child $3/2; ⊗8am-6pm Mon-Sat, to 7pm Sun, services 8:30am, 11am & 6pm Sun; 🚍1, 🚋California) San Francisco's reinforced-concrete Gothic hilltop cathedral took 40

The Mission & Potrero Hill

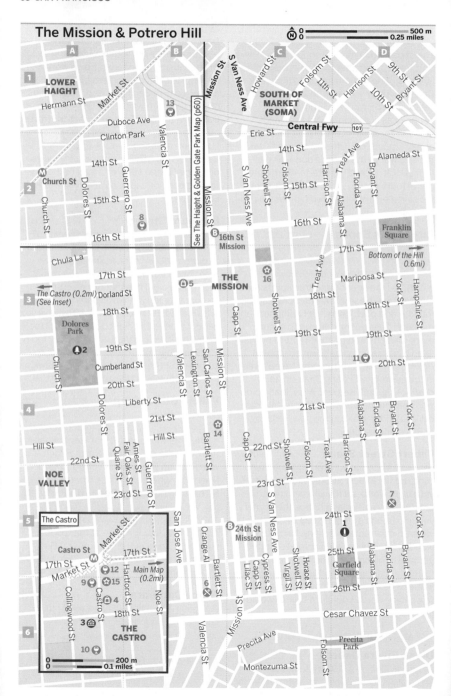

Ⓝ 0 ⌐━━━━━━━ 500 m
0 ⌐━━━━━━━ 0.25 miles

LOWER HAIGHT

Hermann St

Market St

Duboce Ave

Clinton Park

13

Valencia St

14th St

Ⓜ Church St

Dolores St

Guerrero St

15th St

Church St

16th St

8

Chula La

17th St

The Castro (0.2mi)
(See Inset)

Dorland St

18th St

Dolores Park

Church St

19th St

Cumberland St

20th St

Dolores St

Liberty St

21st St

Hill St

Hill St

22nd St

NOE VALLEY

Ames St
Fair Oaks St
Quane St

23rd St

Guerrero St

San Jose Ave

Mission St

S Van Ness Ave

Howard St

Folsom St

11th St

Harrison St

9th St

Bryant St

10th St

SOUTH OF MARKET (SOMA)

Central Fwy [101]

Erie St

14th St

Treat Ave

Alameda St

S Van Ness Ave

Shotwell St

Folsom St

15th St

Harrison St

Florida St

Bryant St

Alabama St

16th St

Treat Ave

17th St

Franklin Square

Ⓑ 16th St Mission

17th St

→ Bottom of the Hill 0.6mi)

5

Ⓐ

THE MISSION

16

Shotwell St

Mariposa St

York St

Hampshire St

18th St

18th St

Capp St

19th St

19th St

11

20th St

Valencia St

Lexington St

San Carlos St

Mission St

21st St

Harrison St

Alabama St

Florida St

Bryant St

York St

Bartlett St

14

Capp St

22nd St

Shotwell St

Folsom St

Treat Ave

23rd St

S Van Ness Ave

7

24th St

1 ❶

Ⓑ 24th St Mission

Orange Al

25th St

Cypress St
Capp St
Lilac St

Shotwell St
Virgil St

Horace St

Garfield Square

Alabama St

Florida St

Bryant St

York St

Bartlett St

6

26th St

Cesar Chavez St

Mission St

Valencia St

Precita Ave

Folsom St

Precita Park

Montezuma St

See The Haight & Golden Gate Park Map (p60)

The Castro

Castro St

Ⓜ

17th St

17th St

Market St

12

Hartford St

Main Map (0.2mi)

9

15

Collingwood St

Castro St

4

18th St

Noe St

3 🏛

THE CASTRO

10

0 ⌐━━━━━━━ 200 m
0 ⌐━━━━━━━ 0.1 miles

The Mission & Potrero Hill

years to complete, with spectacular 'Human Endeavor' stained-glass windows celebrating science – look for Albert Einstein amid swirling nuclear particles. Murals commemorate the 1906 earthquake and 1945 UN charter signing, and Grace's Interfaith AIDS Memorial Chapel features a bronze angel altarpiece by artist-activist Keith Haring – his final work before his 1990 death from AIDS. Locals light candles here and at the feet of Beniamino Bufano's smiling statue of the city's patron saint.

Cathedral artworks honor achievements from Protestant and Catholic faiths alike – Robert Lenz' *Mary Magdalene* is a head-turning modern Greek Orthodox icon, vivid stained-glass windows honor Quaker anti-slavery efforts, and the cathedral doors are exact replicas of Lorenzo Ghiberti's bronze baptistry doors in Florence. Check the website for events, including spectacular choral performances (don't miss Bach's *Magnificat* at Easter) plus inclusive weekly spiritual events, such as yoga, Thursday Evensong and candlelit meditation services. People of all faiths wander indoor and outdoor inlaid-stone labyrinths, meant to guide restless souls through three spiritual stages: releasing, receiving and returning.

⊙ The Mission

Dolores Park   Park
(Map p58; http://sfrecpark.org; Dolores St, btwn 18th & 20th Sts; ⊙6am-10pm; 👪🎾; 🚋14, 33, 49, 🅱16th St Mission, ⓂJ) Welcome to San Francisco's sunny side, the land of street ball and Mayan-pyramid playgrounds, semiprofessional tanning and glorious taco picnics. Grassy slopes are dedicated to the fine art of lolling, while lowlands host soccer, Frisbee, political protests and other local sports. Good weather brings cultural events, including Easter's Hunky Jesus drag contest, free summer movie nights, and fall SF Mime Troupe performances. Fair warning: secondhand highs copped near the refurbished bathroom may have you chasing the *helados* (ice-cream) cart.

⊙ The Haight

Haight & Ashbury   Landmark
(Map p60; 🚌6, 7, 33, 37, 43) This legendary intersection was the epicenter of the psychedelic '60s, and 'Hashbury' remains a counterculture magnet. On average Saturdays here, you can sign Green Party petitions, commission a poem and hear Hare Krishna on keyboards and Bob Dylan on banjo. The clock overhead always reads 4:20 – better known in herbal circles as International Bong-Hit Time. A local clockmaker once fixed the clock; within a week it was stuck again at 4:20.

Haight Street Art Center   Arts Center
(Map p60; 🕾415-363-6150; https://haightstreetart.org; 215 Haight St; ⊙noon-6pm Wed-Sun; 🚌6, 7, 22, ⓂF) **FREE** Jeremy Fish's bronze bunny-skull sculpture guides you into a wonderland of screen-printed posters, San Francisco's signature art form. Glimpse rock-concert posters in progress at the

The Haight & Golden Gate Park

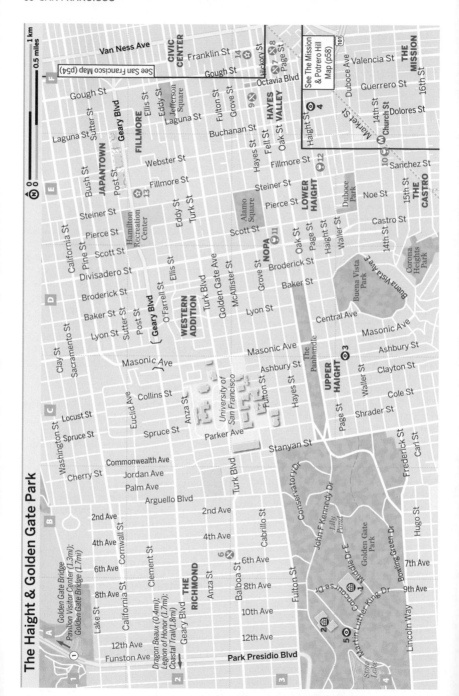

The Haight & Golden Gate Park

on-site screen-printing studio, plus jaw-dropping gallery shows featuring Stanley Mouse's psychedelic Grateful Dead posters and Ralph Steadman's original illustrations for Hunter S Thompson's *Fear and Loathing in Las Vegas*. Gracing the stairwell is a hidden SF treasure: Ruben Kaddish's 1937 WPA fresco *Dissertation on Alchemy,* surely the trippiest mural ever commissioned by the US government.

◎ Golden Gate Park

When San Franciscans refer to 'the park,' there's only one that gets the definite article: Golden Gate Park. Everything San Franciscans hold dear is here: free spirits, free music, redwoods, Frisbee, protests, fine art, bonsai and buffalo.

California
Academy of Sciences   Museum

(Map p60; ☎415-379-8000; www.calacademy. org; 55 Music Concourse Dr; adult/student/ child $36.50/31.25/28; see website for weekday & sustainable transit discounts; ◷9:30am-5pm Mon-Sat, from 11am Sun; 🅿👪; 🚌5, 6, 7, 21, 31, 33, 44, Ⓜ N) ⏺ Architect Renzo Piano's landmark LEED-certified green building houses 40,000 animals in a four-story rainforest, split-level aquarium and planetarium, all under a 'living roof' of wildflowers. Inside, butterflies flit around the Osher Rainforest Dome, giant pink Pacific octopuses roam Steinhart Aquarium, penguins waddle in the African Hall, and Claude the albino alligator stalks the mezzanine swamp. Explore California in the Giants of Land and Sea exhibit – brave an earthquake simula-

tion, virtually climb a redwood and get lost in a fog room.

de Young Museum   Museum

(Map p60; ☎415-750-3600; http://deyoung. famsf.org; 50 Hagiwara Tea Garden Dr; adult/child $15/free, 1st Tue of month free, $2 discount with Bay Area public transit ticket; ◷9:30am-5:15pm Tue-Sun; 🚌5, 7, 44, Ⓜ N) Follow sculptor Andy Goldsworthy's artificial fault line in the sidewalk into Herzog & de Meuron's sleek, copper-clad building that's oxidizing green to blend into the park. Don't be fooled by the camouflaged exterior: shows here boldly broaden artistic horizons, from Oceanic ceremonial mask displays to Frida Kahlo retrospectives, and Black Power movement posters to AI-assisted artwork. Don't miss James Turrell's domed *Skyspace* installation built under the sculpture garden. Ticket includes free same-day entry to the **Legion of Honor** (☎415-750-3600; http://legionofhonor.famsf.org; 100 34th Ave; adult/child $15/free, discount with Muni ticket $2, 1st Tue of month free; ◷9:30am-5:15pm Tue-Sun; 🚌1, 2, 18, 38).

🛍 SHOPPING

Cliff's Variety   Homewares

(Map p58; www.cliffsvariety.com; 479 Castro St; ◷10am-8pm Mon-Sat, to 6pm Sun; Ⓜ Castro St) None of the hardware maestros at Cliff's will raise an eyebrow if you express a dire need for a jar of rubber nuns, some silver body paint, and a case of cocktail toothpicks – though they might angle for an invitation. A community institution since 1936, Cliff's stocks drag supplies galore in

Mission Mural Tours

When Mission muralistas objected to US policy in Latin America in the 1970s, they took to the streets with paintbrushes. Inspired by Diego Rivera's 1930s San Francisco murals, *Mujeres Muralistas* ('Women Muralists') and Placa ('Mark-making') covered Balmy Alley garage doors and back fences with murals of pride and protest. Today Balmy Alley artworks span three decades, from memorials honoring Salvadoran activist Archbishop Romero to a homage to Frida Kahlo. Nonprofit Precita Eyes commissions and upkeeps these murals, plus dozens more throughout the Mission. Take your time wandering the six- to 10-block radius of mural-bedecked Balmy Alley.

Balmy Alley
ENRIQUE MORAN/500PX ©

the annex and celebrates the seasons with gay-gasp-worthy window displays.

Community Thrift   Clothing

(Map p58; ☑415-861-4910; www.communitythriftsf.org; 623 Valencia St; ⊙10am-6:30pm; ☐14, 22, 33, 49, ⒝16th St Mission) ✐ When local collectors and retailers have too much of a good thing, they donate it to nonprofit Community Thrift, where proceeds go to 200-plus local charities – all the more reason to gloat over your $3 porcelain teacup, $9 vintage suede platform heels and $14 aloha-print romper. Donate your cast-offs (until 5pm daily) and show some love to the community.

Recchiuti Confections   Chocolate

(Map p54; ☑415-834-9494; www.recchiuti confections.com; 1 Ferry Bldg, cnr Market St & the Embarcadero; ⊙10am-7pm Mon-Fri, 8am-6pm Sat, 10am-5pm Sun; Ⓜ Embarcadero, ⒝ Embarcadero) ✐ No San Franciscan can resist award-winning Recchiuti: Pacific Heights parts with old money for its *fleur de sel* caramels; foodie Marina kids prefer S'more Bites to the campground variety; North Beach toasts to the red-wine-pairing chocolate box; and the Mission approves SF-landmark chocolates designed by Creativity Explored – proceeds benefit the Mission arts-education nonprofit.

Heath Ceramics   Homewares

(Map p54; ☑415-399-9284; www.heathceramics. com; 1 Ferry Bldg, cnr Market St & the Embarcadero; ⊙10am-7pm Mon-Fri, 8am-6pm Sat, 10am-5pm Sun; Ⓜ Embarcadero, ⒝ Embarcadero) Odds are your favorite SF meal was served on Heath Ceramics, Bay Area chefs' tableware of choice ever since Alice Waters started using Heath's modern, hand-thrown dishes at Chez Panisse. Heath's muted colors and streamlined, mid-century designs stay true to Edith Heath's originals c 1948. Plates are priced for fine dining, but affordable bud vases make fantastic host gifts (hint, hint).

Golden Gate Fortune Cookies   Food & Drinks

(Map p54; ☑415-781-3956; www.goldengatefor tunecookies.com; 56 Ross Alley; ⊙9am-6pm; ☐8, 30, 45, ☐Powell-Mason, Powell-Hyde, ⒨T) Find your fortune at this bakery, where cookies are stamped from vintage presses – just as they were in 1909, when fortune cookies were invented for SF's **Japanese Tea Garden** (Map p60; ☑415-752-1171; www.japaneseteagardensf.com; 75 Hagiwara Tea Garden Dr; adult/child $10/3, Mar-Sep $12/3, before 10am Mon, Wed & Fri free; ⊙9am-5:45pm Mar-Sep, to 4:45pm Oct-Feb; Ⓟ; ☐5, 7, 44, ⒨N). Write your own fortunes for custom cookies (50¢ each), or get cookies with regular or risqué fortunes (or just add 'in bed' to regular ones). Cash only; $1 tip per photo.

⊗ EATING

⊗ The Marina, Fisherman's Wharf & the Piers

Kaiyo Japanese, Peruvian $$

(☑415-525-4804; https://kaiyosf.com; 1838 Union St; small plates $12-28, share plates $19-28; ⊙5-10pm Tue, Wed & Sun, to 11pm Thu & Sat, 10:30am-3pm Sat & Sun; ⊒41, 45) Fusion is more fun at this Nikkei (Japanese-Peruvian) bistro, where Pisco and whiskey cocktails are named for anime characters and neon-green moss streaks like lightning across the dining-room wall. But the real adventure here is the menu, featuring such daring feats of Pacific Rim fusion as smoked duck-breast sashimi, Hokkaido scallop *tiradito,* and *cusquena*-brined, organic Sonoma chicken.

⊗ Downtown & Civic Center

Farm:Table American $

(Map p54; ☑415-300-5652; www.farmtablesf. com; 754 Post St; dishes $6-14; ⊙7:15am-1pm Tue-Fri, 8am-2pm Sat & Sun; ☑; ⊒2, 3, 27, 38) ✐ A ray of sunshine in the concrete heart of the city, this plucky little storefront showcases seasonal California organics in just-baked breakfasts and farmstead-fresh lunches. Daily specials include a rotation of homemade cereals, zesty tuna melts and game-changing toast – mmmm, ginger peach and fresh mascarpone on whole-wheat sourdough! Tiny space, but immaculate kitchen and locally roasted espresso drinks.

Liholiho Yacht Club Hawaiian, Californian $$

(Map p54; ☑415-440-5446; http://lycsf.com; 871 Sutter St; dishes $11-37; ⊙5-10:30pm Mon-Thu, to 11pm Fri & Sat; ⊒2, 3, 27, 38, ⊒California) Who needs yachts to be happy? Aloha comes naturally with Liholiho's pucker-up-tart cocktails and gleefully creative dishes – surefire mood enhancers include spicy beef-tongue *bao,* duck-liver mousse with pickled pineapple on brioche, and Vietnamese slaw with tender squid and crispy tripe. Reservations are tough; arrive early/late for bar dining, or head downstairs to Louie's Gen-Gen Room speakeasy for blissfully indulgent bone-marrow-butter waffles.

Beef-tongue *bao* at Liholiho Yacht Club

JAMES KIRKIKIS/SHUTTERSTOCK ©

Golden Boy

Boulette's
Larder & Boulibar   Californian $$

(Map p54; ☑415-399-1155; www.bouletteslarder.
com; 1 Ferry Bldg, cnr Market St & the Embar-
cadero; mains $18-24; ⊙Larder 8-10:30am
& 11:30am-3pm Tue-Sat, 10am-2:30pm Sun,
Boulibar 11:30am-3pm & 6-9:30pm Tue-Fri,
11:30am-3pm & 4:30-8pm Sat; MEmbarcadero,
BEmbarcadero) Dinner theater can't beat
brunch at Boulette's communal table, stra-
tegically placed inside a working kitchen
amid a swirl of chefs with views of the Bay
Bridge. At adjoining Boulibar, get tangy
Middle Eastern mezze platters, beautifully
blistered wood-fired pizzas and flatbreads
at indoor picnic-style tables – perfect
for people-watching, despite sometimes
rushed service. Get inspiration to go with
Larder spice mixes.

⊗ North Beach & Chinatown
Golden Boy   Pizza $

(Map p54; ☑415-982-9738; www.goldenboy
pizza.com; 542 Green St; slices $3.25-4.25;
⊙11:30am-midnight Sun-Thu, to 2am Fri & Sat;
☐8, 30, 39, 41, 45, ☐Powell-Mason) 'If you don't

see it don't ask 4 it' reads the menu – Gold-
en Boy has kept punks in line since 1978,
serving Genovese focaccia-crust pizza that's
chewy, crunchy and hot from the oven. You'll
have whatever second-generation Sodini
family *pizzaioli* (pizza-makers) are making
and like it – especially pesto and clam-and-
garlic. Grab square slices and draft beer at
the bomb-shelter counter and boom: you're
golden.

Molinari   Deli $

(Map p54; ☑415-421-2337; www.molinarisalame.
com; 373 Columbus Ave; sandwiches $11-14.50;
⊙9am-6pm Mon-Fri, to 5:30pm Sat; ☐8, 10, 12,
30, 39, 41, 45, ☐Powell-Mason, MT) Observe
this quasi-religious North Beach noon ritu-
al: enter Molinari and grab a number. When
your number's called, let wisecracking staff
pile a crusty roll or focaccia with heavenly
fixings: milky buffalo mozzarella, tangy
sun-dried tomatoes, translucent sheets
of prosciutto di Parma, slabs of legendary
house-cured salami, drizzles of olive oil and
balsamic. Enjoy hot from the panini press at
sidewalk tables.

Mister Jiu's   Chinese, Californian $$
(Map p54; ☏415-857-9688; http://misterjius.
com; 28 Waverly Pl; mains $14-45; ☺5:30-
10:30pm Tue-Sat; 🚇30, 🚃California, MT)
Success has been celebrated in this historic
Chinatown banquet hall since the 1880s –
but today, scoring a table is reason enough
for celebration. Build memorable banquets
from chef Brandon Jew's ingenious Chi-
nese–Californian signatures: quail and Mis-
sion-fig sticky rice, hot and sour Dungeness
crab soup, Wagyu sirloin and tuna-heart
fried rice. Don't skip dessert – pastry chef
Melissa Chou's salted plum sesame balls
are flavor bombs.

Nob Hill & Russian Hill
Swan Oyster Depot   Seafood $$
(Map p54; ☏415-673-1101; https://swanoyster
depot.us; 1517 Polk St; dishes $10-28; ☺10:30am-
5:30pm Mon-Sat; 🚇1, 19, 47, 49, 🚃California)
Seafood fresh enough to impress sailors
since 1912. First-timers get oysters mignon-
ette and Dungeness salads with crab-fat
vinaigrette, regulars order secret-menu
specials – try 'dozen eggs' (scallop sashimi
in ponzu puddles) or 'crabsanthemum'
(leg-only crab Louie). Arrive before 11am
or strike up conversations over hour-long
waits for counter stools. Introverts, get your
'salad-sandwich combo' (hollowed-out
sourdough crab salad) to go. Cash only.

Acquerello   Californian, Italian $$$
(Map p54; ☏415-567-5432; www.acquerello.
com; 1722 Sacramento St; 3-/4-/5-course menu
$105/130/150; ☺5:30-9:30pm Tue-Thu, to
10pm Fri & Sat; 🚇1, 19, 47, 49, 🚃California) A
converted chapel is a fitting location for
feasts that turn Italian culinary purists into
true believers in Cal-Italian cuisine. Chef
Suzette Gresham's ingenious handmade
pastas and seasonal signatures include
heavenly abalone risotto, devilish lamb with
sweetbreads, and truffled squab cannelloni.
An anteroom where brides once steadied
their nerves is lined with limited-production
Italian vintages seldom seen outside Tus-
can castles.

Active San Francisco

On sunny weekends, San Francisco is
out kite-flying, surfing or biking. Even
on foggy days, don't neglect sunscreen:
UV rays penetrate San Francisco's thin
cloud cover.

Hit your stride on the 10.5-mile
Coastal Trail (www.californiacoastaltrail.
info; ☺sunrise-sunset; 🚇1,18,38), starting at
Fort Funston, crossing 4 miles of sandy
Ocean Beach and wrapping around
the Presidio to the Golden Gate Bridge.
Casual strollers can pick up the freshly
restored trail near Sutro Baths and
head around the Lands End bluffs for
edge-of-the-world views and glimpses
of shipwrecks at low tide.

Every weekend, thousands of cyclists
cross Golden Gate Bridge to explore the
Marin Headlands and Mt Tamalpais. Since
the 1970s, 'Mt Tam' has been the Bay Ar-
ea's ultimate mountain-biking challenge.

Many SF streets have bicycle lanes
and major parks have bike paths. The
safest places to cycle in SF are Golden
Gate Park (car-free on Sunday), the Em-
barcadero and the wooded Presidio. SF
bikers' favorite street-biking route is the
green-painted, flat bike lane connecting
Market St and Golden Gate Park called
the Wiggle.

The **San Francisco Bicycle Coa-
lition** (☏415-431-2453; www.sfbike.org)
produces the *San Francisco Bike Map &
Walking Guide* ($4), which outlines the
Wiggle route and shows how to avoid
traffic and hills.

Sutro Baths at sunset

🍴 Cheap Eats in the Avenues

Work up an appetite in Golden Gate Park, then haul north for cheap and tasty ethnic eats.

Fog banks and cold wars are no match for the heartwarming powers of the **Cinderella Russian Bakery** (Map p60; ☑415-751-6723; www.cinderellabakery. com; 436 Balboa St; pastries $1.50-3.50, mains $7-14; ⊘7am-7pm; ☖5, 21, 31, 33), serving treats like your baba used to make (just-baked egg-and-green-onion *piroshki*, hearty borscht, decadent dumplings) since 1953.

Hong Kong meets Vegas at San Francisco's most glamorous, decadent Cantonese restaurant, **Dragon Beaux** (☑415-333-8899; www.dragonbeaux.com; 5700 Geary Blvd; dumplings $5-9; ⊘11am-2:30pm & 5:30-9:45pm Mon-Fri, 10am-3pm & 5:30-9:45pm Sat & Sun; ☖2, 38). Say yes to cartloads of succulent roast meats – hello, duck and pork belly – and creative dumplings, especially XO dumplings with plump, brandy-laced shrimp in spinach wrappers.

Piroshki (savory Russian pies)
TASHA_LYUBINA/SHUTTERSTOCK ©

⊗ The Mission

La Palma Mexicatessen   Mexican $

(Map p58; ☑415-647-1500; www.lapalmasf. com; 2884 24th St; tamales, tacos & huaraches $3-10; ⊘8am-6pm Mon-Sat, to 5pm Sun; ☑; ☖12, 14, 27, 48, Ⓑ24th St Mission) ✔ Follow the applause: that's the clapping sound of organic tortilla-making in progress. You've found the Mission mother lode of hand-made tamales, *huaraches* (stuffed masa), and *pupusas* (tortilla pockets) with potato and *chicharones* (pork crackling), *carnitas* (slow-roasted pork), *cotija* (Oaxacan cheese) and La Palma's own tangy tomatillo sauce. Get takeout or bring a small army to finish feasts at sunny sidewalk tables.

Al's Place   Californian $$

(Map p58; ☑415-416-6136; www.alsplacesf.com; 1499 Valencia St; share plates $15-21; ⊘5:30-10pm Wed-Sun; ☑; ☖12, 14, 49, Ⓜ J, Ⓑ24th St Mission) ✔ The Golden State dazzles on Al's plates, featuring heirloom ingredients, pristine Pacific seafood, and meadow-fed meat. Painstaking preparation yields sun-drenched flavors and exquisite textures: goat's-milk curd grits with chanterelles, crispy-skin cod with preserved-lime froth. Dishes are half the size but thrice the flavor of mains elsewhere – get three or the family-style menu (five courses $73), and you'll be California dreaming.

⊗ The Haight & Hayes Valley

RT Rotisserie   Californian $

(Map p60; www.rtrotisserie.com; 101 Oak St; dishes $9-14; ⊘11am-9pm; ☑⚇; ☖5, 6, 7, 21, 47, 49, ⓂVan Ness) ✔ An all-star menu makes ordering mains easy – you'll find bliss with entire chickens hot off the spit, succulent lamb and pickled onions, or surprisingly decadent roast cauliflower with earthy beet-tahini sauce – but do you choose porcini-powdered fries or signature salad with that? A counter staffer calls it: 'Look, I don't normally go for salads, but this one's next-level.' So true. No reservations.

Souvla   Greek $

(Map p60; ☑415-400-5458; www.souvlasf. com; 517 Hayes St; sandwiches & salads $12-15; ⊘11am-10pm; ☖5, 21, 47, 49, ⓂVan Ness) Ancient Greek philosophers didn't think too hard about lunch, and neither should you at Souvla. Step in line for no-fail choices: signature spit-fired lamb atop kale with yogurt dressing, or organic chicken with pickled onion, *mizithra* (sheep's milk) cheese and sweet potatoes. Go early/late for skylit communal seating, or head to Patricia's

JUSTIN SULLIVAN/GETTY IMAGES ©

Sightglass Coffee (p68)

Green park with takeout. Additional locations citywide, including 531 Divisadero; see website.

Rich Table Californian $$
(Map p60; ☎415-355-9085; http://richtablesf.com; 199 Gough St; mains $17-37; ⊙5:30-10pm Sun-Thu, to 10:30pm Fri & Sat; 🚌5, 6, 7, 21, 47, 49, Ⓜ Van Ness) Impossible cravings begin with mind-blowing inventions like porcini doughnuts, sardine chips and burrata funnel cake. Join married co-chefs/owners Sarah and Evan Rich for the world's friendliest culinary competition – Sarah's Southern roots shine in biscuits with chicken-liver mousse and fried chicken skin, while Evan jet-sets from Tokyo to Rome with *cacio e pepe* (cheese and pepper) pasta. For maximum surprise, get the chef's menu ($99).

DRINKING & NIGHTLIFE

For a pub crawl, start with North Beach saloons or Mission bars around Valencia and 16th Sts. The Castro has historic gay bars; SoMa adds dance clubs. Downtown and around Union Sq mix dives with speakeasies. Marina bars are preppy, while Haight bars draw diverse crowds.

The Marina, Fisherman's Wharf & the Piers

Interval Bar & Cafe Bar
(www.theinterval.org; 2 Marina Blvd, Fort Mason Center, Bldg A; ⊙10am-midnight; 🚌10, 22, 28, 30, 47, 49) Lose track of time over aged Tom Collins or freshly roasted coffee at the Interval, specifically designed to stimulate philosophical discussion. The bar-cafe doubles as HQ for nonprofit Long Now Foundation, dedicated to long-term thinking – hence Brian Eno's fourth-dimensional digital artwork over the bar, the interdisciplinary library overhead, and the sculptural prototype of a 10,000-year clock.

Buena Vista Cafe Bar
(Map p54; ☎415-474-5044; www.thebuenavista.com; 2765 Hyde St; ⊙9am-2am Mon-Fri, from 8am Sat & Sun; 📶; 🚌30, 45, 47, 🚋Powell-Hyde) Warm your cockles with a prim little goblet of bitter-creamy Irish coffee, introduced to America at this destination bar that once

served sailors and cannery workers. That old Victorian floor creaks under carousers and families alike, served community-style at round tables overlooking the cable-car turnaround at Victoria Park.

Downtown, Civic Center & SoMa

Sightglass Coffee   Cafe

(Map p54; ☎415-861-1313; www.sightglasscoffee. com; 270 7th St; ⏰7am-7pm; ☐12, 14, 19, ⒷCivic Center, ⓂCivic Center) Follow cult coffee aromas into this sunny SoMa warehouse, where family-grown, high-end coffee is roasted daily. Aficionados sip signature Owl's Howl Espresso downstairs or head directly to the mezzanine Affogato Bar to get ice cream with that espresso. Daredevils should try the sparkling coffee cascara shrub – soda made with the cherry fruit of coffee plants.

Sister operations have opened in the Haight, the Mission, SFMOMA and the Ferry Plaza Farmers Market.

North Beach & Chinatown

Vesuvio   Bar

(Map p54; ☎415-362-3370; www.vesuvio.com; 255 Columbus Ave; ⏰8am-2am; ☐8, 10, 12, 30, 41, 45, ⓇPowell-Mason) Guy walks into a bar, roars and leaves. Without missing a beat, the bartender says to the next customer, 'Welcome to Vesuvio, honey – what can I get you?' Jack Kerouac blew off Henry Miller to go on a bender here and, after you've joined neighborhood characters on the stained-glass mezzanine for 8pm microbrews or 8am Kerouacs (rum, tequila and OJ), you'll see why.

Specs   Bar

(Specs Twelve Adler Museum Cafe; Map p54; ☎415-421-4112; www.facebook.com/specs barsf; 12 William Saroyan Pl; ⏰5pm-2am Mon-Fri; ☐8, 10, 12, 30, 41, 45, ⓇPowell-Mason, ⓂT) The walls here are plastered with merchant-marine memorabilia, and you'll be plastered too if you try to keep up with the salty characters holding court in the back. Surrounded by seafaring mementos

– including a massive walrus organ over the bar – your order seems obvious: pitcher of Anchor Steam, coming right up. Cash only.

Caffe Trieste   Cafe

(Map p54; ☎415-392-6739; www.caffetrieste. com; 601 Vallejo St; ⏰6:30am-10pm Sun-Thu, to 11pm Fri & Sat; ☎; ☐8, 10, 12, 30, 41, 45, ⓂT) Opera on the jukebox, live accordion jams and Beat poetry on bathroom walls: Caffe Trieste remains North Beach at its best, since the 1950s. Linger over espresso drinks and scribble your screenplay under the Sardinian fishing mural just as young Francis Ford Coppola did. Perhaps you've heard of the movie: The Godfather. Cash only.

Nob Hill & Russian Hill

Stookey's Club Moderne   Lounge

(Map p54; www.stookeysclubmoderne.com; 895 Bush St; ⏰4:30pm-2am; ☐1, ⓇPowell-Hyde, Powell-Mason, California) Dangerous dames lure unsuspecting sailors into late-night schemes over potent hooch at this art-deco bar straight out of a Dashiell Hammett thriller. Chrome-lined 1930s Streamline Moderne decor sets the scene for intrigue, and wisecracking white-jacketed bartenders shake the stiffest Corpse Reviver cocktails in town. Arrive early to find room on the hat rack for your fedora, especially on live jazz nights.

The Mission

%ABV   Cocktail Bar

(Map p58; ☎415-400-4748; www.abvsf.com; 3174 16th St; ⏰2pm-2am; ☐14, 22, Ⓑ16th St Mission, ⓂJ) As kindred spirits deduce from the name (the abbreviation for 'percent alcohol by volume'), these cocktail crafters know their Rittenhouse rye from their Japanese malt whiskey. Top-notch hooch is served with zero pretension, including excellent Cali wine and beer, and original historically inspired cocktails like the Sutro Swizzle (Armagnac, grapefruit shrub, maraschino liqueur). Order tasty bar bites early, before the place packs.

Trick Dog   Bar

(Map p58; ☑415-471-2999; www.trickdogbar.
com; 3010 20th St; ☺3pm-2am; ☐12, 14, 49)
Drink in SF inspiration with clever cocktails
inspired by local obsessions like the Whole
Earth Catalog, Mission muralists or Chinese horoscopes. Every six months, Trick
Dog adopts a new theme and the menu
changes – proof you can teach an old dog
new tricks and improve on classics like the
Manhattan. Arrive early for bar stools or hit
the mood-lit loft for high-concept bar bites.

Zeitgeist   Bar

(Map p58; ☑415-255-7505; www.zeitgeistsf.
com; 199 Valencia St; ☺11:30am-2am Mon-Fri,
from 10:30am Sat & Sun; ☐14, 22, 49, ☐16th St
Mission) You've got two seconds flat to order
from tough-gal barkeeps used to putting
macho bikers in their place – but with 48
beers on draft, you're spoiled for choice.
Epic afternoons unfold in the beer garden,
with folks hanging out and smoking at
long tables. SF's longest happy hour lasts
11:30am to 6pm weekdays. Cash only; no
photos (read: no evidence).

🍸 The Haight & Hayes Valley

Madrone Art Bar   Bar

(Map p60; ☑415-241-0202; www.madroneartbar.
com; 500 Divisadero St; cover free-$5; ☺4pm-
2am Tue-Sat, 3pm-1:30am Sun; ☐5, 6, 7, 21,
24) Drinking becomes an art form at this
Victorian parlor crammed with graffiti
installations and absinthe fountains. Daily
4pm-to-7pm happy hours bring $1 off well
drinks, including mules – but nothing beats
monthly Prince/Michael Jackson throw-
down dance parties fueled by Madronis (gin,
Campari, Carpano). Performers redefine
genres: punk-grass (bluegrass/punk), blunt-
funk (reggae/soul) and church, no chaser
(Sunday-morning jazz organ). Cash only.

Toronado   Pub

(Map p60; ☑415-863-2276; www.toronado.com;
547 Haight St; ☺11:30am-2am; ☐6, 7, 22, ☐N)
Glory hallelujah, beer-lovers: your prayers
are answered. Genuflect before the chalk-
board altar that lists 40-plus beers on tap
and hundreds more bottled, including sen-

⚢ LGBT+ San Francisco

It doesn't matter where you're from,
who you love or who's your daddy: if
you're here and queer, welcome home.
San Francisco is America's pinkest city,
and though New York Marys may call it
the retirement home of the young – the
sidewalks roll up early here – there's
nowhere easier to be out and proud.

In San Francisco, you don't need to
trawl the urban underworld for a gay
scene. The intersection of 18th and
Castro is the historic center of the
gay world, but dancing queens head
to SoMa for thump-thump clubs. The
Mission remains the preferred 'hood of
alt-chicks, dykes, trans female-to-males
(FTMs) and flirty femmes.

Pride Parade on Market St
SHEILA FITZGERALD/SHUTTERSTOCK ©

sational seasonal microbrews. Bring cash
and score sausages from the next-door grill
to accompany ale made by Trappist monks.
Sometimes it gets too loud in here to hear
your date talk, but you'll hear angels sing.

🍸 The Castro

Twin Peaks Tavern   Gay

(Map p58; ☑415-864-9470; www.twinpeakstav-
ern.com; 401 Castro St; ☺noon-2am Mon-Fri,
from 8am Sat & Sun; ☐Castro St) The vintage
rainbow neon sign points the way to a local
landmark – Twin Peaks was the world's
first gay bar with windows open to the
street. If you're not here for the Castro's
best people-watching, cozy up to the
Victorian carved-wood bar for cocktails and

conviviality, or grab a back booth to discuss movies at the Castro over wine by the glass.

Ideal for a tête-à-tête after a film, or for cards, Yahtzee or backgammon (BYO).

Blackbird   Gay
(Map p60; ✏415-503-0630; www.blackbirdbar. com; 2124 Market St; ✿3pm-2am Mon-Fri, from 2pm Sat & Sun; ❚33, 37, ⓜF, J, K, L, M) Mysterious tinctures and housemade bitters make creative cocktails with magnetic powers, drawing Castro regulars and straight-friendly after-work crowds to this cozy neighborhood den next to the Church St Muni stop. Mix it up while you wait for your turn at billiards or the photo booth. Happy hours run 5pm to 8pm weekdays; weekends get ear-splittingly loud.

Swirl   Wine Bar
(Map p58; ✏415-864-2262; www.swirloncastro. com; 572 Castro St; ✿1:30-8pm Mon-Thu, to 9pm Fri, noon-9pm Sat, to 8pm Sun; ❚24, 33, ❚F, ⓜK, L, M) Come as you are – pinstripes or leather, gay, straight or whatever – to toast equality with sublime bubbly after **GLBT History Museum** (Map p58; ✏415-621-1107; www.glbthistory.org/museum; 4127 18th St; adult/child $10/free, 1st Wed of month free; ✿11am-6pm Mon-Sat, noon-5pm Sun, closed Tue fall-spring; ⓜCastro St) visits, or find liquid courage for sing-alongs at the **Castro Theatre** (Map p58; ✏415-621-6120; www.castrotheatre.com; 429 Castro St; adult/ child, senior & matinee $13/10; ❚22, 33, ⓜF, K, L, M) in flights of bold reds. This wine shop with a bar in the back has universal appeal, with reliably delicious wine at fair prices in neighborly company.

440 Castro   Gay
(Map p58; ✏415-621-8732; www.the440.com; 440 Castro St; ✿noon-2am; ❚24, 33, ⓜF, K, L, M) The most happening bar on the street, 440 draws bearded, gym-fit 30- and 40-something dudes – especially on scruffy Sundays and weekend nights, when go-go boys twirl – and an odd mix of Peter Pans for Monday's underwear night. If you think the monthly Battle of the Bulges contest has something to do with WWII, this is not your bar, honey.

⊕ ENTERTAINMENT

San Francisco
Symphony   Classical Music
(Map p54; ✏box office 415-864-6000, rush-ticket hotline 415-503-5577; www.sfsymphony.org; Grove St, btwn Franklin St & Van Ness Ave; tickets $20-150; ❚21, 45, 47, ⓜVan Ness, ⒷCivic Center) From the moment cutting-edge conductor and composer Esa-Pekka Salonen raises his baton, the audience is on the edge of their seats for another world-class performance by the Grammy-winning SF Symphony. Don't miss signature Bach and Stravinsky, world premieres of Symphony-commissioned contemporary works, live performances with such films as *Star Trek*, and collaborations with artists from Wynton Marsalis to Renée Fleming.

Fillmore Auditorium   Live Music
(Map p60; ✏415-346-6000; http://thefillmore. com; 1805 Geary Blvd; tickets from $20; ✿box office 10am-3pm Sun, plus 30min before doors open to 10pm show nights; ❚22, 38) Jimi Hendrix, Janis Joplin, the Grateful Dead – they all played the Fillmore, and the upstairs bar is lined with vintage psychedelic posters to prove it. Bands that sell out stadiums keep rocking this historic, 1250-capacity dance hall, and for major shows, free posters are still handed out. To squeeze up to the stage, be polite and lead with the hip.

SFJAZZ Center   Jazz
(Map p60; ✏866-920-5299; www.sfjazz.org; 201 Franklin St; tickets $25-120; ♿; ❚5, 6, 7, 21, 47, 49, ⓜVan Ness) ✐ Jazz legends and singular talents from Argentina to Yemen are showcased at America's largest jazz center. Hear fresh takes on classic jazz albums and poets riffing with jazz combos in downstairs Joe Henderson Lab, and witness main-stage collaborations by Kid Koala and Del the Funky Homosapien, raucous all-women mariachis Flor de Toluache, and tap virtuoso Savion Glover improvising with a jazz trio.

Alamo Drafthouse Cinema   Cinema

(Map p58; 415-549-5959; https://drafthouse.com/sf; 2550 Mission St; tickets $6-20; 14, 24th St Mission) The landmark 1932 New Mission cinema is restored to its original Timothy Pfleuger–designed art-deco glory, and it's on a mission to upgrade dinner-and-a-movie dates. Staff deliver cocktails, beer and pizza to your plush banquette seats while you enjoy premieres, cult revivals (especially Music Mondays) or SF favorites, from *Mrs Doubtfire* to *Dirty Harry* – sometimes followed by filmmaker Q&As.

ODC Theater   Dance

(Oberlin Dance Collective; Map p58; box office 415-863-9834, classes 415-549-8519; www.odctheater.org; 3153 17th St; drop-in classes from $15, shows $20-50; 12, 14, 22, 33, 49, 16th St Mission) For 45 years ODC has been redefining dance with risky, raw performances and the sheer joy of movement. ODC's season runs from September to December, but its stage presents year-round shows featuring local and international artists. Down the block at 351 Shotwell St, ODC Dance Commons offers 200-plus classes a week from flamenco to vogue for all dance levels.

Bottom of the Hill   Live Music

(415-621-4455; www.bottomofthehill.com; 1233 17th St; tickets $5-20; shows generally 9pm Tue-Sat; 10, 19, 22) The bottom of Potrero Hill tops the list for rocking with punk legends the Avengers, Pansy Division and The Dils, and newcomers worth checking out for their names alone (Playboy Manbaby, Try the Pie, The Freak Accident). The patio is covered in handbills and ruled by a cat that prefers music to people –

totally punk rock. Anchor Steam on tap; cash-only bar.

INFORMATION

SF Visitor Information Center (www.sanfrancisco.travel/visitor-information-center) Muni Passports, activities deals, culture and event calendars.

GETTING THERE & AWAY

The Bay Area has three international airports: **San Francisco** (SFO; www.flysfo.com; S McDonnell Rd), Oakland (OAK) and San Jose (SJC). Factor in additional transit time – and cost – to reach San Francisco proper from Oakland or San Jose, and note that what you save in airfare you may wind up spending on ground transportation.

If you've unlimited time, consider taking the train, instead of driving or flying, to avoid traffic hassles and excess carbon emissions.

GETTING AROUND

When San Franciscans aren't pressed for time, most walk, cycle or ride **Muni** (Municipal Transit Agency; 511; www.sfmta.com) bus, streetcar and cable-car lines instead of taking a car or cab. Traffic is notoriously bad at rush hour, and parking is next to impossible in center-city neighborhoods. Avoid driving until it's time to leave town – or drive during off-peak hours.

For Bay Area transit options, departures and arrivals, call 511 or check www.511.org. A detailed *Muni Street & Transit Map* is available free online.

SONOMA VALLEY

Sonoma Valley

Delightfully laid-back, unapologetic and fun-loving, Sonoma Valley, or Valley of the Moon as it's sometimes called, is the down-to-earth alternative to Napa. Rolling hills, dotted with century-old oaks, turn the color of lion's fur under the summer sun and swaths of vineyards carpet hillsides as far as the eye can see. Anchoring the bucolic 17-mile-long valley, the town of Sonoma makes a great jumping-off point for Wine Country. It's less than 50 miles from San Francisco and has storied 19th-century historical sights. Further up the valley, pleasantly tranquil Glen Ellen is straight from a Norman Rockwell painting. The wildfires that devastated vast tracts of northern California in the fall of 2020 affected only a small portion of Sonoma County. More than 450 wineries remain open.

Sonoma Valley in Two Days

Start your Wine Country adventure with coffee in **Sonoma Plaza** (p80). With two days in the area, you'll then have plenty of time to meander around the valley's quaint, vine-lined roads, stopping frequently to taste the vinous wares; be sure to hit California's oldest family-run winery, **Gundlach-Bundschu** (p79). Fans of *The Call of the Wild* should set aside time to visit **Jack London State Historic Park** (p84).

Sonoma Valley in Four Days

With two extra days, it's worth renting a bike and cruising to **Bartholomew Park**, an oak-dotted preserve in a stunning natural setting with a **winery** (p79) on-site. Adventurous types can work off any alcohol-related lassitude hiking the trails of **Sugarloaf Ridge State Park** (p84). On your final evening, celebrate Sonoma Valley produce with a low-food-miles meal at **Cafe La Haye** (p83).

St Helena

10 km
5 miles

St Francis Winery & Vineyards

Rutherford

Santa Rosa

Sugarloaf Ridge State Park

Oakville

Kenwood

Napa Valley

Sonoma Wine Country

Yountville

Glen Ellen

Quarryhill Botanical Garden

Benziger

Napa River

Jack London State Historic Park

Cotati

Sonoma Valley

Bartholomew Estate Winery

Napa

Penngrove

Sonoma

Gundlach-Bundschu Winery

Scribe

Bodega Ave

Cornerstone Sonoma

Petaluma

Sonoma Map (p82)

Arriving in Sonoma Valley

Car Sonoma Valley is a 90-minute drive from San Francisco. Sonoma Hwy (Hwy 12) is lined with wineries and runs from Sonoma, past Glen Ellen, through Kenwood to Santa Rosa, then on to western Sonoma County.

Bus Public transportation will get you to the valley, but is insufficient for vineyard hopping. Call 511 for info or check online (www.transit.511.org).

Sleeping

For the full viticultural experience, stay at one of the many wineries dotted through the region; accommodations are often quaint and romantic. Couples will find a number of cozy cottages and inns in Glen Ellen. There are historic hotels suitable for a midrange budget around Sonoma; those counting pennies will have better luck in Santa Rosa. Off-season rates plummet.

Testing a wine sample in Sonoma Wine Country

Sonoma Wine Country

A bit less fussy and a lot less expensive than its celebrated nearby sister, Napa, this easygoing region is where wine growing began in California more than 200 years ago.

Great For...

ℹ Need to Know

Spring and fall are the best times to visit. Summers are hot, dusty and crowded. Fall brings fine weather, harvest time and the 'crush' (grape pressing).

★ **Top Tip**

Don't be afraid to ask questions. Vintners love to talk. If you don't know how to taste wine, or what to look for, ask the person behind the counter to help you discover what you like.

Wine Tasting

The best way to discover the real Wine Country is to avoid factory wineries; visit family-owned boutique houses (producing fewer than 20,000 annual cases) and midsized houses (20,000 to 60,000 annual cases).

Tastings are called 'flights' and include four to six different wines. In Sonoma Valley, tastings cost about $10 to $20. You must be 21 years old to taste.

To avoid burnout, visit no more than three wineries per day. Most open daily from 10am or 11am to 4pm or 5pm, but call ahead if your heart's set on a particular place. Plan at least five hours to amble from the bottom to the top of Sonoma Valley.

Do not drink and drive. The curvy roads are dangerous and police monitor traffic.

Guided Tours

You have the most flexibility by driving your own vehicle, but to avoid drinking and driving, opt for a tour.

Billed as the anti-wine-snob tour, **Platypus Wine Tours** (www.platypustours.com) specializes in back-road vineyards, historic wineries and family-owned operations. For something a little different, **Active Wine Adventures** (www.activewineadventures. com) pairs wine and food with scenic hikes, local art, literary adventures and, most recently, microbreweries.

Another option is a guided bicycle tour. These start at around $119 per day including bikes, tastings and lunch. Daily rentals with Wine Country Cyclery (p81) cost $30 to $80. Make reservations.

Merlot grapes in Sonoma Wine Country

Wineries

Bartholomew Estate Winery

A great bike-to winery, **Bartholomew Estate Winery** (707-509-0450; www.bartholomewestate.com; 1000 Vineyard Lane; tasting $25, with vineyard tour $45; 11am-4:30pm; P) occupies park-shaded grounds with valley-view hiking. The vineyards were originally cultivated in 1857 and they now yield certified-organic, citrusy sauvignon blanc, cabernet sauvignon softer in style than Napa, and lush zinfandel.

> ☑ **Don't Miss**
>
> The vine-lined byways of the region – perfect for a lazy drive (or cycle).

SHERRI R. CAMP/SHUTTERSTOCK ©

Gundlach-Bundschu Winery

California's oldest family-run **winery** (707-938-5277; www.gunbun.com; 2000 Denmark St; tasting $25-35, incl tour $55-60; 11am-5:30pm Sun-Fri, to 7pm Sat Apr-Oct, to 4:30pm Nov-Mar; P) looks like a castle but has a down-to-earth vibe. Founded in 1858 by a Bavarian immigrant, its signatures are gewürztraminer and pinot noir, but 'Gun-Bun' was the first American winery to produce 100% merlot. Down a winding lane, it's a terrific bike-to winery with picnicking, hiking, a lake and frequent concerts.

St Francis Winery & Vineyards

The vineyards are scenic and all, but the real reason to visit **St Francis** (707-538-9463; www.stfranciswinery.com; 100 Pythian Rd at Hwy 12; tasting $20, wine & food pairing $85; 10am-5pm; P) is the much-lauded food-pairing experience. The mouthwatering, multicourse affair is hosted by amiable and informative wine experts and includes things such as braised Kurobuta pork paired with cab franc and American Wagyu strip loin paired with an old-vine zinfandel.

Scribe

With **Scribe** (707-939-1858; www.scribewinery.com; 2100 Denmark St; tasting $35, food pairing $65; by appointment 11:30am-4pm Thu-Mon), a new generation has found its place in Wine Country. Bantering groups of bespectacled millennials frequent this hip winery designed to resemble a French chateau, and at outdoor picnic tables they hold forth on the terroir-driven rosé or pinot, the skin-fermented chardonnay and the bold cab.

> ✕ **Take a Break**
>
> Buy ready-made boxed lunches at **Sonoma Market** (707-996-3411; www.sonomamarket.net; 500 W Napa St; takeaway boxed lunch $18; 5am-9:30pm) in the morning, then dig in at a pretty winery spot.

Sonoma

Fancy boutiques may lately be replacing hardware stores, but Sonoma still retains an old-fashioned charm, thanks to the plaza, California's largest town square, and its surrounding frozen-in-time historic buildings.

◎ SIGHTS

Sonoma Plaza   Square

(www.sonomaplaza.com; btwn Napa, Spain & 1st Sts) The largest plaza in California showcases everything Sonoma holds dear – food, community, art, history – flanked by indie restaurants, galleries and dozens of wine-tasting rooms. The Mission Revival–style city hall was inaugurated in 1908 with four identical facades, reportedly because plaza businesses all demanded City Hall face their direction. At the plaza's northeast corner, the **Bear Flag Monument** commemorates Sonoma's drunken independence movement. The weekly farmers market (5:30pm to 8pm Tuesdays,

April to October) showcases Sonoma's incredible produce.

Free jazz concerts take place on the plaza every second Tuesday of the month, June to September, 6pm to 8:30pm; arrive early and bring a picnic. (To answer the obvious question here: drinking wine is allowed on Sonoma Plaza from 11:30am until sunset.)

Cornerstone Sonoma   Gardens

(☏707-933-3010; www.cornerstonesonoma.com; 23570 Arnold Dr; ⊘10am-5pm, gardens to 4pm; P⛅⛄) **FREE** The orange Adirondack chair by the road signals your arrival at this Wine Country garden and design showplace, featuring 10 landscape-artist-designed gardens, five kid-friendly experiential-education gardens, local design boutiques, wine-tasting parlors, and on-site Sonoma Valley Visitors Bureau (p83) that's generous with trip advice and tasting-room passes. Stop by for farm-fresh local fare at family-friendly, indoor-outdoor **Palooza Beer Gardens**.

Sonoma Plaza

Sonoma Valley Museum of Art
Museum

(☑707-939-7862; www.svma.org; 551 Broadway; adult/child 13-17yr/family $10/7/15; ◷11am-5pm Wed-Sun; P⚑) From Judy O'Shea's floating costumes to Wanxin Zhang's gas-masked clay warriors, artworks by California and international artists fill rotating gallery shows at this 8000-sq-ft modern- and contemporary-art museum, dedicated to building community around art. Shows here are thoughtful and timely: after the 2017 fires, SVMA commissioned photographers to take portraits of anyone who wanted one – a symbolic but important gift to local families rebuilding their lives and homes in Sonoma. Check online for art-making workshops and kids' events.

✪ ACTIVITIES

Many local inns provide bicycles, and cycling is a great way to visit local wineries.

Vintage Aircraft Company
Scenic Flights

(☑707-938-2444; www.vintageaircraft.com; 23982 Arnold Dr; 20min flight 1/2 people $175/270; ◷Thu & Fri Apr-Oct by appointment, 10:30am-4pm Sat & Sun year round; ⚑) See Sonoma vineyards from above in biplanes, with an option to add aerobatic maneuvers ($50 extra). Daredevils can do loops in open-cockpit biplanes, while gearheads geek out over 1942 navy fighter planes. Weekends are for walk-ins, so you can hop in that cockpit before you change your mind. Flights run 20 minutes, and only take off when weather permits; ages 10-plus.

Wine Country Cyclery
Cycling

(☑707-966-6800; www.winecountrycyclery.com; 262 W Napa St; bicycle rental per day $30-80; ◷11am-4pm Mon, Tue, Thu & Fri, 10am-5pm Sat & Sun) Downtown Sonoma is small, relatively flat and perfect for biking, and this reliable bike shop rents road bikes, electric bikes, hybrids, kids' bikes and even tandem sport bikes (aka 'divorce-makers') to get you

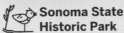

Sonoma State Historic Park

You can time-travel across 200 years of California history, with multiple sites in action-packed downtown Sonoma at **Sonoma State Historic Park** (☑707-938-9560; www.parks.ca.gov; 363 3rd St W; adult/child $3/2; ◷10am-5pm; P), where one ticket allows same-day admission to them all. Start your adventure in 1823 at **Mission San Francisco Solano** (☑707-938-1519; www.sonomaparks.org; 114 E Spain St; adult/child $3/2; ◷10am-5pm), the adobe structure that anchors the plaza where the Native American village of Huichi once stood. **Sonoma Barracks** (☑707-939-9420; www.sonomaparks.org; 20 E Spain St; adult/child $3/2; ◷10am-5pm) captures 19th-century life, and describes how Sonoma's Bear Flag Republic started. The 1886 **Toscano Hotel** (☑707-938-9560; www.sonomaparks.org; 20 E Spain St; adult/child $3/2; ◷10am-5pm) lobby is beautifully preserved – peek inside – and Vallejo's stately 1852 home is a half-mile northwest. Your ticket also includes entry to **Petaluma Adobe State Park** at General Vallejo's former ranch, 15 miles away. Free parking is available behind the barracks.

Petaluma Adobe State Park

JOHN ELK/GETTY IMAGES ©

where you want to go for an hour or all day. Rentals include helmets, handlebar bag, and – crucially – a winery map. Book ahead.

Sonoma

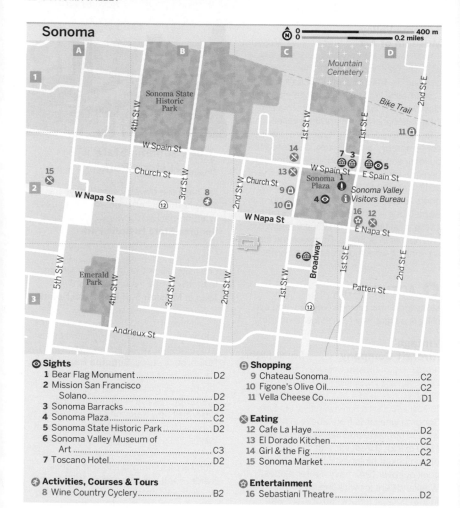

◉ Sights
1 Bear Flag Monument	D2
2 Mission San Francisco Solano	D2
3 Sonoma Barracks	D2
4 Sonoma Plaza	C2
5 Sonoma State Historic Park	D2
6 Sonoma Valley Museum of Art	C3
7 Toscano Hotel	D2

◉ Activities, Courses & Tours
8 Wine Country Cyclery	B2

🛍 Shopping
9 Chateau Sonoma	C2
10 Figone's Olive Oil	C2
11 Vella Cheese Co	D1

✕ Eating
12 Cafe La Haye	D2
13 El Dorado Kitchen	C2
14 Girl & the Fig	C2
15 Sonoma Market	A2

◉ Entertainment
16 Sebastiani Theatre	D2

🔒 SHOPPING

Vella Cheese Co
Food

(☎707-938-3232; www.vellacheese.com; 315 2nd St E; ⏰9:30am-6pm Mon-Fri, to 5pm Sat; 👶) Move over, parmesan: Vella's two-year-aged dry jack is meant for shaving atop rustic dishes, and it has been making spaghetti Western for almost 100 years. The Mezzo Secco is another aged umami bomb, ideal for pairing with Sonoma's hearty reds. Staff graciously provide samples before purchase, and will vacuum-pack for shipping.

Chateau Sonoma
Homewares

(☎707-309-1993; www.chateausonoma.com; 453 1st St W; ⏰10am-5pm) France whimsy meets California quirk at Sarah Anderson's curiosity cabinet of a shop, brimming with unique finds from scouring the countryside across continents. Here home decor doubles as Wine Country installation art – scented soaps spill out of birds' nests, tarnished medicine cabinets hold sleek barware, and vineyard cuttings become centerpieces in vintage enamel pitchers.

Figone's Olive Oil   Food

([📞]707-282-9092; www.figoneoliveoil.com; 483
1st St W; [🕐]11am-5pm Mon-Thu, 10am-6pm Fri-
Sun) Taste the difference Sonoma sunshine
and soil make in Figone's extra-virgin olive
oil, pressed in the family's own olive-oil
mill (tours by reservation; $89 per person
including tasting with small bites). Try oil
infused with natural, seasonal flavors such
as Alba truffle and Meyer lemon – sampling
is encouraged – and dab on olive-enriched
hand lotion.

❌ EATING

Cafe La Haye   Californian $$$

([📞]707-935-5994; www.cafelahaye.com; 140 E
Napa St; mains $26-42; [🕐]5:30-9pm Tue-Sat) [🌿]
Warm feelings are mutual between farmers
and chefs, regulars and visitors at cozy La
Haye, which champions produce sourced
within 60 miles. Neighboring farmers
earn co-star credits on seasonal favorites,
including sherry-basted Wolfe Ranch
quail with sourdough stuffing and hearty
chopped salads with George's farm eggs
and Humboldt Fog goat cheese. Save room
for simple, sensational desserts such as
yuzu-citrus cheesecake.

Girl & the Fig   French $$$

([📞]707-938-3634; www.thegirlandthefig.com;
110 W Spain St; mains $22-36; [🕐]11:30am-10pm
Mon-Thu, from 11am Fri & Sat, from 3pm Sun) [🌿]
French accents aren't required to order up
hearty feasts of rustic fare here – Sondra
Bernstein and her garden keep these bistro
tables loaded with house-cured salami,
velvety duck cassoulet, and aptly named
roast-cauliflower steaks. The all-day and
late-night menus accommodate busy
wine-tasting schedules, including the three-
course prix-fixe menu ($42) and obligatory
Fig Royale (sparkling wine and housemade
fig liqueur).

El Dorado Kitchen   Californian $$$

([📞]707-996-3030; www.eldoradosonoma.com/
kitchen; 405 1st St W; mains lunch $15-24, dinner
$25-35; [🕐]8-11am, 11:30am-2:30pm & 5:30-9pm
Mon-Thu, to 10pm Fri & Sat) [🌿] Chef Armando

Navarro's flavor-packed, casual Californian
dishes are easy to appreciate, but take
a look at that Pacific seafood paella and
Petaluma chicken mole before you dig in –
his technique is sharp and laser-focused
on Sonoma ingredients. Snag a community
table seat in the see-and-be-seen plaza-
front dining room, and you'll be the envy of
passersby (they have no idea).

⭐ ENTERTAINMENT

Sebastiani Theatre   Cinema

([📞]707-996-2020; www.sebastianitheatre.com;
476 1st St E; adult/child $11/9, 3D $14/11; [♿])
Offbeat is what Sonoma does best, and
the plaza's community-run, 1934 Mission
Revival cinema encourages that independent streak with global indie art-house films,
director-led screenings of award contend-
ers, locally produced documentaries on
mushrooms and other Sonoma obsessions,
and outrageously fun events like the Cat
Video Festival – it's no competition, because every video is purr-fect.

ℹ️ INFORMATION

Sonoma Valley Visitors Bureau ([📞]866-966-
1090; www.sonomavalley.com; 453 1st St E;
[🕐]9am-5pm Mon-Sat, from 10am Sun) Offers
guides, maps, pamphlets, merchandise, information on deals and events and more. There's
another branch at **Cornerstone Sonoma** ([📞]707-
996-1090; www.sonomavalley.com; 23570 Hwy
121; [🕐]10am-4pm).

Glen Ellen

Sleepy Glen Ellen is a snapshot of old
Sonoma, with white picket fences and
tiny cottages beside a poplar-lined creek.
When downtown Sonoma is jammed, you
can wander quiet Glen Ellen and feel far
away. It's ideal for a leg-stretching stopover
between wineries or a romantic overnight –
the nighttime sky blazes with stars. The
biggest daytime attractions are Jack
London State Historic Park and Benziger
winery.

JMOOR17/GETTY IMAGES ©

Sugarloaf Ridge State Park

There are 30 miles of fantastic hiking – when it's not blazingly hot – at this **state park** (☏707-833-5712; www. sugarloafpark.org; 2605 Adobe Canyon Rd; per car $8; 🅿🚻) ✎. On clear days, Bald Mountain has drop-dead views to the sea, while the Brushy Peaks Trail peers into Napa Valley. Both are moderately strenuous; plan on a three-hour round-trip. Bikes and horses can use perimeter trails seasonally. The park was impacted by the Glass Fire in the fall of 2020, and during research the backcountry trails had been closed until further notice.

◎ SIGHTS

Jack London State Historic Park — Park

(☏707-938-5216; www.jacklondonpark.com; 2400 London Ranch Rd; per car $10, cottage admission $3; ⊙9:30am-5pm; 🅿🚻) ✎ He wrote the world's longest-running bestseller, *Call of the Wild*, and traveled the world over – but Jack London (1876–1916) claimed his greatest work was rescuing this 1400-acre preserve from early settlers' slash-and-burn farming methods. Beauty Ranch remains as Jack left it: Yokohama sailor shirts overflowing steamer trunks, cowboy hat hanging by his desk. A short but rugged hiking trail leads past Jack's gravesite to ruined Wolf House and House of Happy Walls (10am to 5pm), featuring Jack's rejection letters in the bookshop.

Quarryhill Botanical Garden — Gardens

(☏707-996-3166; www.quarryhillbg.org; 12841 Hwy 12; adult/child 13-17yr $12/8; ⊙9am-4pm) ✎ Just when you thought the vineyards would never end along Hwy 12, along comes this world-renowned 25-acre botanical garden specializing in the flora of Asia. Vines wouldn't grow on this abandoned quarry site, but over 30 years, founder Jane Davenport Jansen and a team of dedicated conservationists cultivated an artful woodland of Asian magnolias, dogwood, lilies and maples – including some that are now endangered in their native lands. Today it's fragrant in spring, colorful in fall and inspiring year-round.

✪ ACTIVITIES

Triple Creek Horse Outfit — Horseback Riding

(☏707-887-8700; www.triplecreekhorseoutfit. com; 2400 London Ranch Rd; 60/90min rides $90/110; ⊙by appointment 9am-5pm Mon-Sat; 🚻) Explore Jack London State Park the way Jack did, on horseback, and see for yourself what the globe-trotting adventure author saw in this place: ancient oaks, stunning vistas over Sonoma Valley, and sunny meadows for roaming and dreaming. Private rides can be followed by lunch at Jack London's cottage farmstead on Beauty Ranch (60/90 minutes $185/210). Reservations required.

✦ EATING

Fig Cafe & Winebar — French, Californian $$

(☏707-938-2130; www.thefigcafe.com; 13690 Arnold Dr; mains $21-27, 3-course meal $39; ⊙dinner from 5pm; 🚻) ✎ With the possible exception of grandma's cooking, Sondra Bernstein's earthy California comfort food is as satisfying as dinner gets. On the seasonal menu, look for succulent Sonoma duck, fig and arugula salad, and decadent steak frites with blue-cheese butter. Service is downright neighborly – through wildfires and Covid-19, these folks kept

Jack London State Historic Park

neighbors and staff fed. No reservations; complimentary corkage.

Glen Ellen Inn & Martini Bar
American $$

(☏707-996-6409; www.glenelleninn.com; 13670 Arnold Dr; mains $16-25; ⊙3-9pm) Start with oysters with Bloody Mary sauce and pre-dinner drinks in the creekside garden, and you may never get around to dinner. Choose from creative vodka martinis (get the cucumber), classic Western gin martinis (dirty, extra olives), or signature Sonoma lavender lemon drop – but get all three and you might fall asleep in your tasty chicken pot pie.

Glen Ellen Star
Californian, Italian $$$

(☏707-343-1384; www.glenellenstar.com; 13648 Arnold Dr; pizzas $17-20, mains $24-50; ⊙5:30-

9pm Sun-Thu, to 9:30pm Fri & Sat; ☑) ✔ The Wine Country star power here is formidable – co-owners are *Food & Wine* star chef Ari Weiswasser and Erinn Benziger-Weiswasser, from **Benziger Winery** (☏707-935-3000; www.benziger.com; 1883 London Ranch Rd; tastings $25-50, tours incl tasting for adults $30-55, kids $10; ⊙11am-5pm Mon-Fri, from 10am Sat & Sun; P🚻) ✔ – yet the vibes are relaxed, with easy banter in the open kitchen and buzzy crowds awaiting wood-fired-oven pizza, roasted fish, and pasta with spring-lamb ragù. Organic produce comes from Benziger gardens; definitely get those bacon-marmalade Brussels sprouts.

REDWOOD FORESTS

In this Chapter

Redwood Forests

The jagged edge of the continent is wild, scenic and even slightly foreboding, where spectral fog and an outsider spirit have fostered the world's tallest trees, most potent weed and a string of idiosyncratic two-stoplight towns. This is a place to traverse valleys of ancient redwood and explore hidden coves with a blanket and a bottle of local wine. The unlikely mélange of residents befits this dramatic clash of land and water: timber barons, tree huggers, pot farmers and radicals of every political persuasion. But come here for the trees – those majestic, otherworldly giants that make our daily problems seem very small indeed.

Redwood Forests in Two Days

With two days to see the redwoods, it's best to road trip to **Humboldt Redwoods State Park** (p93). Stop at the quirky roadside shops along Hwy 101, before strolling agape through the primeval **Rockefeller Forest**, the world's largest grove of old-growth redwood. Spend your nights in a tent under the hushing boughs.

Redwood Forests in Four Days

Keep venturing north to the wild **Redwood National Park** (p90), where the trees are so large that the tiny towns along the road seem even smaller. Along the way, stop for a meal at Eureka's always-busy **Brick & Fire** (p97) and soak away any hiking aches and pains at the **Finnish Country Sauna and Tubs** (p94) in the region's eclectic college town, Arcata.

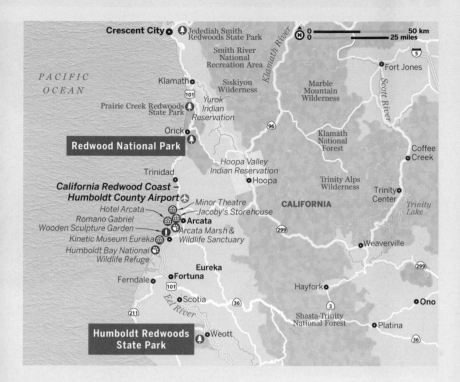

Arriving in the Redwood Forests

Air The California Redwood Coast – Humboldt County Airport (☏707-839-5401; https://humboldtgov.org/1396/Airports; 3561 Boeing Ave; McKinleyville) is located north of McKinleyville on the North Coast. It has regular services to San Francisco and Los Angeles, though flight cancellations due to fog are not uncommon. United Express (www.united.com) is currently the only commercial carrier serving this airport.

Bus Greyhound (www.greyhound.com) runs buses between San Francisco and Eureka (from $35, seven hours, daily) and Arcata (from $39, 7¼ hours, daily).

Sleeping

For comfortable and quaint accommodations, look to stay in Arcata, Eureka and Trinidad. Ferndale is another picture-perfect village in the region with lots of frilly B&Bs. Scores of mid-century motels line Hwy 101, but budget travelers should sleep outdoors if possible. There are plenty of options throughout the region, including backcountry spots in Redwood National Park.

Bull elk, Redwood National & State Parks

TOM REICHNER/SHUTTERSTOCK ©

Redwood National & State Parks

It's hard not to get swept away by the ancient magic of this land of giant trees, some of which predate the Roman Empire by five centuries. Prepare to be impressed.

Great For...

☑ Don't Miss

The magnificent herd of elk at Prairie Creek Redwoods State Park.

Redwood National Park

This **park** (☑707-464-6101, 707-465-7335; www.nps.gov/redw; Hwy 101, Orick) **FREE** is the southernmost of the patchwork of state and federally administered lands under the umbrella of Redwood National & State Parks. A few miles north of Orick along Hwy 101, a trip inland on Bald Hills Rd will take you to **Lady Bird Johnson Grove**, with its 1-mile kid-friendly loop trail, or get you lost in the secluded serenity of **Tall Trees Grove**, which only allows a limited number of cars per day; get permits at the Thomas H Kuchel Visitor Center in Orick.

Prairie Creek Redwoods State Park

Famous for some of the world's best virgin redwood groves and unspoiled coastline, this 14,000-acre **park** (☑707-488-2039; www.

Prairie Creek Redwoods State Park

Jedediah Smith
Redwoods State Park

Crescent City

Del Norte Coast
Redwoods State Park

Klamath

Prairie Creek Redwoods
State Park

*PACIFIC
OCEAN*

Orick

96

101

○ **Redwood
National Park**

❶ Need to Know

Thomas H Kuchel Visitor Center
(☎707-465-7765; www.nps.gov/redw; Hwy
101, Orick; ☺9am-5pm Apr-Oct, to 4pm
Nov-Mar) On Hwy 101, a mile south of the
town of Orick.

✕ Take a Break

Stock up on water, muesli bars and
similar if you are planning on hiking in
any of the parks.

★ Top Tip

Klamath, one of the tiny local settle-
ments, is home to some seriously great
roadside kitsch, for those so inclined.

parks.ca.gov; Newton B Drury Scenic Pkwy) has
spectacular scenic drives and 75 miles of
mainly shady hiking trails, many of which
are excellent for children. A magnificent
herd of elk can often be spied grazing at the
Elk Prairie, signposted from the highway;
the best times to be sure of seeing the elk
are early morning and around sunset.

Del Norte Coast
Redwoods State Park

Marked by steep canyons and dense woods
north of Klamath, this park contains 15
miles of hiking trails and several old logging
roads that are a mountain biker's dream.
The park also fronts 8 miles of rugged
coastline. Hwy 1 winds in from the coast at
dramatic Wilson Beach, and traverses the
dense forest, with groves stretching as far
as you can see. Picnic on the sand at False

Klamath Cove. Heading north, tall trees
cling precipitously to canyon walls that
drop to the rocky, timber-strewn coastline.

Jedediah Smith
Redwoods State Park

The northernmost park, Jedediah Smith
is 9 miles northeast of Crescent City. The
redwood stands are so thick that few trails
penetrate this **park** (☎707-464-6101; www.nps.
gov/redw; Hwy 199, Hiouchi; ☺sunrise-sunset),
but the outstanding 11-mile **Howland Hill
Road scenic drive** cuts through otherwise
inaccessible areas. It's a rough road though,
and unsuitable for RVs. Stop for a stroll
under enormous trees in **Simpson-Reed
Grove**. An easy half-mile trail, departing
from the far side of the campground,
crosses the Smith River via a summer-only
footbridge, leading to **Stout Grove**, the
park's most famous grove.

Humboldt Redwoods State Park

DIANE DIEDERICH/GETTY IMAGES ©

Humboldt Redwoods State Park

Don't miss a magical drive through California's largest redwood park, which covers 53,000 acres – 17,000 of which are old-growth – and contains some of the earth's most magnificent trees.

Great For...

☑ **Don't Miss**

Walking the length of the Dyerville Giant in Founders Grove.

Avenue of the Giants

Exit Hwy 101 when you see the 'Avenue of the Giants' sign and take this smaller alternative to the interstate; it's an incredible 32-mile, two-lane stretch. You'll find free driving guides at roadside signboards at both the avenue's southern entrance, 6 miles north of Garberville, near Phillipsville, and at the northern entrance, south of Scotia, at Pepperwood; there are access points off Hwy 101.

Three miles north of the visitor center, the **California Federation of Women's Clubs Grove** is home to an interesting four-sided stone hearth designed by renowned San Franciscan architect Julia Morgan.

In **Founders Grove**, a mile further north, the Dyerville Giant was knocked over in 1991 by another falling tree. A walk along its

Indian warrior (Pedicularis densiflora)

ROBERT MUTCH/SHUTTERSTOCK ©

ℹ Need to Know

☎707-946-2409; www.parks.ca.gov; Hwy 101; FREE

✗ Take a Break

Stop in at the **Eel River Brewing Company** (☎702-725-2739; http://eelriver brewing.com; 1777 Alamar Way, Fortuna; ⏱11am-11pm) 🍴 for a post-hike selection of all-organic brews.

★ Top Tip

Several towns have simple lodgings along the avenue, but camping is by far the best option.

gargantuan 370ft length helps you appreciate how huge these ancient trees are.

Primeval **Rockefeller Forest**, 4.5 miles west of the avenue via Mattole Rd, appears as it did a century ago. It's the world's largest contiguous old-growth redwood forest and contains about 20% of all such remaining trees. From June to September, when a seasonal bridge is in place, you can tackle the 8-mile **Bull Creek Loop**. You quickly walk out of sight of cars and feel like you have fallen into the time of dinosaurs.

Hiking in Humboldt

The park has more than 100 miles of trails for hiking, mountain biking and horseback riding. Easy walks include short nature trails in Founders Grove and Rockefeller Forest, as well as the 2.4-mile **Drury-Chaney Loop Trail** (with berry picking in

summer). Challenging treks include the popular 14-mile round-trip **Grasshopper Peak Trail**, south of the visitor center, which climbs to the 3379ft fire lookout.

Humboldt Redwoods Visitor Center

Located 2 miles south of Weott, a volunteer-staffed **visitor center** (☎707-946-2263; www.humboldtredwoods.org; Avenue of the Giants; ⏱9am-5pm Apr-Oct, 10am-4pm Nov-Mar) shows videos (three in total), sells maps and also has a sizable exhibition center about the local flora and fauna.

Getting There & Around

Covering Humboldt County, Redwood Transit System operates buses ($3.50) daily between Scotia and Trinidad (2½ hours), stopping en route at Eureka (1¼ hours) and Arcata (1½ hours). To truly explore the park, you will need your own wheels.

Arcata

The North Coast's most progressive town, Arcata surrounds a tidy central square that fills with college students, campers, transients and tourists. Sure, it occasionally reeks of patchouli and its politics lean far left, but its earnest embrace of sustainability has fostered some of the most progressive civic action in America.

Founded in 1850 as a base for lumber camps, today Arcata is defined as a magnet for 20-somethings looking to expand their minds at Humboldt State University (HSU) and/or on the local highly potent marijuana.

◎ SIGHTS

Around Arcata Plaza are two National Historic Landmarks: the 1857 **Jacoby's Storehouse** (☑707-826-2426; ◉hours vary) and the 1915 **Hotel Arcata** (☑707-826-0217; www.hotelarcata.com; 708 9th St). Another great historic building is the 1914 **Minor Theatre** (☑707-822-3456; www.minortheatre. com; 1001 H St; ◉hours vary), which some local

historians claim is the oldest theater in the US built specifically for showing films.

Arcata Marsh & Wildlife Sanctuary   Wildlife Reserve

(www.cityofarcata.org; 569 South G St) FREE On the shores of Humboldt Bay, this sanctuary has 5 miles of walking and biking trails, plus outstanding birding. The **Redwood Region Audubon Society** (☑707-826-7031; www.rras.org; donation welcome) offers guided walks on Saturdays at 8:30am, rain or shine, from the parking lot at I St's south end. Friends of Arcata Marsh offer guided tours Saturdays at 2pm from the **Arcata Marsh Interpretive Center** (☑707-826-2359; www.cityofarcata.org; 569 South G St; ◉9am-5pm Tue-Sun, from 1pm Mon) FREE.

✪ ACTIVITIES

Finnish Country Sauna and Tubs   Spa

(☑707-822-2228; http://cafemokkaarcata. com; 495 J St; per 30min adult/child $10.25/2; ◉11am-11pm Sun-Thu, to midnight Fri & Sat) Like some kind of Euro-crunchy bohemian

Arcata Marsh & Wildlife Sanctuary

dream, these private, open-air redwood hot tubs and sauna are situated around a small frog pond. The staff is easygoing and the facility is relaxing, simple and clean. Reserve ahead, especially on weekends.

⊗ EATING & DRINKING

Slice of Humboldt Pie   Californian $

(☏707-630-5100; 828 I St; pies $4.50-7.50; ⊙11am-6pm Tue-Thu, to 8pm Fri & Sat, closed Sun & Mon) Pies are the mainstays here, ranging from chicken pot pie to Mexican chocolate pecan pie. Savory empanadas also shine and include everything from vegan chipotle black bean to pulled pork with green chili. Ciders are the welcome accompaniment and cover mostly local varieties. The decor is pure industrial chic with exposed pipes and soft gray paintwork.

T's Cafe   Cafe $

(☏707-826-2133; 860 10th St; breakfast $8-15; ⊙7am-2pm; 🛜) Housed in a wonderful early-20th-century mansion; try and grab the table on the front porch if you can. Inside, two cavernous rooms with sage walls, local art, books, toys and magazines provide an informal kickback space for enjoying delicious breakfast classics such as eggs with corned beef hash, stuffed French toast and the specialty: seven kinds of eggs Benedict.

SALT Fish House   Seafood $$

(☏707-630-5300; www.saltfishhouse.com; 7618th St; mains $17-32; ⊙11:30am-10pm Tue-Fri, 4-10pm Sat & Sun; 🛜) ✔ This low-lit, nautical-themed restaurant on the plaza promises sustainably harvested seafood, locally sourced produce and thoughtfully crafted cocktails. It delivers on all three. Come for oysters, chowders, poke bowls and seafood pastas, then stick around for the killer libations.

Redwood Curtain Brewing Company   Microbrewery

(☏707-826-7222; www.redwoodcurtainbrewing. com; 550 S G St; ⊙noon-11pm Sun-Tue, to midnight Wed-Sat; 🎮) This tiny gem of a brewery has gone through a major expansion thanks to its varied collection of rave-worthy craft

The Economics of the Humbolt Herb

With an estimated one-fifth of Humboldt County's population farming its world-famous weed, a good chunk of the economy here has run, for decades, as bank-less, tax-evading and cash only. This is starting to change, albeit slowly, thanks to local incentives aimed at drawing black market farmers out of the forests and into the valleys now that recreational marijuana is – at least in California and some other US states – legal. While the transition hasn't been easy (most farmers remain in the illegal market due to high regulatory fees and plummeting legal marijuana costs) there are several safe and informative ways that visitors can learn about the local industry. **Humboldt Cannabis Tours** (☏707-839-4640; www.humcannabis.com; 215 C St, Ste D1; tours from $55) can take you to the best local dispensaries or out to 'white market' farms where you'll learn about the growing cycle from the Emerald Triangle's longtime cannabis farmers.

Marijuana seedlings

ales. The taproom is family-friendly, invites food trucks to park out back, and has live music or DJs some nights.

ℹ INFORMATION

Arcata Humboldt Welcome Center (☏707-822-3619; www.visitarcata.com; 1635 Heindon Rd; ⊙9am-4pm Mon-Fri) Near the junction of Hwys 299 and 101; has area info.

 Humboldt Bay National Wildlife Refuge

This pristine **wildlife refuge** (☑707-733-5406; www.fws.gov/refuge/humboldt_bay; 1020 Ranch Rd, Loleta; ☉8am-5pm) **FREE** protects wetland habitats for more than 200 species of resident birds and their feathered friends migrating annually along the Pacific Flyway. Between the fall and early spring, when 100,000 Aleutian geese descend en masse to the area, huge numbers might be seen in a cackling gaggle outside the visitor center.

Marsh wren, Humboldt Bay National Wildlife Refuge
PHOTOGRAPHY BY ADRI/SHUTTERSTOCK ©

Eureka

One hour north of Garberville, on the edge of the largest bay north of San Francisco, lies the city of Eureka. With a strip-mall sprawl surrounding a lovely historic downtown, it wears its role as the county seat a bit clumsily. On one hand, it's got a diverse and interesting community of artists, writers, pagans and other free-thinkers. But it's also home to a disturbingly large homeless population. Its main draws are its serene waterfront trail, fantastic restaurants, glorious street murals, and all-around alternative edge. Make for Old Town, a small historic district with good shopping and a revitalized waterfront.

◎ SIGHTS

Romano Gabriel Wooden Sculpture Garden   Public Art
(315 2nd St) **FREE** The coolest thing to gawk at downtown is this collection of whimsical outsider art that's enclosed by aging glass. For 30 years, wooden characters in Gabriel's front yard delighted locals. After he died in 1977, the city moved the collection here.

Kinetic Museum Eureka   Museum
(☑707-786-3443; http://kineticgrandchampi onship.com/kinetic-museum-eureka; 518 A St; admission by donation; ☉2:12-6:32pm Fri-Sun) Come see the fanciful, astounding, human-powered contraptions used in the annual **Kinetic Grand Championship** (☑707-786-3443; www.kineticgrandchampi onship.com; ☉late May) race from Arcata to Ferndale. Shaped like giant fish and UFOs, these colorful piles of junk propel racers over roads, water and marsh during the May event.

✪ ACTIVITIES

Blue Ox Millworks & Historic Park   Historic Building
(☑707-444-3437; www.blueoxmill.com; 1 X St; adult/child 6-12yr $12/7; ☉9am-5pm Mon-Fri year-round, plus 9am-4pm Sat Apr-Nov;) One of only a few of its kind in the US, here antique tools are used to produce authentic gingerbread trim for Victorian buildings, stained glass, decorative gemstones, hand-painted signs and other craft goods from another era. One-hour self-guided tours take you through the mill and historical buildings, including a blacksmith shop and 19th-century skid camp. Peruse the gift shop!

Harbor Cruise   Cruise
(Madaket Cruises; ☑707-445-1910; www.hum boldtbaymaritimemuseum.com; 1st St; narrated cruises adult/child $22/18; ☉1pm, 2:30pm & 4pm Wed-Sat, 1pm & 2:30pm Sun-Tue mid-May– mid-Oct) Board the 1910 *Madaket,* the USA's oldest continuously operating passenger vessel, and learn Humboldt Bay's history. Docked at the foot of C St, it originally ferried mill workers and passengers until the Samoa Bridge opened in 1971. The $10 sunset cocktail cruise (Wednesday to Saturday) serves from the smallest licensed

Boats moored in Eureka

bar in the state. There's also a Sunday morning wildlife cruise.

EATING

Brick & Fire
Californian $$

(☎707-268-8959; www.brickandfirebistro.com; 1630 F St; dinner mains $17-28; ⏰11:30am-9pm Mon & Wed-Fri, 5-9pm Sat & Sun; 🛜) Tucked into an intimate, warm-hued and bohemian-tinged setting, this spot is almost always busy. Choose from thin-crust pizzas, delicious salads (try the pear, bacon and blue cheese), and an ever-changing selection of appetizers and mains that highlight local produce and wild mushrooms. There's a weighty wine list and servers are well-versed in pairings.

Humboldt Bay Provisions
Seafood $$

(☎707-672-3850; www.humboldtbayprovisions. com; 205 G St; half-dozen oysters $13; ⏰4-9pm Mon-Fri, from 1pm Sat & Sun) Sit at the long redwood bar at this rustic-chic establishment and watch as experts shuck local oysters and top them off with intriguing sauces such as habanero and peach juice. The locavore menu also includes charcuterie-style platters and regional wines and ales. If you like what you taste, be sure to ask about the two-hour **Humboldt Bay Oyster Tours** (www.humboldtbayoystertours.com).

Restaurant 301
Californian $$$

(☎707-444-8062; www.carterhouse.com; 301 L St; mains $25-39; ⏰5-9pm) 🍴 Part of the excellent Carter House Inns, romantic, sophisticated 301 serves a contemporary Californian menu, using produce from its organic gardens (tours available). The five-course tasting menu ($70, wine pairings $40) is a good way to sample local seasonal food in its finest presentation.

ℹ INFORMATION

Eureka Visitor Center (☎707-572-4227; www. visiteureka.com; 240 E St; ⏰10am-6pm Tue-Sat, 11am-4pm Sun; 🛜) The main visitor information center for the city of Eureka.

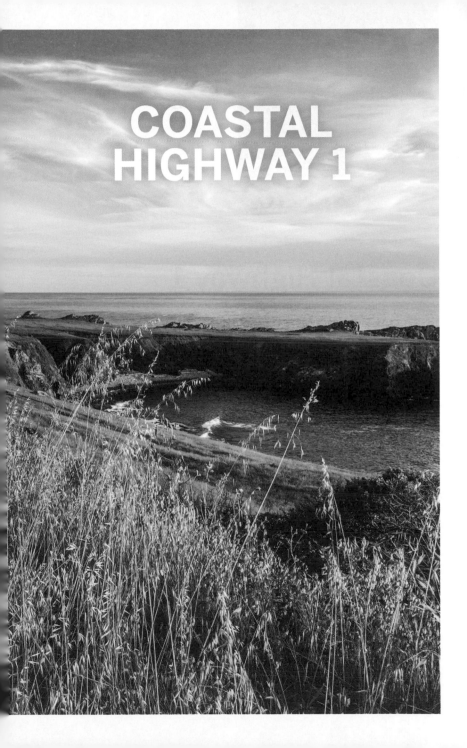

COASTAL
HIGHWAY 1

Coastal Highway 1

Down south it's called the 'PCH,' or Pacific Coast Hwy, but North Coast locals simply call it Hwy 1. However you label it, get ready for a fabulous coastal drive, which cuts a winding course on isolated cliffs high above the crashing surf. Compared to the famous Big Sur coast, the serpentine stretch of Hwy 1 up the North Coast is more challenging, more remote and more real, passing farms, fishing towns and hidden beaches. Drivers use roadside pullouts to scan the hazy Pacific horizon for migrating whales and explore a coastline dotted with rock formations that are relentlessly pounded by the surf.

Coastal Highway 1 in Two Days

With two days, set your sights on **Mendocino** (p102), the most picturesque town on this stretch of coast, and home to the iconic **Café Beaujolais** (p103). Take your time to get here, twisting up Hwy 1 and exploring all the **beaches** along the way (when it's time to go back, cut over to Hwy 101 for a straight shot).

Coastal Highway 1 in Four Days

From Mendocino you can really explore some of California's most rugged coastline in depth. Spend half a day at the **Mendocino Coast Botanical Gardens** (p107) and admiring the sea glass at **Glass Beach** (p108) in Fort Bragg. If you plan to take Hwy 1 back south, make time for a bowl of clam chowder at the **fish market** (p106) in Bodega Bay.

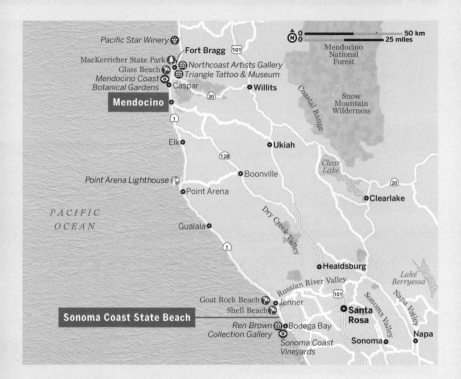

Arriving on Coastal Highway 1

Bus Although Hwy 1 is popular with cyclists and there are bus connections operated by the Mendocino Transit Authority (www.mendocinotransit.org), you will almost certainly need a car to explore this region. Twisty Hwy 1 hugs the coast, then cuts inland and ends at Leggett, where it joins Hwy 101. Neither Amtrak nor Greyhound serve cities on Coastal Hwy 1.

Sleeping

Coastal accommodations (including campgrounds) can fill from Memorial Day to Labor Day (late May to early September) and on fall weekends, and sometimes require two-night stays, so reserve ahead. There is a good choice of places to stay along the highway, although the budget conscious may find a definite lack of chain motels in these parts.

Mendocino

Leading out to a gorgeous headland, Mendocino is the North Coast's salt-washed perfect village, with B&Bs surrounded by rose gardens, white-picket fences and New England–style redwood water towers.

Built by transplanted New Englanders in the 1850s, Mendocino thrived late into the 19th century, with ships transporting redwood timber from here to San Francisco. The mills shut down in the 1930s, and the town was rediscovered in the 1950s by artists and bohemians. Today the culturally savvy, politically aware, well-traveled citizens welcome visitors, but eschew corporate interlopers.

Great For...

☑ Don't Miss

A walk along the headland among berry bramble and wildflowers.

Mendocino Headlands State Park

This **state park** (☎707-937-5804; www.parks.ca.gov) FREE surrounds the village, with trails that crisscross bluffs and rocky coves. Ask at the visitor center about guided weekend walks, including spring wildflower explorations and whale-watching jaunts.

PUS99/GETTY IMAGES ©

Mendocino
Headlands
State Park ⓘ

◉**Mendocino**

Ford House Museum
& Visitor Center

*Mendocino
Bay*

Big River
◉Tidal Estuary

ⓘ Need to Know

Ford House Museum & Visitor Center
(☏707-937-5397; www.mendoparks.org;
45035 Main St; ◷11am-4pm)

✕ Take a Break

Stop by **Fog Eater Cafe** (☏707-397-1806;
https://fogeatercafe.com; 45104 Main St;
mains $13-20; ◷5-8:30pm Wed-Sat, 10am-
2pm & 5-8:30pm Sun; ✐) for a NorCal take
on staples from the American South.

★ Top Tip

To avoid crowds, come midweek or in
the low season, when the vibe is mellow-
er – and prices more reasonable.

Big River Tidal Estuary

Northern California's longest undeveloped
estuary has no highways or buildings,
only beaches, forests, marshes, streams,
abundant wildlife and historic logging sites.
Friendly outfitter **Catch a Canoe** (☏707-937-
0273; www.catchacanoe.com; 10051 S Big River
Rd, The Stanford Inn & Resort; 3hr kayak, canoe
or bicycle rental adult/child $35/15; ◷9am-5pm)
rents bikes, kayaks and canoes (including
redwood outriggers) for trips up the 8-mile
estuary. Bring a picnic, and pack a camera
to capture majestic blue herons and the
ramshackle remnants of century-old train
trestles.

Mendocino Celebrations

Enjoy wine and chowder tastings and
whale-watching at the **Mendocino Whale
Festival** (www.mendowhale.com; ◷early

Mar). During the summer, orchestral and
chamber music concerts take place on the
headlands, as a part of the **Mendocino
Music Festival** (www.mendocinomusic.com;
◷mid-Jul).

Mendocino Dining

The influx of Bay Area weekenders has
fostered an excellent dining scene that
enthusiastically espouses organic, sustainable principles.

For a special-occasion dinner, Mendocino's iconic, beloved country-Cal–French
Café Beaujolais (☏707-937-5614; www.
cafebeaujolais.com; 961 Ukiah St; lunch mains
$11-20, dinner mains $24-50; ◷11:30am-
3pm Wed-Sun, 5:30-9pm daily, closed Jan) ✐
occupies an 1893 farmhouse restyled into
a monochromatic urban-chic dining room.
The locally sourced menu changes with the
seasons, but the dry-aged duck breast is a
gourmand's delight.

Goat Rock

Sonoma Coast State Beach

Bring binoculars, a picnic and a flexible agenda. The hidden coves and rocky headlands of Sonoma Coast make it a stunningly gorgeous place to while away some time.

Great For...

☑ **Don't Miss**

Goat Rock's lethargic colony of harbor seals hauled out on the sand.

Stretching 19 miles north from Bodega Head to Vista Trail, 4 miles north of Jenner, the glorious Sonoma Coast State Beach is actually a series of beaches separated by beautiful rocky headlands. Some beaches are tiny, hidden in little coves, while others stretch far and wide. Most are connected by vista-studded coastal hiking trails along the bluffs.

Exploring the Coast

From Bodega Bay, head to **Salmon Creek Beach** (cnr Bean Ave & Maryanna Dr, Bodega Bay; P), situated around a lagoon and with good waves for surfing. **Portuguese Beach** (cnr Hwy 1 & Eureka Dr; P) is another lovely option and boasts sheltered coves between rocky outcroppings.

    Duncan's Landing (Duncan's Landing Overlook, Bodega Bay; P), by a rocky headland

PHIL HABER PHOTOGRAPHY/GETTY IMAGES ©

❶ Need to Know

Sonoma Coast beaches are beautiful, but the surf is often too treacherous to even wade in; keep an eye on children.

✕ Take a Break

Stop in for a coffee, a pastry and expansive Russian River views at Café Aquatica.

★ Top Tip

Exploring this area makes an excellent day-long adventure, but facilities are nonexistent, so bring water, food and a fully charged cell phone.

where small boats will unload in the morning, is an excellent place to go wandering for wildflowers in the spring. A hop and a skip north, a boardwalk and trail leads out to **Shell Beach** (Shell Beach Rd, Jenner; P), perfect for tide-pooling and beachcombing.

If you only have time for one beach, pull over at **Goat Rock** (Goat Rock Rd, Jenner; P), famous for its colony of harbor seals, lazing in the sun at the mouth of the Russian River. The immense arched sea stack in the distance is said to have earned its name from goat herds that grazed here over a century ago.

Just north of the river in Jenner is the lovely **Café Aquatica** (✆707-865-2251; 10439 Hwy 1; pastries & sandwiches $4-12; ☺8am-5pm; 🛜🅿), the kind of North Coast coffee shop you've been dreaming of, with fresh pastries and fog-lifting organic coffee.

Sonoma Coast Accommodations

Unless you are willing to hammer down tent pegs, you will need to base yourself in Bodega Bay or Jenner.

If you are up for camping, **Wright's Beach** (✆800-444-7275; www.parks.ca.gov; 7095 Hwy 1; tent & RV sites $35-45, day use $8) is the best campground, even though sites lack privacy and there are no hot showers. There are just 27 sites, but they can be booked six months in advance, and numbers one to 10 are right on the beach. Closer to Bodega Bay, **Bodega Dunes** (✆800-444-7275; www.reservecalifornia.com; 2485 Hwy 1, Bodega Bay; tent & RV sites $35, day use $8) is the largest campground in the Sonoma Coast State Beach system of parks with close to 100 sites. Sites are in high dunes and have hot showers, but be warned – the foghorn sounds all night.

Bodega Bay

Bodega Bay is the first pearl in a string of sleepy fishing towns that line the North Coast and was the setting of Hitchcock's terrifying 1963 avian psycho-horror flick *The Birds*. These days the skies are free from bloodthirsty gulls (though you'd best keep an eye on the picnic); it's Bay Area weekenders who descend en masse for extraordinary beaches, tide pools, whale-watching from January to April, fishing, surfing and seafood.

⊙ SIGHTS & ACTIVITIES

Bodega Head Viewpoint

(off Bay Flat Rd) At the peninsula's tip, Bodega Head rises 265ft above sea level. It's great for whale-watching, and there is also a seal colony just offshore. Landlubbers enjoy hiking above the surf, where several good trails include a 3.75-mile trek to Bodega Dunes Campground and a 2.2-mile walk to Salmon Creek Ranch. Head west from Hwy 1 onto Eastshore Rd, then turn right at the stop sign onto Bay Flat Rd.

Ren Brown Collection Gallery Gallery

(☑707-875-2922; www.renbrown.com; 1781 Hwy 1; ⊙10am-5pm Wed-Sun) The renowned collection of modern Japanese prints and California works at this small gallery is a tranquil escape from the elements. Check out the Japanese garden at the back.

Sonoma Coast Vineyards Tasting Room

(☑707-921-2860; www.sonomacoastvineyards. com; 555 Hwy 1; tastings $25; ⊙11am-6pm) Swirl coastal pinot noirs and chardonnays in this sleek tasting room with views over the Pacific to see if you can detect the ocean's strong influence on them. Most bottles are made from small 1- or 2-acre plots (some literally in the backyards of families living within 10 miles of the coast), making it an incredibly bespoke experience.

Chanslor Ranch Horseback Riding

(☑707-589-5040; https://chanslorstables.com; 2660 Hwy 1; rides from $40; ⊙9am-5pm, reduced hours Nov-Feb) Just north of town, this friendly outfit leads horseback expeditions along the coastline and the rolling inland hills. The 90-minute beach rides are justifiably popular, as are trips that combine horseback riding with kayaking.

✖ EATING

Fishetarian Fish Market Californian $

(☑707-875-9092; www.fishetarianfishmarket. com; 599 Hwy 1; mains from $12; ⊙11am-6pm Mon-Thu, to 7pm Fri-Sun; 🐾) This fish market and deli is a great place to eat, with reggae as the soundtrack. It features an outdoor deck near the water and an expansive menu that includes colorful and imaginative organic salads, fried tofu (or calamari) with homemade fries, oysters, fish tacos, crab cakes and a fine clam chowder. Also serves craft beers on tap and decadent desserts.

Spud Point Crab Company Seafood $

(☑707-875-9472; www.spudpointcrab.com; 1910 Westshore Rd; mains $8-13; ⊙9am-5pm) In the classic tradition of dockside crab shacks, Spud Point serves salty-sweet crab sandwiches and *real* clam chowder (that consistently wins local culinary prizes). You can also buy a crab to take home if you fancy. Eat at picnic tables overlooking the marina. Take Bay Flat Rd to get here.

Lucas Wharf Restaurant & Bar Seafood $$

(☑707-875-3522; www.lucaswharfrestaurant. com; 595 Hwy 1; mains $17-32; ⊙11:30am-8:30pm) Located right on the water, this place specializes in sophisticated seafood options, with ingredients such as roasted cherry tomatoes accompanying dishes like Dungeness crab cakes and popcorn shrimp. Founded by a family of commercial fishers, the restaurant originated as a fish market, which is now located next door (along with an upmarket deli). In other words, these folks know their seafood and you can guarantee it is flapping fresh.

Tides Wharf & Restaurant
Seafood **$$**

(☑707-875-3652; www.innatthetides.com; 835 Hwy 1; breakfast $9-24, lunch $15-30, dinner $25-45; ⊗7:30am-9:30pm Mon-Thu, 7:30am-10pm Fri, 7am-10pm Sat, 7am-9:30pm Sun) Enjoy a stunning view of the bay and an upscale atmosphere. The emphasis is on seafood here, but pasta and meat dishes are also available. The black-and-white pics of the Hitchcock days add to the atmosphere and, if you're lucky, you may spy seals and dolphins from the vast picture window.

Drakes
Californian **$$$**

(☑707-875-3525; www.drakesbodegabay.com; 103 Hwy 1, Bodega Bay Lodge & Spa; mains $24-45, appetizers $8-17; ⊗7:30am-8:30pm; 🛜) This fancy spot offers a choice of dining experiences. The Drakes Sonoma Coast kitchen' menu runs from breakfast to dinner, the latter concentrating on hearty staples like braised short ribs or more intriguing creations like crab risotto. The aptly named Fireside Lounge offers a relaxed setting for lighter bites, including charcuterie plates or garlic fries.

ℹ️ INFORMATION

Sonoma Coast Visitor Center (☑707-377-4459; www.visitbodegabayca.com; 913 Hwy 1; ⊗9am-5pm) Opposite the Tides Wharf. Stop by for the best help on the coast and a copy of the *North Coaster,* a small-press indie newspaper of essays and brilliant insights on local culture.

Fort Bragg

In the past, Fort Bragg was Mendocino's ugly stepsister, home to a lumber mill and blue-collar locals who gave a cold welcome to outsiders. Since the mill closure in 2002, the town has started to reinvent itself, slowly warming to a tourism-based economy. The downtown continues to develop as a wonderfully unpretentious alternative to Mendocino (even if its southern outskirts

 Bloodthirsty Birds of Bodega Bay

Bodega Bay has the enduring claim to fame as the setting for Alfred Hitchcock's *The Birds*. Although special effects radically altered the actual layout of the town, you still get a good feel for the supposed site of the farm owned by Mitch Brenner (played by Rod Taylor). The once-cozy Tides Wharf & Restaurant, where much avian-caused havoc occurs in the movie, is still there, but since 1962 it has been transformed into a vast restaurant complex. Venture 5 miles inland to the tiny town of Bodega and you'll find two icons from the film: the schoolhouse and the church. Both stand just as they did in the movie – a crow overhead may make the hair rise on your neck.

Schoolhouse featured in *The Birds*

are hideous). Drive past the chain stores and you'll find better hamburgers and coffee, old-school architecture and residents eager to show off their little town.

⊙ SIGHTS & ACTIVITIES

Mendocino Coast Botanical Gardens
Gardens

(☑707-964-4352; www.gardenbythesea.org; 18220 N Hwy 1; adult/child/senior $15/8/12; ⊗9am-5pm Mar-Oct, to 4pm Nov-Feb) This gem of Northern California displays native flora, rhododendrons and heritage roses. The succulent display alone is amazing, and the organic garden is harvested by volunteers

Point Arena Lighthouse

This 1908 **lighthouse** (☑707-882-2809; www.pointarenalighthouse.com; 45500 Lighthouse Rd; adult/child $8/1; ☺10am-3:30pm mid-Sep–mid-May, to 4:30pm mid-May–mid-Sep) is the tallest on the US West Coast (tied with nearby Pigeon Point) at 115ft. Check in at the museum and have a look at the Fresnel lens, then climb 145 steps to the top for the jaw-dropping view.

It's around 65 miles north of Bodega Bay and 45 miles south of Fort Bragg.

GARY WEATHERS/GETTY IMAGES ©

to feed area residents in need. The serpentine paths wander along 47 seafront acres south of town. Primary trails are wheelchair accessible.

Pacific Star Winery   Winery
(☑707-964-1155; www.pacificstarwinery.com; 33000 Hwy 1, Westport; tastings $10; ☺noon-5pm Thu-Sun) In a dramatic, rub-your-eyes-in-disbelief-beautiful location on a bluff over the sea, the wines here don't get pros excited but they are perfectly drinkable. The winery's owners are supremely friendly and you're encouraged to picnic at one of the many coast-side tables, stroll some of the short coastal trails along the cliffs and generally enjoy yourself (which isn't hard). No reservation necessary.

Located 12 miles north of Fort Bragg; look for the signs.

Glass Beach   Beach
(Elm St) Named for (what very little is left of) the sea-polished glass in the sand, rem-

nants of its days as a city dump, this beach is now part of **MacKerricher State Park** (☑707-964-9112; www.parks.ca.gov; Fort Bragg) **FREE**. Take the headlands trail from Elm St, off Main St, but leave the glass – visitors are not supposed to pocket souvenirs.

Northcoast Artists Gallery   Gallery
(www.northcoastartists.org; 362 N Main St; ☺11am-5pm) An excellent local arts cooperative where 20 full-time members work in photography, glass, woodworking, jewelry, painting, sculpture, textiles and printmaking. Openings are on the first Friday of the month. Check www.visitmendocino.com for a comprehensive list of galleries throughout Mendocino County.

Triangle Tattoo & Museum   Museum
(☑707-964-8814; www.triangletattoo.com; 356b N Main St; ☺noon-6pm Sun-Thu, to 8pm Fri & Sat) **FREE** This one-off museum has an excellent exhibition of international tattoo art and explains the history in various cultures. You can also get a tattoo done here if you fancy.

Skunk Train   Rail
(☑707-964-6371; www.skunktrain.com; 100 W Laurel St; adult/child from $42/26; ☺9am-3pm) Fort Bragg's pride and joy, this vintage train got its nickname in 1925 for its stinky gas-powered steam engines, but today runs on diesel. One- or two-hour trips pass through the Pudding Creek Estuary for views of blue herons, ospreys, otters and redwood forests. Tracks run to **Willits** (299 E Commercial St; adult/child $50/30; ☺Mar-Dec), where there are also rail journeys, but you cannot travel between the two as bookings are round-trip to either Glen Blair Junction or Crowley and back.

⊗ EATING & DRINKING

Taka's Japanese Grill   Japanese $
(☑707-964-5204; 250 N Main St; mains $10-19; ☺11:30am-3pm & 4:30-9pm) Although it may look fairly run-of-the-mill, this is an exceptional Japanese restaurant. The owner is a

former grader at the Tokyo fish market, so the quality is tops, and he makes a weekly run to San Francisco to source freshly imported seafood. Sushi, teriyaki dishes, noodle soups and pan-fried noodles with salmon, beef or chicken are just a few of the options.

Piaci Pub & Pizzeria — Italian $

(☏707-961-1133; 120 W Redwood Ave; mains $8-14; ⊙11am-9:30pm Mon-Thu, to 10pm Fri & Sat, 4-9:30pm Sun) Fort Bragg's must-visit pizzeria is known for its sophisticated wood-fired, brick-oven pizzas as much as for its long list of microbrews. Try the 'Gustoso' – with chèvre, pesto and seasonal pears, all carefully orchestrated on a thin crust. It's tiny, loud and fun, with much more of a bar atmosphere than a restaurant. Expect to wait at peak times.

Princess Seafood Market & Deli — Seafood $

(☏707-962-3123; www.fvprincess.com; 32410 N Harbor Dr; mains $11-19; ⊙10am-6pm Sun-Thu, to 7pm Fri & Sat; ☏) Sit at picnic tables by the docks and chow down on sustainably caught ocean-to-table delicacies, including Dungeness crab cakes, fish tacos and oysters on the half shell. There's live music on weekends and plenty of local craft beer (or kombucha) to keep you lingering long into the afternoon.

North Coast Brewing Company — American $$

(☏707-964-3400; www.northcoastbrewing.com; 444 N Main St; mains $14-22; ⊙11:30am-9:30pm Sun-Thu, to 10:30pm Fri & Sat; ☏) Though dishes like ceviche and seafood polenta demonstrate that this establishment takes the food as seriously as the bevvies, it's the burgers and garlic fries that soak up the fantastic selection of handcrafted brews. A great stop for serious beer-lovers.

Overtime Brewing — Microbrewery

(☏707-962-3040; http://overtimebrewing. com; 190 E Elm St; ⊙11am-10pm Mon-Sat, from noon Sun; ☏) It may be the new kid on the craft-beer block, but Overtime outshines its stalwart neighbor, North Coast Brewing, when it comes to pushing the envelope. The brews here are far more experimental, and you can pair them with alcohol-soaking mac 'n' cheese, jambalaya or burgers while playing board games or chatting with locals at the horseshoe bar.

❶ INFORMATION

Mendocino Coast Chamber of Commerce
(☏707-961-6300; www.mendocinocoast.com; 332 S Main St; ⊙9am-5pm Mon-Fri, 10am-3pm Sat; ☏) The chamber of commerce has lots of helpful information about this stretch of coast and what's on. Its online guide is also worth checking out.

LAKE TAHOE

Lake Tahoe

Shimmering in myriad shades of blue and green, Lake Tahoe is the USA's second-deepest lake and, at 6255ft above sea level, it is also one of the highest-elevation lakes in the country. The horned peaks surrounding the lake, which straddles the California–Nevada state line, are year-round destinations. The sun shines on Tahoe three out of every four days. Swimming, boating, kayaking, windsurfing, stand-up paddle surfing and other water sports take over in summer, as do hiking, camping and wilderness backpacking adventures. Winter brings bundles of snow, perfect for hitting Tahoe's top-tier ski and snowboard resorts.

Lake Tahoe in Two Days

A two-day itinerary is dependent on the season: in winter you'll want to spend at least one day on the **slopes** (p114), whereas **getting out onto the lake** is essential in summer. Regardless of the season, a long drive along the shore will roll past breathtaking scenery, but be warned: driving the entirety of the spellbinding 72-mile scenic shoreline will give you quite a workout behind the wheel.

Lake Tahoe in Four Days

With two extra days, you'll have more time for exploring the outdoors, either on the winter slopes or on a summer hike to the alpine lakes and high-mountain meadows of the **Desolation Wilderness** (p117). For a little less exertion, head south and explore **Vikingsholm Castle** (p118) in Emerald Bay State Park. Ensure you set aside an evening for superb Italian food at **Cafe Fiore** (p122).

Arriving in Lake Tahoe

Car From late fall through early spring, drivers should always pack snow chains. Chains can be purchased and installed in towns along the I-80 and Hwy 50.

Bus and train Greyhound buses from Reno, Sacramento and San Francisco run to Truckee, and you can also get the daily Zephyr train here from the same destinations. From Truckee, TART (www.tahoetruckeetransit.com) buses run to the north, west and east shore of the lake.

Sleeping

If you're not staying at one of the ski resorts, the best bet is one of the many vacation rentals that are scattered around the lake. These vary wildly, from plush retreats with spas to rustic log cabins. If you're here in summer, ski resort prices plummet, but the most memorable stay will be under the stars in the Desolation Wilderness backcountry.

Snowboarding, Lake Tahoe

ERSLER/GETTY IMAGES ©

Snow Sports

Phenomenal ski slopes beckon from more than a dozen resorts. Winter-sports complexes range from the giant, jet-set slopes of Squaw Valley, Heavenly and Northstar, to enticing insider playgrounds like Sugar Bowl and Homewood.

Ski season generally runs November to April, although it can start as early as October and continue until the last storm whips through in May or even June. All resorts have ski schools, equipment rental and other facilities; check the websites for snow conditions, weather reports and free ski-season shuttle buses from area lodgings.

Top Winter Resorts

Heavenly

The 'mother' of all Tahoe mountains, **Heavenly** (☏775-586-7000; www.skiheavenly.com; 3860 Saddle Rd; adult/child 5-12yr/youth 13-18yr $154/85/126; ⏱9am-4pm Mon-Fri, 8:30am-4pm Sat, Sun & holidays; 👪) boasts the most acreage, the longest run (5.5 miles), great tree skiing and the biggest vertical drop around. Follow the sun by skiing on the Nevada side

Great For...

☑ Don't Miss

The outdoor exhibition skate rink at Squaw Valley's High Camp (p122).

Squaw Valley

DAVID A LITMAN/SHUTTERSTOCK ©

❶ Need to Know

For convivial crowds, head for the south shore; for a quieter getaway, check out the north shore options.

✗ Take a Break

Warm up slopeside in **Le Chamois & Loft Bar** (www.squawchamois.com; 1960 Squaw Valley Rd; mains $8-27; ⊘11am-7pm, bar to 9pm or 10pm mid-Dec–May; 👪🐾) after skiing Squaw Valley.

★ Top Tip

The Bay Area Ski Bus (www.tahoe-skitrips.net) from San Francisco and Oakland runs shuttles to major ski resorts.

in the morning, moving to the California side in the afternoon. Two terrain parks won't strand snowboarders of any skill level, with the High Roller for experts only. Stats: 28 lifts, 3500 vertical feet, 97 runs.

Squaw Valley

This mega-sized, world-class, see-and-be-seen **resort** (📞800-403-0206; www.squawalpine.com; 1960 Squaw Valley Rd, off Hwy 89, Olympic Valley; adult/child 5-12yr/youth 13-22yr $169/110/144; ⊘9am-4pm; 👪) hosted the 1960 Winter Olympic Games. Hard-core skiers thrill to white-knuckle cornices, chutes and bowls, while beginners practice their turns in a separate area on the upper mountain. There's also a great après-ski scene, and relatively short chairlift waits. Stats: 29 lifts, 2850 vertical feet, over 170 runs.

Alpine Meadows

Though now owned by neighboring Squaw (tickets are good at both resorts and a free shuttle connects them), **Alpine** (📞530-452-4356; www.skialpine.com; 2600 Alpine Meadows Rd, off Hwy 89; adult/child under 13yr/youth 13-22yr $169/110/144; ⊘9am-4pm) remains a no-nonsense resort with challenging terrain but without the fancy village, attitude or crowds. It gets more snow than Squaw and it's the most backcountry-friendly around. Boarders jib down the mountain in a terrain park designed by Eric Rosenwald. Stats: 13 lifts, 1800 vertical feet, over 100 runs.

Tahoe Cross Country

Run by the nonprofit Tahoe Cross Country Ski Education Association, this **center** (📞530-583-5475; www.tahoexc.org; 925 Country Club Dr, off N Lake Blvd/Hwy 28; adult/child under 19yr $34/free; ⊘8:30am-5pm; 👪🐾), about 3 miles north of Tahoe City, has 40 miles of groomed tracks (23 trails) that wind through lovely forest, suitable for all skill levels.

Hiking around Lake Tahoe

HAVESEEN/SHUTTERSTOCK ©

Hiking & Backpacking

With stunning granite-topped hills and incredible views, there's no better way to connect with this incredible natural wonderland than to explore it on a hike or overnight backpacking trip.

Great For...

☑ Don't Miss

Hidden alpine lakes – these gorgeous secluded gems are worth the effort to find.

Hiking South Lake Tahoe

Many miles of summer hiking trails start from the top of the gondola at Heavenly (p114). On the Nevada side of the state line, **Lam Watah Nature Trail** meanders for just over a mile each way, winding underneath pine trees and beside meadows and ponds and ending beside Lake Tahoe. It starts off Kahle Dr.

Several easy kid- and dog-friendly hikes begin near the United States Forest Service (USFS) Taylor Creek Visitor Center off Hwy 89, including the **Rainbow Trail** and rolling 1-mile **Moraine Trail** near Fallen Leaf Lake. Up at cooler elevations, the mile-long round-trip to **Angora Lakes** is another popular trek with kids, especially because it ends by a sandy swimming beach and a summer snack bar selling ice-cream treats.

Rainbow Trail

DANITA DELIMONT/SHUTTERSTOCK ©

Eagle Falls get the most traffic, but solitude comes quickly.

Three agencies – the USFS, National Park Service and Bureau of Land Management – provide a helpful overview of outdoor activities in wilderness areas along the spine of the Sierra Nevada Mountains at www.sierrawild.gov.

Hiking the Desolation Wilderness

Sculpted by powerful glaciers aeons ago, this relatively compact **wilderness area** (www.fs.usda.gov/detail/eldorado/specialplaces) spreads south and west of Lake Tahoe and is the most popular in the Sierra Nevada. It's a 100-sq-mile wonderland of polished granite peaks, deep-blue alpine lakes, glacier-carved valleys and pine forests that thin quickly at the higher elevations. In summer, wildflowers nudge out from between the rocks.

All this splendor makes for some exquisite backcountry exploration. Six major trailheads provide access from the Lake Tahoe side: Glen Alpine (near Lily Lake, south of Fallen Leaf Lake), Tallac (opposite the entrance to Baldwin Beach), Echo Lakes (near Echo Summit on Hwy 50), Bayview, Eagle Falls and Meeks Bay. Tallac and

Hiking Around Truckee

Truckee is a great base for treks in the **Tahoe National Forest**, especially around **Donner Summit**. One popular 5-mile hike reaches the summit of 8243ft **Mt Judah** for awesome views of **Donner Lake** (www.donnerlakemarina.com; 🅿🚻) and the surrounding peaks. A longer, more strenuous ridge-crest hike (part of the **Pacific Crest Trail**) links **Donner Pass** to Squaw Valley (15 miles each way), skirting the base of prominent peaks, but you'll need two cars for this shuttle hike.

Sunrise over Emerald Bay

COLIN D. YOUNG/SHUTTERSTOCK ©

Emerald Bay State Park

This gorgeous natural landmark is one of the lake's most beautiful corners, drawing families to its beach in summer and hosting snowshoeing adventures in winter.

Great For...

☑ **Don't Miss**

The gorgeous green-water views from the east window of the teahouse on Fannette Island.

Sheer granite cliffs and a jagged shoreline hem in glacier-carved Emerald Bay, a teardrop cove that will have you digging for your camera. Its most captivating aspect is the water, which changes from cloverleaf green to light jade depending on the angle of the sun. Fannette Island, a picture-perfect speck of granite, is set perfectly in its center. You'll spy panoramic pullouts all along Hwy 89, including at **Inspiration Point**. Just south, the road shoulder evaporates on both sides, revealing a glorious view of Emerald Bay and Cascade Lake to the south.

Vikingsholm Castle

Aside from the natural splendor, the focal point of the park is **Vikingsholm Castle** (🖉530-525-7232; http://vikingsholm.com; tour adult/child 7-17yr $15/12; ☺10:30am-4pm late

Vikingsholm Castle

❶ Need to Know

☏530-541-6498; www.parks.ca.gov; parking $10; ⊗sunrise-sunset

✕ Take a Break

After a morning in the park, re-energize with vegetarian bowls and sandwiches at Sprouts (p121).

★ Top Tip

Start the 9-mile round-trip Rubicon Trail, which links DL Bliss State Park and Emerald Bay State Park, at DL Bliss. This avoids a 1-mile climb to the Vikingsholm parking lot at Emerald Bay.

May-Sep; P), heiress Lora Knight's majestic mansion on the bay, a rare example of ancient Scandinavian-style architecture. Completed in 1929, it has trippy design elements aplenty, including sod-covered roofs that sprout wildflowers in late spring and a three-story tower. The mansion is reached by a steep 1-mile trail, which also leads to a visitor center. A 30-minute tour explores the interior of the house, which still has much of the original furnishings. While Knight is best known today for this incredible building, the eccentric figure was also one of the primary financial backers of Charles Lindbergh's nonstop solo flight across the Atlantic in 1927.

Fannette Island

Knight's tract of land here also included Tahoe's only island, the brush-covered,

uninhabited Fannette. The island holds the vandalized remains of a tiny 1920s teahouse. Knight would occasionally motorboat guests here from the castle. Fannette Island is accessible by boat or kayak, except during Canada goose nesting season (typically February to mid-June). Rent boats at Meeks Bay or South Lake Tahoe; from the latter, you can also catch narrated bay cruises or speedboat tours.

Eagle Falls Trail

For an adventure on land, hit this 2-mile round-trip hiking trail, which gives you a chance to see the summer wildflowers on a steep alpine hike. It's a there-and-back trail from Emerald Bay Rd to Eagle Lake, via spectacular falls. In winter, when Emerald Bay is serene and empty, you can also rent snowshoes to explore the route.

South Lake Tahoe & Stateline

Highly congested and arguably overdeveloped, South Lake Tahoe is a chockablock commercial strip bordering the lake and framed by picture-perfect alpine mountains. At the foot of the world-class Heavenly mountain resort (p114), and buzzing from the gambling tables in the casinos just across the border in Stateline, NV, Lake Tahoe's south shore draws visitors with a cornucopia of activities, lodging and restaurant options, especially for summer beach access and tons of powdery winter snow.

◉ SIGHTS

Inspiration Point   Viewpoint
Swoon-worthy views of Emerald Bay, as the crowds testify.

Tallac Historic Site   Historic Site
(📞530-544-7383; www.tahoeheritage.org; 1 Heritage Way; optional tour adult/child $15/10; ⏰10am-4pm daily late May-Sep; 🐾) **FREE**
Sheltered by a pine grove and bordering a wide, sandy beach, this national historic site sits on the archaeologically excavated grounds of the former Tallac Resort, a swish vacation retreat for San Francisco's high society around the turn of the 20th century. Feel free to just amble or cycle around the breezy forested grounds, today transformed into a community arts hub, where leashed dogs are allowed.

Heavenly Gondola   Cable Car
(www.skiheavenly.com; Heavenly Village; adult/child 5-12yr/youth 13-18yr from $64/39/50; ⏰10am-5pm Jun-Aug, reduced off-season hours; 🐾)
Soar to the top of the world as you ride this gondola, which sweeps you from Heavenly Village some 2.4 miles up the mountain in just 12 minutes. From the observation deck at 9123ft, get gobsmacking panoramic views of the entire Tahoe Basin, the Desolation Wilderness and Carson Valley, then jump back on for the final, short hop to the top.

From here there's a range of activities to enjoy (climbing, ziplining, tubing) and decent eating at **Tamarack Lodge** restaurant and bar (mains $14 to $20), or jump on the

Kiva Beach

CHRISTY PETIT/SHUTTERSTOCK ©

Tamarack Express chairlift to get all the way to the mountain summit.

ACTIVITIES

Nevada Beach
Swimming

(per car $8) A sweeping sandy beach with a timber picnic area and a shack selling ice creams and drinks. The Lam Watah Nature Trail ends here.

Pope Beach
Swimming

(1209 Pope Beach Dr; per car $8) With pine trees behind it and water and mountains ahead, this sandy strand is pretty idyllic.

Kiva Beach
Swimming

(Tallac Point Rd) A gorgeous little sandy beach with mountain views.

Camp Richardson Corral & Pack Station
Horseback Riding

(530-541-3113; www.camprichardsoncorral. com; Emerald Day Rd/Hwy 89, trail rides $54-95;) In continuous operation since 1934, this camp offers trail and wagon rides and magical winter sleigh trips.

Zephyr Cove Resort & Marina
Water Sports

(775-589-4901; www.zephyrcove.com; 760 Hwy 50, NV) Rents powerboats, pedal boats, wave runners, Jet Skis, canoes, kayaks and stand-up paddleboards; also offers single and tandem parasailing flights.

🔒 SHOPPING

Grass Roots Natural Foods
Food & Drinks

(http://grassrootstahoe.com; 2030 Dunlap Dr; 9am-8pm) 🍃 This store sells a wealth of organic produce, lifestyle products and grocery goods, as well as sandwiches and fresh pizzas.

🍴 EATING & DRINKING

Sprouts
Vegetarian $

(530-541-6969; www.sproutscafetahoe.com; 3123 Harrison Ave; mains $8-12; 8am-8pm;

 Take a Cruise on Lake Tahoe

A paddle steamer operated by **Lake Tahoe Cruises** (775-586-4906; www. zephyrcove.com; 760 Hwy 50; adult/child from $68/38) plies Lake Tahoe's 'big blue' year-round with a variety of sightseeing, drinking, dining and dancing cruises, including a narrated two-hour daytime trip to Emerald Bay.

STUART DEE/GETTY IMAGES ©

) Cheerful chatter greets you at this energetic, mostly organic cafe that gets extra kudos for its juices and smoothies. A healthy menu will have you noshing happily on satisfying soups, rice bowls, sandwiches, burrito wraps, tempeh burgers and fresh salads. The kids menu offers eight items under $7.

Sugar Pine Cakery
Bakery $

(http://sugarpinecakery.com; 3564 Lake Tahoe Blvd; pastries $1-5; 8am-5pm Tue-Sat, 8am-4pm Sun) Organic crunchy baguettes, ooey-gooey cinnamon rolls, fruit tarts and choco-chunk cookies.

Getaway Cafe
American $$

(570-577-5132; www.facebook.com/TheGet-awayCafe; 3140 Hwy 50, Meyers; mains $12-17; 7am-3pm;) On the outskirts of town, just south of the agriculture inspection checkpoint, this place really lives up to its name. Friendly waitstaff sling heaped-up buffalo chicken salads, barbecue burgers, chile relleno, coconut-encrusted French toast and more. Avoid the weekend crowds.

High Camp, the Olympic Museum & Via Ferrata

At the end of a steep cable-car ride in Squaw Valley, **High Camp** (☑800-403-0206; http://squawalpine.com; cable car adult/child 5-17yr $49/29, all-access adventure pass adult/child 5-17yr $59/34; ☺11am-4pm daily Nov–mid-May & Jul-Aug, Sat & Sun Sep; ☺) boasts a heated seasonal outdoor swimming lagoon, an 18-hole disc-golf course and a roller-skating rink that doubles as an ice-skating rink in winter. Prices for activities vary. Several hiking trails radiate out from here. Cable-car tickets include admission to the **Olympic Museum** (11am to 4pm Saturday and Sunday), a fun retro exploration of the 1960 Olympics, featuring a film and much memorabilia.

Adventurers can now scale the enormous cliff overlooking the Village, known as the Tram Face, on one of two new via ferrata routes with **Tahoe Via Ferrata** (☑877-873-5376; www.tahoevia.com; 1985 Squaw Valley Rd; half-day/full day $99/149). Climbers are clipped to cables, which ascend the rocks across a network of steel anchors – there's more than 1000ft of elevation gain. Trips are run by Alpenglow Expeditions and begin at the Village. Climbers must be at least 10 years old.

Lagoon, High Camp

Naked Fish — Sushi $$

(☑530-541-3474; www.thenakedfish.com; 3940 Lake Tahoe Blvd; sushi $6-12, mains $16-23; ☺5-10pm Mon-Thu, 5-10:30pm Fri & Sat) With sushi chefs in ski caps, 'Rock the Casbah' rolling from the speakers and eclectic sushi-themed art adorning the walls, it's easy to feel not quite cool enough as you enter this oft-recommended raw fish joint. But then you taste the Hidden Dragon roll – with its delicious Cajun ahi – and you know you're right where you should be.

Freshie's — Fusion $$

(☑530-542-3630; www.freshiestahoe.com; 3330 Lake Tahoe Blvd; mains lunch $13-18, dinner $14-28; ☺11:30am-9pm; ☑) From vegans to seafood-lovers, everybody should be able to find a favorite on the extensive menu at this Hawaiian fusion joint with sunset upper-deck views. Most of the produce is local and organic, and the blackened fish tacos are South Lake Tahoe's best. Check the webcam to see if there's a wait.

Cold Water Brewery & Grill — American $$

(☑530-544-4677; www.tahoecwb.com; 2544 Hwy 50; mains $17-22; ☺11am-9pm Mon-Thu, 11am-10pm Fri & Sat) The vibe is welcoming and the gourmet pub grub is delicious at this airy brewery, which is earning raves as far away as Reno. Chase down the hearty roasted pork banh mi with the malty and easy-drinking Mr Toad's Wild Rye.

Cafe Fiore — Italian $$$

(☑530-541-2908; www.cafefiore.com; 1169 Ski Run Blvd; mains $24-43; ☺5:30-10pm) Serving upscale Italian without pretension, this tiny romantic eatery pairs succulent pasta, seafood and meats with an award-winning 300-vintage wine list. Swoon over the veal scaloppine, homemade white-chocolate ice cream and near-perfect garlic bread. With only seven tables (a baker's dozen in summer when the candlelit outdoor patio opens), reservations are essential.

South Lake Brewing Co
Microbrewery

(✆530-578-0087; www.southlakebeer.com; 1920 Lake Tahoe Blvd; ◷2-9pm Mon-Thu, noon-10pm Fri & Sat, noon-9pm Sun) Your tasting flight arrives on a ski at big-windowed South Lake Brewing, where crusty mountain men, parents with babies, dogs and their owners and connoisseurs of good beer commune in late afternoon. The citrusy Pebble Wrestler Pale Ale – with a 'marshmallow mouth feel' they say – is always a good choice. Up to 16 beers on tap daily.

Brewery at Lake Tahoe
Brewery

(www.brewerylaketahoe.com; 3542 Lake Tahoe Blvd; ◷11am-9pm Sun-Thu, 11am-10pm Fri & Sat) This popular brewpub pumps its signature Bad Ass Ale into grateful local patrons, who may sniff at bright-eyed out-of-towners. Burgers, sandwiches, pizza and BBQ ribs on the menu, and a roadside patio in summer. Don't leave without a bumper sticker!

MacDuffs Pub
Pub

(✆530-542-8777; www.macduffspub.com; 1041 Fremont Ave; ◷11:30am-9:30pm) With excellent beers rotating on tap, a dartboard on the wall, and fish-and-chips and shepherd's pie (as well as gourmet burgers and wood-fired pizzas) on the menu, this dark and bustling gastropub wouldn't look out of place in Edinburgh. Sports fans and beer drinkers, step right up.

ⓘ INFORMATION

Lake Tahoe Visitors Authority (✆775-588-4591; www.tahoesouth.com; 169 Hwy 50, Stateline, NV; ◷9am-5pm Mon-Fri) **A full range of tourist information.**

Tahoe City

The western shore's commercial hub, Tahoe City straddles the junction of Hwys 89 and 28, making it almost inevitable that you'll find yourself breezing through here at least once during your round-the-lake sojourn. The town is handy for grabbing food and supplies and renting sports gear. It's also the closest lake town to Squaw Valley (p115). The main drag, N Lake Blvd,

South Lake Tahoe

ANJELIKA GRETSKAIA/GETTY IMAGES ©

From left: Stand-up paddleboarding, Commons Beach;
Gatekeeper's Museum & Marion Steinbach Indian
Basket Museum; Truckee River in winter

is chockablock with outdoor outfitters,
touristy shops and cafes.

◎ SIGHTS

Gatekeeper's Museum & Marion Steinbach Indian Basket Museum   Museum

(☑530-583-1762; www.northtahoemuseums.org;
130 N Lake Blvd/Hwy 89; adult/child under 13yr
$5/free; ☺10am-5pm daily late May–mid-Oct,
11am-4pm Wed-Sat mid-Oct–Apr; P) In a recon-
structed log cabin close to town, this museum has a small but fascinating collection
of Tahoe memorabilia, including Olympics
history and relics from the early steamboat
era and tourism explosion around the lake.
In the museum's newer wing, uncover an
exquisite array of Native American baskets
collected from more than 85 indigenous
California tribes.

Commons Beach   Park

(400 N Lake Blvd) Commons Beach is a small,
attractive park with sandy and grassy
areas, picnic tables, barbecue grills, a
climbing rock and playground, as well as

free summer concerts (www.concertsat-
commonsbeach.com; mid-June to August)
and outdoor movie on Wednesday nights in
July and August.

Fanny Bridge   Bridge

Just south of the always-jammed Hwy
89/28 traffic stoplight junction, the Truckee River flows through dam floodgates and
passes beneath this bridge, cutely named
for the most prominent feature of people
leaning over the railings to look at fish (in
American slang, 'fanny' means your rear
end). The adjacent park and nearby dam
display interpretive markers, historical
photos and hydrological facts.

⊕ ACTIVITIES

Truckee River Raft Rentals   Rafting

(☑530-583-0123; www.truckeeriverraft.com;
185 W River Rd; adult/child 6-12yr $45/35;
☺trips 8:30am-2:30pm Jul-early Sep; ⋓) The
Truckee River here is gentle and wide as it
flows northwest from the lake – perfect for
novice paddlers. This outfit rents rafts for
the 5-mile float from Tahoe City to the River

RON AND PATTY THOMAS/GETTY IMAGES ©

Ranch Lodge (p126), including transportation back to town. Reservations strongly advised.

🔒 SHOPPING

North Tahoe Arts Gift
Shop & Gallery   Arts & Crafts
(www.northtahoearts.com; 380 N Lake Blvd; ⊗11am-4pm) Peruse paintings, ceramics and jewelry from local artists. Open until 5pm in warmer months.

✖ EATING & DRINKING

Fat Cat   Californian $
(📞530-583-3355; www.fatcatrestaurants.com; 599 N Lake Blvd; mains $12-38; ⊗noon-8pm Sun-Thu, 11:30am-9:30pm Fri, 11am-9:30pm Sat & Sun, bar open later; 🚲) This casual, family-run restaurant with local art splashed on the walls does it all: from-scratch soups, heaped salads, sandwiches, incredible burgers, pasta, steak, salmon, a paleo bowl and plenty of fried munchies for sharing. Look for live indie music on Friday and Saturday nights.

Tahoe House Bakery   Bakery $
(www.tahoe-house.com; 625 W Lake Blvd; pastries $1-3, sandwiches $9; ⊗6am-4pm; 🛜) Before you take off down the western shore for a bike ride or hike, drop by this mom-and-pop shop that opened in the 1970s. Their motto: 'While you sleep, we loaf.' Sweet cookies, European pastries, fresh-baked deli sandwiches and homemade salads and soups will keep you going all afternoon on the trail.

New Moon
Natural Foods   Deli, Health Food $
(www.newmoonnaturalfoods.com; 505 W Lake Blvd; mains $7-12; ⊗9am-8pm Mon-Sat, 9am-7pm Sun; 🚲) 🌱 A tiny but well-stocked natural-foods store with a gem of a deli that concocts scrumptious food to go, all packaged in biodegradable and compostable containers. Try the fish tacos or Thai salad with organic greens and spicy peanut sauce.

Rosie's Cafe   American $$
(www.rosiescafe.com; 571 N Lake Blvd; breakfast $10-16, lunch & dinner $13-28; ⊗7:30am-9:30pm; 🚲) With antique skis, shiny bikes and

Homewood looks over Lake Tahoe

lots of pointy antlers belonging to stuffed wildlife mounted on the walls, this quirky place serves breakfast until 2:30pm. The all-American hodgepodge menu with items such as Yankee pot roast is all right, but the convivial atmosphere is a winner. Popular locals bar.

River Ranch Lodge   Modern American $$
(📱530-583-4264; http://riverranchlodge.com; 2285 River Rd, Hwy 89 at Alpine Meadows Rd; mains patio & cafe $8-10, restaurant $38-44; ⏱lunch Jun-Sep, dinner year-round, call for seasonal hours) This stone-built riverside dining room is a popular stop, drawing rafters and bikers to its patio for summer barbecue lunches.

Christy Hill   American $$$
(📱530-583-8551; www.christyhill.com; 115 Grove St; most small plates $14-16, mains $25-42; ⏱5:45-7:30pm, bar from 5pm) Slip into your fanciest mountain-town duds for the finest dining experience in Tahoe City. Seasonal American dishes come with a creative spin, and all are accompanied by a big-windowed lake view. Solo diners can enjoy the whole experience at the bar, where sampling small plates from the happy-hour menu (5pm to 6pm; $4 to $13) is quite pleasant. The house-smoked trout is a treat.

Bridgetender Tavern & Grill   Pub
(📱530-583-3342; www.tahoebridgetender. com; 65 W Lake Blvd; ⏱11am-11pm Sun-Thu, 11am-midnight Fri & Sat) Après-ski crowds gather for beer, burgers and chili-cheese or garlic waffle fries at this woodsy bar (mains $10 to $13). In summer, grab a seat on the open-air patio.

ℹ INFORMATION

Tahoe City Downtown Association (📱530-583-3348; www.visittahoecity.org; 425 N Lake Blvd; ⏱9am-5pm Mon-Fri) Tourist information and online events calendar.

Tahoe City Visitors Information Center (📱530-581-6900; www.gotahoenorth.com; 100 N Lake Blvd; ⏱9am-5pm) At the Hwy 89/28 split.

GETTING THERE & AWAY

Just south of the Hwy 28/89 split, the modern new **Tahoe City Transit Center** (www.tahoetruc keetransit.com; off W Lake Blvd) is the main bus terminal, with a comfy waiting room. Behind it you'll find trailhead parking for the **Tahoe Rim Trail** (www.tahoerimtrail.org) `FREE` and various bike path routes. Regular buses connect the town with other spots on the lake.

Homewood

This quiet and very alpine-looking resort hamlet, associated with the ski resort of the same name, is popular with summertime boaters and, in winter, skiers and snow-boarders. West Shore Sports rents out all the winter and summer gear you'll need.

ACTIVITIES

Homewood Snow Sports

(530-525-2992; www.skihomewood.com; 5145 Westlake Blvd, off Hwy 89; adult/child 5-12yr/youth 13-19yr $134/69/94; 9am-4pm;) Larger than it looks from the road, this gem, 6 miles south of Tahoe City, proves that bigger isn't always better. Locals and in-the-know visitors cherish the awesome lake views, laid-back ambience, smaller crowds, tree-lined slopes, open bowls (including the excellent but expert 'Quail Face') and a high-speed quad that gets things moving.

Families love the wide, gentle slopes. It's also the best place to ski during stormy weather. Stats: eight lifts, 1650 vertical feet, 67 runs.

West Shore Sports Outdoors

(530-525-9920; www.westshoresports.com; 5395 W Lake Blvd; 8am-5pm) Hires bicycles, kayaks, paddle surfing gear and snow-sports equipment.

EATING

West Shore Café Californian $$$

(530-525-5200; www.westshorecafe.com; 5160 W Lake Blvd; mains lunch $17-22, dinner $29-52; 11am-9pm mid-Jun–Sep, noon-3pm, 5-8pm Oct–mid-Jun) At the **West Shore Inn's** (r/ste from $299/429,) cozy destination restaurant, executive chef Rob Wyss whips up worthy meals using fresh produce and ranched meats, from juicy burgers to seared scallops with crab and parmesan couscous. Dinner reservations recommended.

GETTING THERE & AWAY

Tahoe Truckee Area Rapid Transit (TART; 530-550-1212; https://tahoetruckeetransit. com; 10183 Truckee Airport Rd; most routes free) `FREE` operates buses along the north shore as far as Incline Village.

YOSEMITE
NATIONAL PARK

Yosemite National Park

The jaw-dropping head-turner of America's national parks, and a Unesco World Heritage Site, Yosemite (yo-sem-it-ee) garners the devotion of all who enter. From the waterfall-striped granite walls buttressing Yosemite Valley to the skyscraping sequoias of Mariposa Grove, the place inspires a sense of awe. But lift your eyes above the crowds and you'll feel your heart instantly moved by unrivaled splendors: the haughty profile of Half Dome, the hulking presence of El Capitan, the drenching mists of Yosemite Falls and the gemstone lakes of the high country's subalpine wilderness.

Yosemite National Park in Two Days

With two days in Yosemite, you'll want to head straight to the valley, where you can stand agape at the twin marvels of **Half Dome** (p134) and El Capitan, and enjoy a drink or two at the comfortable and remodeled **Ahwahnee Bar** (p135). Make the most of day two with a hike to see some of the valley's **waterfalls** (p136).

Yosemite National Park in Four Days

Get deeper into this incredible park by cruising the twisting two-lane blacktop of CA 120 to Yosemite's high country and **Tuolumne Meadows** (p139). On the way, make time for the incredible views at **Olmsted Point** (p134). If you're particularly ambitious, hike up to **Glacier Point** (p132) for a bird's-eye view of the valley's monuments or try a night or two in the backcountry.

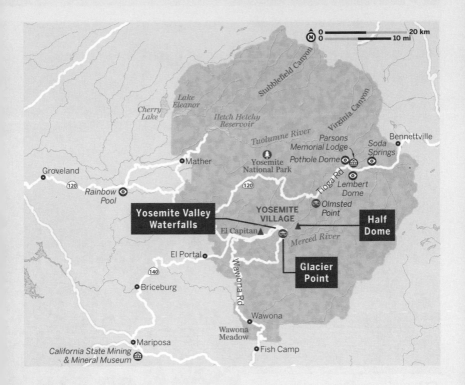

Arriving in Yosemite National Park

Car Yosemite is accessible year-round from the west (via Hwys 120 W and 140) and south (Hwy 41), and also in summer from the east (via Hwy 120 E). Yosemite's entrance fee is $35 per vehicle (or $20 for cyclists or pedestrians) and is valid for seven consecutive days.

Bus and train Yosemite is easily reached by public transportation. Greyhound buses and Amtrak trains serve Merced, west of the park, where they are met by buses operated by Yosemite Area Regional Transportation System (p139).

Sleeping

Camping, even in a busy campground near Yosemite Village, enhances the being-out-in-nature feeling. Backcountry wilderness camping is for the prepared and adventurous. All noncamping reservations within the park are handled by Aramark/Yosemite Hospitality (www.travelyosemite.com); reservations are critical from May to early September. There are a few quality hotels in Groveland proper, a variety of accommodations to the east along Hwy 120 in the Stanislaus National Forest, and numerous hotels and motels in Mariposa.

Glacier Point

With granite peaks stretching out into the distance, Glacier Point offers one of the most commanding views in the state, including a bird's-eye view of El Capitan and Half Dome.

Great For...

☑ **Don't Miss**

The granite faces of the Sierra bathed in warm, golden light at sunset.

History

Almost from the park's inception, Glacier Point has been a popular destination. It used to be that getting up here was a major undertaking. That changed once the Four Mile Trail opened in 1872. A wagon road to the point was completed in 1882, and the current Glacier Point Rd was built in 1936. The cozy Glacier Point Trailside Museum was one of the park's first projects, a humble little stone hut that offers a great shelter from a passing storm.

The View

If you drove up here, the views from 7214ft Glacier Point might make you feel like you cheated – superstar sights present themselves with minimal physical effort. A quick mosey up the paved path from the parking lot and you'll find the entire eastern

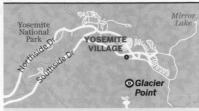

❶ Need to Know

The road to the point is closed in winter; the best time to visit is late spring, as soon as the road is cleared, for the best waterfall flows.

✕ Take a Break

Enjoy a picnic at the Glacier Point amphitheater, an ideal setting with incredible panoramas.

★ Top Tip

To escape Glacier Point crowds, hike down the first half-mile of the Four Mile Trail. You'll round a corner to a view of El Capitan and Yosemite Valley's western half.

Yosemite Valley spread out before you, from **Yosemite Falls** to **Half Dome**, as well as the distant peaks that ring Tuolumne Meadows. Half Dome looms practically at eye level and, if you look closely, you can spot hikers on its summit.

To the left of Half Dome lies the glacially carved **Tenaya Canyon**. To its right are the wavy white ribbons of **Nevada Falls** and **Vernal Falls**. On the valley floor, the Merced River snakes through green meadows and groves of trees. If you're not afraid of heights, sidle up to the railing, hold on tight and peer 3200ft straight down at Half Dome Village. **Basket Dome** and **North Dome** rise to the north of the valley, and **Liberty Cap** and the **Clark Range** can be seen to the right of Half Dome.

At the tip of the point is **Overhanging Rock**, a huge granite slab protruding from the cliff edge like an outstretched tongue, defying gravity. It once provided a scenic stage for daredevil extroverts performing handstands, high kicks and other wacky stunts on the rock. The precipice is now off-limits.

Sentinel Dome

The shortest and easiest trail up one of Yosemite's granite domes is the nearby path to the summit of **Sentinel Dome** (8122ft). Sentinel offers an outstanding 360-degree perspective of Yosemite's wonders, and the 2.2-mile round-trip hike only takes about an hour. A visit at sunrise or sunset or during a full moon is spectacular.

Half Dome

Yosemite's most distinctive natural monument, this beautifully broken slab of granite is 87 million years old and has a 93% vertical grade – the sheerest cliff in North America.

Great For...

☑ Don't Miss

The view of the back side of Half Dome from **Olmsted Point**, midway between the May Lake turnoff and Tenaya Lake.

The Story of Half Dome

According to Native American legend, one of Yosemite Valley's early inhabitants went down from the mountains to Mono Lake, where he wed a Paiute named Tesaiyac. The journey back to the valley was difficult, and by the time they reached what was to become Mirror Lake, Tesaiyac had decided that she wanted to go back to her people at Mono Lake. However, her husband refused to live on such barren land.

With a heart full of despair, Tesaiyac began to run toward Mono Lake, and her husband followed her. When the powerful spirits heard quarreling in Yosemite, they became angry and turned the two into stone: he became North Dome and she became Half Dome. The tears she cried made marks as they ran down her face, thus forming Mirror Lake.

ⓘ Need to Know

Rangers check for valid permits at the base of the Half Dome cables.

✕ Take a Break

Settle in for a drink at the cozy **Ahwahnee Bar** (☑209-372-1489; www.travelyosemite.com; Ahwahnee, 1 Ahwahnee Dr, Yosemite Valley; ⊙11:30am-11pm) inside the majestic Yosemite Hotel.

★ Top Tip

If you want to climb the dome, check www.nps.gov/yose/planyourvisit/hd-permits.htm for the latest information.

Climbing & Hiking

Climbers come from around the world to grapple with Half Dome's legendary north face, but good hikers can reach its summit via a 17-mile round-trip trail from Yosemite Valley. The trail gains 4900ft in elevation and has cable handrails for the final 200yd climb, which shoots up the harrowingly steep eastern slope of the dome.

The hike can be done in a day but is more enjoyable if you break it up by camping along the way (Little Yosemite Valley is the most popular spot).

Half Dome Permits

To stem lengthy lines (and increasingly dangerous conditions) on the vertiginous cables of Half Dome, the park now requires that all day hikers obtain a permit in advance.

Preseason permit lottery (www.recreation.gov) Lottery applications ($10) for 225 of the 300 daily spots must be completed in March, with confirmation notification sent in mid-April; an additional fee of $10 per person confirms the permit. Applications can include up to six people and seven alternate dates.

Daily lottery Approximately 50 additional permits are distributed by lottery two days before each hiking date. Apply online or by phone (☑877-444-6777) between 7am and 9pm Pacific Time; notification is available late that same evening. It's easier to score weekday permits.

Backpackers Those with Yosemite-issued wilderness permits that reasonably include Half Dome can request Half Dome permits (also $10 per person) without going through the lottery process.

Yosemite Falls

Yosemite Valley Waterfalls

Yosemite's waterfalls mesmerize even the most jaded traveler, especially when the spring runoff turns them into spectacularly thunderous cataracts.

Great For...

☑ **Don't Miss**

Cooling off in the refreshing mist of Vernal Falls in the peak of summer.

Yosemite Falls

West of Yosemite Village, Yosemite Falls is considered among the tallest waterfalls in North America, dropping 2425ft (740m) in three tiers. Because it faces the open meadows, you'll be able to see this gorgeous cascade from vantage points throughout the valley. A slick trail leads to the bottom or, if you prefer solitude, you can clamber up the Yosemite Falls Trail, which puts you atop the falls after a grueling 3.4 miles. The falls are usually captivating, but most are reduced to a trickle by late summer.

Bridalveil Fall

At the southwestern end of the valley, Bridalveil Fall tumbles 620ft. The Ahwahneechee people call it *Pohono* (Spirit of the Puffing Wind), as gusts often blow the fall

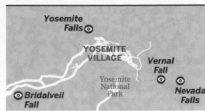

⊙ Need to Know

People have been swept away in Yosemite's falls; be extremely cautious around wet footpaths and railings.

✕ Take a Break

The **Village Store** (Yosemite Village; ⊙8am-8pm, to 10pm summer) has health-food items and organic produce to fuel a waterfall-bound walk.

★ Top Tip

Bring rain gear or expect to get soaked when the falls are heavy.

---

from side to side, even lifting water back up into the air. The waterfall usually runs year-round, though it's often reduced to a whisper by midsummer.

Park at the large lot where Wawona Rd (Hwy 41) meets Southside Dr. From the lot, it's a quarter-mile walk to the base of the fall. The path is paved but probably too rough for wheelchairs, and there's a somewhat steep climb at the very end. Avoid climbing on the slippery rocks at the fall's base – no one likes a broken bone.

Vernal & Nevada Falls

At Vernal Falls, one of Yosemite's most iconic, the thundering waters of the Merced River tumble 317ft down on the way to meet Yosemite Valley below. Mist Trail, the paved path to the falls, is one of the park's most popular. It begins near the Happy

Isles shuttle stop. At the top of the falls, the view is jaw-dropping (and a little scary). Continue a short distance further on the trail and you'll come to Emerald Pool and Silver Apron. Both of these may look tempting on a sweltering summer day, but stay out; it is extremely dangerous to swim here. You can continue over a small bridge and take in a short stretch of the famed John Muir Trail, which will lead back to Yosemite Valley in about 4 miles. This alternate return has big rewards with incredible views of Liberty Cap (look for climbers in summer) and Nevada Falls.

Spectacular views await from Nevada Falls, ricocheting 594ft as part of the 'Giant Staircase' leading the Merced River down into Yosemite Valley. Most people take the Mist Trail (you pass Vernal Fall on the way), which is 5.4 miles round-trip, but the John Muir Trail also gets you to the top.

ⓘ INFORMATION

DANGERS & ANNOYANCES

Yosemite is prime black-bear habitat. Follow park rules on proper food storage and utilize bear-proof food lockers when parked overnight. Mosquitoes can be pesky in summer, so bug spray's not a bad idea. And please don't feed those squirrels. They may look cute but they've got a nasty bite.

MEDICAL SERVICES

Yosemite Medical Clinic (📞209-372-4637, emergency 911; 9000 Ahwahnee Dr, Yosemite Village; ◷9am-7pm Mon-Fri early Jun-early Jul, 9am-7pm Mon-Sat late Jul–mid-Sep, to 5pm Mon-Fri late Sep-late May) A 24-hour emergency service is available.

TOURIST INFORMATION

Yosemite Valley Visitor Center (📞209-372-0200; www.nps.gov/yose; 9035 Village Dr, Yosemite Village; ◷9am-5pm) The main tourist-information center, with exhibits and free film screenings in the **theater** (www.yosemite conservancy.org/yosemite-theater; ◷9:30am-4:30pm; ♿; 🚌shuttle stops 5 & 9). Give yourself plenty of time, as lines are long in summer. Helps with self-issued wilderness permits from November to April when the Wilderness Center is closed.

Yosemite Valley Wilderness Center (📞209-372-0308; Yosemite Village; ◷8am-5pm May-Oct) The park's busiest wilderness information office is located between the Ansel Adams Gallery and the post office. Backpacking permits are issued here and bear canisters are available for rent ($5 for seven days).

ⓘ GETTING THERE & AWAY

CAR

Yosemite is accessible year-round from the west (via Hwys 120 W and 140) and south (Hwy 41), and in summer also from the east (via Hwy 120 E). Roads are plowed in winter, but snow chains may be required at any time. In 2006 a mammoth rockslide buried part of Hwy 140, 6 miles west of the park; traffic there is restricted to vehicles under 45ft. Big Oak Flat Rd was

Vernal Falls (p137)

closed for several months after a 'slide,' really of an entire hillside, in February 2017.

Gas up year-round at Wawona inside the park (you'll pay dearly), at El Portal on Hwy 140 just outside its western boundary or Lee Vining at the junction of Hwys 120 and 395 outside the park in the east. Gas is also sold at Crane Flat. There is no gas for sale in Tuolumne Meadows.

PUBLIC TRANSPORTATION

Yosemite is one of the few national parks that can easily be reached by public transportation. Greyhound (p310) buses and Amtrak (p310) trains serve Merced, west of the park, where they are met by buses operated by the **Yosemite Area Regional Transportation System** (YARTS; ☑877-989-2787; www.yarts.com), and you can buy Amtrak tickets that include the YARTS segment all the way into the park. Buses travel to Yosemite Valley along Hwy 140 several times daily year-round, stopping along the way.

In summer (roughly June through September), another YARTS route, called the Trans-Sierra Connection, runs from Mammoth Lakes along Hwy 395 to Yosemite Valley via Hwy 120. One-way tickets to Yosemite Valley are $19 ($9 child and senior, three hours) from Merced and $26 ($15 child and senior, 3½ hours) from Mammoth Lakes, less if boarding in between.

YARTS fares include the park entrance fee, making them a super bargain, and drivers accept credit cards.

GETTING AROUND

BICYCLE

Bicycling is an ideal way to take in Yosemite Valley. You can rent a wide-handled cruiser (per hour/day $12/34) or a bike with an attached child trailer (per hour/day $20/61) at the **Yosemite Valley Lodge** (per hr/day $12/34; ⊘8am-6pm summer only, weather dependent) or Half Dome Village (p140). Strollers and wheelchairs are also rented here. Or download the Yosemite Bike Share mobile app, which has several pickup locations throughout the valley, including at **Camp 4** (www.nps.gov/yose; Northside Dr; shared tent sites per person $6; ⊘year-round).

Dazzling Tuolumne Meadows

About 55 miles from Yosemite Valley via Tioga Rd (or Hwy 120 E), 8600ft **Tuolumne Meadows** is the largest subalpine meadow in the Sierra. It provides a dazzling contrast to the valley, with its lush open fields, clear blue lakes, ragged granite peaks and domes, and cooler temperatures. If you come during July or August, you'll find a painter's palette of wildflowers decorating the shaggy meadows.

The **main meadow** is about 2.5 miles long and lies on the northern side of Tioga Rd between **Lembert Dome** and **Pothole Dome**. The 200ft scramble to the top of the latter – preferably at sunset – gives you great views of the meadow. An interpretive trail leads from the stables to muddy **Soda Springs**, where carbonated water bubbles up in red-tinted pools. The nearby **Parsons Memorial Lodge** has a few displays.

Hikers and climbers will find a paradise of options around Tuolumne Meadows, which is also the gateway to the High Sierra camps.

Bigelow's sneezeweed, Yosemite National Park
GARY SAXE/SHUTTERSTOCK ©

CAR

Roadside signs with red bears mark the many spots where bears have been hit by motorists, so think before you hit the accelerator and follow the poky posted speed limits – they are strictly enforced. Valley visitors are advised to park and take advantage of the Yosemite Valley Shuttle

 Activities in Yosemite

One easy way to explore Yosemite Valley is by bicycle. Stop by the **Half Dome Village Bike Stand** (per hr/day $12/34; ☺10am-4pm Mar-Oct) for rentals.

Ready for an extended adventure? Take a trek with popular **Yosemite High Sierra Camps Saddle Trips** (☑freight 209-372-8348, lottery 888-413-8869; www.travelyosemite.com/lodging/high-sierra-camps; per person adult/child from $1320/1068, freight per pound $5) – mules will be schlepping you and all the supplies. These four- to six-day trips include all meals and visit the spectacular high-sierra camps circuit. They fill up months in advance; check the park concessionaire's website for details.

To learn how to rock climb, sign up for a course with **Yosemite Mountaineering School** (☑209-372-8344; www.travelyosemite.com; Half Dome Village; ☺8:30am-5pm Apr-Oct), which offers topflight instruction for novice to advanced climbers, plus guided climbs and bouldering instruction.

Rock climbing, Yosemite National Park
ALEX EGGERMONT/GETTY IMAGES ©

Bus. Even so, traffic in the valley can feel like rush hour in LA.

Glacier Point and Tioga Rds are closed in winter.

Village Garage (☑209-372-8320; Village Dr; ☺9am-5pm, towing 24hr) provides emergency repairs and even gasoline when you're in an absolute fix.

Groveland

From the Big Oak Flat entrance to Yosemite, it's 22 miles to Groveland, an adorable town with restored gold rush-era buildings and lots of visitor services.

◎ SIGHTS & ACTIVITIES

Rainbow Pool   Natural Pool
(www.fs.usda.gov/stanislaus; Ⓟ) **FREE** About 15 miles east of Groveland, in the Stanislaus National Forest, Rainbow Pool is a popular swimming hole with a small cascade; it's signed on the south side of Hwy 120. It has vault toilets and limited parking. The road to the pools may be closed in winter; in this case, park and walk to the waterfall.

ARTA River Trips   Rafting
(☑209-962-7873, 800-323-2782; www.arta.org; 24000 Casa Loma Rd; 1-/2-/3-day Tuolumne River rafting $299/539/719; ☺office hours vary) Contact ARTA for one-day and multiday Tuolumne River trips or for day trips on Merced River. Nonprofit ARTA provides all equipment (rafting gear and camping kit), plus food for the trip. The guides will take you into untouched scenery and find rapids to swim in and rocks to jump off. Tip: the overnight trips are not to be missed.

Sierra Mac   Rafting
(☑209-591-8027; www.sierramac.com; 27890 Hwy 120; 1-/2-/3-day rafting $379/779/969; ☺hours vary Apr-Oct) One of two outfitters running the experts-only Cherry Creek trips also offers other Tuolumne and Merced River trips. Marty McDonnell, Sierra Mac's owner, has been river guiding since the 1960s. The office is perched on a hill 13 miles east of town, but best to call ahead before you show up.

✕ EATING & DRINKING

Burgers, sandwiches and pizza aren't in short supply. Groveland also has a good meat market deli and a Mexican place – both are recommended. If heading to campgrounds or accommodations further east, you can stock up on groceries at **Mar-Val** (209-962-7452; http://marvalfoodstores.org; 19000 Main St; 7am-9pm; P), the town supermarket.

Cocina Michoacana Mexican $

(209-962-6651; 18730 Main St; mains $10-18, à la carte tacos from $4.40; 10am-10pm) Quick and friendly service and large servings of tasty Mexican fare make this long-running restaurant popular with locals. There's a large menu, with familiar dishes such as carne asada, steak ranchero, burritos and fajitas. The chicken mole is especially recommended and there's a good selection of Mexican beer. Decor is simple: wooden tables, and traditional Mexican artifacts on the walls.

Provisions Taproom & Bourbon Bar American $$

(Groveland Hotel, 18767 Main St; mains $16-23) Groveland Hotel's newly redesigned Provisions stocks a wide selection of local wines, craft beers and top flight bourbons (flights $16 to 28). A changing dinner menu of homemade specialties includes dishes like chili honey-glazed pork shank and fettuccine with lamb meatballs. There are a few indoor seats with stools and more on the patio. Cheese and meat boards also available.

Iron Door Grill & Saloon Bar

(209-962-8904; www.irondoorsaloon.com; 18761 Main St; restaurant 7am-10pm, bar 11am-1am, shorter hours winter) Claiming to be the oldest bar in the state (established in 1852, when it served liquor to thirsty miners), the Iron Door is a friendly, atmospheric place, with swinging doors, a giant bar, high ceilings, mounted animal heads and hundreds of dollar bills tacked to the ceiling. It has live music on some weekends and also hosts open-mic and karaoke nights.

Mountain Sage Cafe

(18653 Main St; drinks $2-6, snacks $4-8; 7am-5pm summer, 7am-3pm Thu-Mon winter, later for ad hoc events;) This popular cafe, serving fair-trade coffee and tasty baked treats, is also an art gallery, nursery and live-music venue that runs an excellent summer **concert series**. It's the site of a Saturday

Iron Door Grill & Saloon

Yosemite Valley

farmers market in summertime. Smoothies, homemade quiche, cookies, breakfast burritos, oatmeal and other goodies are also available.

ℹ️ INFORMATION

USFS Groveland Ranger Station (📞209-962-7825; www.fs.usda.gov/stanislaus; 24545 Hwy 120; ⏰8:30am-4pm Mon-Fri Sep-May, 8:30am-4pm Mon-Sat Jun-Aug) About 8 miles east of Groveland; offers recreation information for the surrounding Stanislaus National Forest and nearby Tuolumne Wild and Scenic River Area.

ℹ️ GETTING THERE & AWAY

YARTS (YARTS; 📞209-388-9589, 877-989-2787; www.yarts.com; one way $5-16) buses run year-round along Hwy 140 into Yosemite Valley ($9 one way, 1¾ hours) via the Big Flat entrance. Tickets include admission to Yosemite.

Mariposa

About halfway between Merced and Yosemite Valley, Mariposa (Spanish for 'butterfly') is the largest and most interesting town near Yosemite National Park. Established as a mining and railroad town during the gold rush, it has the oldest courthouse in continuous use (since 1854) west of the Mississippi, loads of Old West pioneer character and a couple of museums dedicated to the area's history.

◎ SIGHTS

California State Mining & Mineral Museum   Museum

(📞209-742-7625; www.parks.ca.gov/?page_id=588; 5005 Fairgrounds Rd; adult/under 13yr $4/free; ⏰10am-5pm Thu-Sun May-Sep, to 4pm Oct-Apr) Rock hounds should drive to the Mariposa County Fairgrounds, 2 miles south of town on Hwy 49, to see the 13lb 'Fricot Nugget' (the largest crystallized gold specimen from the California gold-rush era, dating back to 1864) and other gems and machinery at the California State Mining &

Mineral Museum. There is also a very cool exhibit on glow-in-the-dark minerals.

 EATING & DRINKING

Happy Burger   Diner $
(☑209-966-2719; www.happyburgerdiner.com; cnr 5120 Hwy 140 & 12th St; mains $8-14; ◷6am-9pm; ⏣⏣⏣⏣) Burgers, fries and shakes served with a heavy dose of Americana kitsch. Happy Burger, decorated with old album covers, boasts the largest menu in the Sierra. It's also one of the cheaper meals in town. Besides burgers, there's sandwiches, Mexican food, salads and a ton of sinful ice-cream desserts. Patio games and a 'doggy dining area' can be found outdoors.

Savoury's   American $$
(☑209-966-7677; 5034 Hwy 140; mains $18-43; ◷5-9:30pm; ⏣) Upscale yet casual Savoury's is the best restaurant in town. Black-lacquered tables and contemporary art create tranquil window dressing for dishes like caramelized pork chop prepared with Sierra cider, pan-seared scallops with ginger and orange zest, Cajun-spiced New York steak with pan-seared onions, and crab cakes with cilantro-lime aioli.

ⓘ INFORMATION

John C Fremont Hospital (☑209-966-3631; www.jcf-hospital.com; 5189 Hospital Rd; ◷24hr) Emergency room in Mariposa.

Mariposa Chamber of Commerce and County Visitor Center (☑209-966-2456; www.mariposachamber.org/visitor-center; 5158 Hwy 140, cnr Hwy 49; ◷8am-5pm; ⏣) Helpful staff and racks of brochures; plus it has the **Gold Mine Escape Room** (http://exploremariposa.com/; 5158 Hwy 140, Mariposa Visitor Center; $15; ◷9am-4pm; ⏣) on-site. It has free wi-fi and restrooms.

ⓘ GETTING THERE & AWAY

YARTS (☑209-388-9589, 877-989-2787; www.yarts.com; one way $5-16) buses run year-round

along Hwy 140 from Merced through Mariposa into Yosemite Valley ($10 one-way) via the Rock Arch Entrance. Tickets include admission to Yosemite.

Merced River Canyon

The approach to Yosemite via Hwy 140 is one of the most scenic routes to the park, especially the section that meanders through Merced River Canyon. The springtime runoff makes this a spectacular spot for **river rafting**. Right outside the Arch Rock entrance, and primarily inhabited by park employees, **El Portal** makes a convenient Yosemite base.

 EATING

June Bug Cafe   Californian $$
(☑206-966-6666; www.yosemitebug.com/cafe; Yosemite Bug Rustic Mountain Resort, 6979 Hwy 140, Midpines; mains $8-24; ◷7-10am, 11am-2pm & 6-9pm; ⏣⏣⏣) ⏣ Guests of all ages and backgrounds convene at this friendly eatery, decorated with adventure equipment. While sharing hiking stories, folks eat delicious, freshly prepared meals (or drink beer and wine in the evenings). More than a half-dozen inexpensive healthy and hearty (and almost gourmet!) dishes are on the menu and are served cafeteria-style, so clear and stack your own plate.

ⓘ GETTING THERE & AWAY

While Hwy 140, the road through the canyon, is quite beautiful, unless you're up at the crack of dawn it can get crowded at the height of summer.

YARTS buses travel to Yosemite Valley from Merced along Hwy 140 year-round, with stops in Mariposa, Midpines and El Portal along the way. The cost depends on distance traveled.

BIG SUR

Big Sur

Big Sur is more a state of mind than a place to pinpoint on a map, and when the sun goes down the moon and the stars are the area's natural streetlights. (If summer's fog hasn't extinguished them.) Raw beauty and an intense maritime energy characterize this land shoehorned between the Santa Lucia Range and the Pacific. In the 1950s and '60s, Big Sur became a retreat for artists and writers, including Henry Miller and Beat Generation visionaries such as Lawrence Ferlinghetti. Today Big Sur attracts artists, new-age mystics and city slickers seeking to unplug on this emerald-green edge of the continent.

Big Sur in Two Days

It's easy to spend two days driving Hwy 1 between San Francisco and Los Angeles. The opportunities for jaw-dropping vistas are around every bend, so plan lots of time for pulling the car over to take some pictures. Stop in for a drink at **Alvarado Street Brewery** (p151) in Monterey. Among the many along-the-route beaches, **Pfeiffer Beach** (p149) is the most spectacular.

Big Sur in Four Days

Two extra days on the road will allow more time for beach-combing and photo-snapping. Check out the lighthouse at **Point Sur State Historic Park** (p148), take a hike in the **Los Padres National Forest** (p149) and walk along **Sand Dollar Beach** (p149). Two other essential stops are the **Henry Miller Memorial Library** (p153) and the vainglorious **Hearst Castle** (p154).

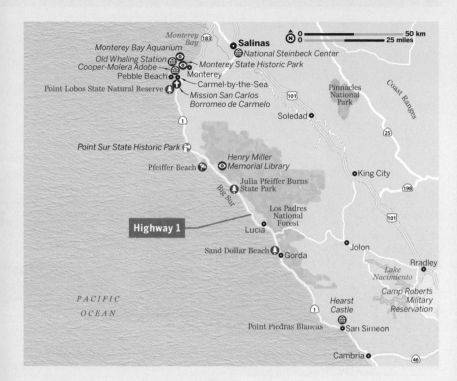

Highway 1

Arriving in Big Sur

Car Big Sur is best explored by car; note that even if your driving skills are up to these narrow switchbacks, others' aren't: expect to average 35mph or less along the route.

Bus MST (www.mst.org) bus 22 ($3.50, 1¼ hours) travels from Monterey via Carmel and Point Lobos as far south as Nepenthe restaurant, stopping en route at Andrew Molera State Park and the Big Sur River Inn.

Where to Stay

Big Sur lodgings are dotted along Hwy 1, but there aren't a lot of rooms overall, so demand often exceeds supply and prices can be steep. In summer and on weekends, reservations are essential. Camping is currently available at two of Big Sur's state parks and two United States Forest Service (USFS) camp-grounds along Hwy 1.

Highway 1, Big Sur

Driving Highway 1

One of the most spectacular drives in North America, Hwy 1 twists along the edge of the continent with rugged coastline, mist-shrouded cliffs, dense forests, crashing waterfalls and remote beaches all waiting to be discovered.

Great For...

☑ **Don't Miss**

Watching waves crash through the rock formation at Pfeiffer State Beach.

Point Sur State Historic Park

Around 6 miles south of **Bixby Bridge** (one of the world's highest single-span bridges), Point Sur rises out of the sea. It looks like an island, but is connected to land by a sandbar. Atop the volcanic rock sits an 1889 stone light station, which was staffed until 1974. During three-hour **guided tours** (✆831-625-4419; www.pointsur.org; off Hwy 1; adult/child 6-17yr from $15/5; ⊙tours 10am & 2pm Wed & Sat, 10am Sun Apr-Sep, 1pm Wed, 10am Sat & Sun Oct-Mar) **FREE**, ocean views combine with tales of the facility's importance in tracking Soviet submarines during the Cold War. Call ahead to confirm tour schedules and show up early because space is limited (no reservations, only credit cards accepted).

ⓘ Need to Know

Driving this narrow highway is very slow going. Allow about three hours to cover the distance between the Monterey Peninsula and San Luis Obispo (excluding stops).

✕ Take a Break

Try to decide which beer to indulge in at the Big Sur Taphouse (p154).

★ Top Tip

Check current highway conditions with CalTrans (www.dot.ca.gov) and fill up your gas tank beforehand.

Pfeiffer Beach

This crescent-shaped, dog-friendly **beach** (☏805-434-1996; www.campone.com; Sycamore Canyon Rd; day use per car $12, cash and credit cards; ⊙9am-8pm; P🚻🎿) is known for its huge double-rock formation, through which waves crash. It's often windy, and the surf is too dangerous for swimming, but dig down into the wet sand: it's purple because manganese garnet washes down from the hillsides above. From Hwy 1, make a sharp right onto Sycamore Canyon Rd.

Julia Pfeiffer Burns State Park

This **state park** (☏831-667-2315; www.parks. ca.gov; Hwy 1; day use per car $10, cash only; ⊙30min before sunrise-30min after sunset; P🚻) 🐾 is named for a Big Sur pioneer. From the parking lot, the 1.3-mile round-trip **Waterfall Overlook Trail** rushes downhill toward the ocean, passing through a tunnel underneath Hwy 1. Everyone photographs 80ft-high **McWay Falls**, which tumble year-round over granite cliffs into the sea – or the beach, depending on the tide. The park entrance is on the east side of Hwy 1, 8 miles south of Nepenthe restaurant (p154).

Los Padres National Forest

The winding 40-mile stretch of Hwy 1 south of Lucia to Hearst Castle (p154) is sparsely populated, rugged and remote, mostly running through national forest lands. Around 5 miles south of Kirk Creek Campground is **Sand Dollar Beach** (http:// campone.com; Hwy 1; per car $10, free with local USFS campground fee; ⊙9am-8pm; 🎿), a crescent-shaped strip of sand protected from winds by high bluffs that is southern Big Sur's longest sandy beach. Nearby is beachcomber-worthy **Jade Cove**, and it's a short drive south to **Salmon Creek Falls**, tucked uphill in a forested canyon.

Monterey

Working-class Monterey is all about the sea. The town's world-class aquarium overlooks Monterey Bay National Marine Sanctuary, which protects dense kelp forests and a sublime variety of marine life.

◎ SIGHTS

Monterey Bay Aquarium   Aquarium
(🖉info 831-648-4800, tickets 866-963-9645; www.montereybayaquarium.org; 886 Cannery Row; adult/child 3-12yr/13-17yr $50/30/40, tours $15; ⊙9:30am-6pm May-Aug, 10am-5pm Sep-Apr; 👪) ✐ Monterey's most mesmerizing experience, this enormous aquarium occupies the site of a humongous sardine cannery. All kinds of aquatic creatures inhabit its halls and outside areas, from sea stars and slimy sea slugs to animated sea otters and surprisingly nimble 800lb tuna. The aquarium is much more than

> *Working-class Monterey is all about the sea*

an impressive collection of glass tanks; thoughtful placards underscore the bay's cultural and historical contexts.

**Monterey State
Historic Park**   Historic Site
(🖉831-649-2907, 831-649-7118; www.parks.ca.gov/mshp; 20 Custom House Plaza; ⊙Pacific House 10am-4pm Tue-Sun) **FREE** Old Monterey is home to an extraordinary assemblage of 19th-century brick and adobe buildings administered as a state park and linked by a 2-mile self-guided walking tour called the 'Path of History.' Pick up a copy at Pacific House Museum, which also doubles as the park HQ. Route highlights are the nearby Custom House and the **Old Whaling Station** (391 Decatur St; ⊙10am-2pm Tue-Fri).

✖ EATING & DRINKING

Alta Bakery & Cafe   Cafe $
(🖉831-920-1018; www.altamonterey.com; 502 Munras Ave; snacks & mains $8-12; ⊙7am-4pm; 🖉👪) ✐ In the restored **Cooper-Molera Adobe** (🖉831-223-0172; www.coopermolera.org;

Fisherman's wharf, Monterey

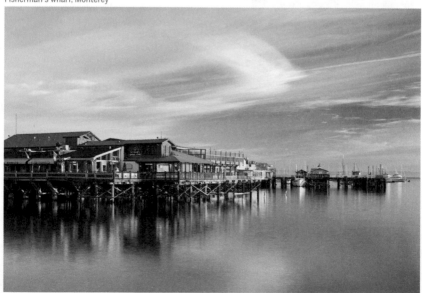

S. GREG PANOSIAN/GETTY IMAGES ©

525 Polk St; ⊙11am-4pm Tue-Sat, to 2:30pm Sun) **FREE**, Alta Bakery & Cafe's excellent baking is showcased with brunch options including orange marmalade and ricotta on sourdough, while daily doughnut, strudel and muffin specials are always worth trying. There's kombucha on tap and organic and fair-trade coffee, and interesting historic photos in the main dining area. In warmer weather, adjourn to the lovely gardens.

Montrio Bistro — Californian $$$

(☑831-648-8880; www.montrio.com; 414 Calle Principal; shared plates $6.50-20, mains $20-46; ⊙4:30-10pm Sun-Thu, to 11pm Fri & Sat; 🐶) 🍴 With 'clouds' hanging from the ceiling and tube sculptures wriggling toward them, it's apparent that much thought has gone into the design of this dining-scene stalwart set inside a 1910 firehouse. Fortunately, the New American fare, prepared with ingredients hunted and gathered locally, measures up nicely. Drink and snack prices during happy hour (daily until 6:30pm) are practically a steal.

Alvarado Street Brewery — Craft Beer

(☑831-655-2337; www.alvaradostreetbrewery. com; 426 Alvarado St; ⊙11:30am-10pm Sun-Thu, to 11pm Fri & Sat) Vintage beer advertising punctuates Alvarado Street's brick walls, but that's the only concession to heritage at this craft-beer pub. Innovative brews harness new hop strains, sour and barrel-aged beers regularly fill the taps, and superior bar food includes pork belly poutine. In summer, adjourn to the alfresco beer garden with a hazy IPA and the excellent Al Pastor pizza.

A Taste of Monterey — Wine Bar

(☑831-646-5446; www.atasteofmonterey. com; 700 Cannery Row; tasting flights $20; ⊙11am-6pm Sun-Thu, to 8pm Fri & Sat) Sample medal-winning Monterey County wines from as far away as the Santa Lucia Highlands while soaking up dreamy sea views, then peruse thoughtful exhibits on barrel-making and cork production. Shared plates, including crab cakes and

 Whale-Watching at Monterey Bay

Whales are off the coast of Monterey Bay year-round. Blue and humpback whales visit from April to early December, while gray whales pass from mid-December to March. **Monterey Bay Whale Watch** (☑831-375-4658; www. gowhales.com; Fisherman's Wharf; 3hr tours adult/child 4-12yr $49/38; 👪🐕) tour boats depart from Fisherman's Wharf, while **Sanctuary Cruises** (☑info 831-917-1042, tickets 831-350-4090; www.sanctuarycruises. com; 7881 Sandholdt Rd; tours $40-55; 👪) 🍴 runs trips from Moss Landing. Reserve at least a day in advance; be prepared for a bumpy, cold ride.

Humpback whale, Monterey Bay
CHASE DEKKER WILD-LIFE IMAGES/GETTY IMAGES ©

smoked salmon, provide a tasty reason to linger, and there's also a good selection of California craft beers.

ⓘ INFORMATION

Monterey Visitor Center (☑831-657-6400; www.seemonterey.com; 401 Camino el Estero; ⊙10am-6pm May-Aug, to 5pm Sep-Apr) Free tourist brochures; ask for information about filming locations for the HBO series *Big Little Lies* (2017–19).

ⓘ GETTING THERE & AWAY

Monterey is 43 miles south of Santa Cruz and 177 miles north of San Luis Obispo.

 Steinbeck in Salinas

Around 20 miles northeast of Monterey, Salinas is the birthplace of Nobel Prize–winning native son, John Steinbeck (1902–68). Tough, funny and brash, he portrayed the troubled spirit of rural, working-class Americans in novels like *The Grapes of Wrath*. Visit the **National Steinbeck Center** (☑831-775-4721; www.steinbeck. org; 1 Main St; adult/child 6-17yr $13/7; ☺10am-5pm, to 9pm 1st Fri of each month; ☝) to explore interactive exhibits and videos chronicling the writer's life in an engaging way. Gems include Rocinante, the camper in which Steinbeck traveled around the USA while researching *Travels with Charley*. Also listen to Steinbeck's Nobel acceptance speech from 1962 – it's grace and power combined.

National Steinbeck Center
JAMES KIRKIKIS/SHUTTERSTOCK ©

Carmel-by-the-Sea

With borderline fanatical devotion to its canine citizens, quaint Carmel has the well-manicured feel of a country club. Founded as a seaside resort in the 1880s – fairly odd, given that its beach is often blanketed in fog – Carmel attracted famous artists and writers including Sinclair Lewis and Jack London, and their hangers-on. Artistic flavor survives in nearly 100 galleries that saturate downtown's immaculate streets and courtyards, but sky-high property values have long obliterated any salt-of-the-earth bohemia.

◉ SIGHTS

Mission San Carlos Borromeo de Carmelo   Church

(831-624-1271; www.carmelmission.org; 3080 Rio Rd; adult/child 7-17yr $10/7; ☺9:30am-5pm; ℗) Carmel's strikingly beautiful mission is an oasis of solemnity with flowering gardens and a thick-walled basilica filled with Spanish Colonial art and artifacts. The mission was originally established by Franciscan friar Junípero Serra in 1770 in nearby Monterey, but poor soil and the corrupting influence of Spanish soldiers forced the move to Carmel two years later. The mission became Serra's home base and he died here in 1784.

Point Lobos State Natural Reserve   State Park

(☑831-624-4909; www.pointlobos.org; Hwy 1; per car $10; ☺8am-5pm, last entry 4:30pm; ℗☝) ✿ They bark, they laze and bathe and they're fun to watch – sea lions are the stars in this state park some 4 miles south of Carmel, along with the dramatically rocky coastline and its excellent tide-pooling. Even a short hike through this spectacular scenery is rewarding. Note that parking inside the reserve is limited to 150 cars, and spaces fill quickly in summer. Arrive before 9:30am or after 3pm to avoid the crowds. Alternatively, park on Hwy 1 and walk in.

The reserve is laced with hiking trails, including several skirting the ocean's edge where you might spot sea lions and sea otters between the crashing waves. A nice short loop is the 0.8-mile Cypress Grove Trail. In the south, Bird Island has impressive views as well, but, frankly, there's not a bad spot anywhere in the reserve.

✪ ACTIVITIES

17-Mile Drive   Scenic Drive

(www.pebblebeach.com; per car/bicycle $10.50/free) Once promoted as 'Mother Nature's Drive-Thru,' the 17-Mile Drive is a spectacularly scenic private toll road (bikers prohibited) that loops around the Monterey

Peninsula, connecting Pacific Grove with Pebble Beach and Carmel-by-the-Sea.

Using the self-guided tour map handed out at the toll gates, you can motor past postcard vistas of the ocean and Monterey cypress trees, world-famous golf courses, a luxury lodge and the bay where Spanish explorer Gaspar de Portolá dropped anchor in 1769.

🍴 EATING & DRINKING

Cultura
Comida y Bebida   Mexican $$
(☏831-250-7005; www.culturacarmel.com; Dolores St btwn 5th & 6th Aves; mains $19-33; ⊙5:30pm-midnight daily, 10:30am-3:30pm Sat & Sun; ⌨) In a brick-lined courtyard, this vivaciously elegant restaurant pairs art and candlelight with food inspired by Oaxacan flavors and an entire library's worth of mezcal. The ambience is upscale but relaxed, and suitable both for a date night or an outing with your posse. The Cultura mole with smoked pork and saffron tortillas is a signature dish.

ℹ️ INFORMATION

Carmel Visitor Center (☏831-624-2522; www.carmelchamber.org; Ocean Ave btwn Junipero & Mission Sts, 2nd fl, Carmel Plaza; ⊙10am-5pm) Maps and brochures available.

ℹ️ GETTING THERE & AWAY

Carmel is about 5 miles south of Monterey via Hwy 1.

Along Highway 1

⊙ SIGHTS

Henry Miller
Memorial Library   Arts Center
(☏831-667-2574; www.henrymiller.org; 48603 Hwy 1; donations accepted; ⊙11am-5pm Wed-Sun) `FREE` Novelist Henry Miller was a Big Sur denizen from 1944 to 1962. More of a beatnik memorial, alt-cultural venue and bookstore, this community gathering spot was never Miller's home. The house belonged to Miller's friend, painter Emil White, until his death and is now run by a nonprofit

Carmel-by-the-Sea

Explore
Hearst Castle

Hilltop **Hearst Castle** (🖉reservations 800-444-4445; www.hearstcastle.org; 750 Hearst Castle Rd; tours adult/child 5-12yr from $25/12; ⊙from 9am, last tour departs 4pm; P⚑) is a wondrous, historic, over-the-top homage to material excess. The estate sprawls across acres of landscaped gardens, accentuated by pools and fountains, statues from ancient Greece and Moorish Spain, and the ruins of what was, in Hearst's day, the world's largest private zoo.

From the 1920s into the '40s, Hearst and Marion Davies, his longtime mistress (Hearst's wife refused to grant him a divorce), entertained a steady stream of the era's biggest movers and shakers. Invitations were highly coveted, but Hearst had quirks – he despised drunkenness and guests were forbidden to speak of death.

California's first licensed female architect, Julia Morgan, based the main building, Casa Grande, on the design of a Spanish cathedral. Over the decades she catered to Hearst's design whims, deftly integrating the spoils of his fabled European shopping sprees.

Tours are mandatory to see this historic monument. There are three main tours: the guided portion of each lasts about an hour, after which you're free to wander the gardens and terraces.

Afterwards, drive to the San Simeon coast to see the elephant seals that hang out on the beach year-round.

group. Stop by to browse and relax on the deck. Concerts are held on a stage in the garden. Check online for listings. The library is 0.4 miles south of Nepenthe restaurant.

Inside are copies of all of Miller's written works, many of his paintings and a collection of Big Sur and Beat Generation material, including copies of the top 100 books Miller said most influenced him.

🟢 ACTIVITIES

Esalen Institute
Hot Springs   Thermal Baths

(🖉831-667-3000; www.esalen.org; 55000 Hwy 1; per person $35; ⊙1am-3am) Writer Hunter S Thompson was the gun-toting caretaker at this new-age hippie camp for adults in the 1960s. Today it still offers the gamut of esoteric workshops but is mostly famous for its ocean-facing hot tubs fed by a natural hot spring. They're open to the public from 1am to 3am only. Same-day online-only reservations start at 9am and are often booked by 9:03am.

The entrance is on the ocean side of Hwy 1, just over 12 miles south of Big Sur village and 10 miles north of Lucia.

🟢 EATING & DRINKING

Big Sur Deli &
General Store   Sandwiches $

(🖉831-667-2225; www.bigsurdeli.com; 47520 Hwy 1, Big Sur Village; sandwiches $5-11; ⊙7am-8pm; P⚑⚑) Put together a picnic of freshly made sandwiches from this family-owned deli and pair them with drinks and chips from the attached store, which also carries other essentials from beer to batteries. Easily the best-value food along this part of Hwy 1.

Nepenthe   Californian $$$

(🖉831-667-2345; www.nepenthebigsur.com; 48510 Hwy 1; mains lunch $18-25, dinner $18-53; ⊙11:30am-10pm; ⚑⚑⚑) Nepenthe comes from a Greek word meaning 'isle of no sorrow,' and indeed it's hard to feel blue while sitting by the fire pit on this aerial terrace. Just-OK California cuisine (try the renowned Ambrosia burger) takes a back seat to the views and Nepenthe's history – Orson Welles and Rita Hayworth briefly owned a cabin here in the 1940s. Kids menu available.

Big Sur Taphouse   Bar

(🖉831-667-2197; www.bigsurtaphouse.com; 47520 Hwy 1, Big Sur Village; ⊙noon-10pm; ⚑) Down California craft beers and regional

Henry Miller Memorial Library (p153)

wines on the back deck or by the fireplace inside this high-ceilinged wooden bar. There are board games, sports on the TVs and balance-restoring pub grub from tacos to artisanal cheeses (dishes $7 to $19).

ⓘ INFORMATION

Big Sur Chamber of Commerce (📞831-667-2100; www.bigsurcalifornia.org; Hwy 1; ◷9am-1pm Mon, Wed & Fri)

Big Sur Station (📞831-667-2315; 47555 Hwy 1; ◷9am-4pm; 🛜) Multiagency ranger station with information about hiking, camping, backpacking and road conditions. It also sells trail maps and guidebooks.

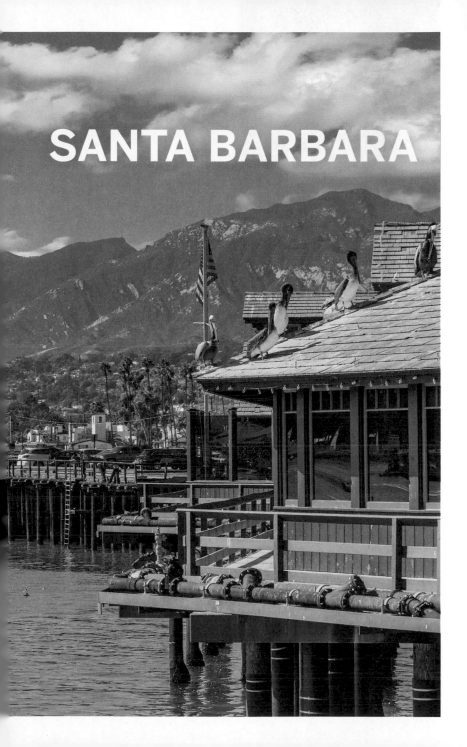

SANTA BARBARA

In this Chapter

Santa Barbara

Locals call Santa Barbara the 'American Riviera,' and honestly that's not too much of a stretch. Waving palm trees, sugar-sand beaches, boats bobbing by the harbor – it'd be a travel cliché if it wasn't the plain truth. California's 'Queen of the Missions' is a beauty, as are downtown's red-roofed, white-washed adobe buildings, all rebuilt in harmonious Spanish Colonial Revival style after a devastating earthquake in 1925. Aspire to the breezy, rich-and-famous lifestyle over a weekend of sipping wine and lazing on the beach. For active travelers there are hiking, biking, surfing, kayaking, scuba-diving and camping opportunities galore.

Santa Barbara in Two Days

Spend your first morning exploring Santa Barbara's historic **mission** (p107). After lunch visit the **county courthouse** (p166) for murals on the 2nd floor and 360-degree views from the clock tower. Then hit **East Beach** (p162), followed by **Stearns Wharf** (p167) for sunset. After dark, follow the siren call of cocktails to **Good Lion** (p173). On day two, Head up to Santa Barbara's Wine Country.

Santa Barbara in Four Days

Spend the morning cycling the coast, surfing or sea kayaking on the Pacific, or hiking in the Santa Ynez foothills. Then drive to posh Montecito for shopping and people-watching. On day four, head east for arty Ojai up in the mountains – it's known for its hot springs and spas. Or book a day trip to explore the rugged Channel Islands by **kayak** (p167).

Santa Barbara Map (p168)

Arriving in Santa Barbara

Santa Barbara Airport (www.flysba. com) Nine miles west of downtown via Hwy 101; a taxi downtown costs $35 to 40 plus tip.

Bus and train Santa Barbara Airbus (www.sbairbus.com) shuttles between Los Angeles International Airport (LAX) and Santa Barbara (one way/round-trip $55/100, 2½ hours). Greyhound operates a few direct buses daily to LA (from $14, three hours) and San Francisco (from $42, nine hours). Amtrak trains run south to LA ($31, 2¾ hours) and north to Oakland (from $57, 8¾ hours).

Sleeping

Prepare for sticker shock: even basic motel rooms by the beach command over $200 in summer. Don't arrive without reservations and expect to find anything reasonably priced, especially on weekends. A good selection of renovated motels is tucked between the harbor and Hwy 101, just about walking distance to everything.

Old Mission Santa Barbara

RON AND PATTY THOMAS/GETTY IMAGES ©

Old Mission Santa Barbara

When the setting sun warms the brick facade and the Pacific breeze carries the scent of eucalyptus from the surrounding hills, California's 'Queen of the Missions' is magical.

Great For...

☑ Don't Miss

Peering into the padre's bedroom, with its thin blanket, chess set and quiet air of contemplation.

Old Mission Santa Barbara reigns above the city on a hilltop perch over a mile north of downtown. Its proud Ionic facade, an architectural homage to an ancient Roman chapel, is topped by an unusual twin bell tower. Inside the mission's 1820 stone church, there are striking examples of Chumash artwork, including a unique abalone-encrusted altar dated to the 1790s. There are also a pair of magnificent paintings, two of the largest of any of the California missions. The *Assumption and Coronation of the Virgin* is thought to have originated in the Mexico City studio of Miguel Mateo Maldonado y Cabrera. The origins of the other, *The Crucifixion,* are unknown. In the cemetery the elaborate mausoleums of early California settlers stand out, while the graves of thousands of Chumash lie largely forgotten.

Interior of Old Mission Santa Barbara

Old Mission
Santa Barbara ◎ — Mission Park — Mission Canyon Rd

State St · Los Olivos St · Garden St · Mission St · Laguna St

❶ Need to Know

☎805-682-4713; www.santabarbaramission.org; 2201 Laguna St; adult/child 5-17yr $15/10; ⊙9am-4:15pm Sep-Jun, to 5:15pm Jul & Aug; ℗

✗ Take a Break

Head back downtown to the Good Lion (p173) for a post-Mission cocktail.

★ Top Tip

Make the most of your visit by joining one of the entertaining and educational docent-led tours.

The mission was established on December 4 (the feast day of St Barbara), 1786, as the 10th California mission. Of California's original 21 Spanish colonial missions, it's the only one that escaped secularization under Mexican rule. Continuously occupied by Catholic priests since its founding, the mission is still an active parish church.

Touring the Mission

The self-guided tour of the mission starts in the pretty garden before heading to the cemetery. Among the graves, you'll find a commemorative plaque inscribed with the Christian baptismal name Juana María, the Native American girl made famous in Scott O'Dell's 1960 Newbery Medal–winning *Island of the Blue Dolphins* novel. She was left behind on San Nicolas Island during the early 19th century, when her people were forced off the Channel Islands, just off the coast. She survived mostly alone on the island for 18 years, living in a whale-bone hut, until she was discovered by a seal hunter in 1853. By the time she was brought to the Santa Barbara Mission she was the last of her people, no one could understand her language and she died just seven weeks later.

Next up is the church itself, followed by a series of rooms turned into a museum and exhibiting Chumash baskets, a missionary's bedroom and time-capsule black-and-white photos showing the last Chumash residents of the Mission and the damage done to the buildings after the 1925 earthquake.

Excellent docent-guided tours are usually given on weekdays at 11am, Saturdays at 10:30am and Sundays at 12:30pm; no reservations are taken.

To get here from downtown, take MTD bus 6 or 11, then walk five blocks uphill.

Santa Barbara sunset

Santa Barbara Beaches

With mile after mile of perfect sand, lots of variety and a Mediterranean vibe, Santa Barbara's beaches are reason enough to visit.

Great For...

☑ Don't Miss

A spot of tide-pooling (low tide only) at Thousand Steps Beach, accessible from Shoreline Park.

East Beach

Santa Barbara's largest and most popular beach is **East Beach** (E Cabrillo Blvd; 🚻), a long, sandy stretch sprawling east of Stearns Wharf, with volleyball nets for pick-up games, a children's play area and a snack bar. On Sunday afternoons, artists set up booths along the sidewalk, near the bike path.

West Beach

West Beach (W Cabrillo Blvd; 🚻) is a central, palm-tree-backed stretch of sand, right next to Stearns Wharf and the harbor (swimming isn't advisable). It's the setting for large outdoor city events such as Fourth of July celebrations. West Beach is also a great place to check out public art. No dogs are allowed.

Leadbetter Beach

GERI LAVROV/GETTY IMAGES ©

❶ Need to Know

Don't expect a sunset over the Pacific; most Santa Barbara beaches face south rather than west.

✖ Take a Break

Stop at Boathouse (p171), right on Arroyo Burro Beach, for cocktails with water views.

★ Top Tip

To cruise from beach to beach, rent a bike from **Wheel Fun Rentals** (☎805-966-2282; http://wheelfunrentalssb.com; 24 E Mason St; ☺8am-8pm Apr–mid-Oct, to 6pm mid-Oct–Mar; 🚲).

Leadbetter Beach

One of Santa Barbara's most popular beaches, **Leadbetter Beach** (☎805-564-5418; Shoreline Dr, cnr Loma Alta Dr; per vehicle per hr $2; P🚻) is always busy with surfers, wind- and kitesurfers, joggers and sunbathers. Facilities include reservable picnic areas and showers. It's also a great place to rent a board from **Paddle Sports Center** (☎805-617-3425; http://paddlesportsca. com; 117 Harbor Way, Suite B; SUP/kayak rental from $25/15; ☺8am-5pm) and try your hand at stand-up paddle surfing.

Shoreline Park

For dazzling views across the city, mountains and ocean (with the chance to spot whales in season and dolphins year-round), come to **Shoreline Park** (Shoreline

Dr; ☺8am-sunset; P🚲) FREE, west of the harbor. There are restrooms, picnic tables and a children's playground, and dogs are welcome.

Arroyo Burro Beach County Park

Swim (lifeguards on duty), stroll or just picnic on this gem of a **stretch of sand** (Hendry's; ☎805-568-2460; www.countyofsb. org/parks/day-use/arroyo-burro-beach.sbc; Cliff Dr, at Las Positas Rd; ☺8am-sunset; P🚻🚲), 5 miles southwest of Santa Barbara. It's wide, away from tourists and great for kids, who can go tide-pooling. It's also a popular local surf spot and the eastern section is dog-friendly. The flat, long beach and selection of driftwood make it perfect for a game of fetch, and there's even a dog wash in the parking lot.

Santa Ynez Valley

RON AND PATTY THOMAS/GETTY IMAGES ©

Santa Barbara Wine Country

Oak-dotted hillsides, winding country lanes, rows of grapevines stretching toward the horizon – it's hard not to gush about the Santa Ynez and Santa Maria Valleys and the Santa Rita Hills wine regions.

Great For...

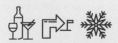

☑ **Don't Miss**

La Purisíma Mission, one of Southern California's most evocative.

This is an area made for do-it-yourself-exploring. With around 100 local wineries, visiting can seem daunting, but simply choose a region and hit the road.

Santa Ynez Valley

One of California's top viticulture regions, the Santa Ynez Valley is a compact area comprising a handful of small towns and dozens of vineyards. Put on the map back in 2004 by the movie *Sideways,* the area still draws the crowds and it's a hugely pleasant place to stay in upmarket lodgings, eat at high-quality restaurants and, of course, enjoy the many fine wines produced here. Los Olivos is the cutest town, Buellton the most down-to-earth, with incongruous Danish Solvang and tiny Santa Ynez and Ballard in between. Popular wineries cluster between Los Olivos and Solvang

Wine, Santa Ynez Valley

INT'L ST CLAIR/GETTY IMAGES ©

⊙ *Rancho Sisquoc Winery*

[101]

⊙ **Foxen**   Los Padres
Los Alamos⊙   **Canyon**   National
            Forest

Los
Olivos
Santa
(246) **Rita Hills**   ⊙
Lompoc   **Santa Ynez Valley**
⊙ ⊙ Buellton⊙   ⊙
(1)   Solvang⊙   ⊙Santa Ynez
                   (154)

❶ Need to Know

Santa Barbara Wine Country (www.
sbcountywines.com) Comprehensive
website with excellent info on tours and
how to make the most of a trip.

✖ Take a Break

Rancho Sisquoc Winery (☎805-934-
4332; www.ranchosisquoc.com; 6600
Foxen Canyon Rd; tastings $15; ☺10am-4pm
Mon-Thu, to 5pm Fri-Sun) is a tranquil gem
worth the extra mileage.

★ Top Tip

Solvang has great restaurants if
you need to fill your stomach before
tastings.

along Alamo Pintado Rd and Refugio Rd,
south of Roblar Ave and west of Hwy 154.

Foxen Canyon

The scenic Foxen Canyon Wine Trail runs
north from Hwy 154, just west of Los Olivos,
deep into the heart of the rural Santa Maria
Valley. It's a must-see for oenophiles or
anyone wanting to get off the beaten path.
For the most part, it follows Foxen Canyon
Rd, though a couple of top spots lie close to
Santa Maria town.

Santa Rita Hills

When it comes to country-road scenery,
eco-conscious farming practices and top-
notch pinot noir, the less-traveled Santa
Rita Hills region holds its own. Almost a
dozen tasting rooms line an easy driving
loop west of Hwy 101 via Santa Rosa Rd and

Hwy 246. Be prepared to share the roads
with cyclists and an occasional John Deere
tractor. More artisan winemakers hide out
in the industrial warehouses of Buellton
near Hwy 101 and further afield in Lompoc,
where you can also visit **La Purísima Mission** (☎805-733-3713; www.lapurisimamis
sion.org; 2295 Purísima Rd, Lompoc; per car $6;
☺park 9am-5pm, visitor center 10am-4pm Tue-
Sun year-round, 11am-3pm Mon Jul & Aug; 🅿🚻)
✎, founded in 1787.

Wine Tours

Full-day wine-tasting tours average $125
to $175 per person; most leave from Santa
Barbara, and some require a minimum
number of participants. Wine Edventures
(www.welovewines.com), Sustainable Vine
Wine Tours (www.sustainablewinetours.
com) and Santa Barbara Wine Country
Cycling Tours (www.winecountrycycling.
com) are great options.

◉ SIGHTS

Santa Barbara
County Courthouse   Historic Building

(☏805-962-6464; http://sbcourthouse.org; 1100
Anacapa St; ⊘8am-5pm Mon-Fri, 10am-5pm Sat
& Sun) FREE Built in Spanish Colonial Revival
style in 1929, the courthouse features
hand-painted ceilings, wrought-iron chan-
deliers and tiles from Tunisia and Spain. On
the 2nd floor, step inside the hushed Mural
Room depicting Spanish-colonial history,
then head up to El Mirador, the 85ft clock
tower, for arch-framed panoramas of the
city, ocean and mountains. Explore on your
own or join a free hour-long tour offered at
2pm daily and 10:30am Monday to Friday,
starting in the Mural Room.

MOXI   Museum

(Wolf Museum of Exploration & Innovation; ☏805-
770-5000; www.moxi.org; 125 State St; adult/
child $16/12; ⊘10am-5pm; ⏶) This next-gen
science museum is an interactive treasure
trove of exhibits and experiences related to
sound, technology, speed, light and color
that are sure to delight and enlighten little
ones. On three floors they can learn about
music (by stepping inside a giant guitar),
build a race car, or recreate sound effects
from famous movie scenes. Don't miss the
views from the Sky Garden roof terrace and
a nerve-challenging walk across a glass
ceiling.

Weekends get very busy, with waits for
many of the exhibits, so try to come during
the week when it's quieter.

Santa Barbara
Historical Museum   Museum

(☏805-966-1601; www.sbhistorical.org; 136 E De
La Guerra St; ⊘10am-5pm Tue-Sat, from noon
Sun) FREE Embracing a romantic clois-
tered adobe courtyard, this peaceful little
museum tells the story of Santa Barbara.
Its endlessly fascinating collection of
local memorabilia ranges from the simply
beautiful, such as Chumash woven baskets
and Spanish-colonial-era textiles, to the
intriguing, such as an intricately carved
coffer that once belonged to Junípero
Serra. Learn about the city's involvement in
toppling the last Chinese monarchy, among
other interesting lessons in local history.

Santa Barbara County Courthouse

NAGEL PHOTOGRAPHY/SHUTTERSTOCK ©

Stearns Wharf   Pier

(www.stearnswharf.org; ⊗8am-10pm; P🚻)

FREE The southern end of State St gives
way to Stearns Wharf, a rough wooden pier
lined with souvenir shops, snack stands
and seafood shacks. Built in 1872, it's the
oldest continuously operating wooden
wharf in California, although the actual
structure has been rebuilt more than
once. During the 1940s it was co-owned
by tough-guy actor Jimmy Cagney and his
brothers. If you have kids, don't miss the
Sea Center.

The first 90 minutes parking on the
wharf are free. The wharf entrance is a
stop on MTD's Downtown and Waterfront
shuttles.

Santa Barbara
Botanic Garden   Gardens

(☑805-682-4726; www.sbbg.org; 1212 Mission
Canyon Rd; adult $14, child 2-12yr $8; youth 13-
17yr $10; ⊗9am-6pm Mar-Oct, to 5pm Nov-Feb;
P🚻🐾) Take a soul-satisfying jaunt around
this 40-acre botanic garden, devoted to
California's native flora. Miles of partly
wheelchair-accessible trails meander past
cacti, redwoods and wildflowers and by the
old mission dam, originally built by Chumash tribespeople to irrigate the mission's
fields. Guided tours (included with admission) depart at 11am and 2pm on Saturday
and Sunday, and 2pm on Monday. Leashed,
well-behaved dogs are welcome.

If you're driving, head north from the
mission to Foothill Blvd/Hwy 192, turn
right and then left to continue on Mission
Canyon Rd; the road is well signed.

✪ ACTIVITIES

Santa Barbara
Adventure Company   Kayaking

(☑805-884-9283; www.sbadventureco.com; 32
E Haley St; ⊗office 8am-5pm Mon-Sat; 🚻) The
name says it all: if you want a company that
provides a whole host of well-organized
adventures then you've come to the right
place. It offers everything from Channel Island kayaking (from $149) to surf and SUP
lessons ($89) to bike tours (from $119).

👪 Santa Barbara for Kids

Santa Barbara abounds with family-
friendly fun for kids of all ages.
MOXI (p166) Santa Barbara's new-
est hands-on, kid-friendly science
attraction.

**Santa Barbara Museum of Natural
History** (☑805-682-4711; www.sbnature.
org; 2559 Puesta del Sol; adult $15, child
2-12yr $9, youth 13-17yr $12, incl planetarium
show $16/12/12; ⊗10am-5pm; P🚻) Giant
skeletons, local bird dioramas and a
backyard museum outside.

Santa Barbara Maritime Museum
(☑805-962-8404; www.sbmm.org; 113 Harbor Way, Suite 190; adult/child 6-17yr $8/5;
⊗10am-5pm Sun-Tue, Thu & Fri, 9am-3pm
Sat; P🚻) Reel in a virtual fish, raise a
sail and visit a tattoo parlor.

Santa Barbara Zoo (☑805-962-6310;
www.sbzoo.org; 500 Ninos Dr; adult $19.95,
child under 13yr $11.95; ⊗10am-5pm; P🚻)
This small zoo has 146 species covering
all creatures great and small.

Sea Center (☑805-962-2526; www.
sbnature.org; 211 Stearns Wharf; adult $10,
child 2-12yr $7, youth 13-17yr $8; ⊗10am-
5pm; P🚻) From touch tanks and
crawl-through aquariums to whale
sing-alongs.

Chase Palm Park (www.santabarbaraca.
gov/gov/depts/parksrec; 323 E Cabrillo Blvd;
⊗sunrise-10pm; 🚻) FREE A shipwreck-
themed playground, a lake with ducks
and a skate park.

Macaw, Santa Barbara Zoo

Santa Barbara

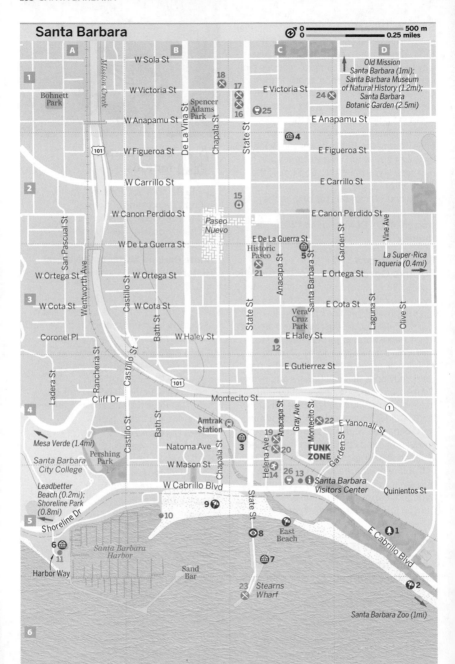

500 m
0.25 miles

A **B** **C** **D**

W Sola St

Old Mission
Santa Barbara (1mi);
Santa Barbara Museum
of Natural History (1.2mi);
Santa Barbara
Botanic Garden (2.5mi)

18

W Victoria St   E Victoria St   24

17   Spencer
16   Adams   25
Park

W Anapamu St   E Anapamu St

4

W Figueroa St   E Figueroa St

101

W Carrillo St   E Carrillo St

15

W Canon Perdido St   Paseo   E Canon Perdido St
Nuevo

La Super-Rica
Taqueria (0.4mi)

W De La Guerra St   E De La Guerra St
Historic
Paseo   5
21

W Ortega St   W Ortega St   E Ortega St

W Cota St   W Cota St   E Cota St

Coronel Pl   Vera
Cruz
Park

W Haley St   E Haley St

12

E Gutierrez St

101

Montecito St

Cliff Dr

Amtrak   22   E Yanonali St
Station
Mesa Verde (1.4mi)   19
Natoma Ave   3   20   FUNK
ZONE
Santa Barbara
City College   Pershing   W Mason St
Park   14
26 13
Leadbetter   W Cabrillo Blvd   Santa Barbara
Beach (0.2mi);   Visitors Center   Quinientos St
Shoreline Park   9
(0.8mi)
Shoreline Dr   10

6   8   East
11   Beach

Harbor Way   Santa Barbara   Sand   7
Harbor   Bar

23 Stearns
Wharf   2

Santa Barbara Zoo (1mi)

Santa Barbara

Surf Happens — Surfing

(☏805-966-3613; http://surfhappens.com; 3825 Santa Claus Lane; 2hr private lesson from $160;) Welcoming families, beginners and 'Surf Happens Sisters,' these highly reviewed classes and camps led by expert staff incorporate the Zen of surfing. In summer you'll begin your spiritual wave-riding journey. Make reservations in advance. Find the office on Santa Claus Lane (just north of Carpinteria).

◉ TOURS

Architectural Foundation of Santa Barbara — Walking

(☏805-965-6307; www.afsb.org; adult/child under 12yr $10/free; ◷10am Sat & Sun weather permitting) Take time out of your weekend for a fascinating two-hour guided walking tour of downtown's art, history and architecture. No reservations required; call or check the website for meet-up times and places.

Santa Barbara Trolley — Bus

(☏805-965-0353; www.sbtrolley.com; adult/child 3-12yr $25/8; ◷10am-3pm; 🖼)∲ Biodiesel-fueled trolleys make a narrated 90-minute one-way loop stopping at 14 major tourist attractions around the city, including the mission and the zoo. They start from the visitor center (hourly departures 10am to

3pm), and the hop-on, hop-off tickets are valid all day (and one consecutive day) – pay the driver directly, or buy discounted tickets online in advance.

One child aged 12 or under rides free with each paid adult rider. Your ticket also gives you savings on admission to several Santa Barbara attractions and shops.

Condor Express — Cruise

(☏805-882-0088; https://condorexpress.com; 301 W Cabrillo Blvd; 150/270min cruises adult from $50/99, child 5-12yr from $30/50; 🖼) Take a whale-watching excursion aboard the high-speed catamaran *Condor Express*. Whale sightings are guaranteed, so if you miss out the first time, you'll get a free voucher for another cruise.

⊜ SHOPPING

Downtown's **State Street** is packed with shops of all kinds, and even chain stores conform to the red-roofed architectural style. For more local art galleries and indie shops, dive into the **Funk Zone**, east of State St, tucked in south of Hwy 101.

Plum Goods — Gifts & Souvenirs

(☏805-845-3900; www.plumgoodsstore.com; 909 & 911 State St; ◷10am-5pm Mon-Thu, to 6pm Fri, to 7pm Sat, 11am-5pm Sun) A go-to shop for ethically and locally made gifts, Plum

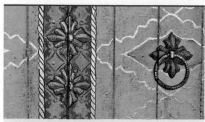

Santa Barbara Art Walks

Prime time for downtown gallery hopping is **First Thursday** (www.santabarbaradowntown.com), from 5pm to 8pm on the first Thursday of every month, when art galleries on and off State St throw open their doors for new exhibitions, artists' receptions, wine tastings and live music, all free. Closer to the beach and similar in aim is the **Funk Zone Art Walk** (http://funkzone.net), happening on a bimonthly basis from 5pm to 8pm, featuring free events and entertainment at offbeat art galleries, bars and restaurants.

The Blue Door, Funk Zone
STOCKIMO/SHUTTERSTOCK ©

Goods curates a playful and quality array of upcycled art, jewelry, skincare, books and homewares. Its newer shop next door is more sartorially focused.

EATING

Corazon Cocina   Mexican $
(⌂805-845-0282; https://corazoncocinasb.com; 38 W Victoria St; mains $5.50-16.50; ⊙11am-9pm Mon-Fri, 10am-9pm Sat & Sun) Mexican regional favorites, elevated: al pastor tacos with pineapple and habanero salsa, delicate wild-shrimp ceviche laden with chili-spiked mango and cucumber, grilled Oaxacan quesadillas featuring local veggies...*sí, por favor*. Head into the Santa Barbara Public Market and prepare to get food drunk (and to wait a while – it's popular for very good reason).

Lucky Penny   Pizza $
(⌂805-284-0358; www.luckypennysb.com; 127 Anacapa St; pizzas $10-16; ⊙11am-9pm Sun-Thu, to 10pm Fri & Sat; ⊘) Shiny exterior walls covered in copper pennies herald a brilliant pizza experience inside this Funk Zone favorite, right beside the Lark (p172). Always jam-packed, it's worth the wait for a crispy pizza topped with a variety of fresh ingredients, many vegetarian-friendly, or a wood-oven-fired lamb-and-pork-meatball sandwich. The coffee is taken seriously too.

Metropulos   Deli $
(⌂805-899-2300; www.metrofinefoods.com; 216 E Yanonali St; dishes $2-10; ⊙8:30am-5pm Mon-Fri, 10am-5pm Sat) Before a day at the beach, pick up custom-made specialty sandwiches (the Harissa Bomb doesn't disappoint), gyros and fresh salads at this perennially popular gourmet deli in the Funk Zone. Artisan crackers, imported cheeses, cured meats, and California olives and wines will be bursting out of your picnic basket.

La Super-Rica Taquería   Mexican $
(⌂805-963-4940; 622 N Milpas St; dishes $1.55-6.80; ⊙11am-9pm Sun-Mon & Thu, to 9:30pm Fri & Sat; 🍴) Although there's plenty of good Mexican food in town, La Super-Rica is deluged daily by locals and visitors keen on tasting the dishes once so loved by the late culinary queen Julia Child. Join the line to tuck into tacos, tamales and other Mexican staples, and see for yourself what the fuss is about.

McConnell's Fine Ice Creams   Desserts $
(⌂805-324-4402; www.mcconnells.com; 728 State St; scoops from $5.25; ⊙11am-10pm Sun-Thu, to 11pm Fri & Sat; 🍴) Just try walking past this place on State St if you have a sweet tooth. A Santa Barbara institution since 1949, McConnell's uses local milk and other ingredients to produce an array of flavors, from the classic such as chocolate and vanilla to the adventurous like Turkish coffee and cardamom and gingersnaps.

Arigato Sushi — Japanese $$

(☏805-965-6074; www.arigatosb.com; 1225 State St; rolls from $7; ⊙5:30-10pm Sun-Thu, to 10:30pm Fri & Sat; ❋☝) Phenomenally popular Arigato Sushi always has people milling around waiting for a table (no reservations taken), but it's worth the wait. Traditional and more unusual sushi, including lots of vegetarian options, plus salads and a dizzying array of hot and cold starters will make you order a sake pronto just to help you get through the menu.

It's noisy and bustling, so not the place for a romantic dinner, unless you nab a table on the small patio on State St.

Santa Barbara Shellfish Company — Seafood $$

(☏805-966-6676; http://shellfishco.com; 230 Stearns Wharf; dishes $4-24; ⊙11am-9pm; ☝☺) 'From sea to skillet to plate' sums up this end-of-the-wharf seafood shack that's more of a buzzing counter joint than a sit-down restaurant. Chase away the seagulls as you chow down on garlic-baked clams, crab cakes and coconut-fried shrimp at wooden picnic tables outside. Awesome lobster bisque, ocean views and the same location for almost 40 years.

Mesa Verde — Vegan $$

(☏805-963-4474; http://mesaverderestaurant. com; 1919 Cliff Dr; shared plates $10-18; ⊙11am-9pm Tue-Fri, 11am-3:30pm & 5-9pm Sat & Sun; ☝) ✿ A top pick for plant-based dining, Mesa Verde has so many delicious, innovative all-vegan sharing plates on the menu that meat-avoiding procrastinators will be in torment. If in doubt, pick a selection and brace yourself for flavor-packed delights. Meat-eaters welcome (and may be converted).

Boathouse — Californian $$

(☏805-898-2628; http://boathousesb.com; 2981 Cliff Dr; mains from $14; ⊙7:30am-close; ☝☺) Water views and ocean air accompany your healthy dining at the Boathouse, right on Arroyo Burro Beach (p163). The patio is great for enjoying a cocktail and fancy salad with other beachgoers, while the walls inside display photos paying homage to the area's surfing and rowing heritage.

Lucky Penny pizza

Municipal Winemakers

Lark Californian $$$

(☑805-284-0370; www.thelarksb.com; 131 Anacapa St; mains $16-38; ☺5-9pm Sun-Thu, to 10pm Fri & Sat; P) ✔ A top spot to savor SoCal's bountiful farm and fishing goodness, chef-run Lark was named after an antique Pullman railway car and is based at a former fish market transformed into a buzzy casual-urban restaurant in the Funk Zone. The menu morphs with the seasons, presenting inspiring flavor combinations such as crispy Brussels sprouts with dates or juniper-smoked duck breast. Make reservations.

Just as much imagination goes into the craft cocktails. Try the Green Goddess, starring chili vodka, arugula, matcha, suze and ginger beer.

Yoichi's Japanese $$$

(☑805-962-6627; www.yoichis.com; 230 E Victoria St; 5-/7-course set menu $80/125; ☺5:30-9pm Tue-Sun) Headline: *kaiseki* (traditional Japanese multicourse dining) comes to Santa Barbara and wows locals. It might have limited hours, take a chunk out

of your wallet and need to be booked way in advance, but none of that has stopped Yoichi's from being hailed as one of Santa Barbara's best (and slightly hidden away) eating experiences.

Bouchon Californian $$$

(☑805-730-1160; www.bouchonsantabarbara. com; 9 W Victoria St; mains $26-36; ☺5-9pm) ✔ The perfect, unhurried follow-up to a day in the Wine Country is to feast on the bright, flavorful California cooking at pretty Bouchon (meaning 'wine cork'). A seasonally changing menu spotlights locally grown farm produce and ranched meats that marry beautifully with almost three dozen regional wines available by the glass. Lovebirds, book a table on the candlelit patio.

🍷 DRINKING & NIGHTLIFE

Figueroa Mountain Brewing Co Craft Beer

(☑805-324-4461; www.figmtnbrew.com; 137 Anacapa St, Suite F; ☺11am-11pm Sun-Thu, to midnight Fri & Sat) Father-and-son brewers have brought their gold-medal-winning hoppy IPA, Danish red lager and potent stout from Santa Barbara's Wine Country to the Funk Zone. Knowledgeable staff will help you choose. Clink glasses below vintage-style posters in the 'surf-meets-Old-West' taproom or on the open-air patio while acoustic acts play.

Enter on Yanonali St. Happy hour runs from 3pm to 6pm Monday to Friday.

Good Lion
Cocktail Bar

(📞805-845-8754; www.goodlioncocktails.com; 1212 State St; ⏰4pm-1am) Order a cocktail at the beautiful blue-tiled bar, then grab a book from the shelves and settle into a leather banquette in this petite place that has a cool turn-of-the-20th-century-Montmartre feel (candles on the tables and absinthe in many of the cocktails help create the Parisian atmosphere).

The drinks are innovative and wittily named (Robb Stark's Revenge made us laugh). It gets very busy with pre– and post–Granada Theatre patrons and whenever live music is on.

Municipal Winemakers
Wine Bar

(📞805-931-6864; www.municipalwinemakers. com; 22 Anacapa St; tastings $12; ⏰1-8pm Thu & Sun, 1-9pm Fri-Sat; 🐾) Muni's winemaker, Dave, studied the oenological arts in Australia and France before applying his knowledge in this industrially decorated tasting room. His fun, accessible blends are hugely popular – enjoy a bottle on the large patio. For food, you can't beat the cheese plate; on weekends, pair your wine selection with East Coast–style lobstah rolls and sea-urchin crudo.

INFORMATION

Santa Barbara Visitors Center (📞805-965-3021; www.santabarbaraca.com; 1 Garden St; ⏰9am-5pm Mon-Sat, to 5:30pm Sun) Pick up maps and brochures while consulting with the helpful but busy staff. The website offers free downloadable DIY touring maps and itineraries, from food-and-drink routes to wine trails, art galleries and outdoors fun.

Driving Highway 154

You'll find a mix of history, scenery and adventure – plus amazing wines – on a drive along Hwy 154, which climbs from Santa Barbara into the rugged Santa Ynez Mountains and Wine Country.

First stop on the route is **Chumash Painted Cave** (📞805-733-3713; www.parks. ca.gov; Painted Cave Rd, off Hwy 154; ⏰dawn-dusk) **FREE**. Created around four centuries ago, the vivid pictographs on the walls here and the views across the whole region reward the rough approach to the cave along a narrow road.

Sidetrack off Hwy 154 again a few miles north of Cold Spring Tavern for a trip to Paradise (road), taking you into **Los Padres National Forest** (📞805-968-6640; www.fs.usda.gov/lpnf; 6750 Navigator Way, Suite 150, Goleta; ⏰8am-noon & 1-4:30pm Mon-Fri). This stretch of the forest holds swimming spots and hikes. For boating and cruising continue along the 154 to **Cachuma Lake** (📞805-568-2460; www. countyofsb.org/parks; per vehicle $10, 90min cruise adult/child $15/10; ⏰6am-sunset; 🐾). It might be artificial (it was created by the construction of a dam in the 1950s), but it's still a pretty spot.

Once past the lake you're in Santa Barbara Wine Country, with vineyards scattered throughout the surrounding area. Enjoy a few tastings before winding up in the incongruous but charming Danish village of Solvang, with plenty of places to indulge a taste for Scandinavian sweets.

Chumash Painted Cave

PALM SPRINGS

In this Chapter

Palm Springs

The Rat Pack is back, baby, or at least its hangout is. In the 1950s and '60s, Palm Springs, some 100 miles east of LA, was the swinging getaway of Sinatra, Elvis and other Hollywood stars. Once the Rat Pack dispersed, the golfing retirees moved in. However, since the mid-1990s new generations have rediscovered the city's retro-chic vibe and elegant mid-century modern structures built by famous architects. Today, retirees and snowbirds mix comfortably with hipsters, hikers and the LGBTIQ+ community on getaways from LA and across the globe.

Two Days in Palm Springs

Start with breakfast at **Cheeky's** (p185), then embark on a self-drive tour of mid-century modern marvels with the **Palm Springs Modern app** (p185). Spend the afternoon at **Sunnylands Estate** (p111). On day two, take the **cable-car ride** (p184) from the desert floor up Mt San Jacinto, then spend the afternoon getting your bliss on at the **Estrella Spa** (p185).

Four Days in Palm Springs

Dedicate much of days three and four to exploring the stunning natural beauty of nearby **Joshua Tree National Park** (p178). Scramble among the **Wonderland of Rocks** and sample the wacky sculptures of the outdoor **Noah Purifoy Desert Art Museum** (p181). Tired but happy, head back into Palm Springs for a refined meal at **Workshop Kitchen + Bar** (p186), followed by cocktails at **Bootlegger Tiki** (p187).

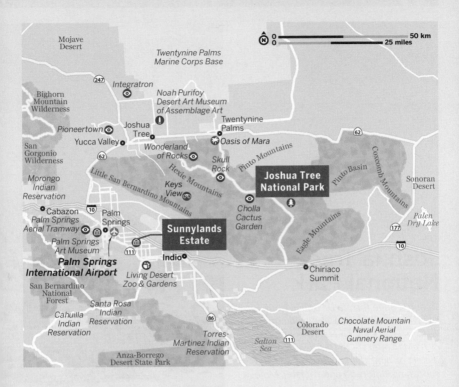

Arriving in Palm Springs

Palm Springs International Airport
(www.palmspringsairport.com) Ask if
your hotel provides free airport trans-
fers; a taxi downtown costs about $12
to $15.

Car Palm Springs is just over 100 miles
east of Los Angeles via I-10 and 140
miles northeast of San Diego via I-15
and I-10.

Train Amtrak's Sunset Limited comes
through three times weekly on its route
between New Orleans and Los Angeles.

Where to Stay

Palm Springs offers the gamut of
lodging options, from plain-Jane motels
to vintage-flair boutique hotels and
full-on luxury resorts. Many properties
add a hefty 'resort fee' to the daily rate.
Some places are adults-only (21 and
over). Most are entirely nonsmoking in
both rooms and outside areas. Campers
should head to Joshua Tree National
Park or into the San Jacinto Mountains
(via Hwy 74).

Joshua Tree National Park

Taking a page from a Dr Seuss book, the whimsical Joshua trees welcome visitors – be they hikers, rock climbers or road trippers – to this mystical desert park at the convergence of the scorching Colorado and moister Mojave Deserts.

Great For...

❶ Need to Know

760-367-5500; www.nps.gov/jotr; 7-day pass per car $30;

★ **Top Tip**
The park's northern half harbors most of the natural attractions, including all the Joshua trees.

Wonderland of Rocks

This striking rock **labyrinth** (📞760-367-5500; www.nps.gov/jotr; 🅿️) of whimsically eroded rocks and boulders extends roughly from Indian Cove in the north to Hidden Valley on Park Blvd. For a quick but satisfying impression, saunter along the 0.6-mile Indian Cove Trail or the 1-mile Hidden Valley Trail.

Oasis of Mara

A half-mile loop trail behind the Oasis Visitor Center leads to an **oasis** (📞760-367-5500; www.nps.gov/jotr; Utah Trail, Twentynine Palms; 🅿️) **FREE** with the original 29 palm trees that gave Twentynine Palms its name. They were planted by indigenous Serranos who named the area Mara, meaning 'the place of little springs and much grass.'

Keys View

From Park Blvd, it's an easy 20-minute drive up to 5185ft **Keys View** (📞760-367-5500; www.nps.gov/jotr; Keys View Rd; 🅿️) for a panoramic gander at the entire Coachella Valley – with any luck you should be able to see as far as the shimmering Salton Sea. Looming in the distance are Mt San Jacinto (10,834ft) and Mt San Gorgonio (11,500ft), Southern California's highest peaks. Below, you can spot a section of the San Andreas Fault.

Cholla Cactus Garden

A dense grove of 'teddy bear' cholla cactus and ocotillo plants, this **garden** (📞760-367-5500; www.nps.gov/jotr; Pinto Basin Rd; 🅿️) delivers a welcome break from the foreboding harshness of the Colorado Desert in the

Cholla Cactus Garden

park's southern reaches. A quarter-mile loop trail meanders through the patch.

Skull Rock

Much-photographed **Skull Rock** (☑760-367-5500; www.nps.gov/jotr; Park Blvd; P) stares out over Park Blvd from eye sockets hollowed out by rainwater over eons of time. A 1.7-mile loop trail starting at this roadside attraction runs past more rock formations and the Jumbo Rocks campground.

✗ Take a Break

Gobble up globally inspired dishes at farm-to-table **La Copine** (☑760-289-8537; www.lacopinekitchen.com; 848 Old Woman Springs Rd, Flamingo Heights; dishes $8-19; ☺noon-6pm Thu-Mon Sep-Jun; P ✳) ✐.

SARAPORN/SHUTTERSTOCK ©

What's Nearby?

Noah Purifoy Desert Art Museum of Assemblage Art

The 'Junk Dada' assemblage sculptures of African American artist Noah Purifoy (1917–2004) are collected by the world's finest museums, but some of his coolest works can be seen for free at his former outdoor **desert studio** (www.noahpurifoy.com; 63030 Blair Lane, Joshua Tree; ☺dawn-dusk; P) **FREE**. Toilets, tires, monitors, bicycles and beds are among the castoffs Purifoy turned variously into political statements, social criticism or just plain nonsense.

Integratron

It may look like just a **white-domed structure** (☑760-364-3126; www.integratron.com; 2477 Belfield Blvd, Landers; sound baths weekdays/weekends $40/45; ☺Wed-Sun Feb-Jul & Sep-Dec; P), but in reality it's an electrostatic generator for time travel and cell rejuvenation. Ahem! At least that's what its creator, aerospace engineer George Van Tassel (1910–78), believed when building the place in the 1950s after receiving telepathic instructions from extraterrestrials. Book way ahead to pick up on the spacey vibes during a one-hour 'sound bath' in the wooden dome.

Pioneertown

More than 50 movies were filmed at **Pioneertown** (https://visitpioneertown.com; Pioneertown Rd; ☺24hr; P) **FREE**, built in 1946 as a Hollywood Western movie set. These days, it's fun to stroll down 'Mane St,' perhaps popping into the little shops, the film museum or the honky-tonk. Weekends, when free gunfight and wild west shows kick up their spurs, are best for visiting.

☑ Don't Miss

Hiking through the magical, eye-popping geological marvel of the Wonderland of Rocks.

Sunnylands Center

Sunnylands Estate

Sunnylands is the mid-century modern winter retreat of Walter and Leonore Annenberg, one of America's 'first families.' It was here that they entertained US presidents, royalty, Hollywood celebrities and heads of state.

Great For...

☑ Don't Miss

Auguste Rodin's sensual statue *Eve* in the estate's foyer.

Historic House

The masterpiece of Los Angeles–based modernist architect A Quincy Jones and designer William Haines, this pink-roofed 1966 estate is considered a jewel of mid-century design. Harmoniously tied to the landscape, the building features overhanging roof lines to shield the interiors from direct sun and huge glass walls that allow the desert brightness to illuminate the rooms. Upon entering, Auguste Rodin's *Eve* leaves a lasting impression.

Gardens

The estate gardens host 70 species of plants from North and South America, the Mediterranean and Africa in an exquisitely manicured 9 acres. Hundreds of bird species have been spotted here, as well as fluttering monarch butterflies who stop on

Sunnylands Estate gardens

❶ Need to Know

☎760-202-2222; www.sunnylands.org; 37977 Bob Hope Dr, Rancho Mirage; visitor center & gardens free; ⏱house tours Wed-Sun, birding tours 8:45am Thu & Sat, visitor center & gardens 8:30am-4pm Wed-Sun mid-Sep–early Jun; 🅿 ✐

✕ Take a Break

Enjoy a light lunch with garden and mountain views at the Sunnylands Center cafe.

★ Top Tip

Don't fret if you can't snag a tour ticket. The free gardens and exhibits also deliver a sightseeing punch.

their annual migration to feast on the milkweed. The garden design was inspired by the Annenbergs' collection of Impressionist and post-Impressionist paintings.

Sunnylands Center

With its overhanging roof, columns and stone walls, Sunnylands visitor center is essentially a contemporary riff on the estate's mid-century modern aesthetic. It's an excellent introduction to the estate and its founders. Start by watching the 20-minute historic documentary before taking in the current art exhibit and admiring the garden and mountain views.

Visiting the Estate

The only way to get inside the historic house is on a 90-minute tour ($48, no children under 10). Tickets for this and the

Birding on the Estate tour ($38) are released at 9am on the 15th of the preceding month and sell out quickly.

Tickets for the 45-minute Open-Air Experience, a shuttle tour of the grounds and golf course that runs from September to April ($21), are sold first-come, first-served at the visitor center (credit cards only).

Neither the birding nor the open-air tour give access to the house.

What's Nearby?

Living Desert Zoo & Gardens

This **popular park** (☎760-346-5694; www. livingdesert.org; 47900 Portola Ave, Palm Desert; adult/child $25/15; ⏱8am-5pm Oct-May, 7am-1:30pm Jun-Sep; 🅿👪) showcases desert plants and animals alongside exhibits on regional geology and Native American culture. Camel encounters, giraffe feeding, the butterfly garden, a spin on the endangered species carousel and a hop-on, hop-off shuttle cost extra.

⊙ SIGHTS

Palm Springs
Aerial Tramway   Cable Car

(☎760-325-1391; www.pstramway.com; 1 Tram
Way; adult/child $27/17, parking $8; ⊙1st tram
up 10am Mon-Fri, 8am Sat & Sun, last tram up
8pm, last tram down 9:45pm daily, varies seasonally; P♿) Since 1963, the 2.5-mile ride
aboard the Palm Springs Aerial Tramway's
rotating gondolas has been the coolest
trip in town. Enjoy uplifting views as you're
whisked through five vegetation zones –
dusty Sonoran desert floor to pine-scented
Mt San Jacinto State Park (☎951-659-
2607; www.parks.ca.gov/msjsp) FREE – in just
10 minutes. It's about 30°F to 40°F (up
to 22°C) cooler at the mountain station
(8561ft), so don't go up in flip-flops and
tank top, especially if you plan on hitting
a trail.

There are exhibits, food, viewing
platforms and gift shops at both ends.
Good-value Ride 'n' Dinner deals are available after 4pm.

The valley station is 3.5 miles off Hwy
111; the turnoff is about 3 miles north
of downtown Palm Springs. Cable cars
depart at least every 30 minutes. Online
tickets are available from six weeks to 24
hours in advance and are highly recommended to avoid often horrendous wait
times. A contingent of on-site tickets is
available on a first-come, first-served
basis.

Palm Springs
Art Museum   Museum

(☎760-322-4800; www.psmuseum.org; 101
Museum Dr; adult/student/under 18yr $14/6/
free; ⊙10am-5pm Fri-Tue, noon-8pm Thu; P) Art
fans should not miss this museum and
its changing exhibitions drawn from a
stellar collection of international modern
and contemporary painting, sculpture,
photography and glass art. The permanent
collection includes works by Henry Moore,
Ed Ruscha, Mark di Suvero, Frederic Rem-
ington and many more heavy hitters. Other
highlights are glass art by Dale Chihuly
and William Morris and a collection of pre-
Colombian figurines. Free entry from 4pm
to 8pm Thursdays.

Indian Canyons

🟢 ACTIVITIES

Indian Canyons
Hiking

(📞760-323-6018; www.indian-canyons.com; 38520 S Palm Canyon Dr; adult/child $9/5; ⏱8am-5pm daily Oct-Jun, Fri-Sun Jul-Sep, last entry 4pm year-round) Sacred to the Agua Caliente Band of Cahuilla Indians, these canyons sustain rich plant life fed by seasonal streams flowing from the San Jacinto Mountains. The most famous is the 15-mile-long Palm Canyon, where you can picnic, meditate or hike beneath a canopy of magnificent fan palms. Quiz the folks at the trading post for other hiking ideas such as the 4.7-mile Murray Canyon trail to a seasonal waterfall or the 1.2-mile Andreas Canyon loop trail past photogenic rock formations.

To get to the trading post from downtown Palm Springs, follow Palm Canyon Dr south for about 2 miles to the reservation toll gate and then head on for another 3 miles.

Palm Springs Historical Society Walking Tours
Tours

(📞760-323-8297; www.pshistoricalsociety.org; 221 S Palm Canyon Dr; tours $25) The Palm Springs Historical Society (PSHS) runs this bouquet of seven tours lasting between one and 2½ hours and covering history, architecture, Hollywood stars and more. Check the website for the schedule and to purchase advance tickets. Tickets are also sold at the PSHS office.

Estrella Spa at Avalon Palm Springs
Spa

(📞760-318-3000; www.avalon-hotel.com/palm-springs/estrella-spa; 415 S Belardo Rd; 60/90min massage from $155/225; ⏱10am-3pm Mon-Fri, from 9am Sat & Sun) A tranquil vibe permeates this stylish retreat that's big on natural options, including such next-gen treatments as a CBD Spa Experience, a Vichy shower (massage shower with multiple shower heads) and the Milky Way manicure/pedicure that starts with a warm fresh-milk soak (vegan version available).

 Palm Springs in Your Palm

The **Palm Springs Modern App** for iPhone and Android covers more than 80 iconic mid-century modern private homes and public buildings in Palm Springs on three tours enhanced with videos, audio and photographs. Download the app for free from your app store.

Modern Architecture, Palm Springs
STEPHANIE BRACONNIER/SHUTTERSTOCK ©

🍴 EATING

A lineup of zeitgeist-capturing restaurants has seriously elevated the level of dining in Palm Springs. The most exciting, including several with eye-catching design, flank N Palm Canyon Dr in the Uptown design district.

Cheeky's
Californian $

(📞760-327-7595; www.cheekysps.com; 622 N Palm Canyon Dr; mains $9-15; ⏱8am-2pm; ❄🍴👪🐾) Waits can be long at this hip breakfast and lunch spot, but the farm-to-table dishes dazzle with witty inventiveness. The offerings change on a weekly basis but faves such as custardy scrambled eggs, grass-fed burger with pesto fries, and bacon flights never rotate off the list. No reservations.

The spicy Bloody Mary – served in a cowboy-boot-shaped glass – is an Insta-worthy eye-opener. Kids menu available.

Counter Reformation

Rooster & the Pig
Vietnamese $

(📞760-832-6691; www.roosterandthepig.com; 356 S Indian Canyon Dr; plates $7-19; ⏱5-9pm Wed-Mon; ❄🍴🍽) A vibe of understated cool permeates this popular progressive-Vietnamese place tucked away in a strip mall. Boundary-pushing dinner winners like jasmine-tea-leaf salad, lemongrass meatballs or green papaya spring roll are good for sharing, while season-linked specials keep the menu in flux. Eccentric cocktails, craft beer and wine, but no reservations or cash.

Farm
French $$

(📞760-322-2724; www.farmpalmsprings.com; 6 La Plaza; breakfast & lunch mains $7-18, dinner prix-fixe $56; ⏱8am-2pm daily, 6-9pm Fri & Sat; ❄🍴🍽) Farm is so fantastically Provençal, you expect to see lavender fields pop up in the desert. Greet the day with fluffy crêpes or omelets, tuck into a salad or sandwich for lunch or book ahead for the three-course prix-fixe surprise dinner. It's in the heart of Palm Springs, yet secluded thanks to its country-style courtyard.

Workshop Kitchen + Bar
American $$$

(📞760-459-3451; www.workshoppalmsprings. com; 800 N Palm Canyon Dr; small plates $12-22, mains $32-42; ⏱5-10pm Mon-Thu & Sun, to 11pm Fri & Sat, 10am-2pm Sun; ❄🍴🍽) 🍃 Hidden away in the back of the ornate 1920s El Paseo building, a large patio with olive trees leads to this starkly beautiful space. At its center is a long, communal table flanked by mood-lit booths. The kitchen crafts market-driven American classics, mostly from locally hunted and foraged ingredients, and injects them with 21st-century sassiness. Matching liquid treats from the bar.

🍷 DRINKING & NIGHTLIFE

Drinking has always been in style in Palm Springs and many bars and restaurants have popular happy hours that sometimes run all day. A handful of speakeasy bars spice up the cocktail scene and craft beer continues to be a draw. Friday is the big night out for the LGBTIQ+ crowd. The city's main 'gayborhood' is the block of Arenas Rd east of S Indian Canyon Dr, with about a dozen gay-themed bars, cafes and shops. Other venues are scattered throughout town.

Bootlegger Tiki
Cocktail Bar

(📞760-318-4154; www.bootleggertiki.com; 1101 N Palm Canyon Dr; ⊗4pm-2am) Crimson light bathes even pasty-faced hipsters with a healthy glow in this bat cave of a tiki bar in the original 1953 Don the Beachcomber restaurant. Beware: after a couple of their pretty but potent cocktails, those blowfish lamps may look downright trippy.

Happy hour runs from 4pm to 6pm and again from midnight to 2am, perfect for ringing in or capping off a night on the town.

Counter Reformation
Wine Bar

(📞760-770-5000; www.parkerpalmsprings.com; 4200 E Palm Canyon Dr; ⊗3-11pm Thu-Mon) If you worship at the altar of Bacchus (the Roman god of wine), you'll be singing his praises in this dimly lit clandestine boîte at the **Parker Palm Springs resort** (d from $309; 🅿⊖❄🛜🛉🐕). The handpicked menu features just 17 reds, whites and champagne from small vineyards around the world.

All have the same price, perfect for sampling several varietals. A small tapas menu provides sustenance.

ℹ INFORMATION

Palm Springs Visitors Center (📞760-778-8418; www.visitpalmsprings.com; 2901 N Palm Canyon Dr; ⊗9am-5pm) Well-stocked and well-staffed official visitor center in a 1965 Albert Frey–designed gas station at the Palm Springs Aerial Tram turnoff, 3 miles north of downtown. Pick up self-guided tour brochures: *Public Art and Historic Sites* (free), *Modernism* ($5) and *Stars' Homes* ($5).

LOS ANGELES

In this Chapter

Los Angeles

Welcome to sunny Los Angeles, a shiny city of reinvention where small talk always starts with a question: 'Where are you from?' This is a city of incredible energy, architectural riches and some of the best places to eat and drink in the nation. Despite the plastic clichés, LA is one of the world's great cultural cities, home to exceptional art collections, world-shaking architecture and an extraordinary melting pot of cultures. But it's the incomparable beauty of its setting that makes it special. Here, the rat race comes with sweeping beaches, mountain vistas and bewitching sunsets.

Los Angeles in Two Days

Start your LA adventure by finding all your favorite stars and then walking right over them on the **Hollywood Walk of Fame** (p195). Spend the afternoon at the **Griffith Observatory** (p196), then (hopefully) spot more stars over dinner at **Connie & Ted's** (p219). On day two, spend an hour or six discovering modern masterpieces at **Broad** (p209) or **MOCA Grand** (p206). Earmark the evening for craft beers and jazz at **Blue Whale** (p223).

Los Angeles in Four Days

With two more days in town, you'll want to get a taste of beach life – take in all the sights at the **Santa Monica Pier** (p193), then rent a bike and cruise all the way to Venice. Hungry? Pop a few blocks inland to **Gjusta** (p220). On day four, prepare for more incredible art at the **Getty Center** (p205) or join the locals in the great outdoors with a **Runyon Canyon** (p213) hike. Keep up the healthy vibe and dine at vegan restaurant **Crossroads** (p218).

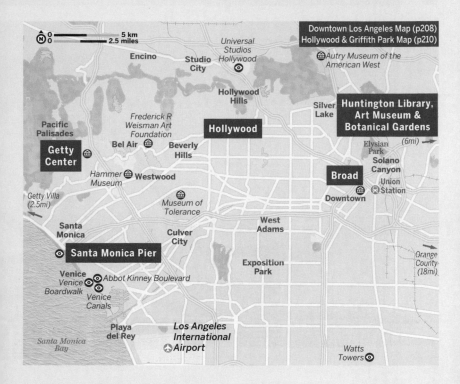

Arriving in Los Angeles

Los Angeles International Airport LAX FlyAway (www.lawa.org/FlyAway) buses run to Union Station (Downtown), Hollywood, Van Nuys and Long Beach. Fares range from $8 to $9.75. Taxis to Downtown LA and Hollywood cost around $60, around $35 to Venice and around $40 to Santa Monica (excluding tip).

Train Amtrak (www.amtrak.com) trains roll into Downtown LA's historic Union Station. Interstate trains stopping in the city are the daily *Coast Starlight* to Seattle (via Oakland and Portland), the daily *Southwest Chief* to Chicago and the thrice-weekly *Sunset Limited* to New Orleans.

Sleeping

From rock-and-roll Downtown digs to fabled Hollywood hideaways, LA serves up a dizzying array of slumber options. The key is to plan well ahead. Do your research and find out which neighborhood best appeals to your style and interests. For seaside life, base yourself in Santa Monica or Venice; cool-hunters and party people will be happiest in Hollywood or WeHo (West Hollywood); culture vultures in Downtown LA.

Santa Monica Pier

Santa Monica Pier

Once the very end of Route 66, Santa Monica Pier dates to 1908 and is the city's most compelling landmark. Extending almost a quarter-mile over the Pacific, it's all about the view: stroll to the edge and gaze out over the rolling blue-green sea.

Great For...

☑ Don't Miss

The beautiful, hand-painted horses of the 1922 carousel at the entrance to the pier.

Carousel

Near the pier entrance, nostalgic souls and their offspring can giddy up the beautifully hand-painted horses (and one rabbit and one goat) of the **carousel** (☏310-394-8042; adult/child $2/1; ⊙hours vary; 🚻). The 1916 Hippodrome building housing the carousel was featured in the movie *The Sting*.

Aquarium

Peer under the pier – just below the carousel – for Heal the Bay's **Santa Monica Pier Aquarium** (☏310-393-6149; www.healthebay. org; 1600 Ocean Front Walk; adult/child $5/ free; ⊙2-6pm Mon-Thu, 12:30-6pm Fri-Sun; 🚻; Ⓜ Expo Line to Downtown Santa Monica) 🍃. Sea stars, crabs, sea urchins and other critters and crustaceans scooped from the bay stand by to be petted – ever so gently – in their adopted touch-tank homes.

Original Muscle Beach

LOKIBAHO/GETTY IMAGES ©

❶ Need to Know

☎310-458-8901; www.santamonicapier.org; 👪

✕ Take a Break

Arrive early for excellent coffee and breakfast burritos at **Dogtown Coffee** (www.dogtowncoffee.com; 2003 Main St; ⊘5:30am-5pm Mon-Fri, from 6:30am Sat & Sun).

★ Top Tip

Santa Monica's free Twilight Concert Series features music to move you at the pier on Thursdays in summer.

Trapeze School New York

Ever wanted to learn how to fly on the trapeze? In a cordoned-off and netted area on the pier, **Trapeze School** (☎310-394-5800; www.trapezeschool.com; 370 Santa Monica Pier; 2hr classes \$40-70; ⊘class schedule varies) will give you the chance. Chalk up and leave your inhibitions and fear of heights at the door. The public is watching.

Pacific Park

Kids (and kids at heart) get their kicks at **Pacific Park** (☎310-260-8744; www.pacpark.com; 380 Santa Monica Pier; per ride \$5-10, all-day pass adult/child under 8yr \$35/19; ⊘daily, seasonal hours vary; 👪; Ⓜ E Line to Downtown Santa Monica), a small, classic Americana amusement park, with a solar-powered Ferris wheel, kiddy rides, midway games

and food stands. Check the website for discount passes.

What's Nearby?

South of the pier is the **Original Muscle Beach** (www.santamonica.com/original-muscle-beach-santa-monica/; 1800 Ocean Front Walk; ⊘sunrise-sunset), where the Southern California exercise craze began in the mid-20th century. New equipment now draws a fresh generation of fitness fanatics. Close by, the search for the next Bobby Fischer is on at the **International Chess Park** (☎310-458-8450; www.smgov.net; 1652 Ocean Front Walk; ⊘sunrise-sunset). Anyone can join in. Following the **South Bay Bicycle Trail** (⊘sunrise-sunset; 👪), a paved bike and walking path, south for about 1.5 miles takes you straight to Venice Beach. Bikes and in-line skates are available to rent on the pier and at beachside kiosks.

Hollywood

No other corner of LA is steeped in as much mythology as Hollywood. You'll find the Walk of Fame, Capitol Records and Grauman's Chinese Theatre, where the entertainment deities have been immortalized in concrete.

Great For...

☑ Don't Miss

Stepping into the shoe prints of your favorite movie star at Grauman's Chinese Theatre.

Grauman's Chinese Theatre

Ever wondered what it's like to be in George Clooney's shoes? Just find his footprints in the forecourt of this world-famous **movie palace** (Map p210; ☎323-461-3331, guided tours 323-463-9576; www.tclchinesetheatres. com; 6925 Hollywood Blvd; ⊕; ⓂB Line to Hollywood/Highland) **FREE**. The exotic pagoda theater – complete with temple bells and stone heaven dogs from China – has shown movies since 1927.

Dolby Theatre

The Academy Awards are handed out at the **Dolby Theatre** (Map p210; ☎323-308-6300; www.dolbytheatre.com; 6801 Hollywood Blvd; tours adult/child $25/19; ⊗10:30am-4pm; Ⓟ; ⓂB Line to Hollywood/Highland). Guided tours will show you the auditorium, a VIP room and an Oscar statuette.

SEAN PAVONE/SHUTTERSTOCK ©

Hollywood Blvd · Hollywood/Vine · Hollywood/Western

Grauman's Chinese Theatre; Dolby Theatre; Hollywood Walk of Fame · **Hollywood Museum** · HOLLYWOOD · Santa Monica Blvd

Hollywood Forever Cemetery · Paramount Pictures · Melrose Ave

❶ Need to Know

Find maps near the intersection of Hollywood Blvd and Highland Ave.

✕ Take a Break

Musso & Frank Grill (p217), Hollywood's oldest eatery, appeared in Quentin Tarantino's *Once Upon a Time...in Hollywood*.

★ Top Tip

The Metro Red Line has three stops along Hollywood Blvd. Hollywood/Vine and Hollywood/Highland stations are especially useful for Hollywood sights.

Hollywood Museum

For a taste of Old Hollywood, don't miss this musty **museum** (Map p210; ☑323-464-7776; www.thehollywoodmuseum.com; 1660 N Highland Ave; adult/senior & student/child $15/12/5; ☺10am-5pm Wed-Sun; 👫; Ⓜ B Line to Hollywood/Highland), its four floors crammed with movie and TV costumes and props. It's housed inside the 1914 Max Factor Building.

Hollywood Walk of Fame

Big Bird, Bob Hope, Marilyn Monroe and Aretha Franklin are among the stars being sought out, photographed and stepped on along the **Hollywood Walk of Fame** (Map p210; www.walkoffame.com; Hollywood Blvd; Ⓜ B Line to Hollywood/Highland). Since 1960 more than 2600 performers have been honored with a pink-marble sidewalk star; check online for upcoming ceremonies.

Hollywood Forever Cemetery

With paradisiacal landscaping, vainglorious tombstones and epic mausoleums this **cemetery** (Map p210; ☑323-894-9507; www.hollywoodforever.com; 6000 Santa Monica Blvd; ☺8:30am-5pm Mon-Fri, to 4:30pm Sat & Sun, guided tours 10am most Sat; Ⓟ👫; 🚊Metro Line 4, DASH Hollywood/Wilshire Route) **FREE** is an appropriate resting place for some of Hollywood's most iconic dearly departed. For a full list of residents, purchase a map ($5) at the flower shop.

Paramount Pictures

Star Trek, *Indiana Jones* and *Shrek* are among the blockbusters that originated at **Paramount** (Map p210; ☑323-956-1777; www.paramountstudiotour.com; 5555 Melrose Ave; regular/VIP tours $60/189, After Dark tours $99; ☺tours 9am-3:30pm; 🚊DASH Hollywood/Wilshire Route), the country's second-oldest movie studio and the only one still in Hollywood proper. Two-hour tours of the studio complex are offered year-round, taking in the back lots and sound stages.

Hollywood sign

LINDA MOON/SHUTTERSTOCK ©

Griffith Park

A gift to the city in 1896 by mining mogul Griffith J Griffith, and five times the size of NY's Central Park, Griffith Park is one of the country's largest urban green spaces. It contains a major outdoor theater, a zoo, an observatory, 53 miles of hiking trails and the Hollywood sign.

Great For...

☑ Don't Miss

The sweeping Hollywood Hills views from the observatory roof.

Griffith Observatory

LA's landmark 1935 **observatory** (Map p210; ☎213-473-0890; www.griffithobservatory. org; 2800 E Observatory Rd; admission free, planetarium shows adult/student & senior/child $7/5/3; ⊙noon-10pm Tue-Fri, 10am-10pm Sat & Sun; P⚿; ⊟DASH Observatory/Los Feliz Route) opens a window onto the universe from its perch on the southern slopes of Mt Hollywood. Its planetarium claims the world's most advanced star projector, while its astronomical touch displays explore some mind-bending topics, from the evolution of the telescope and the ultraviolet x-rays used to map our solar system to the cosmos itself. Then, of course, there are the views, which (on clear days) take in the entire LA basin, surrounding mountains and Pacific Ocean.

Griffith Observatory, designed by architect John C. Austin

LAUREN ORR/SHUTTERSTOCK ©

Ventura Fwy

Ⓜ Universal
City

Griffith Park
◎

Golden State Fwy

❶ Need to Know

Map p210; ☏323-644-2050; www.laparks.
org/griffithpark; 4730 Crystal Springs Dr;
⊙5am-10:30pm, trails sunrise-sunset; P 👬

✕ Take a Break

Fuel up for a hike with pub grub at **Mess
Hall** (Map p210; ☏323-660-6377; www.
messhallkitchen.com; 4500 Los Feliz Blvd, Los
Feliz; mains $17-32; ⊙9am-10pm Sun-Thu,
to 11pm Fri & Sat; P 🛜 ✍ 👬; 🚊Metro Lines
180, 181).

★ Top Tip

Access to the park is easiest via the
Griffith Park Dr or Zoo Dr exits off I-5.
Parking is plentiful and free.

The public is welcome to peer into the
Zeiss Telescope on the east side of the roof
where sweeping views of the Hollywood
Hills and the gleaming city below are especially spectacular at sunset. After dark,
staff wheel additional telescopes out to the
front lawn for stargazing.

Downstairs, the Leonard Nimoy Event
Horizon Theater screens a fascinating
23-minute documentary about the observatory's history.

Autry Museum of the American West

Established by singing cowboy Gene Autry,
this expansive **museum** (☏323-667-2000;
www.theautry.org; 4700 Western Heritage
Way, Griffith Park; adult/senior & student/child
$14/10/6, 2nd Tue of month free; ⊙10am-4pm
Tue-Fri, 10am-5pm Sat & Sun; P 👬; 🚊Metro

Line 96) offers contemporary perspectives
on the history and people of the American West, as well as their links to the
region's contemporary culture. Permanent
exhibitions explore everything from Native
American traditions to the cattle drives of
the 19th century and daily frontier life.

Hollywood Sign

LA's most famous landmark first appeared
in the hills in 1923 as an advertising gim-
mick for a real-estate development called
'Hollywoodland.' Each letter is 50ft tall
and made of sheet metal. Once aglow with
4000 light bulbs, the sign even had its own
caretaker who lived behind the 'L' until 1939.

The last four letters were lopped off in
the '40s as the sign started to crumble.
In the late '70s Alice Cooper and Hugh
Hefner joined forces with fans to save the
famous symbol, and Hef was back at it
again in 2010 when the hills behind the sign
became slated for a housing development.

Getty Center

KEN WOLTER/SHUTTERSTOCK ©

Getty Center

Designed by Pritzker Prize–winning architect Richard Meier, the billion-dollar Getty showcases centuries of glorious creativity inside its hilltop perch. Spectacular gardens feature blazing flowers, world-famous sculptures and trickling water.

Great For...

☑ Don't Miss

Gorgeous city views from the lovely Cactus Garden on the remote South Promontory.

Lofty Views

On clear days, you can enjoy breathtaking bird's-eye views of the city and ocean. A great time to visit is in the late afternoon after the crowds have thinned. Sunsets create a remarkable alchemy of light and shadow and are especially magical in winter.

Collections

The bulk of the permanent collection is displayed chronologically in four pavilions. The North Pavilion houses the oldest works, including medieval and Renaissance decorative arts, Titian's glorious *Venus and Adonis* and treasures from the country's second-largest collection of illustrated manuscripts. The East and South Pavilions showcase 17th- and 18th-century European art. In the former, seek out Gentileschi's

Getty Center gardens

ORHAN CAM/SHUTTERSTOCK ©

❶ Need to Know

☏310-440-7300; www.getty.edu; N Sepulveda Blvd & Getty Center Dr, off I-405 Fwy; ☺10am-5:30pm Tue-Fri & Sun, 10am-9pm Sat; P ♿; ▯Metro Lines 234, 734; FREE

✕ Take a Break

Drop down to Beverly Hills for superlative, MSG-free Chinese food at **Joss Cuisine** (☏310-277-3888; www.josscuisine.com; 9919 S Santa Monica Blvd, Beverly Hills; mains $16.50-48; ☺noon-3pm Mon-Fri, 5:30-10pm daily; ▯Metro Lines 4, 16, 316, 704).

★ Top Tip

Admission is free, but parking is $20 ($15 after 3pm).

Danaë and the Shower of Gold. Nineteenth-century masterpieces shine in the West Pavilion, including Van Gogh's *Irises*, Monet's *Wheatstacks, Snow Effect, Morning* and Degas' extraordinary pastel, *Russian Dancers*.

Architecture & Gardens

From the sprawling arrival plaza – reached by a driverless tram – a natural flow of walkways, stairs, fountains and courtyards encourages a leisurely wander on the 110-acre campus. Cubic forms and horizontal lines define the modernist creation, with walls, floors, windows and exterior paving all organized in a grid of 30in squares. The complex is clad in 16,000 tons of cleft-cut, beige-colored travertine sourced from the same Italian quarry used to construct Rome's ancient Colosseum. The bold shapes, openness and light of Meier's design complement the 134,000-sq-ft Central Garden. Designed by artist Robert Irwin, its striking form includes a stream that flows down into a central pool adorned with a floating maze of azaleas.

Beyond the Collections

Concerts, lectures, films and other cultural events for grown-ups keep the space buzzing with locals. Most are free, but some require reservations (or try standby). In summer, the free Saturday evening concert series Off the 405 (p222) serves up some tremendous progressive pop and world-music acts in the Getty Courtyard.

For the Children

Children can visit the interactive Family Room, enjoy a multimedia Family Tour, or browse the special kids' bookstore.

Japanese Garden

ANUP CHAUHAN/500PX ©

Huntington Library, Art Collections & Botanical Gardens

The Huntington Library complex is a precious treasure, home to celebrated European and American artworks and exquisite, themed gardens. The hefty collection in the library itself includes extraordinary rare works.

Great For...

☑ Don't Miss

High tea at the Rose Garden Tea Room.

History

How did the Huntington get here, you may ask? It began in 1903 when railroad, utility and real-estate tycoon Henry Huntington and his wife, Arabella, purchased a ranch and gradually transformed it into a genteel country estate. In 1919, it opened to the public as a scholarly and cultural institution.

The Library

Only a fraction of its six million rare books and related items can possibly go on display at any one time, but they're pretty darned impressive: a Gutenberg Bible, a manuscript of the *Canterbury Tales* by Geoffrey Chaucer, books by Marco Polo and Christopher Columbus and numerous items relating to the US Civil War, westward

The Huntington's interior

E California Blvd

**SAN
MARINO**   Orlando Rd

**Huntington Library,
Art Museum &
Botanical Gardens**

Oxford Rd

Sierra Madre Blvd

Huntington Dr

❶ Need to Know

📅626-405-2100; www.huntington.org;
1151 Oxford Rd, San Marino; adult weekday/
weekend & holidays $25/29, student & senior
$21/24, youth 4-11yr $13; ⊙10am-5pm Wed-
Mon; ⓟ

✖ Take a Break

Dig into an old-school soda fountain at
Fair Oaks Pharmacy (📅626-799-1414;
www.fairoakspharmacy.net; 1526 Mission St,
South Pasadena; sundaes $7-10; ⊙9am-9pm
Mon-Sat, 10am-7pm Sun; ⓟ🍴🚻).

★ Top Tip

The first Thursday of each month is free
with advance ticket.

expansion, women's suffrage and early
California.

The Galleries

In the galleries of European and American
art, you can lose yourself in the brush-
strokes of Thomas Gainsborough's *The
Blue Boy* and Thomas Lawrence's *Pinkie,*
or take in American classics by the likes of
Mary Cassatt, Edward Hopper, Andy Warhol
and Frank Stella. There are also decorative
arts, from intricately patterned furniture to
porcelain and gleaming silver service.

The Gardens

Then there are the gardens – about a
dozen – meticulously curated like museums
themselves. Among our favorites is the
Chinese Garden, where the Jade Ribbon
Bridge straddles a pond surrounded by

rockeries and a cafe. In the Japanese Gardens, hills, valleys and waterways are lined
with precision-pruned pine trees around a
1904 Japanese house, and paths lead to a
Zen garden and courtyards of bonsai. The
landscapes of the Desert Garden are surprisingly full of life, and in the **Rose Garden**
(📅626-405-2236; www.huntington.org/dining;
⊙11am-4pm Mon & Wed-Fri, 10:30am-5pm Sat &
Sun; 🍴) guests can enjoy high tea in the tea
room (reservations recommended).

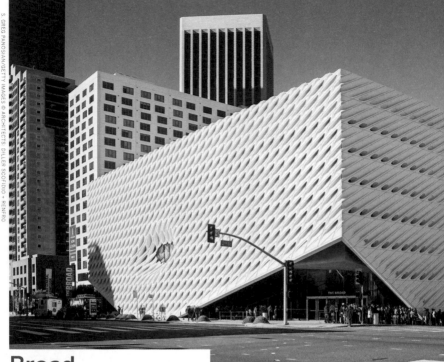

S. GREG PANOSIAN/GETTY IMAGES © ARCHITECTS: DILLER SCOFIDIO + RENFRO

Broad

The Broad's collection of modern and contemporary art is among the world's finest, packed with pop-art paintings, video art and sculpture. The museum itself is a lattice-work behemoth from the future.

What do you do when you've got too much A-list art to handle? Build a cutting-edge museum, fill it with your blockbuster acquisitions and share it with the city. That's exactly what LA philanthropist and billionaire real-estate honcho Eli Broad and his wife Edythe did.

The Building

The striking museum building is an attraction in itself. Designed by New York–based firm Diller Scofidio + Renfro (designers of Manhattan's iconic High Line) in collaboration with SF-based firm Gensler, it's shrouded in a white lattice-like shell that lifts at the corners, allowing visitors to access the cavernous, undulating lobby.

Inside, the building bucks the museum tradition of hiding away its storage facilities. Here, 'The Vault' becomes an integral

Great For...

☑ Don't Miss

The Broad's excellent smartphone app gives further descriptions of the art and artists.

JAMES LEYNSE/GETTY IMAGES © ARCHITECTS: DILLER SCOFIDIO + RENFRO

❶ Need to Know

Map p208; ☎213-232-6200; www.thebroad. org; 221 S Grand Ave; ⏰11am-5pm Tue & Wed, 11am-8pm Thu & Fri, 10am-8pm Sat, 10am-6pm Sun; Ⓟ🚻; ⓂB/D Lines to Civic Center/ Grand Park; FREE

✕ Take a Break

Indulge you gastronomic fancy at the global array of stalls and counter at Grand Central Market (p216).

★ Top Tip

Reserve a timed ticket online to avoid any queues in the walk-up line.

part of the design experience. Hovering between the 1st- and 3rd-floor galleries, it's pierced by the escalator connecting the gallery floors and visible through glass panels, offering visitors a voyeuristic peek at museum artworks lying dormant.

Infinity Mirrored Room

You can (and should) register to experience Yayoi Kusama's super-popular *Infinity Mirrored Room*. When it's your turn to view the installation, you will receive a text message from the museum; arrive by early afternoon for your best shot of viewing the room and check your phone regularly, as wait times are sometimes shorter than estimated. Registration is in the museum lobby.

Permanent Collection

An escalator whisks visitors up from the lobby through a narrow tunnel to the 35,000-sq-ft 3rd-floor gallery, where Jeff Koons charms visitors with his giant bunch of stainless-steel tulips. The surrounding galleries rotate works from the Broad's permanent collection – the world-class stash of more than 2000 postwar pieces belonging to Eli and Edythe Broad. There are dozens of heavy hitters, including Cindy Sherman, Andy Warhol, Roy Lichtenstein, Robert Rauschenberg, Keith Haring, Kara Walker and a second interactive installation by Yayoi Kusama, *Longing for Eternity*.

Walking Tour: Architecture Downtown

Filled with amazing buildings, eateries and museums, Downtown LA is one of the most exciting neighborhoods for a stroll.

Start Verve
Distance 2.5 miles
Duration 3 hours

3 The **Millennium Biltmore Hotel** boasts on-screen cameos in *Ghostbusters*, *Fight Club* and *Mad Men*.

2 Architect Claud Beelman's extraordinary 1929 **Eastern Columbia Building** is a masterpiece of art moderne architecture.

1 Start the tour with a perfect cup of joe from microroastery **Verve**.

Take a Break See the Damian Hirst mural and sip an extraordinary cocktail at **Otium** (p216).

Classic Photo A selfie outside the glittering facade of Gehry's Walt Disney Concert Hall.

5 Frank Gehry's showstopping masterpiece, the **Walt Disney Concert Hall** (p206), is home to the LA Philharmonic.

6 The beaux-arts **Grand Central Market** (p216) has been satisfying appetites since 1917.

4 Gape in wonder at **Broad** (p202), Downtown's most extraordinary.

W 1st St
N Broadway
101
Civic Center/
Grand Park
S Olive St
E Temple St
S Broadway
E 1st St
S Main St
E 2nd St
FINISH
E 3rd St
E 4th St
E 5th St

0 — 500 m
0 — 0.25 miles

◎ SIGHTS

◎ Downtown LA

Grammy Museum   Museum

(Map p208; ☑213-765-6800; www.grammymuse
um.org; 800 W Olympic Blvd; adult/child $15/13;
⏱10:30am-6:30pm Sun, Mon, Wed & Thu,
10am-8pm Fri & Sat; P♿; MA/E Lines to Pico)
The highlight of **LA Live** (☑213-763-5483;
www.lalive.com), this museum's interactive
exhibits explore the evolution of the world's
most famous music awards, as well as define, differentiate and link musical genres.
Spanning three levels, its rotating treasures
might include iconic threads from the ward-
robes of Michael Jackson, Whitney Houston
and Beyoncé, scribbled words from the
hands of Count Basie and Taylor Swift, and
instruments once used by world-renowned
rock legends.

Walt Disney
Concert Hall   Notable Building

(Map p208; ☑323-850-2000; www.laphil.org;
111 S Grand Ave; P; MB/D Lines to Civic Center/
Grand Park) **FREE** A molten blend of steel,
music and psychedelic architecture, this
iconic concert venue is the home base
of the Los Angeles Philharmonic, but has
also hosted contemporary bands such as
Phoenix, and classic jazz musicians such
as Sonny Rollins. The 2003 concert hall's
visionary architect, Frank Gehry, pulled out
all the stops for this building, a gravity-
defying sculpture of heaving and billowing
stainless steel.

MOCA Grand   Museum

(Museum of Contemporary Art; Map p208;
☑213-626-6222; www.moca.org; 250 S Grand
Ave; ⏱11am-6pm Mon, Wed & Fri, 11am-8pm Thu,
11am-5pm Sat & Sun; ♿; MB/D Lines to Civic
Center/Grand Park) **FREE** MOCA's notable art
collection focuses mainly on works created
from the 1940s to the present. There's no
shortage of luminaries, among them Mark
Rothko, Dan Flavin, Willem de Kooning, Joseph Cornell and David Hockney, in regular
and special exhibits. Their creations are
housed in a 1986 building by 2019 Pritzker
Prize–winning Japanese architect Arata
Isozaki. Galleries are below ground, yet sky-
lit bright. Special exhibits usually cost $18
($10 for children).

Petersen Automotive Museum (p209)

SUNFLOWERMOMMA/SHUTTERSTOCK ©

City Hall
Historic Building

(Map p208; ☎213-485-2121; www.lacity.org; 200 N Spring St; ⊙9am-5pm Mon-Fri; ♿; ⓂB/D Lines to Civic Center/Grand Park) **FREE** Until 1966 no LA building stood taller than the 1928 City Hall, which appeared in the *Superman* TV series and 1953 sci-fi thriller *War of the Worlds*. On clear days you'll have views of the city, the mountains and several decades of Downtown growth from the observation deck. On the way up, stop off on level three to eye up City Hall's original main entrance, which features a breathtaking, Byzantine-inspired rotunda graced with marble flooring and a mosaic dome.

Hauser & Wirth
Gallery

(Map p208; ☎213-943-1620; www.hauserwirthlosangeles.com; 901 E 3rd St; ⊙11am-6pm Tue-Sun; ⓂL Line to Little Tokyo/Arts District) **FREE** The LA outpost of internationally acclaimed gallery Hauser & Wirth hosts museum-standard exhibits of modern and contemporary art. It's a huge space, occupying 116,000 sq ft of a converted flour mill complex in the Arts District. Past exhibits have showcased the work of luminaries such as Lucio Fontana, Louise Bourgeois and LA-based Larry Bell. The complex is also home to a standout art bookstore and gift store.

◉ West Hollywood & Mid-City

Academy Museum of Motion Pictures
Museum

(Map p210; ☎323-930-3000; www.academymuseum.org; cnr Wilshire Blvd & Fairfax Ave, Mid-City; ♿; 🚇Metro Lines 20, 217, 720, 780, DASH Fairfax Route) Designed by Italian starchitect Renzo Piano, this 300,000-sq-ft blockbuster celebrates LA's greatest passion: movies. The museum's permanent exhibition offers an immersive, state-of-the-art journey through cinema's evolution, with priceless props and costumes that include Dorothy's ruby slippers from *The Wizard of Oz*. Temporary exhibitions explore diverse aspects and figures of the industry, while daily screenings include anything from world movies to weekend children's matinees. The

Top 10 Los Angeles Beaches

Leo Carrillo Families love this summer-camp-style beach with its tide pools, cliff caves, nature trails and great swimming.

El Matador Arguably Malibu's most stunning beach, this intimate, remote hideaway has sandstone spires.

Zuma Two miles of pearly sand. Mellow swells make for perfect bodysurfing.

Westward Beach Malibu locals favor this wide, blonde beach for crystal-clear water, resident dolphin pods and sea lion colonies.

Santa Monica Wide slab of sand where beach-umbrella-toting families descend like butterfly swarms on weekends.

Venice Beach The wide beaches south of the Venice Pier are oft-ignored gems with excellent bodysurfing.

Manhattan Beach A brassy SoCal beach with a high flirt factor and hardcore surfers hanging by the pier.

Hermosa Beach LA's libidinous, seemingly never-ending beach party with hormone-crazed hard bodies getting their game on.

Malaga Cove This crescent-shaped, cliff-backed shoreline is the only sandy Palos Verdes beach easily accessible by the hoi polloi.

Abalone Cove Hunt for starfish, anemones and other tide-pool critters in and around this eco-preserve.

Hermosa Beach
DEREK HANCHI / EYEEM/GETTY IMAGES ©

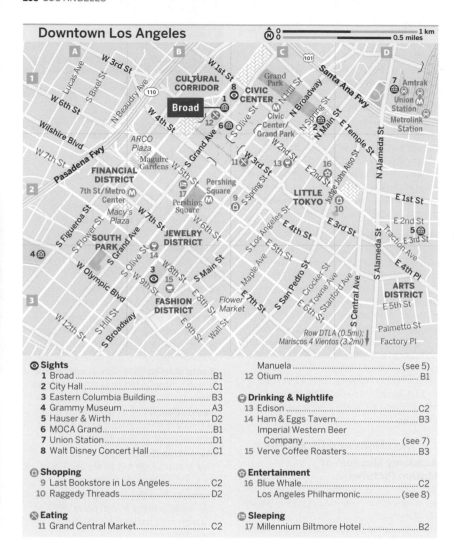

Downtown Los Angeles

Row DTLA (0.5mi);
Mariscos 4 Vientos (3.2mi)

museum's Dolby Family Terrace offers a suitably cinematic panorama of the world's entertainment capital.

The museum was due to open in late April 2021.

Los Angeles County Museum of Art
Museum

(LACMA; Map p210; ☏323-857-6000; www.lacma.org; 5905 Wilshire Blvd, Mid-City; adult/senior/student/child $25/21/21/free, 2nd Tue of month free; ⊙11am-5pm Mon, Tue & Thu, 11am-8pm Fri, 10am-7pm Sat & Sun; ℗⛟; ⊒Metro Lines 20, 217, 720, 780, DASH Fairfax Route) The depth and wealth of the collection at the largest art museum in the western US is stunning. LACMA holds all the major players – Rembrandt, Cézanne, Magritte, Mary Cassatt, Ansel Adams – plus millennia worth of Chinese, Japanese, pre-Columbian and ancient Greek, Roman and Egyptian sculpture. Due to major redevelopment works (due for completion in 2024), only the Broad Contemporary Art Museum (BCAM) and Resnick Pavilion galleries are currently open, hosting world-class temporary exhibitions and a reduced selection of its permanent hoard.

Petersen Automotive Museum   Museum

(Map p210; ☏323-930-2277; www.petersen.org; 6060 Wilshire Blvd, Mid-City; adult/senior/student/child $16/14/14/11; ◷10am-5pm Mon-Fri, to 6pm Sat & Sun; P♿; ▣Metro Lines 20, 217, 720, 780, DASH Fairfax Route) A four-story ode to the auto, this is a treat even for those who can't tell a piston from a carburetor. A headlights-to-brake-lights futuristic makeover (by Kohn Pederson Fox) in 2015 saw the museum swag the prestigious American Architecture Award for significant new buildings. While we love its skin of undulating bands of stainless steel on a hot-rod-red background, it's what's inside that counts: four gripping, themed floors exploring the history, industry and artistry of motorized transportation.

Original Farmers Market   Market

(Map p210; ☏323-933-9211; www.farmers-marketla.com; 6333 W 3rd St, Fairfax District; ◷9am-9pm Mon-Fri, to 8pm Sat, 10am-7pm Sun; P♿; ▣Metro Lines 217, 218, DASH Fairfax Route) Long before LA was flooded with farmers markets, there was *the* farmers market. Once a dusty lot of of produce-laden pickup trucks, the 1934 landmark is now packed with over 100 stalls peddling fresh produce, cheeses, roasted nuts and ready-to-eat bites from around the globe. It's a fun, family-friendly place to browse, people watch and graze. One of our favorite vendors is 1946 veteran Patsy D'Amore's Pizza, once frequented by Rat Pack icons Dean Martin and Frank Sinatra.

La Brea Tar Pits & Museum   Museum

(Map p210; ☏213-763-3499; https://tarpits.org; 5801 Wilshire Blvd, Mid-City; adult/student/senior/child $15/12/12/7, every Tue in Sep & 1st Tue of month Oct-Jun free; ◷9:30am-5pm; P♿; ▣Metro Line 20, DASH Fairfax Route) Mammoths, saber-toothed cats and dire wolves roamed LA's savanna in prehistoric times. We know this because of an archaeological trove of skulls and bones unearthed here, at one of the world's most fecund and famous fossil sites. Generations of young dino hunters have come to seek out fossils and learn about paleontology from docents and demonstrations in on-site labs at the museum that now sits here.

◎ Beverly Hills & Around

Museum of Tolerance   Museum

(☏reservations 310-772-2505; www.museumoftolerance.com; 9786 W Pico Blvd; adult/senior/student/child $15.50/12.50/11.50/11.50, Anne Frank Exhibit $15.50/13.50/12.50/12.50; ◷10am-5pm Sun-Wed & Fri, 10am-9.30pm Thu Apr-Oct, 10am-5pm Sun-Wed, 10am-9.30pm Thu, 10am-3.30pm Fri Nov-Mar, closed Sat; P♿; ▣Big Blue Bus Line 7) Run by the Simon Wiesenthal Center, this powerful, deeply moving museum uses interactive technology to engage visitors in discussion and contemplation around racism and bigotry. Particular focus is given to the Holocaust, with a major basement exhibition that examines the social, political and economic conditions that led to the Holocaust as well as the experience of the millions persecuted. On the museum's 2nd floor, another major exhibition offers an intimate look into the life and impact of Anne Frank.

The third Tuesday of the month is free for general admission (does not include Anne Frank exhibit).

Frederick R Weisman Art Foundation   Museum

(☏310-277-5321; www.weismanfoundation.org; 265 N Carolwood Dr, Holmby Hills; ◷1¾hr guided tours 10:30am & 2pm Mon-Fri, by appointment only; ▣Metro Lines 2, 302) FREE The late entrepreneur and philanthropist Frederick R Weisman had an insatiable passion for art, a fact confirmed when touring his former Holmby Hills home. From floor to ceiling, the mansion (and its manicured grounds)

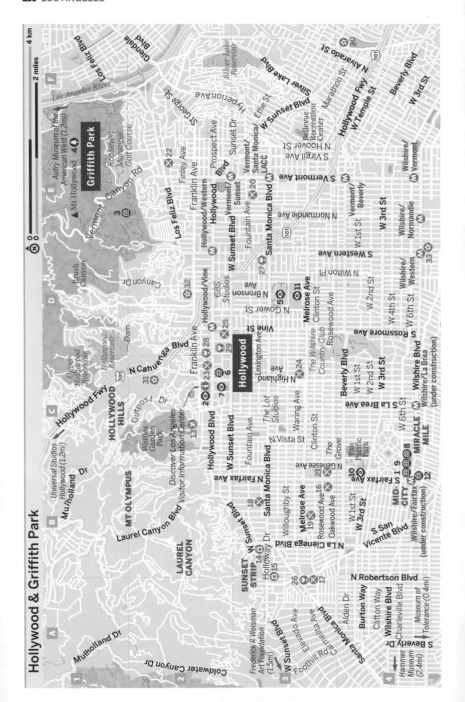

Hollywood & Griffith Park

Hollywood & Griffith Park

bursts with extraordinary works from visionaries such as Picasso, Kandinsky, Miró, Magritte, Rothko, Warhol, Rauschenberg and Ruscha. There's even a motorcycle painted by Keith Haring. Tours should be reserved at least a few days ahead.

Hammer Museum   Museum
(☏310-443-7000; https://hammer.ucla.edu; 10899 Wilshire Blvd, Westwood; ⊙11am-8pm Tue-Fri, 11am-5pm Sat & Sun; 🅿; 🚇Metro Lines 2, 234, 302, Big Blue Bus Lines 1, 2, 8) FREE Originally a vanity project of the late oil tycoon Armand Hammer, this expanding, UCLA-affiliated museum is one of LA's most underrated cultural highlights. The museum really shines in cutting-edge contemporary exhibits featuring local, under-represented and controversial artists. The Made in LA biennial, showcasing a diverse spectrum of LA-area artists in even-numbered years, is headquartered here. It all stands in counterpoint to Armand Hammer's personal collection of Renaissance to early-20th-century European and American art. All that, and it's free.

⊙ Malibu & Pacific Palisades

Getty Villa   Museum
(☏310-430-7300; www.getty.edu; 17985 Pacific Coast Hwy, Pacific Palisades; ⊙10am-5pm Wed-Mon; 🅿🚻; 🚇Metro Line 534 to Coastline Dr) FREE Stunningly perched on an ocean-view hillside, this museum in a replica 1st-century Roman villa is an exquisite, 64-acre showcase for Greek, Roman and Etruscan antiquities. Dating back 7000 years, they were amassed by oil tycoon J Paul Getty. Galleries, peristiles, courtyards and lushly landscaped gardens ensconce all manner of friezes, busts and mosaics, along with millennia-old cut, blown and colored glass and brain-bending geometric configurations in the Hall of Colored Marbles. Other highlights include the Pompeii fountain and Temple of Herakles.

El Matador State Beach   Beach
(☏818-880-0363; www.parks.ca.gov; 32215 Pacific Coast Hwy, Malibu; 🅿) At arguably Malibu's most stunning beach (known as the place swimsuit-model photo shoots take place), you park on the bluffs and stroll down a trail to sandstone rock towers that rise from emerald coves. Sunbathers stroll

Universal Studios Hollywood

Although **Universal** (☎800-864-8377; www.universalstudioshollywood.com; 100 Universal City Plaza, Universal City; 1-/2-day from $109/149, child under 3yr free; ⊘daily, hours vary; P🚗; MB Line to Universal City) in the San Fernando Valley is one of the world's oldest continuously operating movie studios, the big draw is the theme park in and around the studio's back lot. It remains popular for generations of visitors and locals alike, thanks to an entertaining, regularly updated mix of thrill rides, live-action shows and a tram tour.

ANTON_IVANOV/SHUTTERSTOCK ©

through the tides, and dolphins breech the surface beyond the waves. It's been impacted by coastal erosion, but you can still find a sliver of dry sand tucked against the bluffs.

◎ Venice

Abbot Kinney Boulevard Area
(🚌Big Blue Bus Line 18) Abbot Kinney, who founded Venice in the early 1900s, would probably be delighted to find that one of Venice's best-loved streets bears his name. Sort of a seaside Melrose with a Venetian flavor, the mile-long stretch of Abbot Kinney Blvd between Venice Blvd and Main St is full of upscale boutiques, galleries, lofts and sensational restaurants. Some years back, *GQ* named it America's coolest street, and that cachet has only grown since.

Venice Boardwalk Waterfront
(Ocean Front Walk; Venice Pier to Rose Ave) Life in Venice moves to a different rhythm and nowhere more so than on the famous Venice Boardwalk, officially known as Ocean Front Walk. It's a freak show, a human zoo and a wacky carnival alive with Hula-Hoop magicians, old-timey jazz combos, solo distorted garage rockers and artists (good and bad) – as far as LA experiences go, it's a must.

Venice Canals Area
Even many Angelenos have no idea that just a couple of blocks from the Boardwalk madness is an idyllic neighborhood that preserves 3 miles of Abbot Kinney's canals. The **Venice Canal Walk** threads past eclectic homes, over bridges and along waterways where ducks preen and locals lollygag in little rowboats. It's best accessed from either Venice or Washington Blvds.

◎ Exposition Park & South LA

Watts Towers Landmark
(☎213-847-4646; www.wattstowers.org; 1761-1765 E 107th St, Watts; P; MA Line to 103rd St) The three 'Gothic' spires of the fabulous Watts Towers rank among the world's greatest monuments of folk art. In 1921 Italian immigrant Simon Rodia set out to 'make something big' and then spent 33 years cobbling together this whimsical free-form sculpture from concrete, steel and a motley assortment of found objects: green 7Up bottles to sea shells, tiles, rocks and pottery.

⊕ ACTIVITIES

Despite spending a lot of time jammed on freeways, Angelenos love to get physical. Theirs is a city made for pace-quickening thrills, with spectacular mountain hikes, one of the country's largest urban nature reserves and surf-pounded beach. Add to this almost 300 days of sunshine and you'll forgive the locals for looking so, so good. Studio tours are a fun way to discover the truth behind the Hollywood magic.

Runyon Canyon Hiking

(Map p210; www.laparks.org/runyon; 2000 N Fuller Ave; ⏰dawn-dusk) A chaparral-draped cut in the Hollywood Hills, this 130-acre public park is as famous for its buff runners and exercising celebrities as it is for the panoramic views from the upper ridge. Follow the wide, partially paved fire road up, then take the smaller track down to the canyon, where you'll pass the remains of the Runyon estate.

Mishe Mokwa Trail & Sandstone Peak Hiking

(www.nps.gov/samo; 12896 Yerba Buena Rd, Malibu) On warm spring mornings, when the snowy blue *ceonothus* perfumes the air with honeysuckle, there's no better place to be than this 6-mile loop trail beyond the end of Malibu. It winds through a red-rock canyon dotted with climbers, into the oak oasis at **Split Rock** and up to Mt Allen (aka Sandstone Peak), the tallest peak in the Santa Monica Mountains.

Venice Skatepark Skateboarding

(www.veniceskatepark.com; 1500 Ocean Front Walk, Venice; ⏰dawn-dusk; 🚌Metro Line 733, 🚌Big Blue Bus Line 1) Long the destination of local skate punks, the concrete at this skate park has now been molded and steel-fringed into 17,000 sq ft of vert, tranny and street terrain with unbroken ocean views. The old-school-style skate run and the world-class pool are most popular for high flyers and gawking spectators. Great photo ops, especially as the sun sets.

Warner Bros Studio Tour Tour

(☎818-972-8687, 877-492-8687; www.wbstudiotour.com; 3400 Warner Blvd, Burbank; tours adult/child 8-12yr from $69/59; ⏰8:30am-3:30pm year-round, extended hours Jun-Aug; 🚌155, 222, 501 stop about 400yd from tour center) This tour offers the most fun, yet authentic, look behind the scenes of a major movie studio. The two-hour standard tour kicks off with a video of WB's greatest film hits (*Rebel Without a Cause, Harry Potter* etc), before a tram whisks you around 110 acres of sound stages, back-lot sets including *Friends* and the *Big Bang Theory,*

Venice Canals

ADAMKAZ/GETTY IMAGES ©

Last Bookstore in Los Angeles

and technical departments, including props, costumes and the paint shop, and a collection of Batmobiles.

🅐 SHOPPING

Consider yourself a disciplined shopper? Get back to us after your trip. LA is a pro at luring cards out of wallets. After all, how can you not bag that super-cute vintage-fabric frock? Or that tongue-in-cheek tote? Creativity and whimsy drive this town, right down to its racks and shelves.

Last Bookstore in Los Angeles
Books

(Map p208; ☎213-488-0599; www.lastbook-storela.com; 453 S Spring St; ☺10am-10pm Sun-Thu, 10am-11pm Fri & Sat; ♿; Ⓜ B/D Lines to Pershing Sq) What started as a one-person storefront is now California's largest new-and-used bookstore. And what a bookstore! Across two sprawling levels of an old bank building, you'll find everything from cabinets of rare books to an upstairs horror-and-crime book vault, book tunnel and smattering of art galleries. The store

also houses a terrific vinyl collection and cool store-themed merch.

Row DTLA
Shopping Center

(☎213-988-8890; www.rowdtla.com; 1320 E 7th St; ☺8am-10pm, individual shops & eateries vary; 🛜♿; 🚆Metro Lines 60, 62, 760) Row DTLA has transformed a sprawling industrial site into a sharp edit of specialty retail and dining. It's like Tribeca, with better weather. Saunter pedestrianized streets for discerning apparel and accessories, designer homewares, niche fragrances, even Japanese bicycles. Top picks include stationery purveyor **Hightide Store DTLA** (☎213-935-8135; www.hightidestoredtla.shop; Garage Retail, Shop 140; ☺11am-7pm Mon-Sat, 11am-5pm Sun), affordable design store **Poketo** (☎213-372-5686; www.poketo.com; Shop 174; ☺11am-5pm) and progressive unisex fashion label **Shades of Grey** (www.shadesofgreyclothing. com; Suite 110; ☺noon-5pm Mon-Fri, 11am-6pm Sat & Sun).

The complex hosts weekly street-food festival **Smorgasburg** (http://la.smorgas-burg.com/info; Alameda Produce Market, 777 Alameda St, Row DTLA; ☺10am-4pm Sun; ♿)

A SAMSON/SHUTTERSTOCK ©

on Sundays and is home to **M.Georgina**
([📞]213-334-4113; www.mgeorgina.com; B1 Suite
114, 777 S Alameda St, Row DTLA; mains $22-34;
[🕙]5-9pm Tue-Thu, 5-10pm Fri & Sat, 3-9pm Sun;
[P][🍷]; [🚇]Metro Lines 60, 62, 760), one of LA's
top restaurants.

Fred Segal
Fashion & Accessories

(Map p210; [📞]310-432-0560; www.fredsegal.
com; 8500 Sunset Blvd, West Hollywood; [🕙]10am-
7pm Mon-Sat, 11am-6pm Sun; [🚇]Metro Lines
2, 302) No LA shopping trip is complete
without a stop at Fred's. This is its flagship
store, 21,000-sq-ft of chic, Cali-casual
threads, accessories, beauty products and
homewares hip enough for cashed-up celebs. The space also hosts regular product
drops, trunk shows and live music. Alas,
the only time you'll see bargains (sort of) is
during the summer and January sales.

Sika
Art

([📞]323-295-2502; 4330 Degnan Blvd, Leimert
Park; [🕙]noon-6pm) It would be hard to find
a better collection of antiques, masks,
clothes and jewelry outside of West Africa
than the one found in this owner-operated
treasure chest, a pillar of Leimert Park.
It's also known for nose piercings. It co-
sponsors a three-day **Leimert Park Village
Heritage Festival** in the lot next door.

Mystery Pier Books
Books

(Map p210; [📞]310-657-5557; www.mystery
pierbooks.com; 8826 W Sunset Blvd, West
Hollywood; [🕙]11am-6pm Mon-Sat, noon-5pm Sun;
[🚇]Metro Lines 2, 302) The charming Louis and
Harvey have no shortage of fans (including
famous ones) thanks to their remarkable
WeHo bookstore. Famed for stocking
signed shooting scripts from blockbusters,
it also sells rare and obscure 1st editions,
from Shakespeare ($3500 to $9000) and
Salinger ($10,000) to JK Rowling ($30,000
and up).

Raggedy Threads
Vintage

(Map p208; [📞]213-620-1188; www.raggedy
threads.com; 330 E 2nd St, Little Tokyo; [🕙]noon-
8pm Mon-Sat, to 6pm Sun; [🚇]DASH Downtown
A Route, [M]L Line to Little Tokyo/Arts District)
A tremendous vintage Americana store

 **Rose Bowl
Flea Market**

Every month, rain or shine, since the
1960s, the Rose Bowl football field
has hosted 'America's Marketplace of
Unusual Items,' with rummaging hordes
seeking the next great treasure. Over
2500 vendors and some 20,000 buyers
converge on the **market** (www.rgcshows.
com; 1001 Rose Bowl Dr, Pasadena; admission
from $9; [🕙]9am-4:30pm 2nd Sun each month,
last entry 3pm, early admission from 5am;
[♿]; [🚇]Metro Lines 51, 52), and it's always
a great time. Street-fair-style refresh-
ments (burgers, dogs, fries, sausages,
sushi – this is LA – lemonade, cocktails
etc) are on hand to fuel your shopping.

PAUL MOUNCE/CORBIS VIA GETTY IMAGES ©

just off the main Little Tokyo strip. There's
plenty of beautifully ragged denim, with a
notable collection of pre-1950s workwear
from the US, Japan and France. You'll also
find a good number of Victorian dresses,
soft T-shirts and a wonderful turquoise
collection at decent prices.

EATING

Bring an appetite. A big one. LA's cross-
cultural makeup is reflected at its table,
which is an epic global feast. And while
there's no shortage of just-like-the-
motherland dishes – from Cantonese
xiao long bao to Ligurian *farinata* – it's the
takes on tradition that really thrill. Ever
tried Korean-Mexican tacos? Or a vegan
cream-cheese doughnut with jam, basil

🍽️ Five Standout Los Angeles Bites

Petit Trois (p217) Decadent Bic Mec double cheeseburger.

Mariscos 4 Vientos (p216) Flawless deep-fried shrimp tacos.

Cassia (p220) Vietnamese pot-au-feu with short ribs, veggies and bone marrow.

Crossroads (p218) Vegan artichoke 'oysters.'

Salt & Straw (p220) Almond brittle with salted ganache ice cream.

FARKNOT ARCHITECT/SHUTTERSTOCK ©

and balsamic reduction? LA may be many things, but a culinary bore isn't one of them.

⊗ Downtown LA

Mariscos 4 Vientos   Mexican $

(☎323-266-4045; www.facebook.com/Mariscos 4Vientos; 3000 E Olympic Blvd; dishes $2.25-15; ⊙9am-5:30pm Mon-Thu, to 6pm Fri-Sun; 👶) You'll find the greatest shrimp taco of your life at cash-only Mariscos 4 Vientos. Order from the truck (if you're time poor) or grab a table inside the friendly, no-frills dining room. Either way, praise those corn tortillas, stuffed with fresh shrimp, then fried and smothered in *pico de gallo* (fresh salsa). If you love spice, order the fiery La Poseida tostada.

Grand Central Market   Market $

(Map p208; www.grandcentralmarket.com; 317 S Broadway; ⊙8am-10pm; 🛜; Ⓜ B/D Lines to Pershing Sq) Designed by prolific architect

John Parkinson and once home to an office occupied by Frank Lloyd Wright, LA's beaux arts market hall has been satisfying appetites since 1917 and today is DTLA's gourmet mecca. Lose yourself in its bustle of neon signs, stalls and counters, peddling everything from fresh produce and nuts, to sizzling Thai street food, hipster breakfasts, modern deli classics, artisanal pasta and specialty coffee.

Manuela   Modern American $$$

(Map p208; ☎323-849-0480; www.manuela-la. com; 907 E 3rd St, Arts District; mains lunch $16-32, dinner $22-49; ⊙5:30-10pm Mon, 11:30am-3:30pm & 5:30-10pm Tue-Thu, 11:30am-3:30pm & 5:30-11pm Fri, 10am-3:30pm & 5:30-11pm Sat, 10am-3:30pm & 5:30-10pm Sun; 🛜; ⌨DASH Downtown A Route, Ⓜ L Line to Little Tokyo/Arts District) Part of the Hauser & Wirth (p207) arts complex, buzzing, loft-like Manuela remains a standout dining destination in DTLA. Staff are knowledgeable and happy to navigate you around an oft-tweaked menu that beautifully fuses local meats, seafood and produce with smoky Southern accents. The result is polished, attention-grabbing dishes like barbecued oysters with Calabrian-chili butter and wood-grilled sunchokes with cider-candied bacon and dill buttermilk.

Otium   Californian $$$

(Map p208; ☎213-935-8500; http://otiumla. com; 222 S Hope St; lunch dishes $15-36, dinner mains $21-75; ⊙5:30-9pm Mon, 11:30am-2:30pm & 5:30-9pm Tue & Wed, 11:30am-2:30pm & 5:30-10pm Thu, 11:30am-2:30pm & 5-11pm Fri, 11am-2:30pm & 5-11pm Sat, 11am-2:30pm & 5-9pm Sun; 🛜; Ⓜ Red/Purple Lines to Civic Center/Grand Park) Chef Timothy Hollingsworth (ex-French Laundry) helms this fun, sophisticated, evergreen hotspot, set in a modernist pavilion beside the Broad (p209). Prime ingredients conspire in unexpected ways, from the crunch of wild rice and amaranth in an eye-candy salad of avocado, beets and pomegranate, to rainbow trout paired with almonds and grapes.

Grand Central Market

🌀 Hollywood

Stout Burgers & Beers   Burgers $

(Map p210; ☑323-469-3801; www.stoutburger
sandbeers.com; 1544 N Cahuenga Blvd; burgers
$12-15, salads $8-12; ⊘11:30am-4am; P 🛜 🛒;
M B Line to Hollywood/Vine) Woody, pub-
inspired Stout flips gourmet burgers and
pours great craft brews. The beef is ground
in-house, the chicken is free range and the
veggie patties are made fresh daily. The Six
Weeker burger (Brie, fig jam and caramel-
ized onions) and onion rings are standouts,
while the hugely popular happy hour (4pm
to 6pm weekdays) slashes food prices in
half.

Petit Trois   French $$$

(Map p210; ☑323-468-8916; www.petittrois.com;
718 N Highland Ave; mains $18-39; ⊘noon-10pm
Sun-Thu, to 11pm Fri & Sat; P; 🚃Metro Line 10)
Good things come in small packages...like
tiny, no-reservations Petit Trois! Owned by
acclaimed TV chef Ludovic Lefebvre, its two
long counters (the place is too small for
tables) are where food-lovers squeeze in
for smashing, honest, Gallic-inspired grub,

from a ridiculously light Boursin-stuffed
omelet to standout escargot and a showstopping 'Big Mec' double cheeseburger
served with foie gras–infused red-wine
Bordelaise.

Found Oyster   Seafood $$$

(Map p210; ☑323-486-7920; www.foundoyster.
com; 4880 Fountain Ave; dishes $7-28; ⊘4-10pm
Tue-Thu, 4-11pm Fri, noon-11pm Sat, noon-10pm
Sun; 🚃DASH Hollywood Route, Metro Lines 2,
175) Bonhomie and exceptional seafood are
on the menu at this tiny, always-packed
clam shack. Squeeze in among foodies and
East Hollywood hipsters for straightfor-
ward, produce-driven offerings including
Littleneck clams, live Maine scallops, New
England–style chowder, lobster bisque rolls
and a daily-changing selection of East and
West Coast oysters. Head in early (by 5pm
in the evenings) or midweek to minimize
any wait.

Musso & Frank Grill   European $$$

(Map p210; ☑323-467-7788; www.mussoand-
frank.com; 6667 Hollywood Blvd; mains $17-55;
⊘11am-11pm Tue-Sat, 4-9pm Sun; P; M B Line

to Hollywood/Highland) Hollywood history hangs in the thick air at Musso & Frank Grill, Tinseltown's oldest eatery (since 1919). Charlie Chaplin used to knock back vodka gimlets, Raymond Chandler penned scripts in the high-backed booths, and movie deals were made on the old phone at the back. The menu favors bistro classics, from shrimp cocktail and lobster thermidor, to steaks and a decent burger.

✖ West Hollywood & Mid-City

Crossroads   Vegan $$

(Map p210; ☎323-782-9245; www.cross roadskitchen.com; 8284 Melrose Ave, Mid-City; brunch mains $12-15, dinner mains $14-24; ⊙11am-2:30pm & 5-11:30pm Mon-Thu, 11am-2:30pm & 5pm-midnight Fri, 10am-2pm & 5pm-midnight Sat, 10am-2pm & 5-11:30pm Sun; ℙ🖉; 🚇Metro Line 10) Tal Ronnen didn't get to be a celebrity chef (Oprah, Ellen) by serving ordinary vegan fare. Instead, seasonal creations include 'crab cakes' made from hearts of palm, artichoke 'oysters,' and 'bechamel'-smothered eggplant, alongside pizzas and pastas incorporating innovative 'cheeses' made from nuts. Is that Jane Fonda? Tobey Maguire? Probably. The place is a hit with celebs; leave the Birkenstocks at home.

Canter's   Deli $$

(Map p210; ☎323-651-2030; www.cantersdeli. com; 419 N Fairfax Ave, Mid-City; mains $9-29; ⊙24hr; ℙ🖉🖟; 🚇Metro Lines 217, 218, DASH Fairfax Route) As old-school delis go, Canter's is hard to beat. A fixture in the traditionally Jewish Fairfax district since 1931, seen-it-all waitresses serve up the requisite pastrami, corned beef and matzo-ball soup, plus 24-hour breakfast, in a retro space deserving of its own '70s sitcom.

Jon & Vinny's   Italian $$

(Map p210; ☎323-334-3369; www.jonandvin nys.com; 412 N Fairfax Ave, Mid-City; breakfast $10-21, lunch & dinner pasta $15-24, mains $18-26; ⊙8am-10pm; 🖟; 🚇Metro Lines 217, 218, DASH Fairfax Route) ✐ It might look like a Finnish sauna, but this oak-clad evergreen is all about simple, modern Italian cooked smashingly. Charred pizzas and the housemade pastas are the standouts, with soul-soothing meatballs also worth an encore. If it's breakfast, start right with

From left: Salt & Straw ice cream (p220); Catch LA; Musso & Frank Grill (p217)

olive-oil fried eggs with grilled kale, crispy potato, 'nduja (spicy Calabrian paste) and preserved Meyer lemon. Reserve well ahead, especially for dinner.

Connie & Ted's   Seafood $$$

(Map p210; ☎323-848-2722; www.connie andteds.com; 8171 Santa Monica Blvd, West Hollywood; mains $15-46; ⊙4-10pm Mon & Tue, 11:30am-10pm Wed & Thu, 11:30am-11pm Fri, 10am-11pm Sat, 10am-10pm Sun; [P]; [Q]Metro Lines 4, 218) ✔ Acclaimed chef Michael Cimarusti is behind this buzzing, homely take on the New England seafood shack. Freshness and sustainability underscore the offerings, with up to a dozen oyster varieties at the raw bar, as well as superb, authentic renditions of northeast classics such as lobster rolls (served cold with mayo or hot with drawn butter), clam cakes, chowder and steamers.

For brunch, look for faves such as crab and lobster omelet or the Nor'easter breakfast sandwich with bacon and fried clams, and oyster Bloody Mary shooters (Bloody Mary with a raw oyster inside) that will rock your boat and maybe your world.

Pair your choice with a craft beer, Rhode Island coffee milk, or something crisp and dry from the wine list. Valet parking is $8.

Catch LA   Fusion $$$

(Map p210; ☎323-347-6060; http://catchres taurants.com/catchla; 8715 Melrose Ave, West Hollywood; dinner mains $39-79; ⊙11am-3pm Sat & Sun, 5pm-2am daily; [P][🛜][✎]; [Q]Metro Lines 10, 30, 330, 705) You may well find sidewalk paparazzi stalking celebrity guests and a door attendant to check your reservation, but all that's forgotten once you saunter into this oh-so-hot, 3rd-floor rooftop restaurant/bar. Graze on East–West, surf-centric share plates, from pickled-onion-spiked wonton tacos to decadent Cantonese lobster with sake and oyster sauce. Solid if not groundbreaking, with an optional vegan menu, excellent cocktails and fabulous people-watching.

⊗ Santa Monica

Santa Monica
Farmers Markets   Market $

(www.smgov.net/portals/farmersmarket; Arizona Ave, btwn 2nd & 3rd Sts; ⊙8:30am-1:30pm

Wed, 8am-1pm Sat; 🖈) 🖉 You haven't really experienced Santa Monica until you've explored one of its outdoor farmers markets stocked with organic fruits, vegetables, flowers, baked goods and freshly shucked oysters. The mack daddy is the Wednesday market, around the intersection of 3rd and Arizona – it's the biggest and arguably the best for fresh produce, and is often patrolled by leading local chefs.

Milo & Olive   Italian $$

(📞310-453-6776; www.miloandolive.com; 2723 Wilshire Blvd; mains breakfast $11-15, lunch & dinner $17-24; ⊘7am-11pm) We love this place for its small-batch wines, incredible pizzas, terrific breakfasts (creamy polenta and poached eggs, anyone?), breads and pastries, all of which you may enjoy at the marble bar or shoulder to shoulder with new friends at one of two common tables. It's a cozy neighborhood joint so it doesn't take reservations.

Cassia   Southeast Asian $$$

(📞310-393-6699; www.cassiala.com; 1314 7th St; appetizers & sides $16-24, mains $37-39; ⊘5-10pm Sun-Thu, 5-11pm Fri & Sat; 🅿) Open, airy Cassia has made about every local and national 'best' list of LA restaurants. Chef Bryant Ng draws on his Chinese-Singaporean heritage in dishes such as *kaya* toast (with coconut jam, butter and a slow-cooked egg), 'sunbathing' prawns, and the encompassing Vietnamese pot-au-feu: short-rib stew, veggies, bone marrow and delectable accompaniments.

⊗ Venice

Salt & Straw   Ice Cream $

(📞310-310-8429; www.saltandstraw.com; 1357 Abbot Kinney Blvd, Venice; ice cream from $4.15; ⊘11am-11pm; 🚌Big Blue Bus Line 18) There always seems to be a line out the door at this branch of the cool Portland-based ice-cream fantasy land. Maybe it's because there's always something new to try (adventurous, seasonally themed flavors change monthly – think farmers-market veggies to late-summer harvest) in addition

to year-round classics. Check the website for current offerings.

Gjusta   Californian $$

(📞310-314-0320; www.gjusta.com; 320 Sunset Ave, Venice; mains $7.50-20; ⊘7am-9pm; 🚌Big Blue Bus Lines 1, 18) The folks behind the standard-setting **Gjelina** (📞310-450-1429; www.gjelina.com; 1429 Abbot Kinney Blvd, Venice; mains $10-35; ⊘8am-midnight; 🚌Big Blue Bus Line 18) have opened this very casual, very gourmet, *very* Venice bakery, cafe and deli behind a nondescript storefront on a hidden side street. The menu changes regularly, but if we say lunches of chicken, cabbage and dumpling soup, house-cured charcuterie and fish (such as gravlax, smoked Wagyu brisket and leg of lamb), does that help?

🍸 DRINKING & NIGHTLIFE

Abbey   Gay & Lesbian

(Map p210; 📞310-289-8410; www.theabbeyweho.com; 692 N Robertson Blvd, West Hollywood; ⊘11am-2am Mon-Thu, from 10am Fri, from 9am Sat & Sun; 🛜; 🚌Metro Lines 4, 704) It's been called the best gay bar in the world, and who are we to argue? Once a humble coffeehouse, the chichi Abbey has expanded into the bar/club/restaurant of record in WeHo. It has so many different-flavored martinis and mojitos that you'd think they were invented here, plus a menu of upscale pub food (brunch $14 to $22, dinner mains $16 to $22).

Edison   Cocktail Bar

(Map p208; 📞213-613-0000; https://theneverlands.com/edison; 108 W 2nd St; ⊘5pm-2am Thu & Fri, from 7pm Sat; 🛜; Ⓜ B/D Lines to Civic Center/Grand Park) Accessed through easy-to-miss Harlem Pl alleyway, this extraordinary basement lounge sits in a century-old power plant. It's like a dimly lit, steampunk wonderland, punctuated with vintage generators, handsome leather lounges and secret nooks. Look for celebrity signatures in the original coal furnace and stick around for the live tunes (anything from jazz to folk), burlesque or aerialist performances.

High — Rooftop Bar

(☑424-214-1062; www.highvenice.com; 1697 Pacific Ave, Hotel Erwin, Venice; ☺3-10pm Mon-Thu, 3pm-midnight Fri, noon-midnight Sat, noon-10pm Sun) Venice's only rooftop bar is quite an experience, with 360-degree views from the shore to the Santa Monica Mountains – if you can take your eyes off the beautiful people. High serves creative seasonal cocktails (blood-orange julep, lemon apple hot toddy, Mexican hot chocolate with tequila) and dishes including beef or lamb sliders, meze plates and crab dip. Reservations recommended.

Ham & Eggs Tavern — Bar

(Map p208; www.hamandeggstavern.com; 433 W 8th St; ☺5pm-1am Sun-Thu, to 2am Fri & Sat; 🚇, Ⓜ B/D Lines to 7th St/Metro Center) Our favorite rock 'n' roll dive has it all: affable barkeeps, decent beer and vino, and a gritty, house-party vibe channeling Downtown pre-gentrification. It's tiny, dark and loud (especially later at night), serving up regular live rock and punk to a come-one, come-all crowd of fun-loving regulars. It's also easy enough to miss, masked behind the shopfront of a long-gone Chinese diner.

No Vacancy — Bar

(Map p210; ☑323-465-1902; www.novacancyla. com; 1727 N Hudson Ave; ☺8pm-2am; 🚇; Ⓜ B Line to Hollywood/Vine) If you prefer your cocktail sessions with plenty of wow factor, make a reservation online, style up (no sportswear, shorts, logos or shiny shirts) and head to this old shingled Victorian. It's a vintage-Hollywood scene of dark timber panels and elegant banquettes, with bars tended by clever barkeeps while burlesque dancers and porch-playing musicians entertain the droves of party people.

La Descarga — Lounge

(Map p210; ☑323-466-1324; www.ladescargala. com; 1159 N Western Ave; ☺8pm-2am Tue-Sat; 🚇Metro Lines 175, 207) This mixed-age, reservations-only rum and cigar lounge is a revelation. Behind the marble bar sit more than 1060 types of rum from across the globe. The bartenders mix specialty cocktails,

⬆ Take a Tour in Los Angeles

Whatever your pleasure – dark or light, tragic or profane, sweet or salty – LA has a guided tour for you.

Los Angeles Conservancy (☑213-623-2489; www.laconservancy.org; adult/child $15/10; 👪) Nonprofit walking tours of architectural pearls in Downtown LA.

Esotouric (www.esotouric.com; tours $64) Bus tours that explore the city's hypnotic underbelly, from real-life crime stories to the seedy LA of Chandler and Bukowski.

TMZ Celebrity Tour (Map p210; ☑844-869-8687; www.tmz.com/tour; 6822 Hollywood Blvd; adult/child $52/31; ☺tours depart 10am-5pm most days; 👪; Ⓜ B Line to Hollywood/Highland) Irreverent celeb-culture bus tours of Hollywood and Beverly Hills.

Dearly Departed (☑855-600-3323; www. dearlydepartedtours.com; tours $45-85; 👪) A bus tour of scandal and blood, because life and Hollywood can be dark and tragic.

Pride Explorer (www.thelavendereffect. org/tours) Closeted heart-throbs, underground bars and brave radicals are all celebrated on these fascinating self-guided walking tours of LGBTIQ+ Hollywood and Downtown LA.

Hollywood Walk of Fame (p195)

but you'd do well to order something aged, and sip it neat as you enjoy live salsa and bachata tunes and, Thursday to Saturday, burlesque ballerinas. Book two weeks ahead for Friday and Saturday.

Imperial Western Beer Company
Microbrewery

(Map p208; ☑213-270-0035; www.imperial western.com; Union Station, 800 N Alameda St; ◎3pm-midnight Mon-Thu, 3pm-2am Fri, noon-2am Sat, noon-midnight Sun; ☎; Ⓜ B/D/L Lines to Union Station) Even New York's Grand Central Terminal can't claim an in-house craft brewery, but that's exactly what awaits at Union Station. Occupying a glorious hall with original, Navajo-inspired floor tiles, the fun, sprawling space pours everything from single-hop and unfiltered IPAs, to ales, dubbels, oyster stouts and goses. Bonuses include decent $1 happy-hour oysters (3pm to 7pm weekdays).

Sayers Club
Club

(Map p210; ☑323-871-8233; www.facebook. com/TheSayersClub; 1645 Wilcox Ave; cover varies; ◎10pm-2am Wed, Fri & Sun, 9pm-2am Thu; ☎; Ⓜ B Line to Hollywood/Vine) When established stars such as the Black Keys, and even movie stars such as Joseph Gordon-Levitt, decide to play secret shows in intimate environs, they come to the back room at this brick-house, speakeasy-style Hollywood nightspot, where the sofas are leather, the lighting moody and the music always satisfying. Dress to impress.

⭐ ENTERTAINMENT

Geffen Playhouse
Theater

(☑310-208-5454; www.geffenplayhouse.com; 10886 Le Conte Ave, Westwood; Ⓜ Metro Lines 2, 17, 302, Big Blue Bus Lines 1, 2, 8) Entertainment megamogul David Geffen forked out over $17 million to get his Mediterranean-style playhouse back into shape. The center's season includes both American classics and freshly minted works, and it's not unusual to see well-known film and TV actors treading the boards.

Hollywood Bowl
Concert Venue

(Map p210; ☑323-850-2000; www.hollywood bowl.com; 2301 N Highland Ave; rehearsals free, performance costs vary; ◎late May–mid-Oct; Ⓜ Metro Line 237) Summers in LA just wouldn't be the same without alfresco melodies under the stars at the Bowl, a huge natural amphitheater in the Hollywood Hills. Its annual season – which usually runs from late May to September – includes symphonies, jazz bands and iconic acts such as Bob Dylan, Diana Ross, the B52s and Pet Shop Boys. Bring a sweater or blanket as it gets cool at night.

Echo
Live Music

(Map p210; www.spacelandpresents.com; 1822 W Sunset Blvd, Echo Park; cover varies; Ⓜ Metro Lines 2, 4, 302, 704) Eastsiders hungry for an eclectic alchemy of sounds pack this crowded dive, basically a sweaty bar with a stage and a back patio. On the music front, expect anything from indie and electronica, to dub reggae and dream and power pop. Monday nights are dedicated to up-and-coming local bands, with regular club nights including Saturday's always-a-blast Funky Sole party.

Off the 405
Live Music

(www.getty.edu; Getty Center; ◎6-9pm Sat May-Sep) FREE On selected Saturdays from May to September, the Getty Center (p205) courtyard fills with evening crowds for a delicious collision of art, brilliant live acts and beat-pumping DJ sets.

Upright Citizens Brigade Theatre
Comedy

(Map p210; ☑323-908-8702; https://franklin. ucbtheatre.com; 5919 Franklin Ave; tickets $5-12; Ⓜ Metro Line 207) Founded in New York by *Saturday Night Live* alums Amy Poehler and Ian Roberts along with Matt Besser and Matt Walsh, this sketch-comedy group cloned itself in Hollywood in 2005. With numerous nightly shows spanning anything from stand-up comedy to improv and sketch, it's arguably the best comedy hub in town. Valet parking costs $7.

Wiltern Theatre
Theater

(Map p210; ☑213-388-1400; www.wiltern.com; 3790 Wilshire Blvd; Ⓜ D Line to Wilshire/Western)

Soaring confidently at the intersection of Wilshire and Western Blvds (get it?), this extraordinary, turquoise-hued deco landmark started life as a movie theater (*West Side Story* premiered here). These days it's an epic venue for live music, comedy and occasional screenings of cult-status movies: recent live acts have included Japanese rockers Radwimps and comics Chelsea Handler and Ronny Chieng.

Blue Whale   Jazz
(Map p208; ☑213-620-0908; www.blue-whalemusic.com; 123 Onizuka St, Suite 301, Little Tokyo; prices vary; ☺8pm-2am; Ⓜ L Line to Little Tokyo/Arts District) An intimate space on the top floor of Weller Court in Little Tokyo, Blue Whale serves top-notch jazz nightly from 9pm to around midnight. The crowd is eclectic, the beers craft and the spirits focused on small batch. Acts span from emerging and edgy to established, and the acoustics are excellent. The cover charge varies, but is generally between $15 and $30.

Los Angeles Philharmonic   Classical Music
(Map p208; ☑323-850-2000; www.laphil.org; 111 S Grand Ave; Ⓜ B/D Lines to Civic Centre/Grand Park) The world-class LA Phil performs classics and cutting-edge works at the Walt Disney Concert Hall (p206), under the baton of Venezuelan phenom (and Grammy award-winning) Gustavo Dudamel.

ⓘ INFORMATION

Discover Los Angeles Visitor Information Center (Map p210; 6801 Hollywood Blvd; ☺9am-10pm Mon-Sat, 10am-7pm Sun; ☎) The main tourist office for Los Angeles, located in Hollywood. Maps, brochures and public transportation information, plus tickets to attractions.

ⓘ GETTING THERE & AWAY

The main LA gateway is **Los Angeles International Airport** (LAX; www.flylax.com; 1 World Way). Its nine terminals are linked by the free LAX Shuttle A, leaving from the lower (arrival) level of each terminal. Cabs and hotel and car-rental shuttles stop here as well. A free minibus for travelers with disabilities can be ordered by calling 310-646-6402. Ticketing and check-in are on the upper (departure) level.

Two Amtrak trains – the *Coast Starlight* to Seattle and the *Southwest Chief* to Chicago – stop daily at **Union Station** (Map p208; www.unionstationla.com; 800 N Alameda St; Ⓟ; Ⓜ B/D/L Lines to Union Station) in Downtown LA. The thrice-weekly *Sunset Limited* to New Orleans also stops here. For a scenic coastal ride, hop aboard the *Pacific Surfliner*, which travels numerous times daily between San Diego, Santa Barbara and San Luis Obispo via LA.

ⓘ GETTING AROUND
CAR & MOTORCYCLE

Unless time is short – or money is extremely tight – you will probably want to spend some time behind the wheel, although this means contending with some of the worst traffic in the country. Avoid rush hour (7am to 9am and 3:30pm to 6pm).

Parking at motels and cheaper hotels is usually free, while fancier ones charge anywhere from $10 to around $55 for the privilege. Valet parking at nicer restaurants and hotels is commonplace, with rates ranging from $3.50 to $10 (plus tip).

PUBLIC TRANSPORTATION

Most public transportation, including buses, metro lines and light rail, is handled by **Metro** (☑323-466-3876; www.metro.net), which offers maps, schedules and trip-planning help through its website.

To ride Metro trains and buses, buy a reusable TAP card. Available from TAP vending machines at Metro stations with a $2 surcharge, the cards allow you to add a preset cash value or day passes.

ORANGE COUNTY

In this Chapter

Orange County

LA and Orange County are the closest of neighbors, but in some ways they couldn't be more different. If LA is about stars, the OC is about surfers. LA, ever more urban; OC, proudly suburban, built around cars, freeways and shopping malls. If LA is SoCal's seat of liberal thinking, the OC's heritage is of mega-churches and ultraconservative firebrands. If LA is Hollywood glam, the OC is Real Housewives. Tourism is dominated by Disneyland in Anaheim in northern OC, and beach communities promising endless summer – and very different lifestyles – as you progress down the coast.

Orange County in Two Days

Spend one day at **Disneyland Park** (p228), meeting Mickey, screaming your head off on Hyperspace Mountain and ensuring 'It's a small world,' is stuck in your head forevermore. On day two, head south for a classic California day at the beach. Aim for **Huntington Beach** (p240), where you can end the night with a bonfire after a day of killer waves.

Orange County in Four Days

With a couple more days, you'll probably want to add **Disney California Adventure** (p230) to your Disneyland Resort experience, or sample a stretch of sand (or three) in **Laguna Beach** (p236). On day four, prepare to be awed by Spanish colonial history at the beautiful **Mission San Juan Capistrano** (p235), the jewel of the missions.

Huntington Beach Map (p242)

Arriving in Orange County

Air Orange County has its own airport, John Wayne Airport, although if you're flying into Los Angeles International Airport (LAX) it's usually not worth the time and expense to catch a connecting flight. If you do arrive at LAX, it's barely an hour by road. Super Shuttle (www.supershuttle.com) operates from LAX to Disney resort hotels from $17 each way (more expensive to Disneyland proper).

Sleeping

Accommodations along Orange County's beaches range from midrange to very expensive indeed (and probably worth it). The further you go inland, say to Costa Mesa or Anaheim, the cheaper your stay. Anaheim makes a convenient base to explore Disneyland Resort and the region. Disneyland hotels can be part of the experience, but add to the cost; there are less expensive options just outside the parks' gates.

Disney store, Disneyland Resort

AARON P/BAUER-GRIFFIN/GC IMAGES ©

Disneyland Resort

Welcome to the 'Happiest Place on Earth,' a magical 'imagineered' hyper-reality where the streets are always clean, employees – called 'cast members' – are always upbeat and there are parades every day.

Since opening his Disneyland home in 1955, Mickey has been a thoughtful host to millions of guests. In 2001 a second theme park, Disney's California Adventure (DCA), designed to salute the state's most famous natural landmarks and cultural history, was added. Downtown Disney, an outdoor pedestrian mall packed with shops, restaurants, bars, hotels and entertainment venues, makes up the Disneyland Resort triumvirate.

Disneyland Park

Spotless, wholesome Disneyland is still laid out according to Walt's original plans. It's here you'll find plenty of rides and some of the attractions most associated with the Disney name – Main Street, U.S.A., Sleeping Beauty Castle and Tomorrowland.

Main Street, U.S.A., gateway to the park, is a pretty thoroughfare lined with

Great For...

☑ Don't Miss

Tomorrowland's Autopia – one of the original rides from 1955.

Mickey Mouse balloons

JONATHAN ALCORN/BLOOMBERG VIA GETTY IMAGES ©

Disneyland Park
Frontierland   Fantasyland
Adventureland   Tomorrowland
Downtown Disney   **Disneyland Resort**
Grizzly Peak   Disney California
  Adventure
Pixar Pier   Cars Land
ANAHEIM

❶ Need to Know

☏714-781-4636; www.disneyland.com; 1313
Harbor Blvd; 1-day pass adult $104-149, child
3-9yr $96-141, 2-day pass adult/child 3-9yr
$225/210; ⊙open daily, seasonal hours vary

✕ Take a Break

Make a booking for refined dining at
Napa Rose (☏714-300-7170; https://
disneyland.disney.go.com/dining; Grand
Californian Hotel & Spa; mains $38-58;
⊙5:30-10pm; 🚻).

★ Top Tip

The Disneyland mobile app lets you purchase tickets, make reservations, view
wait times and locate characters.

old-fashioned Americana ice-cream parlors
and shops. Though kids will make a beeline
for the rides, adults may enjoy lingering
on Main Street for the antique photos and
history exhibit.

At the far end of the street is **Sleeping
Beauty Castle**, an obligatory photo op
and a central landmark worth noting – its
towering blue turrets are visible from many
areas of the park. The different sections of
Disneyland radiate from here like spokes
on a wheel.

Tomorrowland

How did 1950s imagineers envision the future? As a galaxy-minded community filled
with monorails, rockets and Googie-style
architecture, apparently. In 1998 this 'land'
was revamped to honor three timeless fu-
turists: Jules Verne, HG Wells and Leonardo

da Vinci. These days, though, the *Star Wars*
franchise gets top billing. **Space Mountain**, Tomorrowland's signature attraction
and one of the USA's best roller coasters,
hurtles you into complete darkness at
frightening speed, and **Star Wars Launch
Bay** shows movie props and memorabilia.

Just outside the Tomorrowland monorail
station, children (and their grown-ups) will
want to drive their own miniature cars in
the classic **Autopia** ride.

Fantasyland

Fantasyland is filled with the characters
of classic children's stories. If you only
see one attraction here, visit **'It's a small
world,'** a boat ride past hundreds of
Audio-Animatronics dolls of children from
different cultures all singing an earworm of
a theme song.

Another classic, the **Matterhorn Bob-
sleds** is a steel-frame roller coaster that
mimics a bobsled ride down a mountain.

Frontierland

This Disney 'land' is a salute to old Americana: there's the Mississippi-style paddle-wheel **Mark Twain Riverboat**, the 18th-century replica **Sailing Ship Columbia**, a rip-roarin' Old West town with a shooting gallery, and the **Big Thunder Mountain Railroad**, a mining-themed roller coaster.

Adventureland

Loosely deriving its jungle theme from Southeast Asia and Africa, Adventureland has a number of attractions, but the hands-down highlight is the safari-style **Indiana Jones Adventure**. Nearby, little ones love climbing the stairways of **Tarzan's Treehouse**.

Adventureland's **Pirates of the Caribbean** is the longest ride in Disneyland (17 minutes) and provided 'inspiration' – thin as that inspiration may be – for the popular movies.

Disney California Adventure

Across the plaza from Disneyland Park, this ode to California's geography, history and culture – or at least a sanitized G-rated version – covers more acres than Disneyland and feels less crowded. It also has more modern rides and attractions inspired by coastal amusement parks, the inland mountains and redwood forests, the magic of Hollywood, and car culture by way of the movie *Cars*.

Cars Land

This land gets kudos for its incredibly detailed design based on the popular Disney•Pixar *Cars* movies. Top billing goes

Pixar Pier

to the wacky **Radiator Springs Racers**, a race-car ride that bumps and jumps around a track painstakingly decked out like the Great American West.

Grizzly Peak

Grizzly Peak is broken into sections high-lighting California's natural and human achievements. Its main attraction, **Soarin' Around the World**, is a virtual hang-gliding ride using Omnimax technology that 'flies' you over famous landmarks. Enjoy the light

breeze as you soar, keeping your nostrils open for aromas blowing in the wind.

Grizzly River Run takes you 'rafting' down a faux Sierra Nevada river – you will get wet, so come when it's warm.

Pixar Pier

If you like carnival rides, you'll love Pixar Pier, designed to look like a combination of all the beachside amusement piers in California. The state-of-the-art **California Screamin'** roller coaster resembles an old wooden coaster, but it's got a smooth-as-silk steel track: it feels like you're being shot out of a cannon. Just as popular is **Toy Story Midway Mania!** – a 4D ride where you earn points by shooting at targets while your carnival car swivels and careens through an oversize, old-fashioned games arcade.

Downtown Disney

Downtown Disney is a triumph of market-ing. Once in this open-air pedestrian mall, sandwiched between the two parks and the hotels, it may be hard to extract yourself. There are plenty of opportunities to drop cash in stores (not just Disney stuff either), restaurants and entertainment venues. Apart from the Disney merch, a lot of it is shops you can find elsewhere, but in the moment it's still hard to resist. Most shops here open and close with the parks.

Tickets

There is a multitude of Disneyland Resort ticket options. Single-day ticket prices are $104 to $149 for adults and $96 to $141 for a children's ticket for either Disney-land or DCA, and a variety of multiday and 'park-hopper' passes are available.

> ### ❶ Need to Know
>
> Disneyland Resort is open 365 days a year. Hours vary seasonally and sometimes daily, but generally you can count on at least 10am to 8pm. Check the current schedule (www.disneyland.com) in advance.

PAUL HIFFMEYER © DISNEY

> ### ★ Top Tip
>
> For information or help inside the parks, just ask any cast member or visit Dis-neyland's City Hall or Disney California Adventure's guest relations lobby.

Children's tickets apply to kids aged from three to nine.

FASTPASS

Disney's FastPass can significantly cut wait times at some of the resorts' most popular attractions. If you have purchased MaxPass, you can book FastPasses on the Disneyland app. If you haven't purchased MaxPass:

○ Find a FastPass ticket machine – located near the entrance to the ride – and insert your park entrance ticket or annual passport. You'll receive a ticket showing the 'return time' for boarding (at least 40 minutes later). If you're traveling with others, each person needs their own FastPass.

○ Show up within the window of time on the ticket and join the line for FastPass holders. There'll still be a wait, but it's shorter (typically 15 minutes or less). Hang on to your FastPass ticket until you board.

○ If you miss the time window printed on your FastPass ticket, you can still try joining the FastPass line, although showing up before your FastPass time is a no-no.

You're thinking, what's the catch, right? When you get a FastPass, you will have to wait before getting another one (check the 'next available' time at the bottom of your ticket).

So, make it count. Before getting a FastPass, check the return time. If it doesn't fit your schedule, a FastPass may not be worth it. Ditto if the ride's current wait time is just 15 to 30 minutes.

Disney Dining

From stroll-and-eat Mickey-shaped pretzels ($7.25) and jumbo turkey legs ($12) to deluxe, gourmet dinners (sky's the limit), there's no shortage of eating options, though most are pretty expensive and targeted to mainstream tastes. Restaurant hours vary seasonally, sometimes daily. Check the Disneyland app or Disney Dining website for same-day hours.

Outside the parks proper, Downtown Disney has a number of dining and drinking options.

Food & Drink Tips

○ Technically, you can't bring any food or drinks into the parks, but security-inspection staff usually look the other way at small water bottles and a few snacks.

○ Store soft-sided coolers and nonperishable food in lockers by the not-so-appealing picnic area outside the main entrance.

○ Within the parks, reservations are recommended at top-end restaurants. If you haven't made reservations, plan on eating at off-peak times (eg outside the noon to 3pm lunch rush, and before 6pm or after 9pm for dinner).

Flo's V8 Cafe, Disney California Adventure Park

• Convenient, if overpriced, fast food and carnival-style snacks are sold everywhere in the parks.

• Park maps indicate restaurants and cafes where you can find healthy food options – look for the apple icon.

• For better-value eats and wider menu options, exit the parks and walk (or ride the monorail) to Downtown Disney.

• Drinking fountains are everywhere, so bring a refillable water bottle.

Getting There & Away

Disneyland and Anaheim can be reached by car (off the I-5 Fwy) or Amtrak or Metrolink trains at Anaheim's ARTIC (p247) transit center. From here it's a short taxi, ride share or shuttle with **Anaheim Resort Transportation** (ART; ☎888-364-2787; www.rideart.org; adult/child fare $3/1, day pass $6/2.50, multiple-day passes available) to Disneyland proper.

★ **Top Tip**

To beat the crowds, arrive when parking lots and ticket booths open, an hour before the theme parks' official opening times.

★ **Local Knowledge**

Disneyland may be the happiest place on earth, but it ain't because of alcohol; no booze is allowed or served in the park. For that you have to go to DCA, Downtown Disney or one of the Disneyland hotels.

FROZENSHUTTER/GETTY IMAGES ©

Mission San Juan Capistrano

California's Missions

California's gracious Spanish missions stand as quiet reminders of the state's tumultuous past. Established by Spanish missionaries between 1769 and 1823, they still offer a chance to step into California's complex history.

Great For...

☑ **Don't Miss**

The whitewashed Serra Chapel, believed to be the oldest standing building in the state.

From California's first mission at San Diego de Alcalá, which was founded in 1769, to the state's last, the 1823 Mission San Francisco Solano, the 21 California missions were built as the first European effort to colonize the Pacific Coast. These military and religious fortresses gave Spain a foothold in the New World, and signaled the downfall of California's once-thriving indigenous population. Indeed, legend has it that ghosts still pace the cloisters of many missions, built by Native Californian conscripts, many of whom didn't survive to see their completion.

Mission San Juan Capistrano

Famous for its swallows that fly back to town every year on March 19 (though sometimes they're just a bit early), San Juan Capistrano is home to its eponymous

Basilica at Mission San Juan Capistrano

BPPERRY/GETTY IMAGES ©

mission (📞949-234-1300; www.missionsjc.com; 26801 Ortega Hwy; adult/child $10/7; ⊙9am-5pm; ♿), nicknamed the 'jewel of the California missions.' Founded by peripatetic priest Junípero Serra in 1776, and built around a series of 18th-century arcades, the mission complex encloses stone arcades, bubbling fountains and flowery gardens. Archaeologists, engineers and restoration artists have done an exquisite job of keeping the mission alive. Plan on spending at least an hour or two poking around the sprawling grounds and stately buildings, including the padre's quarters, soldiers' barracks and cemetery.

Particularly moving are the towering remains of the **Great Stone Church**, almost completely destroyed by a powerful earthquake on December 8, 1812. The **Serra Chapel** (1782) – whitewashed outside with restored frescoes inside – is believed to be the oldest existing building in California. It's certainly the only one still standing in which Junípero Serra gave Mass.

Admission includes a worthwhile free audio tour with interesting stories narrated by locals.

California Mission Trail

California's 21 missions are strung like pearls along the well-marked Historic Mission Trail. They are all located on or near Hwy 101 and roughly trace 'El Camino Real,' named in honor of the Spanish monarchy that financed their construction as a way to expand their empire. If you're traveling through California today, the missions make an excellent detour and you'll find stunningly renovated buildings from San Diego in the south to Solano in the north.

Laguna Beach coastline

Laguna Beach

Secluded coves, romantic cliffs, azure waves and waterfront parks imbue Laguna Beach with a classic Riviera-like feel. Public sculptures, art festivals and free summer shuttles are thoughtful and much-appreciated touches.

Great For...

ℹ Need to Know

Shops, restaurants and bars are concentrated in downtown's 'village,' along three parallel streets: Broadway, Ocean Ave and Forest Ave.

★ **Top Tip**

Stop by the **visitor center** (☏ 949-497-9229; www.lagunabeachinfo.com; 381 Forest Ave; ⊙10am-5pm; 🛜) for free brochures on everything from hiking trails to self-guided walking tours.

One of the earliest incorporated cities in California, Laguna has a strong tradition in the arts, starting with the plein air Impressionists who lived and worked here in the early 1900s. Today it's the home of renowned arts festivals, galleries, a well-known museum and exquisitely preserved arts-and-crafts cottages and bungalows that come as a relief after seeing endless miles of suburban beige-box architecture. It's also the OC's most prominent gay enclave (even if the gay nightlife scene is a shadow of its former self).

Separated from the inland flatlands by a long steep canyon, Laguna stretches about 7 miles along Pacific Coast Hwy.

Laguna Art Museum

This breezy **museum** (📞949-494-8971; www.lagunaartmuseum.org; 307 Cliff Dr; adult/student & senior/child under 13yr $7/5/free, 5-9pm 1st Thu of month free; 🕙11am-5pm Fri-Tue, to 9pm Thu) has changing exhibitions featuring contemporary California artists, and a permanent collection heavy on California landscapes, vintage photographs and works by early Laguna bohemians.

Beaches

With 30 public beaches sprawling along 7 miles of coastline, Laguna Beach is perfect for do-it-yourself exploring. There's always another stunning view or hidden cove just around the bend. For a bird's-eye view of the shoreline, head to the grassy, bluff-top **Heisler Park** (375 Cliff Dr), where you'll find vistas of craggy coves and deep-blue sea.

Near downtown's village, **Main Beach** (🚻) has volleyball and basketball courts, a playground and restrooms. It's the first beach

Surfing, Laguna Beach

you see as you come down Laguna Canyon Blvd from the 405 Fwy, and it's Laguna's best beach for swimming. Just north of Main Beach, **Picnic Beach** is too rocky to surf but has excellent tide-pooling.

South of downtown, locals' favorite **Aliso Beach County Park** (☎949-923-2280; http://ocparks.com/beaches/aliso; 31131 S Pacific Coast Hwy; parking per hr $1; ☺6am-10pm; P🚻) is popular with surfers, boogie boarders and skimboarders. With picnic

tables, fire pits and a play area, it's also good for families.

South again, **West Street Beach** (West St) has long been a hangout for Laguna's (and the OC's) LGBTIQ+ community (with an emphasis on the G).

Jealously guarded by locals, **Thousand Steps Beach** (off 9th Ave) is hidden off Hwy 1 just south of Mission Hospital. At the south end of 9th St, more than 200 steps (way less than 1000) lead down to the sand. Though rocky, the beach is great for sunbathing, surfing and bodysurfing.

Diving & Snorkeling

With its coves, reefs and rocky outcroppings, Laguna is one of the best SoCal beaches for diving and snorkeling. One of the most famous spots is **Divers Cove** just below Heisler Park. It's part of the **Glenn E Vedder Ecological Reserve**, an underwater park stretching to the northern border of Main Beach. Also popular is **Shaw's Cove**. Check weather and surf conditions with the city's **marine safety forecast line** (☎949-494-6573) beforehand, as drownings have happened. The visitors bureau has tide charts.

Kayaking

Take a guided kayaking tour of the craggy coves of Laguna's coast with **La Vida Laguna** (☎949-275-7544; www.lavidalaguna. com; 1257 S Coast Hwy; 2hr guided tour from $95) and you might just see a colony of sea lions. Reservations required.

FOCQUS/SHUTTERSTOCK ©

Huntington Beach

'No worries' is the phrase you'll hear over and over in Huntington Beach, the town that goes by the trademarked nickname 'Surf City USA.' In 1910, real-estate developer and railroad magnate Henry Huntington hired Hawaiian-Irish surfing star George Freeth to give demonstrations. When legendary surfer Duke Kahanamoku moved here in 1925, the town's status as a surf destination was set.

HB remains a quintessential spot to celebrate the hang-loose SoCal coastal lifestyle: consistently good waves, surf shops, a surf museum, bonfires on the sand, a canine-friendly beach and hotels and restaurants with killer views.

◎ SIGHTS

Bolsa Chica
Ecological Reserve   Nature Reserve

(📞714-846-1114; http://bolsachica.org; 18000 Pacific Coast Hwy; ⊗sunrise-sunset; 🅿) You'd be forgiven for overlooking Bolsa Chica, at least on first glance. Against a backdrop of nodding oil derricks, this flat expanse of wetlands doesn't exactly promise the unspoiled splendors of nature. However, more than 200 bird species aren't so aesthetically prejudiced, either making the wetlands their home throughout the year, or dropping by mid-migration. Simply put, the restored salt marsh is an environmental success story.

This 'Little Pocket' (*bolsa chica* in Spanish) of estuarine tidal saltwater marsh – home to loons, ducks, terns, sandpipers and rare species such as the white pelican – is largely untouched, other than two circular embedded gun batteries (a legacy of WWII fears of Japanese invasion). Preservation didn't come easily, however: decades of arm-wrestling between developers and conservationists resulted, in 1997, in the state buying up some 800 acres for the reserve. Eventually, about 1450 acres were saved by a band of determined locals from numerous development projects.

The park's small interpretive center has lots of information about the reserve and leads occasional tours. On your own, there

Common yellowthroat, Bolsa Chica Ecological Reserve

SUSANGARYPHOTOGRAPHY/GETTY IMAGES ©

are multiple trails for about a 5-mile loop if you cover the whole reserve.

Sadly, Bolsa Chica is one of the last remaining coastal wetlands in SoCal – over 90% has already succumbed to development.

Bolsa Chica State Beach   Beach

(📞714-377-5691; www.parks.ca.gov/bolsachica; Pacific Coast Hwy, btwn Seapoint & Warner Aves; parking $15; ⊙6am-10pm; 🅿)A3-mile-longstrip of sand favored by surfers, volleyball players and fishers, Bolsa Chica State Beach stretches alongside Pacific Coast Hwy between **Huntington Dog Beach** (📞714-841-8644; www.dogbeach.org; btwn Goldenwest & Seapoint Sts; ⊙5am-10pm; 🅿) to the south and Sunset Beach to the north. Even though it faces a monstrous offshore oil rig, Bolsa Chica gets mobbed on summer weekends. You'll find picnic tables, fire rings and beach showers, plus a bike path running north to Anderson Ave at Sunset Beach and south to Huntington State Beach.

Huntington City Beach   Beach

(www.huntingtonbeachca.gov; ⊙5am-10pm; 🅿🚻) One of SoCal's best beaches, the sand surrounding the pier at the foot of Main St gets packed on summer weekends with surfers, volleyball players, swimmers and families. Bathrooms and showers are located north of the pier at the back of the snack-bar complex. In the evening volleyball games give way to beach bonfires.

If you want to build a bonfire or have a barbecue, stake out one of the 1000 cement fire rings early in the day, especially on holiday weekends, when you should plan to arrive when the beach opens. To indicate that it's taken, surround the ring with your gear. You can buy firewood from concessionaires on the beach.

Huntington Beach Pier   Historic Site

(cnr Main St & Pacific Coast Hwy; ⊙5am-midnight) The 1853ft Huntington Pier is one of the West Coast's longest. It has been here – in one form or another – since 1904, though the mighty Pacific has damaged giant sections or completely demolished

Huntington Beach Festivals

Every Tuesday brings **Surf City Nights** (www.surfcityusa.com/things-to-do/attractions/surf-city-nights/; 1st 3 blocks Main St; ⊙5-9pm Tue), a street fair with about 90 vendors doing sidewalk sales for the grown-ups, and live music and farmers-market goodies for everyone.

Car buffs get up early on Saturday mornings for the **Donut Derelicts Car Show** (www.donutderelicts.com; cnr Magnolia St & Adams Ave), a weekly gathering of woodies, beach cruisers and pimped-out street rods.

Surf City Nights farmers market
DAVID TONELSON/SHUTTERSTOCK ©

it multiple times since then. The current concrete structure was built in 1983 to withstand 31ft waves or a 7.0-magnitude earthquake, whichever hits HB first. On the pier you can rent fishing gear from **Let's Go Fishing** (📞714-960-1392; 21 Main St; fishing sets per hr/day $6/15; ⊙hours vary) bait and tackle shop.

International Surfing Museum   Museum

(📞714-960-3483; www.huntingtonbeachsurfingmuseum.org; 411 Olive Ave; $3; ⊙noon-5pm Tue-Sun) Look for the world's biggest surfboard next to this small museum, an entertaining stop for surf-culture enthusiasts. Temporary exhibits chronicle the sport's history with photos, vintage surfboards, movie memorabilia and surf music. For the best historical tidbits, spend a minute chatting with the all-volunteer staff. That surfboard? It's 42ft

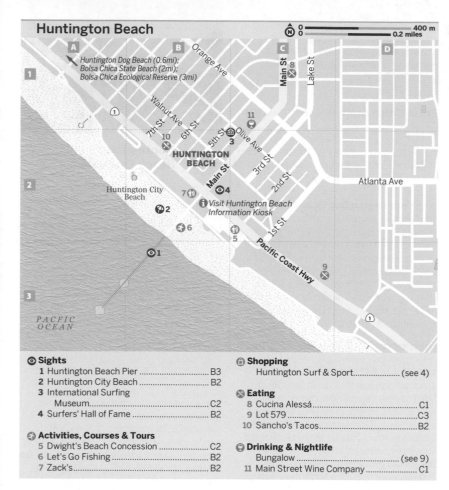

Huntington Beach

Huntington Dog Beach (0.6mi);
Bolsa Chica State Beach (2mi);
Bolsa Chica Ecological Reserve (3mi)

HUNTINGTON BEACH

Huntington City Beach

Visit Huntington Beach Information Kiosk

Atlanta Ave

PACIFIC OCEAN

Sights
1 Huntington Beach Pier B3
2 Huntington City Beach B2
3 International Surfing
  Museum.. C2
4 Surfers' Hall of Fame B2

Activities, Courses & Tours
5 Dwight's Beach Concession C2
6 Let's Go Fishing B2
7 Zack's.. B2

Shopping
Huntington Surf & Sport.................... (see 4)

Eating
8 Cucina Alessá... C1
9 Lot 579 ....C3
10 Sancho's Tacos.. B2

Drinking & Nightlife
Bungalow .... (see 9)
11 Main Street Wine Company C1

long, weighs 1300lb, and holds 66 people and the Guinness World Record.

⊕ ACTIVITIES

Dwight's Beach Concession
Surfing

(☑714-536-8083; www.dwightsbeachconcession.com; 201 Pacific Coast Hwy; surfboard rentals per hr/day $10/40, bicycle rentals from $10/30; ⊕9am-5pm Mon-Fri, to 6pm Sat & Sun) Rents surfboards, bodyboards, bikes and other beach gear at competitive rates. It's HB's longest-running business, since 1932.

Zack's
Surfing

(☑714-536-0215; www.zackssurfcity.com; 405 Pacific Coast Hwy; group lessons $85, surfboard rentals per hr/day $12/35, wetsuits $5/15) This well-established outfit by the pier offers surfing lessons and rents all sorts of beach equipment. Lessons include equipment rental for the day.

Vans Off the Wall Skatepark
Outdoors

(☑714-379-6666; www.vans.com/skateparks-hb.html; 7471 Center Dr; helmet & pad set rentals $5; ⊕9am-8pm daily) **FREE** This custom-built facility by the OC-based sneaker and skatewear company has plenty of ramps, bowls, dips, boxes and rails for boarders to catch air. BYOB (board). Helmets and pads required for visitors under 18.

🅐 SHOPPING

Huntington
Surf & Sport   Sports & Outdoors
(www.hsssurf.com; 300 Pacific Coast Hwy; ⊗8am-9pm Sun-Thu, to 10pm Fri & Sat) Towering behind the statue of surf hero Duke Kahanamoku, this massive store supports the Surf City vibe with vintage surf photos, the **Surfers' Hall of Fame** (www.hsssurf.com/shof) and lots of tiki-themed decor. You'll also find rows of surfboards to buy or rent, beachwear and surfing accessories.

HSS rents surfboards for $10/30 per hour/day (wetsuits $8/15).

🅧 EATING

Lot 579   Food Hall $
(www.gopacificcity.com/lot579; Pacific City, 21010 Pacific Coast Hwy; ⊗hours vary; P 🛜 ♿) The food court at HB's ocean-view mall offers some unique and fun restaurants for pressed sandwiches (Burnt Crumbs – the spaghetti grilled cheese is so Instagrammable), Vietnamese street food (Phans 55), coffee (Portola) and ice cream (Hans'). For the best views, take your meal to the deck, or eat at American Dream (brewpub) or Bear Flag Fish Company.

Sancho's Tacos   Mexican $
(☑714-536-8226; www.sanchostacos.com; 602 Pacific Coast Hwy; mains $6-10.75; ⊗11am-8pm Mon-Fri, from 10am Sat & Sun; P) There's no shortage of taco stands in HB, but locals are fiercely dedicated to the original location of this local mini-chain, across from the beach. This two-room shack with patio grills flounder, shrimp and tri-tip to order. Trippy Mexican-meets-skater art.

Eat at red leatherette booths or on the outdoor patio across from the ocean.

Cucina Alessá   Italian $$
(☑714-969-2148;http://cucinaalessarestaurants.com; 520 Main St; mains lunch $16-20, dinner $16-35; ⊗11am-10pm) Every beach town needs its favorite go-to Italian kitchen. Alessá wins hearts and stomachs with classics like Neapolitan lasagna, butternut-squash ravioli and chicken marsala. Lunch brings panini, pizzas and pastas, plus breakfasts including 'famous' French toast. Get sidewalk seating, or sit behind big glass windows.

🅠 DRINKING & NIGHTLIFE

Bungalow   Club
(☑714-374-0399; www.thebungalow.com/huntington-beach; Pacific City, 21058 Pacific Coast Hwy, Suite 240; ⊗5pm-2am Mon-Fri, noon-2am Sat, noon-10pm Sun) The second location of this Santa Monica landmark of cool is in Pacific City, and with its combination of lounge spaces, outdoor patio, cozy, rustic-vintage design, specialty cocktails, DJs who know how to get the crowd going and – let's not forget – ocean views, it's setting new standards for the OC. The food menu's pretty great too.

Main Street
Wine Company   Wine Bar
(www.mainstreetwinecompany.com; 301 Main St, Suite 105; ⊗4-9pm Mon, noon-10pm Tue-Thu, noon-11pm Fri, 1-11pm Sat, 1-9pm Sun) Boutique California-wine shop with a sleek bar, generous pours and meet-your-(wine)maker nights.

🅘 INFORMATION

Visit Huntington Beach operates the **Pier Plaza kiosk** (☑714-969-3492, 800-729-6232; www.surfcityusa.com; Pier Plaza, 325 Pacific Coast Hwy; ⊗10:30am-7pm Mon-Fri, from 10am Sat & Sun, shorter hours in winter), which is open daily.

🅘 GETTING THERE & AWAY

Pacific Coast Hwy (PCH) runs alongside the beach. Main St intersects PCH at the pier. Heading

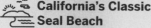

California's Classic Seal Beach

The OC's first beach town driving south from LA County, 'Seal' is one of the last great California beach towns and a refreshing alternative to the more crowded coast further south. Its 1.5 miles of pristine beach sparkle like a crown, and that's without mentioning three-block Main St, a stoplight-free zone with mom-and-pop restaurants and indie shops that are low on 'tude and high on charm.

Although the town's east side is dominated by the sprawling retirement community Leisure World and the huge US Naval Weapons Station (look for grass-covered bunkers), all that fades away along the charming Main St and the oceanfront.

JON BILOUS/SHUTTERSTOCK ©

inland, Main St ends at Hwy 39 (Beach Blvd), which connects north to I-405.

OCTA (www.octa.net) bus 1 connects Huntington Beach with the rest of OC's beach towns every hour; a one-way/day pass is $2/5, payable on board (exact change required).

San Clemente

Just before reaching San Diego County, PCH slows down and rolls past the laid-back surf town of San Clemente. Home to surfing legends, top-notch surfboard companies, a surfing museum and the dearly departed *Surfing* magazine (1964–2017), this unpretentious enclave may be one of the last spots in the OC where you can authentically live the surf lifestyle.

◎ SIGHTS

San Clemente Pier   Pier

(611 Avenida Victoria; ⊘4am-midnight; P) San Clemente City Beach stretches alongside this historic 1296ft-long, wood-built pier. The original 1928 pier, where Prohibition-era bootleggers once brought liquor ashore, was rebuilt most recently in 1985. Surfers go north of the pier, while swimmers and bodysurfers take the south side.

Parking in lots near the pier is $1.50 per hour, but good luck finding a spot during the summer daytime peak or on sunny weekends. If you're not driving, trains stop right in front of the pier.

Surfing Heritage & Culture Center   Museum

(☑949-388-0313; www.facebook.com/surfingheritage; 110 Calle Iglesia; suggested donation $5; ⊘11am-5pm Tue-Sun; P) **FREE** This foundation gives a timeline of surfing history by exhibiting surfboards ridden by the greats, from Duke Kahanamoku to Kelly Slater. Its photo archive has some 100,000 photos (a tiny fraction may be on display at any one time). Temporary exhibits (photos, skateboarding, surf-shop culture and more) change approximately every three months.

It's in an office park in the rolling hills a few miles inland from the beach.

⊗ EATING

Pierside Kitchen & Bar   American $$

(☑949-218-0980; www.piersidesc.com; 610 Avenida Victoria; mains $15-29; ⊘opens 9am daily, closing time varies) The name really says it all at this urbane spot across from the water. Get a table by the window for the best ocean views as you chomp on a modern California menu (kale Caesar salad, bacon-wrapped dates, braised short ribs, ginger soy scallops) with some crazy-cat cocktails like the 'jalapeño business.' Weekend brunch gets rocking with live music.

Fisherman's Restaurant & Bar
Seafood $$$

(☏949-498-6390; www.thefishermansrestaurant.com; 611 Avenida Victoria; breakfast $11-22, mains lunch $17-29, dinner $18-64; ⏱8am-9:30pm Sun-Thu, to 10pm Fri & Sat) Right on the pier, Fisherman's chowders, fish and chips and mesquite-grilled fresh catches come with a side of incomparable ocean views. Generous four-course Fisherman's Feasts ($32 to 62 per person, minimum two people) offer clams, chowder, salad and your choice of fish. Sure, you'll be with tourists, but hey, you're a tourist too, right? Embrace it.

The main dining room is on the left as you enter the pier; to the right are the bar and oyster bar with a more limited menu. No reservations accepted; expect a wait at peak times.

ⓘ GETTING THERE & AWAY

OCTA (www.octa.net) bus 1 heads south from Dana Point about every 60 minutes. At San Clemente's Metrolink station, transfer to OCTA bus 191, which runs hourly to San Clemente Pier. Unless you have a bus pass, you willl need to pay the one-way fare ($2, exact change) twice.

San Clemente is about 6 miles southeast of Dana Point via the Pacific Coast Hwy. Pay-and-display parking at the pier costs $1.50 per hour.

Anaheim

You can't really talk about Anaheim without mentioning Disneyland (p228) – but if that's all you talk about, you're missing out. Anaheim has grown into Orange County's largest city and, particularly in the last decade, has developed some surprising pockets of cool that have nothing to do with the Mouse House.

◎ SIGHTS

Center Street Anaheim
Area

(www.centerstreetanaheim.com; W Center St) This quietly splashy redeveloped neighborhood boasts a futuristic **ice rink** and a couple of

San Clemente

Anaheim Packing House

DAVID TONELSON/SHUTTERSTOCK ©

blocks packed with hipster-friendly shops selling everything from casual clothing and accessories to comic books. There's also food, including healthy junk at, um, **Healthy Junk** (☎714-772-5865; www.thehealthyjunk.com; 201 Center St Promenade; mains $9-14; ⊗10am-9pm; ☑).

⊗ EATING & DRINKING

Anaheim
Packing House   Food Hall $
(☎714-533-7225; www.anaheimpackingdistrict. com; 440 S Anaheim St; prices vary; ⊗opens 9am, closing hours vary; ℗) This 1919 former Sunkist orange packing house has a fabulous new life. Over 20 stalls and restaurants sell both sit-down and stroll-around eats and drinks: fish dinners to ramen, cocktails to shave ice, adventurous ice-cream pops to waffles. It's all airy and modern on the inside, with lots of spaces to hang out.

Umami Burger   Burgers $$
(☎714-991-8626; www.umamiburger.com; 338 S Anaheim Blvd; mains $10.50-17.50; ⊗11am-11pm

Sun-Thu, to midnight Fri & Sat; ℗) The Anaheim outpost of this LA-based minichain anchors the **Packing District** (www.anaheimpack ingdistrict.com; S Anaheim Blvd). Burgers span classic to truffled, Wagyu to vegan 'Impossible' patties. Try the Wag-yu-mami with miso-honey mustard, shredded cabbage, sesame yuzu and kimchi mayo, or the Beefy with beer cheddar and bacon lardons. Get 'em with decadent fries loaded with bacon and jalapeño ranch. The full bar dispenses milkshake cocktails.

Blind Rabbit   Cocktail Bar
(www.theblindrabbit.com; Anaheim Packing House, 440 S Anaheim Blvd; ⊗reservations 5-10:30pm Mon-Fri, from noon Sat & Sun) This chill, dimly lit, atmospheric speakeasy carves its own ice, makes its own juice, does regularly changing (but always creative) cocktails and has live music four nights a week. Reserve online (until 2pm on the same day) and they'll tell you where to show up. A dress code means no flip-flops, shorts or ball caps.

Anaheim Brewery
Brewery

(714-780-1888; www.anaheimbrew.com; 336 S Anaheim Blvd; ☺5-9pm Tue-Thu, to 11pm Fri, noon-11pm Sat, 1-7pm Sun) Anaheim Brewery dates back to 1870 (albeit with a 90-year break after Prohibition in 1920) and reopened in 2010. It serves surprisingly good brews at this simple tasting room in a renovated warehouse in the Packing District. Standouts include the Hefeweizen Red and Coast to Coast IPA with nice citrus notes. You can get food from Umami Burger next door.

Look for events like Wednesday trivia and occasional concerts.

ℹ INFORMATION

Visit Anaheim (855-405-5020; http://visit anaheim.org; 800 W Katella Ave, Anaheim Convention Center) Phone or go online for information.

ℹ GETTING THERE & AWAY

Anaheim's sparkling-new transit center, **ARTIC** (Anaheim Regional Transportation Intermodal Center; 2150 E Katella Ave, Anaheim), connects trains and buses from out of town with local transport. ARTIC is about 3 miles east of the Disney Resort area.

Greyhound (www.greyhound.com) has several daily buses between ARTIC and Downtown LA (from $6, 40 minutes) and San Diego (from $7, 2¼ hours).

Most international travelers arrive at Los Angeles International Airport (LAX) or San Diego (SAN), but for easy-in, easy-out domestic travel, nothing beats nearby **John Wayne Airport** (SNA; www.ocair.com; 18601 Airport Way, Santa Ana), served by all major US airlines and Canada's WestJet. The airport is about 14 miles south of Disneyland, near the junction of Hwy 55 and

 Old Towne Orange

The city of Orange, 7 miles southeast of Disneyland, retains its charming historical center, called Old Towne Orange. Visitors will find it well worth the detour for antiques and vintage clothing shops, smart restaurants and pure SoCal nostalgia.

Orange was originally laid out by Alfred Chapman and Andrew Glassell, who in 1869 received the 1-sq-mile piece of real estate in lieu of legal fees. Orange became California's only city laid out around a central plaza, a traffic circle where present-day Glassell St and Chapman Ave meet, and it remains pleasantly walkable today.

FELIPE SANCHEZ/SHUTTERSTOCK ©

I-405 (San Diego Fwy). Ride-hailing services cost about $20 each way to Anaheim.

Amtrak (www.amtrak.com) has almost a dozen daily trains to/from LA's Union Station ($15.60, 40 minutes) and San Diego ($30.45, 2¼ hours). Less frequent Metrolink (www.metrolink trains.com) commuter trains connect Anaheim to LA's Union Station ($8.75, 50 minutes), Orange ($2.50, six minutes), San Juan Capistrano ($8.50, 40 minutes) and San Clemente ($10, 50 minutes).

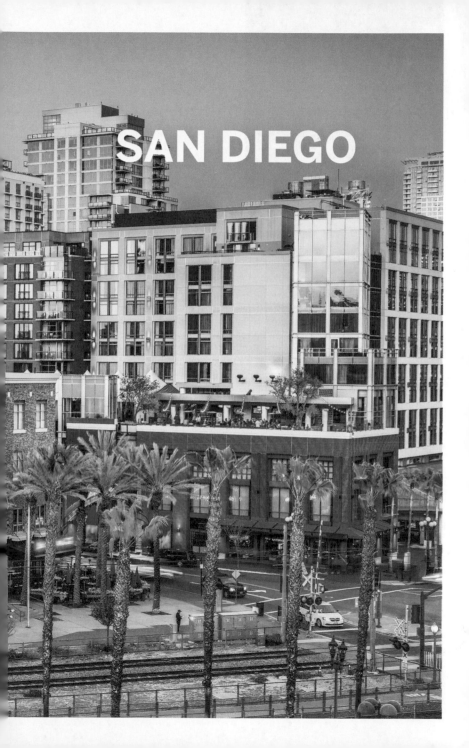

In this Chapter

San Diego

San Diego bursts with world-famous attractions for the entire family, including the zoo, Legoland and the museums of Balboa Park, plus a bubbling Downtown, beautiful hikes for all, more than 60 beaches and America's most perfect weather. Indeed, San Diego calls itself 'America's Finest City' and its breezy confidence filters down to folks you encounter every day on the street. It feels like a collection of villages each with their own personality, but it's the nation's eighth-largest city and we're hard-pressed to think of a place that's more laid-back.

San Diego in Two Days

Fill your belly (for the whole day) with breakfast at **Hash House a Go Go** (p262), then make tracks for Balboa Park and the **San Diego Zoo** (p253). If you manage to tear yourself away from the animals, check out the fascinating exhibits at the **San Diego Museum of Man** (p254). Spend day two rambling around the **Old Town San Diego State Historic Park** (p256) and hit **Prohibition Lounge** (p264) for some jazz in the evening.

San Diego in Four Days

Day three is beach day – head to **Mission and Pacific Beaches** (p256) for a spot of people-watching and be seduced by the sand till sunset. Back in town, seek out **Bang Bang** (p263) for tasty eats and delicious cocktails. If you've kids in tow, spend day four among the bricks at **Legoland** (p257). Otherwise, grab supplies from **Liberty Public Market** (p261), then get out of town and join the locals hiking **Los Penasquitos Canyon Trail** (p259).

Previous page: Gaslamp Quarter, Downtown San Diego
SEAN PAVONE/SHUTTERSTOCK ©

San Diego Map (p258)

Arriving in San Diego

San Diego International Airport Bus 992 (the Flyer, $2.50 one-way) operates at 15-minute intervals between the airport and Downtown most of the day, with stops along Broadway. The route takes roughly 15 minutes. A taxi to Downtown typically costs between $11 and $18 and takes 10 minutes.

Train Amtrak runs the *Pacific Surfliner* several times daily from Anaheim (2¼ hours), LA (three hours) and Santa Barbara (5¾ hours) into the historic Santa Fe Depot (p265).

Where to Stay

Downtown is San Diego's most convenient place to stay, for its wealth of restaurants and hotels and its easy access to transit. It's also a pricier area. Base yourself in San Diego's Old Town, and you may not need a car; many lodgings offer free airport shuttles and there are convenient transit links on the other side of the state park. Staying in Coronado Village puts you close to the beach, shops and restaurants.

Balboa Park Gardens

RON AND PATTY THOMAS/GETTY IMAGES ©

Balboa Park & San Diego Zoo

San Diego Zoo is a highlight of any trip to California and essential for first-time visitors. The zoo is at the heart of Balboa Park, a 1200-acre space with more than 16 museums and cultural institutions, and expansive gardens.

Great For...

☑ **Don't Miss**

The endangered red panda draws crowds in Panda Canyon.

Balboa Park History

Early plans for San Diego included a 1400-acre city park at the northeastern corner of what was to become Downtown, which at the time was all bare hilltops and deep arroyos. Enter Kate O Sessions, a UC Berkeley botany graduate who in 1892 started a nursery on the site to landscape fashionable gardens for the city's emerging elite. The city granted her 30 acres of land in return for planting 100 trees a year in the park and donating 300 more for placement throughout the city. By the early 20th century, Balboa Park had become a well-loved part of San Diego.

Balboa Park Gardens

Balboa Park includes a number of gardens, reflecting different horticultural styles and environments, including Alcazar Garden, a

Gerenuk, San Diego Zoo

DON HUTTER/500PX/GETTY IMAGES ©

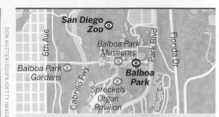

San Diego Zoo
6th Ave
Balboa Park Museums
Park Blvd
Florida Dr
Balboa Park Gardens
Cabrillo Fwy
Balboa Park
Spreckels Organ Pavilion

ⓘ Need to Know

Balboa Park Visitors Center (☏619-239-0512; www.balboapark.org; House of Hospitality, 1549 El Prado; ⏱9:30am-4:30pm)

✖ Take a Break

Get a civilized lunch, afternoon cocktails or appetizers in the bar at **Prado** (☏619-557-9441; www.pradobalboa.com; 1549 El Prado; mains lunch $10-19, dinner $24-37; ⏱11:30am-3pm Mon-Fri, 11am-3pm Sat & Sun, 5-9pm Tue-Sun).

★ Top Tip

Balboa Park is easily reached from Downtown on bus 7 along Park Blvd.

formal Spanish-style garden; Palm Canyon, with more than 50 species of palms; Japanese Friendship Garden; Australian Garden; Rose Garden; and Desert Garden. Florida Canyon gives an idea of the San Diego landscape before Spanish settlement.

San Diego Zoo

Located in the northern part of Balboa Park, this justifiably famous **zoo** (☏619-231-1515; https://zoo.sandiegozoo.org; 2920 Zoo Dr; day pass adult/child 3-11yr from $58/48, 2-visit pass zoo &/or safari park adult/child 3-11yr $92.80/82.80; ⏱9am-9pm mid-Jun–early Sep, to 5pm or 6pm rest of year; 🅿🚻) 🐾 is one of SoCal's biggest attractions. It hosts more than 4000 animals representing more than 650 species in a beautifully landscaped setting. Its sister park is San Diego Zoo Safari Park in northern San Diego County.

The zoo's bioclimatic environments include the Conrad Prebys Australian Outback exhibit, with the largest colony of koalas outside Australia, the 7.5-acre Elephant Odyssey and the Tiger Trail. Get a close-up view of polar bears swimming at the Northern Frontier and hippos grazing in the water through thick panes of glass on the Hippo Trail.

The Monkey Trail takes you on an elevated path into the tree canopy, where you can see capuchin, colobus and spot-nosed monkeys swinging around, while the large, impressive Scripps Aviary has well-placed feeders to allow some close-up viewing. Finally, don't miss Africa Rocks, an 8-acre exhibit for African plants and animals.

To get a grip on all of this, there's a guided double-decker bus tour that gives a good overview of the zoo, with informative commentary: sitting downstairs puts you closer to the animals. The Skyfari cable car goes right across the park and can save you some walking time, though there may be a line to get on it.

Key Balboa Park Museums

San Diego Museum of Man (☎619-239-2001; www.museumofman.org; Plaza de California, 1350 El Prado; adult/child under 5yr $13/free; ⊙10am-5pm; 👪) This anthropological museum is packed with exhibits spanning everything from ancient Egypt to local indigenous Kumeyaay people, beer and even monsters. The California Tower atop the building, with 360-degree views of the park, can be climbed for a separate fee (45-minute tours adult $23, child six to 17 years $20).

San Diego Museum of Art (SDMA; ☎619-232-7931; www.sdmart.org; 1450 El Prado; adult/student/child under 17yr $15/8/free; ⊙10am-5pm Mon, Tue, Thu & Sat, 10am-8pm Fri, noon-5pm Sun) Pride of place in SDMA's permanent collection goes to its Spanish old masters (El Greco,

Goya) and a respectable selection of works by other international heavy hitters from Matisse to Magritte and Cassatt to Rivera. American landscape paintings are another focus, and the Asian galleries have some eye-catchers.

Timken Museum of Art (☎619-239-5548; www.timkenmuseum.org; 1500 El Prado; ⊙10am-4:30pm Tue-Sat, from noon Sun) **FREE** Don't skip the Timken, home of a small but impressive collection of American and European paintings. It features works by Rembrandt and Rubens.

San Diego Natural History Museum (The Nat; ☎877-946-7797, 619-232-3821; www.sdnhm.org; 1788 El Prado; adult/child 3-17yr/under 2yr $19.95/11.95/free; ⊙10am-5pm; 👪)The 'Nat' houses 7.5 million specimens, including rocks, fossils and taxidermy animals, as well as an impressive dinosaur skeleton and a California fault-line exhibit, all in beautiful spaces.

Balboa Park Gardens (p252)

Fleet Science Center (🗗619-238-1233; www. rhfleet.org; 1875 El Prado; adult/child 3-12yr incl IMAX film $22/19, VR ride $8; ⏱10am-5pm Mon- Thu, 10am-6pm Fri-Sun; 👪) One of Balboa Park's most popular venues, this hands-on science museum features interactive displays and a toddler room. The biggest draw is the Giant Dome Theater, which screens several different films each day.

San Diego History Center (🗗619-232-6203; www.sandiegohistory.org; 1649 El Prado, Suite 3; $5 donation recommended; ⏱10am-5pm) **FREE** The San Diego Historical Society operates this center, with permanent and temporary exhibitions on city history.

San Diego Air & Space Museum (🗗619-234-8291; www.sandiegoairandspace.org; 2001 Pan American Plaza; adult/youth 3-11 yr/child under 2yr $20/11/free; ⏱10am-5pm, last entry 4:30pm; 👪) The round building at the southern end of the plaza houses an excellent museum with extensive displays of aircraft throughout history – originals, replicas, models – plus memorabilia from legendary aviators, including Charles Lindbergh and astronaut John Glenn.

Spreckels Organ Pavilion

Going south from Plaza de Panama, you can't miss this **pavilion** (🗗619-702-8138; http://spreckelsorgan.org; ⏱concerts 2-3pm Sun) **FREE**, with its circle of seating and curved colonnade, in front of the band shell housing the organ said to be the world's largest outdoor pipe organ. Donated by the Spreckels family of sugar fortune and fame, the pipe organ came with the stipulation that San Diego must always have an official organist. Make a point of attending the free concerts, held throughout the year at 2pm Sundays.

★ **Top Tip**

Free tours of Balboa Park depart from the visitor center on Tuesdays at 11am; see www.balboapark.org visitor-center-tours.

DANCESTROKES/SHUTTERSTOCK ©

ⓘ Need to Know

The multiday explorer pass (adult/child $103/68) covers admission to 16 of Balboa Park's museums and one day at the zoo; it's valid for seven days.

◎ SIGHTS

San Diego's Downtown is the region's main business, financial and convention district. Whatever intense urban energy Downtown generally lacks, it makes up for in spirited shopping, dining and nightlife in the historic Gaslamp Quarter, while the East Village and North Park are hipster havens. The waterfront Embarcadero is good for a stroll, and in the northwestern corner of Downtown vibrant Little Italy is full of good eats. Old Town is the seat of local history.

The city of Coronado – with its landmark **Hotel del Coronado** (☎619-435-6611, tours 619-522-8100; www.hoteldel.com; 1500 Orange Ave; tours $40; ⊙tours 10am daily plus 2pm Sat & Sun; P) FREE, built in 1888, and top-rated **beach** (opposite Hotel del Coronado; P♿) – sits across San Diego Bay from Downtown. At the entrance to the bay, Point Loma has sweeping views across sea and city from the Cabrillo National Monument (p260). The coast to the northwest, including Ocean, Mission and Pacific Beaches, epitomizes the SoCal beach scene.

Mission & Pacific Beach Boardwalks   Beach

(Parallel to Mission Blvd) FREE Central San Diego's best beach scene is concentrated in a narrow strip of land between the ocean and Mission Bay. There's great people-watching along the **Ocean Front Walk**, the boardwalk running from South Mission Beach Jetty to the Pacific Beach pier. It's crowded with joggers, in-line skaters and cyclists any time of the year. On warm summer weekends, the beaches are packed with oiled bodies frolicking in sand and sea.

Old Town San Diego State Historic Park   Historic Site

(☎619-220-5422; www.parks.ca.gov; 4002 Wallace St; ⊙visitor center & museums 10am-5pm May-Sep, 10am-4:30pm Oct-Apr; P♿) FREE On the site of San Diego's first European settlement, Old Town consists of a cluster of restored or rebuilt historic 19th-century buildings filled with quaint exhibits, souvenir stores and cafes. A good place to start is at the visitor center in 1853 **Robinson-Rose House**; see the neat model of the pueblo in 1872 and pick up a self-guided

Mission Beach Boardwalk

GREGOBAGEL/GETTY IMAGES ©

tour pamphlet (or download one for free at www.parks.ca.gov). Staff also run free guided walking tours daily at 11am and 2pm.

California Surf Museum   Museum

(☎760-721-6876; www.surfmuseum.org; 312 Pier View Way; adult/student/child under 12yr $5/3/free, 1st Tue of month $1; ◷10am-4pm Fri-Wed, 10am-8pm Thu; 🖈) It's easy to spend an hour in this heartfelt museum of surf artifacts, from a timeline of surfing history to surf-themed art and a radical collection of boards, including the one chomped by a shark when it ate the arm of surfer Bethany Hamilton. Exhibits change frequently; previous themes have included Women of Surfing, Adaptive Surfing and Surfers of the Vietnam War.

Maritime Museum   Museum

(☎619-234-9153; www.sdmaritime.org; 1492 N Harbor Dr; adult/child 3-12yr/child under 3yr $20/10/free; ◷9am-9pm late May-early Sep, 9am-8pm rest of year; 🖈) Next to the new Waterfront Park, this collection of 11 historic sailing ships, steam boats and submarines is easy to spot: just look for the 100ft-high masts of the iron-hulled square-rigger *Star of India,* a tall ship launched in 1863 to ply the England–India trade route. Also moored here is a replica of the *San Salvador* that brought explorer Juan Rodríguez Cabrillo to San Diego's shore in 1542. It's easy to spend hours looking at exhibits and clambering around vessels.

New Children's Museum   Museum

(☎619-233-8792; www.thinkplaycreate.org; 200 W Island Ave; admission $15.50, parking Mon-Thu $10, Fri-Sun $15; ◷10am-5pm Mon-Sat, 9:30am-4pm Sun; 🖈) This interactive children's museum offers endless activities for kids. Installations are designed by artists, so the future generation can learn the principles of movement and physics while simultaneously being exposed to art and working out the ants in their pants. Exhibits change every 18 months or so, so there's always something new. Workshops rotate daily and include clay and paint sessions.

Legoland
California Resort

This **amusement park** (☎760-203-3604, 888-690-5346; www.legoland.com/california; 1 Legoland Dr; adult/child 3-12yr from $101/95, parking $25; ◷10am-5pm; 🅿🖈) is a fantasy environment built largely of those wonderful little plastic blocks from Denmark. Many of the rides and attractions are targeted to elementary schoolers: a junior 'driving school,' a jungle cruise lined with Lego animals, and fairy-tale-, princess-, pirate-, adventurer- and dino-themed escapades. The whole family will probably get a kick out of Miniland USA, recreating the skylines of New York, San Francisco, Las Vegas and Washington, DC entirely of Lego blocks, alongside many world monuments.

From I-5, take the Legoland and Cannon Rd exit and follow the signage. Parking is $25.

USS Midway Museum   Museum

(☎619-544-9600; www.midway.org; 910 N Harbor Dr; adult/child 6-12yr/child under 6yr $26/12/free; ◷10am-5pm, last admission 4pm; 🅿🖈) The hulking aircraft carrier USS *Midway* was one of the navy's flagships from 1945 to 1991, last playing a combat role in the First Gulf War. On the flight deck, walk right up to some two dozen restored aircraft, including an F-14 Tomcat and F-4 Phantom jet fighter. Admission includes an audio tour along the narrow confines of the upper decks to the bridge, the admiral's

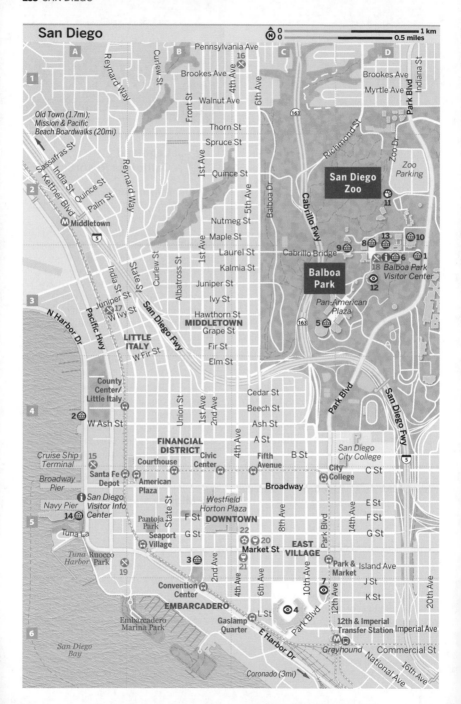

San Diego

Old Town (1.7mi);
Mission & Pacific
Beach Boardwalks (20mi)

Pennsylvania Ave

Brookes Ave

Walnut Ave

Thorn St

Spruce St

Quince St

Nutmeg St

Maple St

Laurel St

Kalmia St

Juniper St

Ivy St

Hawthorn St

Grape St

Fir St

Elm St

Cedar St

Beech St

Ash St

A St

B St

Broadway

Curlew St

Front St

4th Ave

6th Ave

1st Ave

5th Ave

Balboa Dr

Brookes Ave

Myrtle Ave

Indiana St

Park Blvd

Richmond St

Cabrillo Fwy

Zoo Dr

Zoo Parking

San Diego Zoo

Balboa Park

Cabrillo Bridge

Pan-American Plaza

Balboa Park Visitor Center

Reynard Way

Sassafras St

India St

Kettner Blvd

Quince St

Palm St

Middletown

Reynard Way

1st Ave

Curlew St

Albatross St

State St

India St

Juniper St

W Ivy St

Pacific Hwy

San Diego Fwy

N Harbor Dr

MIDDLETOWN

LITTLE ITALY

W Fir St

County Center/
Little Italy

W Ash St

Union St

1st Ave

2nd Ave

4th Ave

FINANCIAL DISTRICT

Courthouse

Civic Center

Fifth Avenue

San Diego City College

City College

C St

San Diego Fwy

Cruise Ship Terminal

Broadway Pier

Santa Fe Depot

American Plaza

State St

Westfield Horton Plaza

DOWNTOWN

8th Ave

E St

F St

14th Ave

G St

Navy Pier

San Diego Visitor Info Center

Pantoja Park

F St

Market St

EAST VILLAGE

Park & Market

Park Blvd

Island Ave

20th Ave

Tuna La

Seaport Village

2nd Ave

4th Ave

6th Ave

10th Ave

J St

Tuna Ruocco Harbor Park

Convention Center

EMBARCADERO

Gaslamp Quarter

L St

E Harbor Dr

K St

12th & Imperial Transfer Station

Imperial Ave

Embarcadero Marina Park

San Diego Bay

Greyhound

Commercial St

National Ave

16th Ave

Coronado (3mi)

San Diego

war room, and below deck to the sick bay, galley, laundry and engine room.

San Diego Main Library   Library

(☑619-236-5800; www.sandiego.gov/public-library; 330 Park Blvd; ⊙9:30am-7pm Mon-Thu, 9:30am-6pm Fri & Sat, noon-6pm Sun) FREE A couple of blocks east of **Petco Park** (☑619-795-5000; www.mlb.com/padres/ballpark/tours; 100 Park Blvd; tours adult/child under 13yr/senior $22/19/19; ⊙tours 10:30am, 12:30pm & 3pm; ♿), this city landmark is a beauty. Crowned by a steel-and-mesh dome, the futuristic, nine-story library features art-filled public spaces and plenty of learning opportunities – it has the second-largest collection of baseball memorabilia in the US. It's fully open to the public for a wander and you can even log on to the free wi-fi. The architect? Rob Wellington Quigley, who also designed the New Children's Museum (p257).

❸ ACTIVITIES

There are plenty of hikes in San Diego, but most outdoor activities involve the ocean. These waters are a dream for surfers, paddle boarders, kayakers and boaters.

Los Penasquitos Canyon Trail   Hiking

(☑county ranger 858-538-8066; www.sandiego.gov/park-and-recreation/parks/osp/lospenasquitos; entry via Park Village Rd & Celome Way; ⊙sunrise-sunset) FREE A 20-minute drive inland finds a series of wonderful, mostly flat, shady and sunny paths snaking through a lush valley and past a cascading waterfall surrounded by volcanic rock. The main 7-mile pathway is moderately trafficked with runners, walkers and mountain bikers. Look out for butterflies, mule deer and bobcats. Stay alert when exploring – rattlesnakes also favor these arid pathways. Download the very useful (and free!) Easy2Hike app before you set off, for maps and trail info.

Torrey Pines State Natural Reserve   Hiking

(☑858-755-2063; https://torreypines.org; 12600 North Torrey Pines Rd; ⊙visitor center 9am-6pm) FREE Walkers and hikers explore 8 miles of hillside sandy **trails** in a wilderness oasis of 2000 acres. Choose from routes of varying difficulties in this well-trodden coastal state park. The 0.7-mile Guy Fleming Trail has panoramic sea views and paths through wildflowers, ferns and cacti. Meanwhile, the 1.4-mile Razor Point Trail offers a good whale-spotting lookout during winter months.

Flora and fauna is abundant in this protected area. During quieter times, with fewer stomping feet, quiet walkers may spot raccoons, rabbits, bobcats, skunks and foxes among plenty of other types of wildlife. Parking $12 to $25 per vehicle (demand-based pricing).

 Whale-Watching in San Diego

Gray whales pass San Diego from mid-December to late February on their way south to Baja California, and again in mid-March on their way back up to Alaskan waters. Their 12,000-mile round-trip journey is the longest migration of any mammal on earth.

Cabrillo National Monument
(☑619-557-5450; www.nps.gov/cabr; 1800 Cabrillo Memorial Dr; per car/walk-in/motorcycle $20/10/15; ☺9am-5pm, tide pools to 4:30pm, bayside trail to 4pm; P⏵) ☞ is the best place to see the whales from land. Here you'll also find exhibits, whale-related ranger programs and a shelter from which to watch the whales breach (bring binoculars).

Half-day whale-watching boat trips are offered by most of the companies that run daily fishing trips, including **Seaforth Sportfishing** (☑619-224-3383; www.seaforthlanding.com; 1717 Quivira Rd, Mission Bay; half-day whale-watching trips $36-48; ☺shop 5am-6pm), whose half-day whale-watching trips cost $36 to $48 per person, depending on the day of the week (weekends are more expensive). Trips sometimes offer ticket refunds if you don't spot any whales; sightings are sometimes guaranteed.

SKODONNELL/GETTY IMAGES ©

San Diego-La Jolla Underwater Park
Snorkeling, Diving
(☑619-525-8213; 8302 Camino Del Oro) Some of California's best and most accessible diving is in this reserve, accessible from La Jolla Cove and La Jolla Shores. With an average depth of 20ft, the 6000 acres of look-but-don't-touch underwater real estate are great for snorkeling, too. Ever-present are the spectacular bright-orange garibaldi fish – California's official state fish and a protected species (there's a hefty fine for poaching one).

Further out you'll see forests of giant California kelp (which can increase its length by up to 3ft per day) and the 100ft-deep La Jolla Canyon. A number of commercial outfits conduct scuba-diving courses, sell or rent equipment, fill tanks, and conduct boat trips to nearby wrecks and islands.

🔒 SHOPPING

San Diego is chock-full of shops selling everything from local-pride souvenirs, Mexican gifts, adventure goods, beachwear and interesting antiques. Keep your eyes peeled in neighborhood streets for independent shops and boutiques trading in local wares. Farmers markets are also a big hit around town.

Pangaea Outpost
Fashion & Accessories
(☑858-224-3195; http://pangaeaoutpost.com; 909 Garnet Ave, Pacific Beach; ☺10am-7pm Sun-Thu, to 8pm Fri-Sat) Like a mini-world unto themselves, the 70-plus merchants here offer a supremely eclectic selection of clothing, jewelry, wraps, handbags and art from all around the world.

Adams Avenue
Antiques
There are fewer antique shops than there once were, but this street is still known as San Diego's 'antique row,' and features shops selling furniture, art and antiques from around the world. The road cuts across some of San Diego's less-visited neighborhoods. Take a rest from all the shopping at the Blind Lady Ale House (p263), serving pizzas and craft beers.

EATING

San Diego has a thriving dining culture, with an emphasis on Mexican, Californian and seafood. San Diegans eat dinner early, usually around 6pm or 7pm, and most restaurants are ready to close by 10pm. There's a burgeoning farm-to-table and gourmet scene all over the county.

Oscars Mexican Seafood   Mexican $

(☑858-488-6392; www.oscarsmexicanseafood. com; 703 Turquoise St; tacos/ceviche from $2.25/6.75) This phenomenal California-Mexican hole-in-the-wall joint is lauded by locals in the know. The perfectly tangy mixed fish and shrimp ceviche (served with fresh avocado and crispy tortillas) is probably the best we've ever tasted. The fish soup is also seriously good, and all heaped tacos are super fresh. Smother them with the punchy housemade green hot sauce. Chase with a craft soda.

Liberty Public Market   Market $

(☑619-487-9346; www.bluebridgehospitality. com; 2820 Historic Decatur Rd, Point Loma; dishes $5-20; ☉11am-9pm; P ⊛ ☑) The culinary heart of a 1920s-era naval training center turned artistic urban playground, this hip food hall presents around 30 local artisan vendors who sling everything from ramen and bulging tacos to lobster sandwiches, pasta and poke bowls. Pick your fave, then follow it up with craft beer or innovative cocktails in the bustling bar in the former mess hall.

You can easily spend a couple of hours wandering around and sampling the finest bites each has to offer. Core hours are 11am to 7pm but many vendors open earlier or stay open later.

Ocean Beach People's Market   Vegetarian $

(☑619-224-1387; www.obpeoplesfood.coop; 4765 Voltaire St; dishes around $8, salads per lb from $8.49; ☉8am-9pm; ☑) ✿ For strictly vegetarian groceries and fabulous prepared meals and salads north of central Ocean Beach, this organic cooperative does bulk foods and excellent (incredibly good-value) counter-service soups, sandwiches, salads and mains by weight. Order dishes such as cashew cranberry quinoa, vegan Greek salad or dhal curry and rice, plus tasty chocolate and coconut cookies to finish.

Liberty Public Market

USS Midway Museum (p257)

Hash House a Go Go   American $

(☑619-298-4646; www.hashhouseagogo.com; 3628 5th Ave, Hillcrest; mains $9-24; ⊗7:30am-2pm & 5:30-9pm Thu-Sun, 7:30am-2:30pm Mon-Wed) This buzzing bungalow, with its old-school dining room, busy bar and breezy patio, dishes up rib-sticking 'twisted farm food' straight from the American Midwest. Towering Benedicts, succulent sage-fried chicken, large-as-your-head pancake stacks and – wait for it – hash six different ways will keep you going for the better part of the day.

Other menu stars include a stuffed burger and an award-winning meatloaf sandwich.

Carnitas' Snack Shack   Californian, Mexican $

(☑619-696-7675; http://carnitassnackshack. com; 1004 N Harbor Dr; mains $8-13; ⊗11am-9pm Mon-Thu, 11am-10pm Fri, 9am-1pm Sat & Sun) Eat honestly priced, pork-inspired slow food on a cute outdoor patio on the Embarcadero. The tangy triple-threat pork sandwich comes with schnitzel, pepperoncini, pickle relish, shack aioli and a brioche bun. Wash

it down with local craft ales. Look out for regular events on the website, including pigs 'n' pups (for dog-lovers) and live music on Taco Tuesdays.

Puesto at the Headquarters   Mexican $$

(☑610-233-8880; www.eatpuesto.com; 789 W Harbor Dr; mains from $14; ⊗11am-10pm) In the old San Diego Police Headquarters, this vibrant eatery serves modern Mexican street food that will knock your *zapatos* off. Start with some creamy guacamole before moving on to innovative tacos, such as chicken in hibiscus-chipotle sauce with avocado and pineapple-habanero salsa in a blue-corn tortilla. Sit on the spacious patio or inside amid murals and floating potted plants.

Juniper & Ivy   Californian $$$

(☑619-269-9036; www.juniperandivy.com; 2228 Kettner Blvd; small plates $15-28, mains $20-48; ⊗5-10pm Sun-Thu, 5-11pm Fri & Sat) Spearheading a crop of Little Italy fine-dining restaurants, J&I is the collaboration of owner Michael Rosen and star chef Richard

Blais, who performs culinary sorcery with whatever is fresh, in season and locally available. While the menu is always in flux, the sharing concept and creative dishes are constants. It's all beautifully presented in the spacious setting of an open-beamed warehouse.

Reserve in advance, or try for a seat at the bar (great cocktails, too).

🍸 DRINKING & NIGHTLIFE

Coin-Op Game Room   Bar
(☎619-255-8523; www.coinopsd.com; 3926 30th St, North Park; ⊙4pm-2am Mon-Fri, noon-2am Sat & Sun) Dozens of classic arcade games on rotation – from pinball and Mortal Kombat, Pac-Man and Big Buck Safari to Beer Pong Master – line the walls of this hipster bar in North Park. All the better to quaff craft beers and cocktails like the Rum DMC (white rum, Averna, allspice and lemon) and chow on truffle-parm tots, fried pickle spears and fried Oreos.

Polite Provisions   Cocktail Bar
(☎619-677-3784; www.politeprovisions.com; 4696 30th St, North Park; ⊙3pm-2am Mon-Thu, 11:30am-2am Fri-Sun) With a French-bistro feel and plenty of old-world charm, Polite Provisions' hip clientele sip cocktails at the marble bar, under a glass ceiling, and in a beautifully designed space, complete with a vintage cash register, wood-paneled walls and tiled floors. Many cocktail ingredients, syrups, sodas and infusions are homemade and displayed in apothecary-esque bottles.

Grass Skirt   Cocktail Bar
(☎858-412-5237; http://thegrassskirt.com; 910 Grand Ave; ⊙5pm-2am Mon-Sat, 11am-2am Sun) Through a secret doorway, disguised as a refrigerator in the next-door **Good Time Poke** cafe, you'll step into a lost Hawaiian world with Polynesian wood carvings, thatched verandahs, fire features and tiki-girl figurines made into lamps. Sip your daiquiri or mai tai and wait for more surprises to come...listen out for immersive weather sounds and lighting effects.

 Traveling Over the Border to Tijuana

A passport is required to cross the border, and to re-enter the United States. By public transportation from San Diego, the San Diego Trolley runs from Downtown to **San Ysidro border crossing** (☎619-690-8900; www.cbp.gov/contact/ports/san-ysidro-class; 720 E San Ysidro Blvd; ⊙24hr). By car, take I-5 south and look for either signs to Mexico or for the last US exit, where you can park at one of the many lots in the area (from $10 for five hours, from $20 for 24 hours). To cross the border on foot, follow the signs to Mexico, and a turnstile, which you walk through into Mexico. Then follow signs reading 'Centro Downtown.'

San Ysidro border crossing
4KCLIPS/SHUTTERSTOCK ©

Blind Lady Ale House   Pub
(☎619-225-2491; https://blindladyalehouse.com; 3416 Adams Ave; ⊙5pm-midnight Mon-Thu, from 11:30am Fri-Sun) A superb neighborhood pub, with creative decor like beer cans piled floor to ceiling and longboard skateboards attached to the walls. It sells craft ales on the pump and prepares fresh pizza (from $9). Vegetarians should try the meat-free Mondays offering pies with inventive flavors.

Bang Bang   Club
(☎619-677-2264; www.bangbangsd.com; 526 Market St; cover $10-30; ⊙5pm-midnight Wed, Thu & Sun, 5pm-2am Fri & Sat) This Gaslamp hot spot serves sushi and Asian bites five nights a week and turns into a steamy

From left: San Diego-La Jolla Underwater Park (p260); Torrey Pines State Natural Reserve (p259); San Diego skyline

dance club (EDM, minimal, deep house) on Fridays and Saturdays. Enter via a tiled Tokyo subway-style staircase to mingle with shiny happy people below a giant disco ball or share a giant punch bowl with your posse. Cocktails $15.

⭐ ENTERTAINMENT

Check out the San Diego *City Beat* or *San Diego Union Tribune* for the latest movies, theater, galleries and music gigs around town.

Prohibition Lounge   Cocktail Bar

(☑619-501-1919; http://prohibitionsd.com; 548 5th Ave; ⊘8pm-1:30am Tue-Sun) Find the unassuming doorway on 5th Ave with 'Eddie O'Hare's Law Office' on it, then flip the light switch on to alert the door staff, who'll guide you into a sensuously lit basement exuding a 1920s Prohibition vibe. Enjoy live jazz and blues while sipping innovative craft cocktails. Dress nicely and keep that cell phone off.

Shout House   Live Music

(☑619-231-6700; www.facebook.com/The ShoutHouseSanDiego; 655 4th Ave; Mon-Wed free, Thu & Sun after 8pm $5, Fri $10, Sat $12; ⊘7pm-late Sun-Thu, 6pm-late Fri & Sat) Good, clean fun at this cavernous Gaslamp bar with dueling pianos. Talented players have an amazing repertoire, including classics, rock and more. We once heard a dirty version of 'Part of Your World' from *The Little Mermaid* (OK, maybe the fun's not so clean). The lively crowd ranges from college age to conventioneers. Requests encouraged.

ℹ️ INFORMATION

DISCOUNT CARDS

The Go San Diego card offers up to 55% off big-ticket attractions. The three-day pass (adult/child $207/189) includes one premium attraction (SeaWorld), plus San Diego Zoo, Legoland and many of Balboa Park's museums.

TOURIST INFORMATION

San Diego Visitor Info Center (☑619-236-1242; www.sandiegovisit.org; 996 N Harbor Dr; ⊙9am-4pm) Pick up local info, maps and tickets at the tourist office.

ⓘ GETTING THERE & AWAY

Most flights to **San Diego International Airport** (SAN; ☑619-400-2400; www.san.org; 3325 N Harbor Dr; 🛜) are domestic. The airfield sits just 3 miles west of Downtown.

Allow at least two hours to drive the 125 miles between San Diego and LA in nonpeak traffic. With traffic, it's anybody's guess. If there are two or more passengers in your car, you can use the high-occupancy vehicle lanes, which will shave off a fair amount of time in heavy traffic.

Amtrak runs the *Pacific Surfliner* several times daily between Anaheim, Los Angeles, Santa Barbara and the historic **Santa Fe Depot** (Amtrak Station; ☑800-872-7245; www.amtrak. com; 1050 Kettner Blvd), built in 1915 for the Panama-California Exposition. Within San Diego County, *Surfliner* trains also stop in Solana Beach, Oceanside, San Clemente and San Juan

Capistrano. Fares start from around $31 and the coastal views are glorious.

Greyhound (☑619-515-1100; www.greyhound. com; 1313 National Ave; ⊙5am-11:45pm; 🛜) serves San Diego from cities across North America from its Downtown location.

ⓘ GETTING AROUND

While most people get around San Diego by car, it's possible to have an entire vacation here using municipal buses and trolleys run by the Metropolitan Transit System, and your own two feet. The **MTS Transit Store** (☑619-234-1060; www. sdmts.com; 1255 Imperial Ave; one-way adult/child $2.50/1.25; ⊙8am-5pm Mon-Fri) is a one-stop shop for route maps, tickets and Compass Cards – there's an initial fee of $2, then $6 for day passes for regional MTS trolleys and buses or $15 for day passes including regional Coaster services. There's also a new Compass Cloud mobile ticketing app for easy online purchases and tickets delivered right to your phone. Same-day passes are available from bus drivers. At trolley stations, purchase tickets from vending machines.

View from Zabriskie Point

Death Valley National Park

The name evokes all that is harsh, hot and hellish, but don't be fooled: Death Valley delivers a spectacular mosaic of sensuous sand dunes, water-sculpted canyons, volcanic craters, palm-shaded oases and plenty of endemic wildlife.

Death Valley holds the US records for hottest temperature (134°F/57°C), lowest point (Badwater, 282ft below sea level) and largest national park outside Alaska (more than 5300 sq miles). Furnace Creek is its commercial hub, home to the visitor center, gas station, ATM, post office, lodging and restaurants.

Zabriskie Point

Early morning is the best time to visit Zabriskie Point for spectacular views across ethereally glowing, golden badlands eroded into waves, pleats and gullies.

Dante's View

At 5475ft, the view of the entire southern Death Valley basin from the top of the Black Mountains is absolutely brilliant, especially at sunrise or sunset.

Great For...

☑ **Don't Miss**

Sunrise at Zabriskie Point where the cover of U2's *Joshua Tree* album was shot.

❶ Need to Know

☎760-786-3200; www.nps.gov/deva; 7-day-pass per car $30; 🅿️ 🚻 ♿

✗ Take a Break

The lounge at the **Inn at Death Valley** (www.oasisatdeathvalley.com) is perfect for sunset cocktails and nibbles.

★ Top Tip

Watch the *Seeing Death Valley* movie at the **Furnace Creek Visitor Center** (⊙8am-5pm 📶).

Badwater Basin

The lowest point in North America (282ft below sea level) is a hauntingly beautiful landscape of crinkly salt flats. A boardwalk takes you out over this constantly evaporating bed of salty, mineralized water.

Mesquite Flat Sand Dunes

This gracefully undulating sea of sand rises up to 100ft high and is at its photogenic best at sunrise or sunset, when bathed in soft light and accented by long, deep shadows.

Artists Drive & Palette

The 9-mile, one-way **Artists Drive** (☎760-786-3200; www.nps.gov/deva; Badwater Rd) delivers 'wow' moments around every turn. About 5 miles in, you'll pass the Artists Palette, where oxidized metals tinge the mountains into hues from rose to green and purple; view them at their luminous best right before sunset.

Titus Canyon Road

Check road conditions at the visitor center before tackling grandiose but tricky Titus Canyon Rd by vehicle or mountain bike. For a rough 27 miles, it climbs, dips and winds to a crest in the Grapevine Mountains, then descends back to the desert floor past a ghost town, petroglyphs and canyon narrows.

Ubehebe Crater

An impressive geological feature in the northern park, 600ft-deep Ubehebe Crater is believed to have formed some 2100 years ago in a single eruptive event by the meeting of fiery magma and cool groundwater. Its martian beauty is easily appreciated from the parking lot, but for closer inspection embark on the 1.5-mile trek along the rim (not recommended if vertigo-prone).

Hiking

The best time for hiking is November to March. Stay off the trail in summer, except on higher-elevation mountain trails, which are usually snowed in during winter. Constructed paths are rare and all but the easiest hikes may require some scrambling or bouldering. An adequate water supply is essential; one gallon per day per person in summer and half a gallon in winter are recommended.

Golden Canyon

Don't miss a spin around this winding wonderland of golden canyons between Badwater Rd and Zabriskie Point. The most popular route is a 3-mile in-and-back trek from the main trailhead off Badwater Rd to the oxidized iron cliffs of Red Cathedral.

Mosaic Canyon

A 2.3-mile gravel road deadends at the mouth of Mosaic Canyon, from where a 4-mile in-and-out trail meanders past polished marble walls carved from 750-million-year-old rocks.

Telescope Peak

Views from the park's highest summit – Telescope Peak (11,049ft) – plummet all the way to the desert floor. The 14-mile round-trip trail clocks a 3000ft elevation gain from the Mahogany Flat campground. Summiting in winter requires an ice-axe, crampons and winter-hiking experience. By June, the trail is usually free of snow.

Eating

There are restaurants as well as stores for stocking up on basic groceries and camp-

Badwater Basin (p267)

ing supplies in Furnace Creek, Stovepipe
Wells Village and Panamint Springs.

Inn Dining Room

This formal **restaurant** (☏760-786-2345;
www.oasisatdeathvalley.com; Inn at Furnace
Creek, Hwy 190; breakfast $15-21, mains lunch
$14-28, dinner $32-71; ◷7-10:30am, 11:30am-
2:30pm year-round, 5-9pm Oct-Apr, 6-10pm May-
Sep; P❄🛜) delivers continental cuisine with
stellar views of the Panamint Mountains.
Reservations are key for dinner, when a 'no
shorts or tank tops' policy kicks in.

★ **Top Tip**

(Expensive) gas is available 24/7 at Furnace Creek and Stovepipe Wells Village,
and from 7am to 9:30pm in Panamint
Springs.

MICHAEL VER SPRILL/GETTY IMAGES ©

Last Kind Words Saloon

The menu is meat-centric Americana, from
chili and burgers to steaks and ribs, at this
high-ceilinged **dining den** (☏760-786-3335;
www.oasisatdeathvalley.com; Town Sq, Ranch
at Furnace Creek; mains lunch $19-25, dinner
$24-105; P❄🛜) with Disney-esque Wild West
decor. It's at the Ranch at Death Valley in
Furnace Creek.

Toll Road Restaurant

Above-par cowboy cooking happens at
this **ranch house** (☏760-786-7090; www.
deathvalleyhotels.com; 51880 Hwy 190, Stovepipe
Wells Village; mains $12.50-31; ◷7-10am &
5:30-9pm; P❄) in Stovepipe Wells. Many
of the mostly meaty mains are made with
local ingredients, such as mesquite honey,
prickly pear and piñons.

Sleeping

Camping is plentiful but if you're looking
for a place with a solid roof, in-park options
are limited, pricey and often fully booked
in springtime. Alternative bases are the
gateway towns of Beatty (40 miles from
Furnace Creek), Lone Pine (40 miles),
Death Valley Junction (30 miles), Shoshone
(60 miles) and Tecopa (70 miles). Options
a bit further afield include Ridgecrest (120
miles) and Las Vegas (140 miles).

Getting There & Away

The park's main roads (Hwys 178 and
190) are paved and in great shape, but
if your travel plans include dirt roads, a
high-clearance vehicle and off-road tires
are highly recommended and essential on
many routes. 4WD is often necessary after
rains. Always check with the visitor center
for current road conditions, especially
before heading to remote areas.

✕ **Take a Break**

Try a Timbisha Taco, made with fry
bread instead of a tortilla, by the local
Timbisha Shoshone tribe in Indian
Village behind Furnace Creek.

Aerial view of Lombard Street, San Francisco (p57)

In Focus

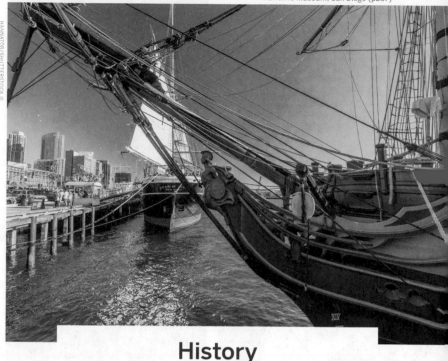

Maritime Museum, San Diego (p257)

History

Native American nations called this land home for millennia before the Europeans arrived. Spanish conquistadors and priests sought gold and god, but soon relinquished their flea-plagued missions to Mexico. The unruly territory was handed off to the US mere months before gold was discovered in 1848. Generations of dreamers continue to make the trek for gold, glory and self-determination.

13,000–6000 BCE
Native communities settle this land, from Yurok redwood houses in the north to Kumeyaay thatch-domed dwellings in the south.

1542–43 CE
Portuguese navigator Juan Rodríguez Cabrillo and his Spanish crew are among the first Europeans to sail California's coast.

1769
Franciscan friar Junípero Serra and Captain Gaspar de Portolá lead an expedition to establish missions.

Mission San Diego de Alcalá (p274)

NAGEL PHOTOGRAPHY/SHUTTERSTOCK ©

Native Californians

Humans were settling California as early as 19,000 years ago, leaving behind traces of early California cuisine in large middens of seashells along the beaches and campfire sites on the Channel Islands.

Native Californians spoke at least 100 distinct languages, and passed knowledge of hunting grounds and turf boundaries from generation to generation in song. Northern coastal fishing communities such as the Ohlone, Miwok and Pomo built subterranean roundhouses and sweat lodges, where they held ceremonies and told stories. Northern hunting communities, including the Hupa, Karok and Wiyot, constructed big houses and redwood dugout canoes, while the Modoc lived in summer tipis and winter dugouts – but all their paths converged during California's seasonal salmon runs. Kumeyaay and Chumash villages dotted the central coast, where they fished and paddled canoes as far out into the Pacific as the Channel Islands. Southern Mojave, Yuma and Cahuilla nations made sophisticated pottery and developed irrigation systems for farming in the desert.

1781	1821	1835
Spanish governor Felipe de Neve and a tiny band of settlers set down stakes at the future Los Angeles.	Mexican independence ends Spanish colonization of California. Mexico inherits 21 missions.	An emissary of Andrew Jackson·offers to buy Alta California, but Mexico tries to unsuccessfully sell it to Britain instead.

Old Mission Santa Barbara (p160)

BILL PERRY/SHUTTERSTOCK ©

★ Best Historical Sites

Autry Museum of the American West (p197), Los Angeles

Old Mission Santa Barbara (p160)

Maritime National Historical Park (p52), San Francisco

La Brea Tar Pits & Museum (p209), Los Angeles

When English sea captain Sir Francis Drake harbored briefly on Miwok land north of San Francisco in 1579, the English were taken to be the dead returned from the afterworld, and shamans saw the arrival as a warning of apocalypse. The omens weren't far wrong: within a century of the arrival of Spanish colonists in 1769, California's indigenous population would plunge by between 80% and 90%, falling to just 20,000 due to foreign diseases, conscripted labor, violence, marginalization and hunger in their own fertile lands.

The Spanish Mission Period

In the 18th century, when Russian and English trappers began trading valuable pelts from Alta California, Spain concocted a plan for colonization. For the glory of God and the tax coffers of Spain, missions would be built across California. According to plan, these missions would be going concerns run by local converts within 10 years. This venture was approved by quixotic Spanish colonial official José de Gálvez of Mexico, who was known for wild schemes.

Almost immediately after Spain's missionizing plan was approved in 1769, it began to fail. When Franciscan friar Junípero Serra and Captain Gaspar de Portolá made the overland journey to establish **Mission San Diego de Alcalá** in 1769, only half the sailors on their supply ships survived. Portolá had heard of a fabled cove to the north, but failing to recognize Monterey Bay in the fog, he gave up and turned back.

Portolá reported to Gálvez that if the Russians or English wanted California, they were welcome to it. But Serra wouldn't give up, and secured support to set up presidios (forts) alongside missions. In exchange for their forced labor, Native Californians were promised one meal a day and a place in God's kingdom – which came much sooner than expected, due to diseases such as smallpox and syphilis that the Spanish introduced.

California's indigenous nations often rebelled against the Spanish colonists, and the missions barely managed to become self-sufficient. Spanish colonists gave up, other foreigners moved in, and more Native Californians died than were converted.

1848

Gold is discovered near Placerville by mill employees, a San Francisco tabloid spreads the news and the gold rush is on.

1850

With hopes of solid-gold tax revenues, the US declares California the 31st state.

1869

On May 10 the 'golden spike' is nailed in place at Promontory, Utah, completing the first transcontinental railroad.

California Under Mexican Rule

Spain wasn't sorry to lose California to Mexico in the 1810–21 Mexican War of Independence – and Californian settlers known as *rancheros* (ranchers) saw an opportunity. The Spanish, Mexican and American ranchers who had intermarried with Native Californians had become a sizable constituency known as 'Californios,' but the best grazing land was still reserved for the missions. So in 1834 Californios convinced Mexico to secularize the missions.

Californios quickly snapped up deeds to privatized mission property, and capitalized on the growing market for cowhides and tallow (a key ingredient in soap). Only a few dozen Californios were literate in the entire state, so boundary disputes were settled with muscle, not paper. By law, half the lands were supposed to go to Native Californians who worked at the missions, but few actually received their entitlements.

Through marriage and other mergers, most of the land and wealth in California was held by just 46 *ranchero* families by 1846. The average *rancho* (ranch) was now 16,000 acres, having grown from cramped shanties to elegant haciendas where women were ordered to stay confined to quarters at night. But *rancheras* (ranch women) weren't so easily bossed around: women owned some Californian ranches, rode horses as hard as men and caused romantic scandals worthy of modern *telenovelas* (soap operas).

Still, the US saw potential in California. When US president Andrew Jackson offered the financially strapped Mexican government $500,000 for the territory in 1835, the offer was tersely rejected. The Mexican–American War was declared in 1846, lasting two years with very little fighting in California. Hostilities ended with the Treaty of Guadalupe Hidalgo, in which Mexico ceded much of its northern territory (including Alta California) to the US. Just a few weeks after the US took possession of California, gold was discovered.

Fierce Queen Calafía, California's Namesake

Have you heard the one about the sunny island of Amazon women armed with gold weapons, who flew griffins fed with their own sons? This isn't a twisted *Wonder Woman* remake. It's the plot of Garci Rodríguez de Montalvo's 16th-century novel *Las Sergas de Esplandían* – the legend that inspired explorer Hernán Cortés, who claimed in a 1524 letter that he hoped to find the island northwest of Mexico.

Montalvo and Cortés weren't entirely wrong. Across the water from mainland Mexico was a peninsula Spanish colonists called Baja (Lower) California after Queen Calafía, Montalvo's legendary queen of the Amazons. Above it was Alta (Upper) California, where gold was discovered 50 years after the Spaniards quit their search.

1882

The US Chinese Exclusion Act suspends new immigration from China and denies citizenship to those already in the country.

1906

An earthquake levels entire blocks of San Francisco in 42 seconds, setting off fires that rage for three days.

1928

The Jazz Singer premieres – as the first feature-length 'talkie' movie, it kicks off Hollywood's Golden Age.

The Gold Rush

The gold-rush era in California began with a bluff. Real-estate speculator, lapsed Mormon and wily tabloid publisher Sam Brannan was looking to unload some California swampland in 1848 when he heard rumors of gold flakes found near Sutter's Mill in the Sierra Nevada foothills. Figuring this news should sell some newspapers and raise real-estate values, Brannan published the rumor as fact.

At first Brannan's story didn't generate much excitement – gold flake had surfaced in southern California as far back as 1775. So he ran another story, this time verified by Mormon employees at Sutter's Mill who had sworn him to secrecy. Brannan kept his word until he reached San Francisco, where he legendarily ran through Portsmouth Sq brandishing gold entrusted to him as tithes for the Mormon church, shouting, 'Gold on the American River!'

Other newspapers around the world weren't scrupulous about the facts either, hastily publishing stories of gold near San Francisco. By 1850 – the year California was fast-tracked for admission as the 31st US state – California's non-native population had ballooned from 15,000 to 93,000.

With each wave of new arrivals, profits dropped and gold became harder to find. In 1848 each prospector earned an average of about $300,000 in today's terms. By 1849 earnings were less than half that, and by 1865 they had dipped to $35,000. When surface gold became scarce, miners picked, shoveled and dynamited through mountains. The work was grueling and dangerous and, with few doctors around, injuries often proved lethal. The cost of living in cold, filthy mining camps was sky-high – and with only one woman for every 400 men in some camps, many turned to paid company, booze and opium for consolation.

Vigilantes, Robber Barons & Railroads

Gold prospectors who did best arrived early and got out quick, while those who stayed too long either lost fortunes searching for the next nugget or became targets of resentment. Native Californian laborers who helped miners strike it rich were denied the right to hold claims. Successful Peruvians and Chileans were harassed and denied renewals to their mining claims, and most left California by 1855. The 'Chilecito' neighborhood they established in San Francisco is now called Jackson Sq, but you can still order the drink these early settlers brought to San Francisco circa 1848: Pisco punch.

As mining became industrialized, fewer miners were needed. Jobless prospectors turned their anger toward Chinese workers. Frozen out of mining claims, many Chinese opened service-based businesses that survived when mining ventures went bust. By 1860 enough Chinese pioneers had endured to become the second-most populous group in California after Mexicans, but this hard-won resilience met with irrational resentment. Discriminatory Californian laws restricting housing, employment and citizenship for anyone

1942
Executive Order 9066 sends nearly 120,000 Japanese Americans to internment camps.

1955
Disneyland opens in Anaheim on July 17. As crowds swarm the park, plumbing breaks and Fantasyland springs a gas leak.

1965
The National Guard suppresses the Watts civil unrest in LA. Six days of clashes result in death and $40 million in damage.

born in China were passed and extended with the 1882 US Chinese Exclusion Act, which remained law until 1943.

Inter-ethnic rivalries obscured the real competitive threat posed not by fellow workers, but by those who controlled the means of production: California's 'robber barons.' These Californian speculators hoarded the capital and industrial machinery necessary for deep-mining operations. Laws limiting work options for Chinese arrivals served the needs of robber barons, who needed cheap labor to build railroads to their mining claims and East Coast markets.

To blast tunnels through the Sierra Nevada, workers were lowered down sheer mountain faces in wicker baskets, planted lit dynamite sticks in rock crevices then urgently tugged the rope to be hoisted out of harm's way. With little other choice of legitimate employment, an estimated 12,000 Chinese laborers blasted through the Sierra Nevada, meeting the westbound end of the transcontinental railroad in 1869.

The Bear Flag Republic

In June 1846, American settlers tanked up on liquid courage declared independence in the northern town of Sonoma. Not a shot was fired – instead, they captured the nearest Mexican official and hoisted a hastily made flag. Locals awoke to discover they were living in the independent 'Bear Republic,' under a flag painted with a grizzly that looked like a drunken dog. The Bear Flag Republic lasted only a month before US orders telling settlers to stand down arrived.

Oil & Water

During the US Civil War (1861–65), California couldn't count on food shipments from the East Coast, and started growing its own. California recruited Midwestern homesteaders to farm the Central Valley with shameless propaganda. The hype worked: more than 120,000 homesteaders came to California in the 1870s and '80s.

These homesteaders soon discovered that California's gold rush had left the state badly tarnished. Hills were stripped bare, vegetation wiped out, streams silted up and mercury washed into water supplies. Cholera spread through open sewers of poorly drained camps, claiming many lives. Smaller mineral finds in Southern California mountains diverted streams, turning the green valleys below into deserts. Recognizing at last that water, not gold, was the state's most precious resource, Californians passed a pioneering law preventing dumping into rivers in 1884.

With the support of budding agribusiness and real-estate concerns, Southern Californians passed bond measures to build aqueducts and dams that enabled large-scale farming and real-estate development. By the 20th century, the lower one-third of the state claimed two-thirds of available water supplies, inspiring Northern California's calls for secession.

1966	**1967**	**1968**
Ronald Reagan is elected governor of California, setting a career precedent for fading entertainment figures.	The Summer of Love kicks off in Golden Gate Park, where draft cards are used as rolling papers.	Presidential candidate and civil rights ally Robert Kennedy is fatally shot in Los Angeles.

★ **Best for California History**

Slouching Towards Bethlehem (Joan Didion; 1968)

Alice: Memoirs of a Barbary Coast Prostitute (Ivy Anderson and Devon Angus; 2016)

California: A History (Kevin Starr; 1980)

The banner of the Bear Flag Republic (p277)

CALIFORNIA REPUBLIC

While pastoral Southern California was urbanizing, Northern Californians who had witnessed mining and logging devastation firsthand were jump-starting the nation's first conservation movement. Scottish immigrant John Muir moved to San Francisco to make his living, but found his true calling as a naturalist on a week-long trip to the Yosemite Valley. Muir founded the Sierra Club in 1892 and devoted his life to defending Yosemite and vast tracts of California's wilderness against the encroachments of dams and pipelines to urban centers.

Reforming the Wild West

When a massive earthquake struck San Francisco in 1906, it unearthed a terrible truth. The earthquake sparked fires across town, but there was no water to put them out. In a city surrounded by water on three sides, there were only two functioning water mains: a fountain donated by opera star Lotta Crabtree at Market and Kearny Sts, and a Mission hydrant atop Dolores Park (still painted gold today, in honor of its service). For three days, fires swept across the city. When the smoke lifted, one thing was clear from this unnatural disaster: it was time for the Wild West to change its ways.

While San Francisco was rebuilt at a rate of 15 buildings a day, political reformers set to work on city, state and national policies, one plank at a time. Californians concerned about public health and the trafficking of women pushed for the passage of the 1914 Red Light Abatement Act, which shut down brothels statewide.

California's Civil Rights Movement

Before the 1963 march on Washington, DC, the civil rights movement was well under way in California. When almost 120,000 Japanese Americans living along the West Coast were ordered into internment camps by President Roosevelt in 1942, the Japanese American Citizens League immediately filed suits that advanced all the way to the US Supreme Court. These lawsuits established groundbreaking civil rights legal precedents, and in 1992

1969

Native American activists symbolically reclaim Alcatraz until ousted by the FBI in 1971.

1977

San Francisco Supervisor Harvey Milk becomes the first openly gay man elected to public office in California.

1989

The Loma Prieta Earthquake collapses a two-level section of Interstate 880 and results in 63 deaths and 4000 injuries.

internees received reparations and an official letter of apology signed by President George HW Bush.

Adopting the nonviolent resistance practices of Mahatma Gandhi and Martin Luther King Jr, labor leaders César Chávez and Dolores Huerta formed United Farm Workers in 1962 to champion the rights of immigrant laborers. Four years later Chávez and Californian grape pickers marched on Sacramento, bringing the issue of fair wages and the health risks of pesticides to the nation's attention. When Bobby Kennedy was sent to investigate, he sided with Chávez, bringing Latinos into the US political fold.

California was again on the front lines during the fight for marriage equality. In open defiance of the 1996 US Defense of Marriage Act (DOMA) that defined marriage as between opposite-sex partners, the San Francisco mayor Gavin Newsom (and future California governor) began issuing marriage certificates to same-sex couples in 2004. Court cases were appealed all the way to the Supreme Court, where the court found in favor of the California couples, and marriage equality became the law of the land nationwide.

Today civil rights remains top of mind in California, where immigrants and first-generation Americans represent over half the population – yet Immigration and Customs Enforcement (ICE) raids, border camps, and other federal initiatives treat neighbors as criminals. Some California cities refuse to cooperate, citing long-standing sanctuary laws including Berkeley's trailblazing 1971 sanctuary resolution and San Francisco's 1989 city-wide sanctuary law (the world's first). Under sanctuary laws, police stations, schools and hospitals don't have to assist federal authorities in deporting undocumented Californians who aren't charged with any crime. Despite threats by the Trump administration in 2017 to withhold federal funds, San Francisco and Berkeley reaffirmed their sanctuary policies – and California state legislators responded by declaring all of California a sanctuary state.

Hollywood & California Counterculture

By the 1920s California's greatest export was the sunny, wholesome image it projected to the world through its homegrown film and TV industry. With consistent sunlight and versatile locations, Southern California proved to be an ideal movie location. Early in its career, SoCal was a stand-in for more exotic locales, and got dressed up for period-piece productions such as Charlie Chaplin's *Gold Rush* (1925). But with its beach sunsets and palm-lined drives, California soon stole the scene in Technicolor movies and iconic TV shows. California shed its bad-boy Wild West reputation to become a movie star, dominating the screen behind squeaky-clean beach boys and bikini-clad blondes.

But Northern Californians didn't picture themselves as extras in *Beach Blanket Bingo* (1965). The Navy discharged WWII sailors for insubordination and homosexuality in San Francisco, as though that would teach them a lesson. Instead they found themselves at home in North Beach's jazz clubs, bohemian coffeehouses and City Lights Books.

The final button of convention was popped not by San Francisco artists, but by the CIA. To test psychoactive drugs intended to create the ultimate soldier, the CIA gave LSD

1992	**1994**	**2003**
Four white police officers charged with assaulting Rodney King are acquitted, sparking violent clashes with police in Los Angeles.	The 6.7-magnitude Northridge earthquake strikes LA on January 17, killing 72 and causing $20 billion in property damage.	Republican Arnold Schwarzenegger is elected governor of California.

to writer Ken Kesey. He saw the potential not for war but for a wild party, and spiked the punch at the 1966 Trips Festival organized by Stewart Brand. The psychedelic era hit an all-time high at the January 14, 1967 Human Be-In in Golden Gate Park, where trip-master Timothy Leary urged a crowd of 20,000 hippies to dream a new American dream and 'turn on, tune in, drop out.'

Northern California had the more attention-grabbing counterculture from the 1940s to '60s, but nonconformity in sunny SoCal shook the country to the core. In 1947, when Senator Joseph McCarthy attempted to root out suspected communists in the film industry, 10 writers and directors refused to admit to communist alliances or to name names. The 'Hollywood Ten' were charged with contempt of Congress and barred from working in Hollywood, but their impassioned defenses of the US Constitution were heard nationwide. Major Hollywood players boldly voiced dissent and hired blacklisted talent until lawsuits finally curbed McCarthyism in the late 1950s.

Geeking Out

When Silicon Valley introduced the first personal computer in 1968, advertisements breathlessly gushed that Hewlett-Packard's new 'light' (40lb) machine could 'take on roots of a fifth-degree polynomial, Bessel functions, elliptic integrals and regression analysis' – all for just $4900 (over $33,000 today). Consumers didn't know quite what to do with such computers, but Trips Festival organizer Stewart Brand had a totally psychedelic idea: what if all that technology could fit into the palm of your hand? Maybe then, the technology governments used to run countries could empower ordinary people.

By the mid-1990s an entire dot-com start-up industry boomed in Silicon Valley, and suddenly people were getting everything – mail, news, pet food and, yes, sex – online. But when dot-com profits weren't forthcoming, venture-capital funding evaporated. Fortunes in stock options disappeared when the Nasdaq plummeted on March 10, 2000, popping the dot-com bubble. Overnight, 26-year-old vice-presidents and Bay Area service-sector employees alike found themselves jobless.

Meanwhile, California's biotech industry was quietly booming. An upstart company called Genentech, founded in a San Francisco bar in 1976, quickly got to work cloning human insulin and introducing the hepatitis B vaccine. In 2004 California voters approved a $3-billion bond measure for stem-cell research, and by 2008 California had become the USA's biggest funder of stem-cell research, as well as the focus of Nasdaq's new Biotechnology Index. With cloud computing to store and access data, machine learning can now make rapid advancements in healthcare. Covid-19 is putting these advancements to the test, combining mass-testing and harm reduction strategies established in San Francisco during the HIV/AIDS epidemic with new technology-assisted testing and tracing protocols.

So will machines save us all, or surpass us? Sounds like a Hollywood movie – or at least a far-out conversation in a California marijuana dispensary (legal as of 2017). No matter what happens, you can say you saw it coming in California.

2005	2017	2020
Antonio Villaraigosa is elected mayor of LA, becoming the first Latino to hold that office since 1872.	Threatened with defunding from the federal government, over a dozen California cities reinforce their sanctuary statutes.	California declares quarantine early in response to Covid-19. Historic wildfires burned a record 4 million-plus acres.

Santa Monica (p192)

The Way of Life

In a California dreamworld, you wake up with an espresso and a side of wheatgrass and roll down to the beach while the surf's up. You skateboard down the boardwalk to your yoga class, where everyone admires your downward dog. A food truck pulls up serving sustainable fish tacos topped with organic mango chipotle salsa...and then you wake up.

Regional Identity

Now for the reality check. Any Northern Californian hearing your California dream is bound to get huffy. What, political protests and Silicon Valley start-ups don't factor in your dreams? But Southern Californians will also roll their eyes at these stereotypes: they didn't create NASA's Jet Propulsion Lab, SpaceX and almost half of the world's movies by slacking off.

But there is some truth to your California dreamscape. Some 70% of Californians live in coastal areas, even though California beaches aren't always sunny or swimmable. Self-help, fitness and body modification are major industries throughout California, successfully marketed since the 1970s as 'lite' versions of religious experience – all the agony and ecstasy of the major religions, without all those heavy commandments. Exercise

Californian Languages

More than 200 different languages are spoken in California, with Spanish, Chinese, Tagalog, Russian, Hindi and Arabic in the top 10. Around 44% of state residents speak a language other than English at home.

and healthy food help keep Californians among the fittest in the nation. At the same time, millions of them apparently see no contradiction in consuming recreational marijuana, which was legalized in the state in 2017. Ahem.

Lifestyle

The charmed existence you dreamed about is a stretch, even in California. Few Californians can afford to spend entire days tanning and networking, what with all the aging UVA/UVB rays and sky-high rents out here. Eight of the 10 most expensive US housing markets are in California, and in one of the most expensive areas, Palo Alto, the average house price is over $3 million.

With a median annual household income of $71,000, buying a home these days is out of reach for many Californians. Indeed, the homeownership rate has dropped to 55%, down from a 60.7% peak in 2006. The high cost of living is also prompting more middle- and low-income Californians (especially millennials) to migrate to other states with more affordable pastures.

If you're a Californian aged 18 to 24, there's a 50-50 possibility that your roomies are your parents. Among adult Californians, one in four live alone, and about half are unmarried. If you're not impressed with your dating options in California, stick around: of those who are currently married, about a third won't be in 10 years. Increasingly, Californians are shacking up together: the number of unmarried cohabiting couples has increased 40% since 1990.

Like most Californians, you effectively live in your car. Californians commute an average of 29 minutes each way to work and spend at least $1 out of every $5 earned on car-related expenses. Small wonder that, according to the American Lung Association, six of the US cities with the highest year-round air-pollution levels are in California. But at least Californians are zooming ahead of the national energy-use curve in their smog-checked cars, buying more hybrid and fuel-efficient cars than any other state.

Population

With almost 40 million residents, California is the most populous US state. One in every eight Americans lives here. It is, however, no longer the fastest-growing state, adding only about 87,500 people in 2019 (0.2% vs 4.1% in Idaho, the current fastest-growing state). In fact, these days more people leave Californa than move here from other states, a trend that began in 2006, slowed around 2011 and picked up again in 2016.

Within California, there's a shift away from the coast to the inland areas, with the Central Valley and the Inland Empire (east of LA) posting especially robust growth rates. LA County, by contrast, lost residents in the last two years, even though it is still California's most populous. Although the High Sierras and southern deserts are sparsely populated, California's overall population density is 251 people per square mile – almost triple the national average.

Immigration & Diversity

Immigration has been key to California's growth since its inception. California was a territory of Mexico and Spain before it became a US state, and has sustained one of the world's most diverse populations ever since. Today, more than 10 million Californians are immigrants. One of every four arrivals settles in California, with twice as many now coming from Asia as from Latin America.

Most newcomers trace their origins to Mexico (four million), followed by the Philippines (848,999), China (798,000), India (532,000) and Vietnam (515,000). Many immigrants move to California to join family members already settled here. An estimated three million undocumented immigrants currently live in California, often with documented or naturalized family members.

Californian culture reflects the composite identity of the state. Latinx surpassed whites as the state's majority ethnic group in 2014 and now constitute 39% of the population (whites 37%). Some 15% of residents are Asian American, which make up about one third of the nation's Asian American population. There are thriving immigrant communities from China, Korea, Vietnam, Japan, Cambodia, Thailand and other parts of Asia. The greatest concentration can be found in the San Francisco Bay Area but many Asian immigrants also settled in Los Angeles, Orange, San Diego and Sacramento Counties.

As relatively late arrivals during the WWII shipping boom, California's African Americans have historically represented just 6% of the population while being a driving force in fields such as popular culture, politics, fashion and sports.

Homelessness

Surging homelessness has been a tragic consequence of the lack of affordable housing and the growing gap between income levels and the cost of living in California. In just one year, 2018 to 2019, the homeless rate jumped a whopping 17%. Living without permanent shelter is now a reality for at least 150,000 residents, or some 25% of the total US homeless population. Even in suburban and rural areas, people sleeping in cars, in tent encampments and under freeway bridges have become a common sight.

Homeless demographics are changing too. The good news: homelessness among military veterans has dropped to half of 2010 levels, helped largely by targeted public housing programs. There are also fewer homeless families with children, although 8000 families and 14,000 children are hardly numbers for rejoicing. Neither is the fact that about one-third of the state's unhoused population is African American.

To counter this disturbing trend, the state government has allocated significant sums of money for emergency shelters, subsidized long-term housing, psychological counseling, job training and other measures. In 2018, voters approved Proposition 1, a $4-billion affordable housing bond, as well as Proposition 2, which funds housing for people with mental illnesses. It remains to be seen if these measures will be sufficient to reverse the crisis or just the proverbial drop in the bucket.

Religion

California is one of the most religiously diverse US states, but also one of the least religious. Less than half of Californians consider religion very important, and a quarter profess no religion at all. Of those Californians who do practice a religion, a third identify as Protestant and about 28% as Catholic. California is home to most of the nation's practicing Hindus, the biggest Jewish community outside New York, a sizable Muslim community and the largest number of Buddhists anywhere outside Asia. Californians have also established their own spiritual practices, including the Church of Satan, EST self-help movement and UFO cults.

Paramount Pictures (p195)

On Location: Film & TV

*Picture Orson Welles whispering 'Rosebud,'
Judy Garland clicking her ruby-red heels, or the
Terminator threatening 'I'll be back': California is
where iconic film images come to life. Shakespeare
claimed 'all the world's a stage,' but in California, it's
a production set. With so many TV shows and movies
shot here annually, every palm-lined boulevard or
beach seems to come with its own IMDb résumé.*

The Industry

You might know it as the TV and movie business, but to Southern Californians it's simply 'the Industry.' It all began in the humble orchards of Hollywoodland, a residential suburb of Los Angeles where entrepreneurial moviemakers established studios in the early 20th century. Within a few years, immigrants turned a humble orchard into Hollywood. In 1915 Polish immigrant Samuel Goldwyn joined with Cecil B DeMille to form Paramount Studios, while German-born Carl Laemmle opened nearby Universal Studios, selling lunch to curious guests to help underwrite his moving pictures. A few years later, a family of Polish immigrants arrived from Canada, and Jack Warner and his brothers soon set up a movie studio of their own.

With perpetually balmy weather and more than 315 days of sunshine a year, So-Cal proved to be an ideal shooting location, and moviemaking flourished. In those early Wild West movie-making days, patent holders such as Thomas Edison sent agents to collect payments, or repossess movie equipment. Fledgling filmmakers saw them coming, and made runs for the Mexican border with their equipment. Palm Springs became a favorite weekend hideaway for Hollywood stars, partly because its distance from LA (just under 100 miles) was as far as they could travel under restrictive studio contracts.

Seemingly overnight, Hollywood studios made movie magic. Fans lined up for premieres in LA movie palaces for red-carpet glimpses of early silent-film stars such as Charlie Chaplin and Harold Lloyd. Moviegoers nationwide celebrated the first big Hollywood wedding in 1920, when swashbuckler Douglas Fairbanks married 'America's sweetheart' Mary Pickford. Years later, their divorce would be one of Hollywood's biggest scandals, but the United Artists studio they founded with Charlie Chaplin endures today. When the silent-movie era gave way to 'talkies' with the 1927 musical *The Jazz Singer,* the world hummed along.

The Art of Animation

In 1923 a young cartoonist named Walt Disney arrived in LA, and within five years he had a hit called *Steamboat Willie* and a breakout star called Mickey Mouse. That film spawned the entire Disney empire, and dozens of other California animation studios have followed with films and TV programs. Among the most beloved are Warner Bros (Bugs Bunny et al in *Looney Tunes*), Hanna-Barbera (*The Flintstones, The Jetsons, Yogi Bear* and *Scooby-Doo*), DreamWorks (*Shrek, Madagascar, Kung-Fu Panda*), Pixar Animation Studios (*Toy Story, Finding Dory, Inside Out*) and Film Roman (*The Simpsons*). Even if much of the hands-on work takes place overseas (in places such as South Korea), concept and supervision still takes place in LA and the San Francisco Bay Area.

Hollywood & Beyond

By the 1920s Hollywood became the Industry's social and financial hub, but it's a myth that most movie production took place there. Of the major studios, only Paramount Pictures is in Hollywood proper, surrounded by block after block of production-related businesses, such as lighting and post-production. Most movies have long been shot elsewhere around LA, in Culver City (at MGM, now Sony Pictures), Studio City (at Universal Studios) and Burbank (at Warner Bros and later Disney).

Moviemaking hasn't been limited to LA either. Founded in 1910, the American Film Manufacturing Company (aka Flying 'A' Studios) churned out box-office hits in San Diego and then Santa Barbara. Balboa Studios in Long Beach was another major silent-era dream factory. Contemporary movie production companies based in the San Francisco Bay Area include Francis Ford Coppola's American Zoetrope, Pixar animation studios and George Lucas' Industrial Light & Magic. Both San Francisco and LA remain major hubs for independent filmmakers and documentarians.

But not every Californian you meet is in the Industry, even in Tinseltown. The high cost of filming has sent location scouts far beyond LA's San Fernando Valley (where most of California's movie and TV studios are found) to Vancouver, Toronto and Montreal, where film production crews are welcomed with open arms (and sweet deals) to 'Hollywood North.' California's five-year tax credit program, which started in 2015 to lure filmmakers back to Cali, seems to have worked – more 2016 TV pilots were shot here than in any other location.

Hollywood Walk of Fame (p195)

★ **Top Film Festivals**

AFI Fest (https://fest.afi.com)

San Francisco International LGBTIQ+ Film Festival (www.frameline.org)

Palm Springs International Film Festival (www.psfilmfest.org)

San Francisco International Film Festival (https://sffilm.org)

Still, for Hollywood dreamers and movie buffs, LA remains *the* place for a pilgrimage. You can tour major movie studios, be part of a live TV studio audience, line up alongside the red carpet for an awards ceremony, catch movie premieres at film festivals, wander the Hollywood Walk of Fame and discover what it's like to live, dine and party with the stars.

California on Celluloid

California is a sneaky scene-stealer in many Hollywood films, stepping out of the background to become a main topic and character in its own right. From sunny capers to moody film-noir mysteries, California has proved its versatility in movie classics ranging from *The Maltese Falcon* (1941) to *Blade Runner* (1982) to *The Big Lebowski* (1998).

The Small Screen

After a year of tinkering, San Francisco inventor Philo Farnsworth transmitted the first television broadcast in 1927 of...a straight line. Giving viewers something actually interesting to watch would take a few more years. The first TV station began broadcasting in Los Angeles in 1931, beaming iconic images of California into living rooms across America and around the world with *Dragnet* (1950s), *The Beverly Hillbillies* (1960s), *The Brady Bunch* and *Charlie's Angels* (1970s), *LA Law* (1980s), and *Baywatch, Buffy the Vampire Slayer* and *The Fresh Prince of Bel-Air* (1990s). *Beverly Hills 90210* (1990s) made that LA zip code into a status symbol, while *The OC* (2000s) glamorized Orange County and *Silicon Valley* (2014–19) satirized NorCal start-ups. Reality-TV fans will recognize Southern California locations from *Top Chef, Real Housewives of Orange County* and *Keeping Up with the Kardashians*.

A suburban San Francisco start-up changed the TV game in 2005, launching a streaming video on a platform called YouTube. With on-demand streaming services competing with cable channels to launch original series, we have entered a new golden age of California television. Netflix Studios (in Silicon Valley and LA), Amazon Studios (Culver City) and Hulu Studios (Santa Monica) are churning out original series, satisfying binge-watching cravings with dark dramas such as *Stranger Things, Man in the High Castle* and *The Handmaid's Tale*. Time will tell if streaming services will also yield breakthrough Californian comedies to compare with Showtime's sharp-witted suburban pot-growing dramedy *Weeds*, its *Californication* adventures of a successful New York novelist gone Hollywood, or HBO's *Curb Your Enthusiasm*, an insider satire of the industry featuring *Seinfeld* co-creator Larry David and Hollywood celebrities playing themselves.

Kamaiyah (p289)

Music & the Arts

When Californians thank their lucky stars – or good karma – that they don't live in New York, they're not just talking about beach weather. This place has long supported thriving music and arts scenes that aren't afraid to be independent, even outlandish. In the US' most racially and ethnically diverse state, expect eclectic playlists, immersive performances and vivid shows of pride and individuality.

Music

In your California dream, you're a DJ – so what kind of music do you play? Beach Boys covers, West Coast rap, bluegrass, original punk, classic soul, hard bop, heavy-metal riffs on opera? To please Californian crowds, try all of the above. To hear the world's most eclectic playlist, just walk down a city street in California.

LA's recording industry has produced countless pop princesses, airbrushed boy bands and brooding balladeers. But the NorCal DIY tech approach is launching YouTube artists daily, not to mention wild dance parties.

Swing, Jazz, Blues & Soul

Swing was California's next big thing. In the 1930s and '40s, big bands sparked a Lindy Hopping craze in LA, and sailors on shore leave hit San Francisco's integrated underground jazz clubs.

As California's African American community grew with the 'Great Migration' during the WWII shipping and manufacturing boom, the West Coast blues sound was born. Texas-born bluesman T-Bone Walker worked in LA's Central Ave clubs before making hit records of his electric guitar stylings for Capitol Records. Throughout the 1940s and '50s, West Coast blues were nurtured in San Francisco and Oakland by guitarists such as Pee Wee Crayton and Oklahoma-born Lowell Fulson.

With Beat poets riffing over improvised bass lines and audiences finger-snapping their approval, the cool West Coast jazz of Chet Baker and Bay Area–born Dave Brubeck emerged from San Francisco's North Beach neighborhood in the 1950s. Meanwhile, in the African American cultural hub along LA's Central Ave, the hard bop of Charlie Parker and Charles Mingus kept SoCal's jazz scene alive and swinging.

In the 1950s and '60s, doo-wop, rhythm and blues, and soul music were all in steady rotation at nightclubs in South Central LA, considered the 'Harlem of the West.' Soulful singer Sam Cooke ran his own hit-making record label, attracting soul and gospel talent to LA.

Rockin' Out

The first homegrown rock-and-roll talent to make it big in the 1950s was San Fernando Valley–born Richie Valens, whose 'La Bamba' was a rockified version of a Mexican folk song. Dick Dale experimented with reverb effects in Orange County in the 1950s, becoming known as 'the King of the Surf Guitar.' He topped the charts with his band the Del-Tones in the early '60s, influencing everyone from the Beach Boys to Jimi Hendrix – you might recognize his recording of 'Miserlou' from the movie *Pulp Fiction*.

Guitar got psychedelic in 1960s California. When Joan Baez and Bob Dylan had their Northern California fling in the early 1960s, Dylan plugged in his guitar and pioneered folk rock. Centered around San Francisco's Fillmore Auditorium, Janis Joplin and Big Brother & the Holding Company developed their own shambling musical stylings in San Francisco, splintering folk rock into psychedelia. Jefferson Airplane turned Lewis Carroll's children's classic *Alice's Adventures in Wonderland* into the psychedelic hit 'White Rabbit.' For many 1960s Fillmore headliners, the show ended too soon with drug overdoses – though for the original jam band, the Grateful Dead, the song remained the same until guitarist Jerry Garcia died in rehab in 1995.

On LA's famous Sunset Strip, LA bands were also blowing minds at the legendary Whisky a Go-Go nightclub – especially the Byrds and the Doors. But the California sound also got down and funky with iconic funk bands War from Long Beach, Tower of Power from Oakland, and San Francisco's Sly and the Family Stone.

Post-Punk to Pop

The 1980s saw the rise of such influential LA crossover bands as Bad Religion (punk) and Suicidal Tendencies (hardcore/thrash), while more mainstream all-female bands the Bangles and the Go-Gos, new wavers Oingo Boingo, and California rockers Jane's Addiction and Red Hot Chili Peppers took the world by storm. Hollywood's Guns N' Roses set the '80s standard for arena rock, while San Francisco's Metallica showed the world how to head bang with a vengeance. Avant-garde rocker Frank Zappa earned a cult following and a rare hit with the 1982 single 'Valley Girl,' in which his 14-year-old daughter Moon Unit taught the rest of America to say 'Omigo-o-od!' like an LA teenager.

By the 1990s California's alternative rock acts took the national stage, including songwriter Beck, political rockers Rage Against the Machine and Orange County's ska-rockers No Doubt, fronted by Gwen Stefani. Hailing from East LA, Los Lobos was king of the Chicano (Mexican American) bands, an honor that has since passed to Ozomatli.

Berkeley's 924 Gilman Street club revived punk in the 1990s, launching the career of Grammy Award–winning Green Day. Riding the wave were Berkeley ska-punk band Rancid, surf-punk Sublime from Long Beach, San Diego–based pop-punksters Blink 182, and Orange County's resident loudmouths, the Offspring.

Rap & Hip-Hop

Since the 1980s, West Coast rap and hip-hop have spoken truth and hit the beat. When the NWA album *Straight Outta Compton* was released in 1989, it launched the careers of Eazy E, Ice Cube and Dr Dre, and established gangsta rap. Dre co-founded Death Row Records, which helped launch megawatt talents such as Long Beach bad boys Snoop Dogg, Warren G and the late Tupac Shakur. The son of a Black Panther leader who'd fallen on hard times, Tupac combined party songs and hard truths learned on Oakland streets until his untimely shooting in 1996 in a suspected East Coast/West Coast rap feud. Feuds also checkered the musical career of LA rapper Game, whose 2009 *R.E.D. Album* brought together an all-star lineup of Diddy, Dr Dre, Snoop Dogg and more.

Throughout the 1980s and '90s, California maintained a grassroots hip-hop scene in Oakland and LA. Reacting against the increasing commercialization of hip-hop in the late 1990s, the Bay Area scene produced underground 'hyphy' (short for hyperactive) artists such as E-40. Political commentary and funk hooks have become signatures of East Bay groups Blackalicious, the Coup and Michael Franti & Spearhead, and Oakland-based Kamaiyah is among today's chart-toppers.

Punk's Not Dead in California

In the 1970s American airwaves were jammed with commercial arena rock that record companies paid DJs to shill like laundry soap. California teens bored with prepackaged anthems started making their own with secondhand guitars, three chords and crappy amps that added a loud buzz to unleashed fury. Punk was born.

LA punk paralleled the scrappy local skate scene with the hardcore grind of Black Flag from Hermosa Beach and LA's the Germs. LA band X bridged punk and new wave from 1977 to 1987 with John Doe's rockabilly guitar, Exene Cervenka's angsty wail, and disappointed-romantic lyrics inspired by Charles Bukowski and Raymond Chandler.

San Francisco's punk scene was arty and absurdist, in rare form with Dead Kennedys singer (and future San Francisco mayoral candidate) Jello Biafra mocking Golden State complacency in 'California Über Alles.'

Architecture

There's more to California than beach houses and boardwalks. Californians have adapted imported styles to the climate and available materials, building cool, adobe-inspired houses in San Diego and fog-resistant redwood-shingle houses in Mendocino to mid-century modern in Palm Springs.

Spanish Missions & Victorian Queens

The first Spanish missions were built around courtyards, using materials that Native Californians and Spaniards found on hand: adobe, limestone and grass. Many missions

Gamble House, Pasadena

★ **Architectural Icons**
Salk Institute, La Jolla
Mission San Juan Capistrano
Sunnylands, Rancho Mirage
Getty Center, LA
Walt Disney Concert Hall, LA
Gamble House, Pasadena
Hearst Castle, San Simeon

crumbled into disrepair as the church's influence waned, but the style remained practical for the climate. Early California settlers later adapted it into the rancho adobe style, as seen in Downtown LA's El Pueblo de Los Angeles and San Diego's Old Town.

Once the mid-19th-century gold rush was on, California's nouveau riche imported materials to construct grand mansions matching European fashions. Many millionaires favored the gilded Queen Anne style, raising the stakes with ornamental excess. Outrageous examples of colorful, gingerbread-swagged Victorian 'Painted Ladies' can be found in San Francisco, Ferndale and Eureka.

But Californian architecture has always had its contrarian streak. Many turn-of-the-20th-century architects rejected frilly Victorian styles in favor of the simpler, classical lines of Spanish designs. Spanish Colonial Revival architecture (also known as Mission Revival style) recalls early California missions with their restrained functional details: arched doors and windows, long covered porches, fountain courtyards, solid walls and red-tile roofs. Downtown Santa Barbara showcases this revival style, as do stately buildings in San Diego's Balboa Park, Scotty's Castle in Death Valley and several SoCal train depots, including those in Downtown LA, San Diego and Santa Barbara.

Arts & Crafts to Art Deco

Simplicity and harmony were hallmarks of California's early-20th-century arts-and-crafts style. Influenced by both Japanese design principles and England's arts-and-crafts movement, its woodwork and handmade touches marked a deliberate departure from the industrial revolution's mechanization. Bernard Maybeck and Julia Morgan in Northern California, and SoCal architects Charles and Henry Greene, popularized the versatile one-story bungalow. Today you'll spot them in Berkeley and Pasadena with their overhanging eaves, airy terraces and sleeping porches harmonizing warm, livable interiors with the natural environment outdoors.

In the 1920s, the international art-deco style took elements from the ancient world – Mayan glyphs, Egyptian pillars, Babylonian ziggurats – and flattened them into modern motifs to cap stark facades and outline streamlined skyscrapers in Oakland, San Francisco and LA. Streamline moderne kept decoration to a minimum, and mimicked the aerodynamic look of ocean liners and airplanes.

Postmodern Evolutions

True to its mythic nature, California couldn't help wanting to embellish the facts a little, veering away from strict high modernism to add unlikely postmodern shapes to the local landscape.

In 1997 Richard Meier made his mark on West LA with the Getty Center, a cresting white wave of a building on a sunburned hilltop. Canadian-born Frank Gehry relocated to Santa

Monica, and his billowing, sculptural style for LA's Walt Disney Concert Hall winks cheekily at shipshape streamline moderne. Also in Downtown LA, the Cathedral of Our Lady of the Angels, designed by Spanish architect Rafael Moneo, echoes the grand churches of Mexico and Europe from a controversial deconstructivist angle. Renzo Piano's signature inside-out industrial style can be glimpsed in the sawtooth roof and red-steel veins of the Broad in Los Angeles.

The Bay Area's iconic postmodern building is the San Francisco Museum of Modern Art, which Swiss architect Mario Botta capped with a black-and-white striped, marble-clad atrium in 1995 and Snøhetta architects expanded with wings shaped like ship sails in 2016. Lately SF has championed a brand of postmodernism by Pritzker Prize–winning architects that magnifies and mimics the great outdoors, especially in Golden Gate Park. Swiss architects Herzog & de Meuron clad the de Young Memorial Museum in copper, which promises to oxidize green to match its park setting. Nearby, Renzo Piano literally raised the roof on sustainable design at the LEED Platinum–certified California Academy of Sciences, capped by a living-roof garden.

Visual Arts

Although the earliest European artists were trained cartographers accompanying Western explorers, their images of California as an outside, almost mythical presence show more imagination than scientific rigor. This mythologizing tendency continued throughout the gold-rush era, as Western artists alternated between caricatures of Wild West debauchery and manifest-destiny propaganda urging pioneers to settle the golden West. The completion of the Transcontinental Railroad in 1869 brought an influx of romantic painters, who produced epic California wilderness landscapes. After the 20th century arrived, home-grown colonies of California impressionist plein-air painters emerged at Laguna Beach and Carmel-by-the-Sea.

With the invention of photography, the improbable truth of California's landscape and its inhabitants was revealed. Pirkle Jones saw expressive potential in California landscape photography after WWII, while San Francisco–born Ansel Adams' sublime photographs had already started doing justice to Yosemite. Adams founded Group f/64 with Edward Weston and Imogen Cunningham in San Francisco. Berkeley-based Dorothea Lange turned her unflinching lens on the plight of Californian migrant workers in the Great Depression and Japanese Americans forced to enter internment camps during WWII, producing poignant documentary photos.

As the postwar American West became crisscrossed with freeways and divided into planned communities, Californian painters captured the abstract forms of manufactured landscapes on canvas. In San Francisco, Richard Diebenkorn and David Park became leading proponents of Bay Area Figurative Art, while San Francisco–born sculptor Richard Serra captured urban aesthetics in massive, rusting monoliths resembling ship prows and industrial Stonehenges. Meanwhile pop artists captured the ethos of conspicuous consumerism, through Wayne Thiebaud's gumball machines, British émigré David Hockney's LA pools and, above all, Ed Ruscha's studies of SoCal pop culture.

Today's California contemporary-art scene brings all these influences together with muralist-led social commentary, an obsessive dedication to craft and cutting-edge technology. LA's Museum of Contemporary Art puts on provocative and avant-garde shows, as does LACMA's Broad, San Francisco's Museum of Modern Art, and the Museum of Contemporary Art San Diego.

City Lights Books (p57)

By the Book

Since its earliest days, California has been a source of fascination for authors and readers alike, and its landscapes and personalities have inspired some unforgettable classics. Today's West Coast remains a magnet, now inhabited by a multicultural literary community.

Early Voices of Social Realism

Arguably the most influential author to emerge from California was John Steinbeck, born in Salinas in 1902 in the heart of Central Valley farm country. He explored the lives and struggles of diverse California communities: Mexican American WWI vets adjusting to civilian life in *Tortilla Flat,* flat-broke wharf characters attempting to throw a party in *Cannery Row,* and migrant farm workers just trying to survive the Great Depression in his Pulitzer Prize–winning book *The Grapes of Wrath*. Acclaimed social realist Eugene O'Neill took his 1936 Nobel Prize money and transplanted himself near San Francisco, where he wrote the autobiographical play *Long Day's Journey into Night*.

Novelists took on the myth of California's self-made millionaires, exposing the tarnish on the Gold State. Classics in this vein include Upton Sinclair's *Oil!,* revealing the schemes of real-life LA oil tycoon Edward Mahoney that resulted in the Teapot Dome Scandal.

California became synonymous with adventure through the talents of early chroniclers such as Mark Twain and Bret Harte. Professional hell-raiser Jack London was a wild child from the Oakland docks who traveled the world with little more than his wits. He became the world's most successful adventurer and travel writer, sailing the seven seas, getting swept up in the Klondike gold rush, and dictating stories of his adventures on his pioneering permaculture ranch in Sonoma onto an early recording device.

Driving Tales

Road-trip through California with local storytellers as your copilots in *My California: Journeys by Great Writers*. Alternatively, get a slice of the state's heartland in *Highway 99: A Literary Journey Through California's Great Central Valley*, edited by Oakland-based writer Stan Yogi. It's full of multicultural perspectives, from early European settlers to 20th-century Mexican and Asian immigrant farmers.

Pulp Noir & Science Fiction

With mysterious fog and neon signs to set the mood, San Francisco and Los Angeles became crime-drama pulp-fiction capitals and the setting of choice for film noir movies. Dashiell Hammett *(The Maltese Falcon)* made a cynical San Francisco private eye into a modern antihero, while hard-boiled crime writer Raymond Chandler set the scene for murder and double-crossing dames in Santa Monica. The masterminds behind California's 1990s neo-noir crime fiction renaissance were James Ellroy *(LA Confidential),* the late Elmore Leonard *(Get Shorty)* and Walter Mosley *(Devil in a Blue Dress),* whose Easy Rawlins detective novels are set in South Central LA.

California technology has long inspired science fiction. Raised in Berkeley, Philip K Dick imagined dystopian futures, including a Los Angeles ruled by artificial intelligence in *Do Androids Dream of Electric Sheep?* It was adapted into the 1982 sci-fi movie classic *Blade Runner*. Berkeley-born Ursula K Le Guin *(The Left Hand of Darkness, A Wizard of Earthsea)* brings feminism to the genre of fantasy, imagining parallel realities where heroines confront forces of darkness.

Social Movers & Shakers

After surviving WWII, the Beat Generation refused to fall in line with 1950s conformity, defying McCarthyism with poignant, poetic truths. San Francisco Beat scene luminaries included Jack Kerouac *(On the Road),* Allen Ginsberg *(Howl)* and Lawrence Ferlinghetti, the Beats' patron publisher who cofounded City Lights Books. Censors called *Howl* obscene, and Ferlinghetti was arrested for publishing it – but he won the trial in a landmark decision for free speech.

But no author has captured California culture with such unflinching clarity as Joan Didion. Her collection of literary nonfiction essays *Slouching Towards Bethlehem* captures 1960s flower power at the exact moment it blooms and wilts. Didion pioneered immersive first-person New Journalism with fellow '60s California chroniclers Hunter S Thompson *(Hells Angels: A Strange and Terrible Saga)* and Tom Wolfe *(The Electric Kool-Aid Acid Test).*

In the 1970s, Charles Bukowski's semiautobiographical novel *Post Office* captured down-and-out Downtown LA, while Richard Vasquez' *Chicano* took a dramatic look at LA's Latino barrio. Bret Easton Ellis followed coked-up 1980s Beverly Hills teenagers in *Less Than Zero*.

More recently, Paul Beatty bagged the Man Booker Prize and National Book Critics Circle Award for his 2015 satirical novel *The Sellout,* set in a downtrodden LA suburb. USC English professor Viet Thanh Nguyen won the 2016 Pulitzer Prize for *The Sympathizer,* about a half-Vietnamese undercover agent, and Tommy Orange was a 2019 Pulitzer Prize nominee for *There There,* about Native Americans living around Oakland.

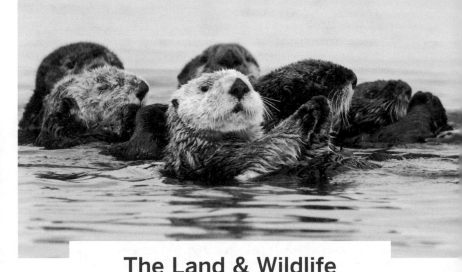

SUZY SIMONS/500PX ©

The Land & Wildlife

You'll never have to leave California for a change of scenery: from snowy peaks to scorching deserts it's the most biodiverse state in the US. Species that are rare elsewhere thrive in this balmy climate, with its dry summers and wet winters. California's population strains natural resources, but for more than 150 years conservation-minded Californians have worked hard to protect the environment.

Lay of the Land

California is the third-biggest US state after Alaska and Texas, covering more than 155,000 sq miles – if it were a country it would rank as the 59th largest in the world. It shares borders with Oregon to the north, Mexico to the south, Nevada and Arizona to the east, and has 840 miles of glorious Pacific shoreline to the west.

Geology & Earthquakes

California is a complex geologic landscape formed from fragments of rock and earth crust squeezed together as the North American continent drifted westward over hundreds of millions of years. Crumpled coastal ranges, fault lines rippling through the Central Valley and jagged, still-rising Sierra Nevada mountains all reveal gigantic forces at work, as the continental and ocean plates crush together.

Everything changed about 25 million years ago, when the ocean plates stopped colliding and instead started sliding against each other, creating the massive San Andreas Fault. This contact zone catches and slips, rattling California with an ongoing succession of tremors and earthquakes.

In 1906 the state's most famous earthquake measured 7.8 on the Richter scale and demolished San Francisco, leaving more than 3000 people dead. The Bay Area was again badly shaken in 1989, when the Loma Prieta earthquake (6.9) caused a section of the Bay Bridge to collapse. In LA the last 'big one' was in 1994, when the Northridge quake (6.7) caused parts of the Santa Monica Fwy to fall down, resulting in damage that made it the most costly quake in US history.

California Burning

According to the OEHHA (California Office of Environmental Health Hazard Assessment), annual air temperatures in California have been increasing since records began in 1895. Over the past 40 years, the mercury has been rising more quickly. Extreme weather events are more common, the winter chill has lessened, and the state has become drier overall. Aggravated by strong winds and drought, the 2018 wildfire season torched more than 2800 sq miles. It was the most destructive season on record – until the nightmare infernos two years later in which more than 6400 sq miles burned.

Shifting fault lines far from the large urban areas periodically register high on the Richter scale, like the 2019 Ridgecrest quake, which at 6.4, along with over 100,000 aftershocks, was the strongest in Southern California in more than 20 years.

The Coast to the Central Valley

Rugged mountains take the brunt of winter storms along California's coast, leaving inland areas more protected. San Francisco marks the midpoint of the Coast Ranges, with fog swirling along the sparsely populated North Coast. To the south, beach communities enjoy balmier climates along the Central and Southern California coasts.

The northernmost reaches of the Coast Ranges get 120in of rain in a typical year, and persistent summer fog contributes another 12in of precipitation in some spots. This may not sound like the best climate for beach-going, but California's northern coastal lowlands are sublime for coastal wine tasting. Nutrient-rich soils and abundant moisture foster towering stands of towering coast redwoods, growing as far south as Big Sur and all the way north to Oregon.

On their eastern flanks, the Coast Ranges taper into gently rolling hills that slide into the sprawling Central Valley. Once an inland sea, this flat basin is now an agricultural powerhouse producing about half of America's fruits, nuts and vegetables. Stretching about 450 miles long and 50 miles wide, the valley sees about as much rainfall as a desert, but gets huge volumes of water runoff from the Sierra Nevada.

Before the arrival of Europeans, the Central Valley was a natural wonderland – vast marshes with flocks of geese that blackened the sky, grasslands carpeted with flowers sniffed by millions of antelopes, elk and grizzly bears. Virtually this entire landscape has been plowed under and replaced with non-native plants (including agricultural crops and vineyards) and livestock ranches. So when you savor your next great California meal, raise a glass to the flora and fauna that came before you.

Mountain Ranges

On the eastern side of the Central Valley looms California's most prominent topographic feature: the Sierra Nevada, nicknamed the 'Range of Light' by conservationist John Muir.

At 400 miles long and 70 miles wide, this is one of the world's largest mountain ranges, punctuated with 13 peaks over 14,000ft high. The vast wilderness of the High Sierra (mostly above 9000ft) is an astounding landscape of shrinking glaciers, sculpted granite peaks and remote canyons. This landscape is beautiful to look at but difficult to access, and it was one of the greatest challenges for 19th-century settlers attempting to reach California.

The soaring Sierra Nevada captures storm systems and drains them of their water, with most of the precipitation above 3000ft turning to snow, creating a premier winter-sports destination. Melting snow flows down into a half-dozen major river systems on the range's western and eastern slopes, providing the vast majority of water needed for agriculture in the Central Valley and for the metro areas of San Francisco and LA.

At its northern end, the Sierra Nevada merges imperceptibly into the volcanic Cascade Mountains, which continue north into Oregon and Washington. At its southern end, the Sierra Nevada makes a funny westward hook and connects via the Transverse Ranges (one of the USA's few east–west mountain ranges) to the southern Coast Ranges.

Climate Challenges

Climate change is already having a significant impact on rural lifestyles, as well as on the tourist industry. With so much at stake, Californians take climate change very seriously. Visit California has spearheaded efforts to reduce car use, the National Park Service (NPS) is moving toward carbon-neutral operations in many California parks, and private businesses are getting creative (from sustainable winemaking to ecofriendly accommodations).

Ski resorts, too, are adopting a plethora of initiatives, like lower-impact snow-making machines and improved public transport links. The Vail resorts (including Heavenly, Northstar and Kirkwood) subscribe to a 'Commitment to Zero' program with a goal of zero waste and zero net emissions by 2030. Squaw Valley has a host of measures, such as an increased carpooling lot and banning plastic water bottles.

California's Flora & Fauna

Although the staggering numbers of animals that greeted the first foreign settlers are now distant memories, you can still easily spot wildlife thriving in California. Some are only shadow populations, and some are actually endangered – all the more reason to take the opportunity to stop by California's designated wildlife areas to appreciate their presence and support their conservation.

Marine Mammals

Spend even one day along California's coast and you may spot pods of bottlenose dolphins and porpoises swimming, canoodling and cavorting in the ocean. Playful sea otters and harbor seals typically stick closer to shore, especially around public piers and protected bays. Since the 1989 earthquake, sea lions have taken to sunbathing on San Francisco's Pier 39, where delighted tourists watch the city's resident beach bums nap, goof off and recover from their seafood dinners. To see more wild pinnipeds, visit Point Lobos State Natural Reserve near Monterey, or Channel Islands National Park in Southern California.

Once threatened by extinction, gray whales now migrate in growing numbers along California's coast between December and April. Adult whales live up to 60 years, grow longer than a city bus and can weigh up to 40 tons, making quite a splash when they leap out of the water. Every year they travel from summertime feeding grounds in the arctic Bering Sea, down to southern breeding grounds off Baja California, then all the way back up again, making a 6000 mile round-trip.

Also almost hunted to extinction by the late 19th century for their oil-rich blubber, northern elephant seals have made a remarkable comeback along California's coast. North of Santa Cruz, Año Nuevo State Reserve is a major breeding ground for northern elephant seals. California's biggest elephant seal colony is found at Piedras Blancas, south of Big Sur. There's a smaller rookery at Point Reyes National Seashore in Marin County.

Land Mammals

Lumbering across California's flag is the state mascot: the grizzly bear. Grizzlies once roamed California's beaches and grasslands in large numbers, eating everything from acorns to whale carcasses. Grizzlies were particularly abundant in the Central Valley, but retreated upslope into the Sierra Nevada as they were hunted to extinction in the 1920s.

California's mountain forests are still home to an estimated 30,000 to 40,000 black bears, the grizzlies' smaller cousins. Despite their name, their fur ranges in color from black to dark brown, auburn or even blonde. These burly omnivores feed on berries, nuts, roots, grasses, insects, eggs, small mammals and fish, but will tend to hang around campgrounds and cabins where food and trash are not secured.

As settlers moved into California in the 19th century, many other large mammals fared almost as poorly as grizzlies. Immense herds of tule elk and antelope in the Central Valley were particularly hard hit, with antelope retreating in small numbers to the northeastern corner of the state, and tule elk hunted into near-extinction. A small remnant herd was moved to Point Reyes, where it has since rebounded.

Mountain lions (also called cougars) hunt throughout California's mountains and forests, especially in areas teeming with deer. Solitary lions can grow 8ft in length and weigh 175lb, and are formidable predators. Few attacks on humans have occurred, happening mostly where suburbs have encroached on the lions' wilderness hunting grounds.

Birds & Butterflies

California is an essential stop on the migratory Pacific Flyway between Alaska and Mexico. Almost half the bird species in North America use the state's wildlife refuges and nature preserves for rest and refueling. Migration peaks during the wetter winter season starting in October/November, when two million fowl gather at the Klamath Basin National Wildlife Refuges for the world's biggest game of duck, duck, goose.

Year-round you can see birds dotting California's beaches, estuaries and bays, where herons, cormorants, shorebirds and gulls gather. Point Reyes National Seashore and the Channel Islands are prime year-round bird-watching spots.

As you drive along the Big Sur coastline, look skyward to spot endangered California condors. You may also spot condors inland, soaring over Pinnacles National Park and Los Padres National Forest.

Desert Critters

California's deserts are far from deserted, but most animals don't hang out in the daytime heat. Most come out only in the cool of the night, as bats do. Roadrunners (black-and-white mottled ground cuckoos) can often be spotted on roadsides – you'll recognize them from their long tails and punk-style Mohawks. Other desert inhabitants include burrowing kit foxes, tree-climbing gray foxes, hopping jackrabbits, kangaroo rats, slow-moving (and endangered) desert tortoises and a variety of snakes, lizards and spiders. Desert bighorn sheep and migrating birds flock to watering holes, often around seasonal springs and native fan-palm oases – look for them in Joshua Tree National Park and Anza-Borrego Desert State Park.

Cholla Cactus Garden (p180)

★ California's Top Parks

Yosemite National Park (p129)

Death Valley National Park (p266)

Redwood National & State Parks (p87)

Joshua Tree National Park (p178)

Monarch butterflies are glorious orange creatures that take epic long-distance journeys in search of milkweed, their only source of food. They winter in California by the tens of thousands, clustering along the Central Coast at Santa Cruz, Pacific Grove, Pismo Beach and Santa Barbara County.

Wildflowers & Trees

Like human Californians, California's 6000 kinds of plants are by turns shy and flamboyant. Many species are so obscure and similar that only a dedicated botanist could tell them apart, but in the spring they merge into shimmering carpets of wildflowers that will take your breath away. The state flower is the native California poppy, which shyly closes at night and unfolds by day in a shocking display of golden orange.

California is also a region of superlative trees: the oldest (bristlecone pines of the White Mountains live to nearly 5000 years old), the tallest (coast redwoods reach 380ft) and the largest (giant sequoias of the Sierra Nevada exceed 36ft across). Sequoias are unique to California, adapted to survive in isolated groves on the Sierra Nevada's western slopes in Yosemite, Sequoia and Kings Canyon National Parks.

An astounding 20 native species of oak grow in California, including live (evergreen) oaks with holly-like leaves and scaly acorns. Other common trees include the aromatic California bay laurel, whose long slender leaves turn purple. Rare native trees include Monterey pines and Torrey pines, gnarly species that have adapted to harsh coastal conditions such as high winds, sparse rainfall and sandy, stony soils. Torrey pines only grow at Torrey Pines State Reserve near San Diego and in the Channel Islands, California's hot spot for endemic plant species.

Heading inland, the Sierra Nevada has three distinct ecozones: the dry western foothills covered with oak and chaparral; conifer forests starting from an elevation of 2000ft; and an alpine zone above 8000ft. Almost two-dozen species of conifer grow in the Sierra Nevada, with mid-elevation forests home to massive Douglas firs, ponderosa pines and, biggest of all, the giant sequoia. Deciduous trees include the quaking aspen, a white-trunked tree with shimmering leaves that turn pale yellow in the fall, helping the Golden State live up to its name in the Eastern Sierra.

Cacti & Other Desert Flora

In Southern California's deserts, cacti and other plants have adapted to the arid climate with thin, spiny leaves that resist moisture loss (and deter grazing animals). Their seed and flowering mechanisms kick into high gear during brief winter rains. Desert flora can bloom spectacularly in spring, carpeting valleys and drawing thousands of onlookers and shutterbugs.

One of the most common species is cholla, which looks so furry that it's nicknamed 'teddy-bear cactus,' but don't be fooled by its cuddly appearance. Cholla will bury extremely sharp, barbed spines in your skin at the slightest touch. Also watch out for the aptly named catclaw acacia, nicknamed 'wait-a-minute bush' because its small, sharp, hooked thorny spikes will try to grab your clothing or skin as you brush past.

> ### John Muir's Sierra Club
>
> Cofounded by naturalist John Muir in 1892, the Sierra Club (www.sierraclub.org) was the USA's first conservation group. It remains the nation's most active, offering educational programs, group hikes, organized trips and volunteer vacations.

You may also recognize prickly pear, a flat, fleshy-padded cacti whose juice is traditionally used as medicine by Native Americans. You can hardly miss spiky ocotillo, which grows up to 20ft tall and has canelike branches that sprout blood-red flowers in spring. Creosote may look like a cactus, but it's actually a small evergreen bush with a distinctive smell.

With gangly arms and puffy green sleeves, Joshua trees look like Dr Seuss characters from afar, but up close you can see they're actually a type of yucca. In spring they burst into blossom with greenish-white flowers. According to local legend, they were named by Mormons who thought their crooked branches resembled the outstretched arms of a biblical prophet.

California's National & State Parks

Most Californians rate outdoor recreation as vital to their quality of life, and the amount of preserved public lands has steadily grown since the 1960s with support from key legislation. The landmark 1976 California Coastal Act saved the coastline from further development, while the controversial 1994 California Desert Protection Act passed over the objections of ranchers, miners and off-highway vehicle (OHV) enthusiasts.

Today, **California State Parks** (www.parks.ca.gov) protects nearly a third of the state's coastline, along with redwood forests, mountain lakes, desert canyons, waterfalls, wildlife preserves and historical sites. In recent decades, state budget shortfalls and chronic underfunding of California's parks have contributed to closures, limited visitor services, increased park entry fees, as well as a near-stoppage on acquiring new lands or expanding the size of the parks. But with state revenues from recreational tourism consistently outpacing resource-extraction industries such as mining, California has a considerable vested interest in protecting its wilderness tracts.

While you could be disappointed to find a park closed or full, bear in mind that some limits to public access are necessary to prevent California's parklands from being loved to death. Too many visitors can stress the natural environment. To avoid the crowds and glimpse wilderness at its most untrammeled, plan to visit popular parks such as Yosemite outside of peak season. Alternatively, less famous natural areas managed by the **National Park Service** (www.nps.gov/state/CA) often receive fewer visitors, which means you won't have to reserve permits, campsites or lodging many months in advance.

There are 18 national forests in California managed by the **US Forest Service** (www.fs.usda.gov/r5), comprising lands around Mt Whitney, Mt Shasta, Lake Tahoe, Big Bear Lake and Big Sur. Beloved by birders, national wildlife refuges (NWR), including the Salton Sea and Klamath Basin, are managed by the **US Fish & Wildlife Service** (www.fws.gov/refuges). More wilderness tracts in California, including the Lost Coast and Carrizo Plain, are overseen by the **Bureau of Land Management** (www.blm.gov/ca/st/en.html).

Huntington Beach Pier (p241)

LUNAMARINA/SHUTTERSTOCK ©

Survival Guide

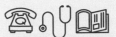

Directory A–Z

Accessible Travel

More populated areas of California are reasonably well equipped for travelers with disabilities, but facilities in smaller towns and rural areas may be limited. Download Lonely Planet's free Accessible Travel guides from http://lptravel.to/AccessibleTravel.

Accessibility

○ Most traffic intersections have dropped curbs and some have audible crossing signals.

○ The Americans with Disabilities Act (ADA) requires public buildings built after 1993 to be wheelchair-accessible, including restrooms.

○ Motels and hotels built after 1993 must have at least one ADA-compliant accessible room; state your specific needs when making reservations.

○ For nonpublic buildings built prior to 1993, including hotels, restaurants, museums and theaters, there are no accessibility guarantees; call ahead to find out what to expect.

○ Most national and many state parks and some other outdoor recreation areas offer paved or boardwalk nature trails that are graded and accessible by wheelchair.

○ Many theme parks go out of their way to be accessible to wheelchairs and guests with mobility limitations and other disabilities.

○ US citizens and permanent residents with a permanent disability qualify for a free lifetime 'America the Beautiful' Access Pass (http://store.usgs.gov/pass/access.html), which waives entry fees to all national parks and federal recreational lands and offers discounts on some recreation fees (eg camping). There's a $10 handling fee.

○ California State Parks' disabled discount pass ($3.50) entitles people with permanent disabilities to 50% off day-use parking and camping fees; for an application, see www.parks.ca.gov.

Communications

○ Telephone companies provide relay operators (dial 711) for the hearing impaired.

○ Many banks provide ATM instructions in braille.

Helpful Resources

A Wheelchair Rider's Guide to the California Coast (www.wheelingcalscoast.org) Free accessibility information covering beaches, parks and trails, plus downloadable PDF guides to the San Francisco Bay Area and Los Angeles and Orange County coasts.

Access Northern California (www.accessnca.org) Extensive links to accessible-travel resources, including outdoor recreation opportunities, lodgings, tours and transportation.

Access Santa Cruz County (www.scaccessguide.com) Free online accessible-travel guide for visiting Santa Cruz and around, including restaurants, lodging, beaches, parks and outdoor recreation.

Achieve Tahoe (http://achievetahoe.org) Organizes summer and winter sports, 4WD adventures and adaptive-ski rental around Lake Tahoe in the Sierra Nevada (annual membership from $50).

California State Parks (http://access.parks.ca.gov) Searchable online map and database of accessible features at state parks.

Disabled Sports Eastern Sierra (http://disabledsportseasternsierra.org) Offers summer and winter outdoor-activity programs around Mammoth Lakes.

Los Angeles for Disabled Visitors (www.discoverlosangeles.com/search/site/disabled) Tips for accessible sightseeing, entertainment, museums and transportation.

Wheelchair Traveling (www.wheelchairtraveling.com) Travel articles, lodging and helpful California destination info.

Yosemite National Park Accessibility (www.nps.gov/yose/planyourvisit/accessibility.htm) Detailed, downloadable accessibility information for Yo-semite National Park, including services for deaf visitors.

Transportation

○ All major airlines, Grey-hound buses and Amtrak trains can accommodate people with disabilities, usually with 48 hours of advance notice required.

○ Major car-rental agencies offer hand-controlled vehi-cles and vans with wheel-chair lifts at no extra charge, but you must reserve these well in advance.

○ For wheelchair-accessible van rentals, also try **Wheel-chair Getaways** (☑888-432-9339; www.wheelchairgetaways.com) in Sacramento, San Diego, San Francisco and LA, or **Mobility Works** (☑877-275-4915; www.mobilityworks.com) in LA, San Diego, San Francisco, Oakland, San Jose and Sacramento.

○ Local buses, trains and subway lines usually have wheelchair lifts.

Book Your Stay Online

For more accommoda-tions reviews by Lonely Planet authors, check out http://hotels.lonely planet.com/california. You'll find independ-ent reviews, as well as recommendations on the best places to stay. Best of all, you can book online.

○ Seeing-eye dogs are permitted to accompa-ny passengers on public transportation.

○ Taxi companies have at least one wheelchair-accessible van, but you'll usually need to call and then wait for one.

Accommodations

California dreaming comes easy at a range of local accommodations, but the sooner you book, the better – especially June to August.

Campgrounds Not just a cheap sleep, but the best way to experience California's great outdoors by the beach, under the redwoods or nestled in desert dunes.

Hostels Budget-friendly dorm stays in key locations, including coastal parks and city centers.

B&Bs Home-style inns range from romantic vineyard cottages to historic Victorian mansions.

Motels Handy for road-trippers and less expensive than hotels; some have swimming pools.

Hotels & Resorts Upscale options come with prime locations, views and deluxe amenities.

Amenities

○ Budget accommodations include campgrounds, hos-tels and motels. Midrange properties generally offer better value for money.

○ Facilities in hostels typi-cally include dorms, semi-

private rooms with shared bathrooms, communal kitchens, lockers, internet access, coin-op laundry and TV lounges.

○ At midrange motels and hotels, expect clean, com-fortable and decent-sized rooms with at least a private bathroom, and standard amenities such as cable TV, direct-dial telephone, a coffee maker, and perhaps a microwave and mini-fridge.

○ Top-end lodgings offer top-notch amenities and perhaps a scenic location, high design, historical ambience, pools, fitness rooms, business centers, full-service restaurants and bars and other convenient facilities.

○ In Southern California, nearly all lodgings have air-conditioning, but in perpetually cool Northern California, most don't. In coastal areas as far south as Santa Barbara, only fans may be provided.

○ Accommodations offering online computer terminals for guests are designated with the internet icon. A fee may apply, including at full-service hotel business centers. Rarely, there may be a fee for wireless internet or in-room access. Look for free wi-fi hot spots in hotel public areas such as the lobby or poolside.

○ Many lodgings are now exclusively nonsmoking. Where they still exist, smoking rooms are often left unrenovated and in less desirable locations. Expect a hefty 'cleaning fee' ($100 or more) if you light up in designated nonsmoking rooms.

o Hotel parking fees can add up quickly, especially in big cities and at resorts.

Rates & Reservations

o Generally midweek rates are lower, except at urban hotels geared toward business travelers. Hotels in Silicon Valley, downtown San Francisco, LA and San Diego may lure leisure travelers with weekend deals.

o Hotel rooms are often priced by the size and number of beds, rather than the number of occupants. A room with one double or queen-size bed usually costs the same for one or two people, while a room with a king-size bed or two double beds costs more.

o Discount membership cards, such as American Automobile Association (AAA) and AARP, may get you about 10% off standard rates at participating hotels and motels.

o Look for freebie-ad magazines packed with hotel and motel discount coupons at gas stations, highway rest areas, tourist offices and online at HotelCoupons (www. hotelcoupons.com).

o High season is June through August everywhere, except the deserts and mountain ski areas, where

December through April are the busiest months.

o Demand and prices spike around major holidays and for festivals, when some properties may impose multiday minimum stays.

o Reservations are recommended for weekend and holiday travel year-round, and every day during high season.

o Bargaining may be possible for walk-in guests without reservations, especially at off-peak times.

o The state park system has a variety of campgrounds. To reserve, check out www. reservecalifornia.com.

Customs Regulations

Currently, non-US citizens and permanent residents may import:

o 1L of alcohol (if you're over 21 years of age)

o 200 cigarettes (one carton) or 100 cigars (if you're over 18 years)

o $100 worth of gifts Amounts higher than $10,000 in cash, traveler's checks, money orders and other cash equivalents must be declared. Don't even think about bringing in illegal drugs.

For more complete, up-to-date information, check the website of **US Customs and Border Protection** (www.cbp.gov).

Electricity

120V/60Hz

Food

o Lunch is generally served between 11:30am and 2:30pm, and dinner between 5pm and 9pm daily, though some restaurants stay open later, especially on Friday and Saturday nights.

o If breakfast is served, it's usually between 7:30am and 11am. Some diners and cafes keep serving breakfast into the afternoon, or all day. Weekend brunch is a laid-back meal, usually available from 11am until 3pm on Saturdays and Sundays.

Eating Price Ranges

The following price ranges refer to an average main course at dinner, unless otherwise stated. These prices don't include taxes or tip, which together can tack another 25% to 30% onto your bill. Note the same dishes at lunch will usually be cheaper.

$ less than $15
$$ $15–25
$$$ more than $25

---

o Californian restaurant etiquette tends to be informal. Only a handful of restaurants require more than a dressy shirt, slacks and shoes that aren't flip-flops. At other places, T-shirts, shorts and sandals are fine.

o Tipping 18% to 20% is expected anywhere you receive table service.

o Smoking is illegal indoors. Some restaurants have patios or sidewalk tables where smoking is tolerated (ask first, or look around for ashtrays), but don't expect your neighbors to be happy about secondhand smoke.

o You can bring your own wine to most restaurants; a 'corkage' fee of $15 to $30 usually applies. Lunches rarely include booze, though a glass of wine or beer is socially acceptable.

o If you ask the kitchen to divide a plate between two (or more) people, there may be a small split-plate surcharge.

o Vegetarians, vegans and travelers with food allergies or dietary restrictions are in luck – many restaurants are used to catering to specific dietary needs.

LGBTIQ+ Travelers

California is a magnet for LGBTIQ+ travelers. Hot spots include the Castro in San Francisco, West Hollywood (WeHo), Silver Lake, Long Beach and Downtown in LA, San Diego's Hillcrest neighborhood, the desert resort of Palm Springs, Guerneville in the Russian River Valley and Calistoga in Napa Valley.

Same-sex marriage is legal in California. Despite widespread tolerance, homophobic bigotry still exists. In small towns, especially away from the coast, tolerance often comes down to a 'don't ask, don't tell' policy.

Helpful Resources

Advocate (www.advocate.com/travel) Online news, gay travel features and destination guides.

Damron (www.damron.com) Classic, advertiser-driven gay travel guides and 'Gay Scout' mobile app.

LGBT National Hotline (☎888-843-4564; www.glbthotline.org) For counseling and referrals of any kind.

Misterb&b (www.misterbandb.com) Online booking site for accommodations friendly to LGBT+ travelers.

Out Traveler (www.outtraveler.com) Free online magazine articles with travel tips, destination guides and hotel reviews.

Health

Health Care & Insurance

o Medical treatment in the USA is of the highest caliber, but the expense could kill you. Many health-care professionals demand payment at the time of service, especially from out-of-towners or international visitors.

o Except for medical emergencies (in which case call 911 or go to the nearest 24-hour hospital emergency room, or ER), phone around to find a doctor who will accept your insurance.

o Keep all medical receipts and documentation for billing and insurance claims and reimbursement later.

o Some health-insurance policies require you to get pre-authorization over the phone for medical treatment before seeking help.

o Overseas visitors with travel-health-insurance policies may need to contact a call center for an assessment by phone before getting medical treatment.

Insurance

Getting travel insurance to cover theft, loss and medical problems is highly recommended. Some policies do not cover 'risky' activities such as scuba diving, motorcycling and skiing, so read the fine print. Make sure the policy at least covers hospital stays and an emergency flight home.

Paying for your airline ticket or rental car with a credit card may provide limited travel accident insurance. If you already have private health insurance or a homeowner's or renter's policy, find out what those policies cover and only get supplemental insurance. If you have prepaid a large portion of your vacation, trip-cancellation insurance may be a worthwhile expense.

Travel insurance is available at www.lonelyplanet. com/travel-insurance. Buy, extend and claim online anytime – even if you're already on the road.

Internet Access

● With branches in major cities and towns, **FedEx** (☏800-463-3339; www.fedex. com/us/office) offers internet access at self-service computer workstations (30¢ to 40¢ per minute) and sometimes free wi-fi.

● Free wi-fi hot spots can almost always be found at major airports, malls, hotels, motels and coffee shops (eg Starbucks) and some tourist information centers, campgrounds (eg KOA), stores (eg Apple), bars and restaurants.

● Free public wi-fi is proliferating and even some of California's state parks are now wi-fi-enabled (get details at www.parks.ca.gov).

Legal Matters

Drugs & Alcohol

● Possession of up to 1oz of marijuana (if you are 21 years or older) for recreational use is no longer a crime in California, but it is still illegal to use marijuana in public (subject to fines of up to $500, as well as mandatory community-service hours and drug-education classes).

● Possession of any other drug or more than 1oz of marijuana is a felony punishable by lengthy jail time. For foreigners, conviction of any drug offense is grounds for deportation.

● Police can give roadside sobriety checks to assess if you've been drinking or using drugs. If you fail, they'll require you to take a breath, urine or blood test to determine if your blood alcohol is over the legal limit (0.08%). Refusing to be tested is treated the same

as if you had taken and failed the test.

● Penalties for driving under the influence (DUI) of drugs or alcohol range from license suspension and fines to jail time.

● It's illegal to carry open containers of alcohol or marijuana inside a vehicle, even if they're empty. Unless they're full and still sealed, store them in the trunk.

● Consuming alcohol anywhere other than at a private residence or licensed premises is a no-no, which puts most parks and beaches off-limits (although many campgrounds legally allow it).

● Bars, clubs and liquor stores often ask for photo ID to prove you are of legal drinking age (21 years). Being 'carded' is standard practice, so don't take it personally.

Police & Security

● For police, fire and ambulance emergencies, dial 911. For nonemergency police assistance, contact the nearest local police station (dial 411 for directory assistance).

● If you are stopped by the police, be courteous. Don't get out of the car unless asked. Keep your hands where the officer can see them (eg on the steering wheel) at all times.

● There is no system of paying fines on the spot.

Attempting to pay the fine to the officer may lead to a charge of attempted bribery.

● For traffic violations, the ticketing officer will explain your options. There is usually a 30-day period to pay a fine; most matters can be handled by mail or online.

● If you are arrested, you have the right to remain silent and are presumed innocent until proven guilty. Everyone has the right to make one phone call. If you don't have a lawyer, one will be appointed to you free of charge. Foreign travelers who don't have a lawyer, friends or family to help should call their embassy or consulate; the police can provide the number upon request.

● Due to security concerns about terrorism, never leave your bags unattended, especially at airports or bus and train stations.

Money

ATMs

● ATMs are available 24/7 at most banks, shopping malls, airports and grocery and convenience stores.

● Expect a minimum surcharge of around $3 per transaction, in addition to any fees charged by your home bank.

● Most ATMs are connected to international networks and offer decent foreign-exchange rates.

● Withdrawing cash from an ATM using a credit card usually incurs a hefty fee and high interest rates; contact your credit-card company for details and a PIN number.

Cash

Most people don't carry large amounts of cash for everyday use, relying instead on credit and debit cards. Some businesses refuse to accept bills over $20.

Credit Cards

● Major credit cards are almost universally accepted. In fact, it's almost impossible to rent a car, book a hotel room or buy tickets over the phone without one. A credit card may also be vital in emergencies.

● Visa, MasterCard and American Express are the most widely accepted credit cards.

Moneychangers

● Exchange money at major airports, bigger banks and currency-exchange offices such as American Express (www.americanexpress.com) or Travelex (www.travelex.com). Always enquire about rates and fees.

● Outside big cities, exchanging money may be a problem, so make sure you have a credit card and sufficient cash on hand.

Taxes

● California state sales tax (7.25%) is added to the

Tipping

Tipping is not optional. Only withhold tips in cases of outrageously bad service.

Airport skycaps & hotel bellhops $2 or $3 per bag, minimum $5 per cart.

Bartenders 15% to 20% per round, minimum $1 per drink.

Concierges Nothing for simple information, up to $20 for securing last-minute restaurant reservations, sold-out show tickets etc.

Housekeeping staff $2 to $4 daily, left under the card provided; more if you're messy.

Parking valets At least $2 when handed back your car keys.

Restaurant servers & room service 18% to 20%, unless a gratuity is already charged (common for groups of six or more).

Taxi drivers 10% to 15% of metered fare, rounded up to the next dollar.

retail price of most goods and services (groceries are exceptions). Local and city sales taxes may tack on up to 3%.

○ Gasoline is heavily and increasingly taxed in California; in January 2020 drivers were paying 79¢ on the gallon.

○ Tourist lodging taxes vary statewide, but average 10.5% to 14% in major cities.

○ No refunds of sales or lodging taxes are available for visitors.

Practicalities

Newspapers *Los Angeles Times* (www.latimes.com), *San Francisco Chronicle* (www.sfchronicle.com), *Mercury News* (www.mercurynews.com), *Sacramento Bee* (www.sacbee.com).

Radio National Public Radio (NPR), lower end of FM dial.

Smoking Smoking is generally prohibited inside all public buildings, including airports, shopping malls and train and bus stations. In some cities and towns, smoking outdoors within a certain distance of any public business is illegal. The minimum age to legally purchase tobacco products (including e-cigarettes) in California is now 21.

TV PBS (public broadcasting); cable: CNN (news), ESPN (sports), HBO (movies), Weather Channel.

Weights & Measures Imperial (except 1 US gallon equals 0.83 imperial gallons).

Opening Hours

Businesses, restaurants and shops may close earlier and on additional days during the winter off-season (November to March). Otherwise, standard opening hours are as follows:

Banks 9:30am–4pm (some later) Monday to Friday, some 9am–noon or later Saturday

Bars 4pm–2am daily

Business hours (general) 9am–5pm Monday to Friday

Nightclubs 10pm–4am Thursday to Saturday

Post offices 8:30am–5pm Monday to Friday, some 8:30am–noon or later Saturday

Restaurants 11am–3pm and 5:30pm–10pm daily, some open later Friday and Saturday

Shops 10am–7pm Monday to Saturday, 11am–6pm Sunday (malls open later)

Supermarkets 8am–9pm or 10pm daily, some 24 hours

Public Holidays

On the following national holidays, banks, schools and government offices (including post offices) are closed, and transportation, museums and other services operate on a Sunday schedule. Holidays falling on a weekend are usually observed the following Monday.

New Year's Day January 1

Martin Luther King Jr Day Third Monday in January

Presidents' Day Third Monday in February

Cesar Chavez Day March 31

Memorial Day Last Monday in May

Independence Day July 4

Labor Day First Monday in September

Indigenous Peoples' Day Second Monday in October

Veterans Day November 11

Thanksgiving Day Fourth Thursday in November

Christmas Day December 25

Safe Travel

Despite its seemingly apocalyptic list of dangers – guns, violent crime, riots, earthquakes – California is a reasonably safe place to visit. The greatest danger is posed by car accidents (buckle up – it's the law), while the biggest annoyances are metro-area traffic and crowds. When hiking or swimming in wilderness areas, be sure to understand the route, bring proper equipment and water, and read up on dangers such as rock slides, flash floods or riptides. Wildlife can also pose a threat.

Earthquakes

Earthquakes happen all the time, but most are so tiny they are detectable only by sensitive seismological instruments. If you're caught in a serious shaker, take precautions:

○ If indoors, get under a desk or table or stand in a doorway.

○ Protect your head and stay clear of windows, mirrors or anything that might fall.

○ Don't head for elevators or go running into the street.

○ If you're in a shopping mall or large public building, expect the alarm and/or sprinkler systems to come on.

○ If outdoors, get away from buildings, trees and power lines.

○ If you're driving, pull over to the side of the road away from bridges, overpasses and power lines. Stay inside the car until the shaking stops.

○ If you're on a sidewalk near buildings, duck into a doorway to protect yourself from falling bricks, glass and debris.

○ Prepare for aftershocks.

○ Turn on the radio and listen for bulletins.

○ Use the telephone only if absolutely necessary.

Wildlife

○ Never feed or approach any wild animal, not even harmless-looking critters – it causes them to lose their innate fear of humans, which in turn makes them dangerously aggressive. Many birds and mammals, including deer and rodents such as squirrels, carry serious diseases that can be transmitted to humans through a bite.

○ Disturbing or harassing specially protected species, including many marine mammals such as whales, dolphins and seals, is a crime, subject to enormous fines.

○ Black bears are often attracted to campgrounds, where they may find food, trash and any other scented items left out on picnic tables or stashed in tents and cars. Always use bear-proof containers where they are provided. For more bear-country travel tips, visit the SierraWild website (http://sierrawild.gov/bears).

○ If you encounter a black bear in the wild, don't run. Stay together, keeping small children next to you and picking up little ones. Keep back at least 100yd. If the bear starts moving toward you, back away slowly off-trail and let it pass by, being careful not to block any of the bear's escape routes or get caught between a mother and her cubs. Sometimes a black bear will 'bluff charge' to test your dominance. Stand your ground by making yourself look as big as possible (eg waving your arms above your head) and shouting menacingly.

○ Mountain lion attacks on humans are rare, but can be deadly. If you encounter a mountain lion, stay calm, pick up small children, face the animal and retreat slowly. Make yourself appear larger by raising your arms or grabbing a stick. If the lion becomes menacing, shout or throw rocks at it. If attacked, fight back aggressively.

○ Snakes and spiders are common throughout California, not just in wilderness areas. Always look inside your shoes before putting them back on outdoors, especially when camping. Snake bites are rare, but occur most often when a snake is stepped on or provoked (eg picked up or poked with a stick). Antivenom is available at most hospitals.

Telephone

Cell Phones

○ You'll need a multiband GSM phone to make calls in the USA. Popping in a US prepaid rechargeable SIM card is usually cheaper than using your network.

○ SIM cards are sold at telecommunications and electronics stores. These stores also sell inexpensive prepaid phones, including some data.

o You can rent a cell phone at San Francisco (SFO) International Airport from **TripTel** (www.triptel.com); pricing plans vary, but typically are expensive.

Dialing Codes

o US phone numbers consist of a three-digit area code followed by a seven-digit local number.

o When dialing a number within the same area code, use the seven-digit number (if that doesn't work, try all 10 digits).

o For long-distance calls, dial 1 plus the area code plus the local number.

o Toll-free numbers (eg beginning with 800, 855, 866, 877 or 888) must be preceded by 1.

o For direct international calls, dial 011 plus the country code plus the area code (usually without the initial '0') plus the local phone number.

o If you're calling from abroad, the country code for the US is 1 (the same as Canada, but international rates apply between the two countries).

Payphones & Phonecards

o Where payphones still exist, they're usually coin-operated, though some may only accept credit cards (eg in state or national parks). Local calls cost 50¢ minimum.

o For long-distance and international calls, prepaid phonecards are sold at convenience stores, supermarkets, newsstands and electronics and convenience stores.

Tourist Information

o For pre-trip planning, peruse the information-packed website **Visit California** (www.visitcalifornia.com).

o The same government agency operates more than a dozen statewide **California Welcome Centers** (www.visitcwc.com), where staff dispense maps and brochures and may be able to help find accommodations.

o Almost every city and town has a local visitor center or a chamber of commerce where you can pick up maps, brochures and information.

Visas

o Visa information is highly subject to change. Depending on your country of origin, the rules for entering the USA keep changing. Double-check current visa requirements *before* coming to the USA.

o Currently, under the US Visa Waiver Program (VWP), visas are not required for citizens of 39 countries for stays up to 90 days (no extensions) as long as you have a machine-readable passport that meets current US standards and is valid for six months beyond your intended stay.

o Citizens of VWP countries must still register with the **Electronic System for Travel Authorization** (ESTA; https://esta.cbp.dhs.gov) at least 72 hours before travel. Once approved, ESTA registration ($14) is valid for up to two years or until your passport expires, whichever comes first.

o For most Canadian citizens traveling with Canadian passports that meet current US standards, a visa for short-term visits (usually up to six months) and ESTA registration aren't required.

o Citizens from all other countries, or whose passports don't meet US standards, need to apply for a visa in their home country. The process has a nonrefundable fee (minimum $160), involves a personal interview and can take several weeks, so apply as early as possible.

o For up-to-date information about entry requirements and eligibility, check the visa section on the website of the **US Department of State** (http://travel.state.gov), or contact the nearest USA embassy or consulate in your home country (for a complete list, visit www.usembassy.gov).

● For information about Covid-19 travel restrictions, visit the website of the **Centers for Disease Control and Prevention** (www.cdc.gov).

Transport

Getting There & Away

Getting to California by air or overland by car, train or bus is easy, although it's not always cheap. Flights, cars and tours can be booked online at www.lonelyplanet.com/bookings.

Entering the Region

Under the US Department of Homeland Security's Orwellian-sounding Office of Biometric Identity Management, almost all foreign visitors to the USA (excluding, for now, many Canadians, some Mexican citizens, children under the age of 14 and seniors over the age of 79) will be digitally photographed and have their electronic (inkless) fingerprints scanned upon arrival.

At the time of writing, Covid-19 travel restrictions prevented the entry of foreign nationals who had in the last 14 days spent time in China, Iran, the UK, Ireland, Brazil and many countries in Europe. For updates, visit the website of the **Centers for Disease Control and Prevention** (www.cdc.gov).

Air

● To get through airport security checkpoints (30- to 45-minute wait times are standard), you'll need a boarding pass and photo ID.

● Some travelers may be required to undergo a secondary screening, involving hand pat downs and carry-on-bag searches.

● Airport security measures restrict many common items (eg pocket knives, scissors) from being carried on planes. Check current restrictions with the **Transportation Security Administration** (TSA; www.tsa.gov).

● Currently TSA requires that all carry-on liquids and gels be stored in 3.4oz or smaller bottles placed inside a quart-sized clear plastic zip-top bag. Exceptions, which must be declared to checkpoint security officers, include medications.

● All checked luggage is screened for explosives. TSA may open your suitcase for visual confirmation, breaking the lock if necessary. Leave your bags unlocked or use a TSA-approved lock.

Airports

California's major international airports are **Los Angeles International Airport** (LAX; Map p191; www.flylax.com; 1 World Way) and **San Diego International Airport** (SAN; Map p251; 619-400-2400; www.san.org; 3325 N Harbor Dr;) in Southern California and **San Francisco International Airport** (SFO; www.flysfo.com; S McDonnell Rd), **Oakland International Airport** (OAK; 510-563-3300; www.oaklandairport.com; 1 Airport Dr; ; Oakland International Airport) and **Sacramento International Airport** (SMF; 916-929-5411; www.sacramento.aero/smf; 6900 Airport Blvd) in Northern California. Smaller regional airports throughout the state are mainly served by domestic US airlines. Many domestic and international air carriers offer direct flights to and from California.

Land

Bus

Greyhound (800-231-2222; www.greyhound.com) is the major long-distance bus company, with routes throughout the USA, including to/from California. Routes trace major highways and may stop only at larger population centers, with services to many small towns having been cut. **FlixBus** (https://global.flixbus.com/bus/united-states) is a new competitor offering service between California and Nevada, Arizona and Utah.

Train

Amtrak (800-872-7245; www.amtrak.com) operates a fairly extensive rail system throughout the USA. Trains are comfortable, if a bit slow, and are equipped with dining and lounge cars and sometimes wi-fi on long-distance routes. Fares vary according to the type of train and seating (eg coach or business class, sleeping compartments).

Amtrak's major long-distance services to/from California:

California Zephyr Daily service between Chicago and Emeryville (from $176, 52 hours), near San Francisco, via Denver, Salt Lake City, Reno, Truckee and Sacramento.

Coast Starlight Travels the West Coast daily from Seattle to LA (from $141, 35 hours) via Portland, Sacramento, Oakland, San Jose, San Luis Obispo and Santa Barbara.

Southwest Chief Daily departures from Chicago and LA (from $118, 43 hours) via Kansas City, Albuquerque, Flagstaff and Barstow.

Sunset Limited Thrice-weekly service between New Orleans and LA (from $136, 48 hours) via Houston, San Antonio, El Paso, Tucson and Palm Springs.

Getting Around

Most people drive themselves around California. You can also fly (it's expensive) or take cheaper long-distance buses or scenic trains. In cities, when distances are too far to walk, hop aboard buses, trains, streetcars, cable cars or trolleys, or grab a taxi or rideshare.

Air

Several major US carriers fly within California. Flights are often operated by their regional subsidiaries, such as American Eagle, Delta Connection and United Express. Alaska Airlines/Virgin America, Frontier Airlines, Horizon Air and JetBlue serve many regional airports, as do low-cost airlines Southwest and Spirit.

Bicycle

Although cycling around California is a nonpolluting 'green' way to travel, the distances involved demand a high level of fitness and make it hard to cover much ground. Avoid the deserts in summer and the mountains in winter.

California Bicycle Coalition (http://calbike.org) links to cycling route maps, events, safety tips, laws, bike-sharing programs and community nonprofit bicycle shops.

Rental

o You can rent bikes by the hour, day or week in most cities and tourist towns.

o Rentals start at around $10 per day for beach cruisers, and up to $45 or more for mountain bikes; ask about multiday and weekly discounts.

o Most rental companies require a large security deposit using a credit card.

Road Rules

o Cycling is allowed on all roads and highways – even along freeways if there's no suitable alternative, such as a smaller parallel frontage road; all mandatory exits are marked.

o Some cities have designated bicycle lanes, but make sure you have your wits about you in traffic.

o Cyclists must follow the same rules of the road as vehicles. Don't expect drivers

Climate Change & Travel

Every form of transport that relies on carbon-based fuel generates CO_2, the main cause of human-induced climate change. Modern travel is dependent on airplanes, which might use less fuel per mile per person than most cars but travel much greater distances. The altitude at which aircraft emit gases (including CO_2) and particles also contributes to their climate change impact. Many websites offer 'carbon calculators' that allow people to estimate the carbon emissions generated by their journey and, for those who wish to do so, to offset the impact of the greenhouse gases emitted with contributions to portfolios of climate-friendly initiatives throughout the world. Lonely Planet offsets the carbon footprint of all staff and author travel.

to always respect your right of way.

● Wearing a bicycle helmet is mandatory for riders under 18 years of age.

● Ensure you have proper lights and reflective gear, especially if you're pedaling at night or in fog.

Bus

Buses are an economical way to travel between major cities and points along the coast, but won't get you off the beaten path or to national parks. Frequency varies, but main routes have service several times daily. **Greyhound** (☑800-231-2222; www.greyhound.com) and new competitor **FlixBus** (https://global.flixbus.com/bus/united-states) offer services between numerous cities in California.

Buses are usually clean, comfortable and reliable. The best seats are near the front, away from the bathroom. Limited on-board amenities include freezing air-con (bring a sweater) and slightly reclining seats; select buses have electrical outlets and wi-fi. Long-distance buses stop for meal breaks and driver changes.

Bus stations are typically dreary places, often in dodgy areas. If you arrive at night, take a taxi into town or directly to your lodgings. In small towns where there's no station, know exactly where and when the bus arrives, be obvious as you flag

it down, and pay the driver with exact change.

Car, Motorcycle & Recreational Vehicle

California's love affair with cars runs deep for at least one practical reason: the state is so big, public transportation can't cover it. For flexibility and convenience, you'll probably want a car, but rental rates and gas prices can eat up a good chunk of your trip budget.

Driver's Licenses

● Visitors may legally drive a car in California for up to 12 months with their home driver's license.

● If you're from overseas, an International Driving Permit (IDP) will have more credibility with traffic police and simplify the car-rental process, especially if your license doesn't have a photo or isn't written in English.

● To ride a motorcycle, you'll need a valid US state motorcycle license, or a specially endorsed IDP.

● International automobile associations can issue IDPs, valid for one year, for a fee. Always carry your home license together with the IDP.

Fuel

● Gas stations in California, nearly all of which are self-service, are ubiquitous, except in national and state parks and some sparsely populated desert and mountain areas.

● Gas is sold in gallons (one US gallon equals 3.78L). At the time of writing, the average cost for mid-grade fuel was around $2.80 a gallon.

Insurance

California law requires liability insurance for all vehicles. When renting a car, check your auto-insurance policy from home or your travel insurance policy to see if you're already covered. If not, expect to pay about $10 to $20 per day.

Insurance against damage to the car itself, called Collision Damage Waiver (CDW) or Loss Damage Waiver (LDW), costs another $10 to $20 or more per day. The deductible may require you to pay the first $100 to $500 for any repairs.

Some credit cards cover CDW/LDW, provided you charge the entire cost of the car rental to the card. Check with your credit-card issuer first to determine the extent of coverage and policy exclusions. If there's an accident you may have to pay the rental-car company first, then seek reimbursement from the credit-card company.

Parking

● Parking is usually plentiful and free in small towns and rural areas, but often scarce and/or expensive in cities.

● When parking on the street, read all posted regulations and restrictions (eg street-cleaning hours, permit-only residential areas) and pay attention to colored curbs, or you may be ticketed and towed.

○ You can pay municipal parking meters and sidewalk pay stations with coins (eg quarters) and sometimes credit or debit cards.

○ Expect to pay $30 to $50 for overnight parking in a city lot or garage.

○ Flat-fee valet parking at hotels, restaurants, nightclubs etc is common in major cities, especially Los Angeles and Las Vegas, NV (don't forget to tip).

Rental

Cars

To rent your own wheels, you'll typically need to be at least 25 years old, hold a valid driver's license and have a major credit card, not a check or debit card. A few companies may rent to drivers under 25 years, but over 21 for a hefty surcharge. If you don't have a credit card, large cash deposits are infrequently accepted.

With advance reservations, you can often get an economy-size vehicle with unlimited mileage from around $30 per day, plus insurance, taxes and fees. Weekend and weekly rates are usually the most economical. Airport locations may have cheaper rates, but higher add-on fees; if you get a fly-drive package, local taxes may be extra when you pick up the car. City-center branches some-

times offer free pickups and drop-offs.

Rates generally include unlimited mileage, but expect surcharges for additional drivers and one-way rentals. Child or infant safety seats are legally required; reserve them when booking for $10 to $15 per day.

If you'd like to minimize your carbon footprint, some major car-rental companies offer 'green' fleets of hybrid or biofueled rental cars, but these fuel-efficient models are in short supply. Reserve them well in advance and expect to pay significantly higher rates.

All of the major car-rental companies are represented in California.

Motorcycles

Motorcycle rentals and insurance are not cheap, especially if you've got your eye on a Harley. Depending on the model, renting a motorcycle costs $100 to $250 per day plus taxes and fees, including helmets, unlimited miles and liability insurance; one-way rentals and collision insurance (CDW) cost extra. Discounts may be available for multiday and weekly rentals. Security deposits can be up to $2000 (credit card required).

Dubbelju (☏ 415-495-2774, 866-495-2774; www.dubbelju. com; 274 Shotwell St; per day from $99; ☺ 9am-6pm Mon-Sat) San Francisco–based; rents Harley-Davidson, Japanese and European imported motorcycles, as well as scooters.

Eagle Rider (☏ 310-321-3180, 888-900-9901; www.eaglerider. com) Nationwide company with 11 locations in California, as well as Las Vegas, NV.

Recreational Vehicles

Gas-guzzling recreational vehicles (RVs) remain popular despite fuel prices and being cumbersome to drive. That said, they do solve transportation, accommodations and cooking needs in one fell swoop. It's easy to find RV campgrounds with electricity and water hookups, yet there are many places in national and state parks and in the mountains they can't go. In cities RVs are a nuisance, because there are few places to park or plug them in.

Book RVs as far in advance as possible. Rental costs vary by size and model, but you can expect to pay more than $100 per day. Rates often don't include mileage, bedding or kitchen kits, vehicle-prep fees or taxes. If pets are allowed, a surcharge may apply.

Cruise America (☏ 800-671-8042, 480-464-7300; www. cruiseamerica.com) Nationwide RV-rental company with two dozen locations statewide.

El Monte (☏ 888-337-2214; www.elmonterv.com) With 11 locations in California, this national RV-rental agency offers AAA discounts.

Escape Campervans (☏ 877-270-8267, 310-672-9909; www.escapecampervans.com) Awesomely painted campervans at economical rates in the

San Francisco Bay Area, LA and Las Vegas.

Jucy Rentals (☏800-650-4180; www.jucyusa.com) Campervan rentals in the San Francisco Bay Area, LA and Las Vegas.

Road Bear (☏818-865-2925, 866-491-9853; www.roadbearrv.com) RV rentals in the San Francisco Bay Area and LA.

Vintage Surfari Wagons (☏714-585-7565; www.vwsurfari.com) VW campervan rentals in Orange County.

Road Conditions & Hazards

For up-to-date highway conditions, including road closures and construction updates, check with the **California Department of Transportation** (CalTrans; ☏800-427-7623; www.dot.ca.gov). For Nevada highways, call 877-687-6237 or check www.nvroads.com.

In places where winter driving is an issue, snow tires and tire chains may be required in mountain areas. Ideally carry your own chains and learn how to use them before you hit the road. Otherwise, chains can usually be bought or rented (but not cheaply) on the highway, at gas stations or in the nearest town. Most car-rental companies don't permit the use of chains and also prohibit driving off-road or on dirt roads.

In rural areas, livestock sometimes graze next to unfenced roads. These areas are typically signed as 'Open Range,' with the silhouette of a steer. Where deer and other wild animals frequently appear roadside, you'll see signs with the silhouette of a leaping deer. Take these signs seriously, particularly at night.

In coastal areas thick fog may impede driving – slow down and if it's too soupy, get off the road. Along coastal cliffs and in the mountains, watch out for falling rocks, mudslides and avalanches that could damage or disable your car if struck.

Road Rules

● Drive on the right-hand side of the road.

● Talking, texting or otherwise using a cell (mobile) phone or other mobile electronic device without hands-free technology while driving is illegal.

● The driver and all passengers must use seat belts in a private vehicle. In a taxi or limo, back-seat passengers are not required to buckle up.

● Infant and child safety seats are required for children under eight years of age, or who are less than 4ft 9in tall.

● All motorcyclists must wear a helmet. Scooters are not allowed on freeways.

● High-occupancy vehicle (HOV) lanes marked with a diamond symbol are reserved for cars with multiple occupants, sometimes only during signposted hours.

● Unless otherwise posted, the speed limit is 65mph on freeways, 55mph on two-lane undivided highways, 35mph on major city streets and 25mph in business and residential districts and near schools.

● Except where indicated, turning right at a red stoplight after coming to a full stop is permitted, although intersecting traffic still has the right of way.

● At four-way stop signs, cars proceed in the order in which they arrived. If two cars arrive simultaneously, the one on the right has the right of way. When in doubt, politely wave the other driver ahead.

● When emergency vehicles (ie police, fire or ambulance) approach from either direction, carefully pull over to the side of the road.

● California has strict anti-littering laws; throwing trash from a vehicle may incur a $1000 fine.

● Driving under the influence of alcohol or drugs is illegal. It's also illegal to carry open containers of alcohol or marijuana, even empty ones, inside a vehicle. Store them in the trunk.

Local Transportation

Except in cities, public transit is rarely the most convenient option, and coverage to outlying towns and suburbs can be sparse. However, it's usually cheap, safe and reliable.

Bicycle

Cycling is a feasible way of getting around smaller cities and towns. Even in metropolitan areas like LA, bikes can be useful for getting around neighborhoods.

Bike-sharing programs are becoming more commonplace and include Breeze Bike Share on LA's Westside (eg Santa Monica, Venice, Beverly Hills), Metro Bike Share (Downtown LA, Hollywood, Koreatown) and Long Beach BikeShare.

Bicycles may be transported on many local buses and trains, sometimes during off-peak, non-commuter hours only.

Bus, Cable Car, Streetcar & Trolley

● Almost all cities and larger towns have reliable local bus systems (average $1 to $3 per ride). Outside of major metro areas, service is limited in the evening and on weekends.

● LA's Metro Rail network consists of two subway

lines, four light-rail lines and two express bus lines.

● In San Diego, municipal trolleys operate on three lines as far south as the Mexican border.

Train

To get around the San Francisco Bay Area, hop aboard Bay Area Rapid Transit (BART) or Caltrain. Sacramento, San Jose and LA also have limited light-rail systems.

Taxi

● Taxis are metered, with flag-fall fees of $2.50 to $3.50 to start, plus around $2 to $3 per mile. Credit cards may be accepted, but bring cash just in case.

● Taxis may charge extra for baggage and airport pickups.

● Drivers expect a 10% to 15% tip, rounded up to the next dollar.

● Taxis cruise the streets of the busiest areas in large cities, but elsewhere you may need to call for one.

● Ridesharing apps are generally cheaper than cabs and often provide better service. During peak times, waits can be long and rides are charged at a premium. This is especially true on Friday and Saturday nights and after major events.

Train

Amtrak (800-872-7245; www.amtrak.com) runs comfortable, if occasionally tardy, trains to major California cities and some towns. At some stations Thruway buses provide onward connections – or replace trains (read schedules carefully). Smoking is prohibited aboard trains and buses.

Behind the Scenes

Acknowledgements

Climate map data adapted from Peel MC, Finlayson BL & McMahon TA (2007) 'Updated World Map of the Köppen-Geiger Climate Classification', *Hydrology and Earth System Sciences*, 11, 1633–44.

Cover photograph: Giant sequoias, California © Larry Gerbrandt/Getty Images

Illustration pp44–45 by Michael Weldon.

This Book

This 2nd edition of Lonely Planet's *Best of California 2* guidebook was researched and written by Amy C Balfour, Brett Atkinson, Andrew Bender, Alison Bing, Cristian Bonetto, Celeste Brash, Jade Bremner, Michael Grosberg, Ashley Harrell, Mark Johanson, Andrea Schulte-Peevers and Wendy Yanagihara. The previous edition was written by Brett Atkinson, Andrew Bender, Sara Benson, Alison Bing, Cristian Bonetto, Jade Bremner, Nate Cavalieri, Michael Grosberg, Ashley Harrell, Josephine Quintero, Andrea Schulte-Peevers, Helena Smith, John A Vlahides and Clifton Wilkinson. This guidebook was produced by the following:

Senior Product Editors Dan Bolger, Grace Dobell

Regional Senior Cartographer Alison Lyall

Product Editor Sandie Kestell

Book Designer Ania Bartoszek

Assisting Editors Victoria Harrison, Anne Mulvaney, Lorna Parkes, Monique Perrin, James Smart

Cover Researcher Fergal Condon

Thanks to Karen Henderson, Genna Patterson, Angela Tinson

Send Us Your Feedback

We love to hear from travelers – your comments keep us on our toes and help make our books better. Our well-traveled team reads every word on what you loved or loathed about this book. Although we cannot reply individually to postal submissions, we always guarantee that your feedback goes straight to the appropriate authors, in time for the next edition. Each person who sends us information is thanked in the next edition, the most useful submissions are rewarded with a selection of digital PDF chapters.

Visit lonelyplanet.com/contact to submit your updates and suggestions or to ask for help. Our award-winning website also features inspirational travel stories, news and discussions.

Note: We may edit, reproduce and incorporate your comments in Lonely Planet products such as guidebooks, websites and digital products, so let us know if you don't want your comments reproduced or your name acknowledged. For a copy of our privacy policy visit lonelyplanet.com/privacy.

Index

Symbols & Map Key

Look for these symbols to quickly identify listings:

- Sights
- Activities
- Courses
- Tours
- Festivals & Events
- Eating
- Drinking
- Entertainment
- Shopping
- Information & Transport

These symbols and abbreviations give vital information for each listing:

- Sustainable or green recommendation
- FREE No payment required

- Telephone number
- Opening hours
- Parking
- Nonsmoking
- Air-conditioning
- Internet access
- Wi-fi access
- Swimming pool
- Bus
- Ferry
- Tram
- Train
- English-language menu
- Vegetarian selection
- Family-friendly

Find your best experiences with these Great For... icons.

- Art & Culture
- Beaches
- Budget
- Cafe/Coffee
- Cycling
- Detour
- Drinking
- Entertainment
- Events
- Family Travel
- Food & Drink
- History
- Local Life
- Nature & Wildlife
- Photo Op
- Scenery
- Shopping
- Short Trip
- Sport
- Walking
- Winter Travel

Sights

- Beach
- Bird Sanctuary
- Buddhist
- Castle/Palace
- Christian
- Confucian
- Hindu
- Islamic
- Jain
- Jewish
- Monument
- Museum/Gallery/ Historic Building
- Ruin
- Shinto
- Sikh
- Taoist
- Winery/Vineyard
- Zoo/Wildlife Sanctuary
- Other Sight

Points of Interest

- Bodysurfing
- Camping
- Cafe
- Canoeing/Kayaking
- Course/Tour
- Diving
- Drinking & Nightlife
- Eating
- Entertainment
- Sento Hot Baths/ Onsen
- Shopping
- Skiing
- Sleeping
- Snorkelling
- Surfing
- Swimming/Pool
- Walking
- Windsurfing
- Other Activity

Information

- Bank
- Embassy/Consulate
- Hospital/Medical
- Internet
- Police
- Post Office
- Telephone
- Toilet
- Tourist Information
- Other Information

Geographic

- Beach
- Gate
- Hut/Shelter
- Lighthouse
- Lookout
- Mountain/Volcano
- Oasis
- Park
- Pass
- Picnic Area
- Waterfall

Transport

- Airport
- BART station
- Border crossing
- Boston T station
- Bus
- Cable car/Funicular
- Cycling
- Ferry
- Metro/MRT station
- Monorail
- Parking
- Petrol station
- Subway/S-Bahn/ Skytrain station
- Taxi
- Train station/Railway
- Tram
- Underground/ U-Bahn station
- Other Transport

Cristian Bonetto

Los Angeles Cristian has contributed to more than 30 Lonely Planet guides to date, including *New York City, Italy, Venice & the Veneto, Naples & the Amalfi Coast, Denmark, Copenhagen, Sweden* and *Singapore*. Lonely Planet work aside, his musings on travel, food, culture and design appear in numerous publications around the world, including *The Telegraph* (UK) and *Corriere del Mezzogiorno* (Italy). When not on the road, you'll find the reformed playwright and TV scriptwriter slurping espresso in his beloved hometown, Melbourne. Instagram: @ rexcat75.

Celeste Brash

Family Travel Like many California natives, Celeste now lives in Portland, Oregon. She arrived, however, after 15 years in French Polynesia, a year and a half in Southeast Asia and a stint teaching English as a second language (in an American accent) in Brighton, England – among other things. She's been writing guidebooks for Lonely Planet since 2005 and her travel articles have appeared in publications from *BBC Travel* to *National Geographic*. She's currently writing a book about her five years on a remote pearl farm in the Tuamotu Atolls and is represented by the Donald Maass Agency, New York.

Jade Bremner

San Diego Jade has been a journalist for more than 15 years. She has lived in and reported on four different regions. It's no coincidence many of her favourite places have some of the best waves in the world. Jade has edited travel magazines and sections for *Time Out* and *Radio Times* and has contributed to *The Times, CNN* and *The Independent*. She feels privileged to share tales from this wonderful planet we call home and is always looking for the next adventure. @jadebremner

Michael Grosberg

Yosemite National Park Michael has worked on over 50 Lonely Planet guidebooks. Other international work included development on Rota in the western Pacific; South Africa where he investigated and wrote about political violence and trained newly elected government representatives; and Quito, Ecuador to teach. He received a Masters in Comparative Literature and taught literature and writing as an adjunct professor.

Ashley Harrell

Survival Guide After a brief stint selling day spa coupons door-to-door in South Florida, Ashley decided she'd rather be a writer. She went to journalism grad school, convinced a newspaper to hire her, and starting covering wildlife, crime and tourism, sometimes all in the same story. Fueling her zest for storytelling and the unknown, she traveled widely and moved often, from a tiny NYC apartment to a vast California ranch to a jungle cabin in Costa Rica, where she started writing for Lonely Planet. From there her travels became more exotic and farther flung, and she still laughs when paychecks arrive.

Mark Johanson

Redwood Forests Mark Johanson grew up in Virginia and has called five different countries home over the last decade while circling the globe reporting for British newspapers (*The Guardian*), American magazines (*Men's Journal*) and global media outlets (*CNN, BBC*). When not on the road, you'll find him gazing at the Andes from his current home in Santiago, Chile. Follow the adventures at www.markjohanson.com.

Andrea Schulte-Peevers

Palm Springs Born and raised in Germany and educated in London and at UCLA, Andrea has travelled the distance to the moon and back in her visits to some 75 countries. She has earned her living as a professional travel writer for over two decades and authored or contributed to nearly 100 Lonely Planet titles as well as to newspapers, magazines and websites around the world. She also works as a travel consultant, translator and editor. She makes her home in Berlin.

Wendy Yanagihara

Santa Barbara Wendy serendipitously landed her dream job of writing for Lonely Planet in 2003 and has spent the intervening years contributing to titles including *Vietnam, Japan, Mexico, Costa Rica, Cuba, Ecuador, Indonesia,* and *Grand Canyon National Park*. In the name of research, she has explored remote valleys of West Papua, explored tiny alleys of Tokyo sprawl, and hiked the Grand Canyon from rim to rim. For work and pleasure, she has traveled six continents and lived in three, Antarctica being the exception to date. Top experiences include gorilla tracking in Uganda, rafting the Nile, spotting pink river dolphins in the Amazon, trekking on a Patagonian glacier, and closer to home in southern California, stand-up paddleboarding with common dolphins. She hopes that writing for LP encourages travelers to connect with indigenous people, cultures, wildlife, and the environment at large to motivate conservation of such rich diversity in the world.

Our Story

A beat-up old car, a few dollars in the pocket and a sense of adventure. In 1972 that's all Tony and Maureen Wheeler needed for the trip of a lifetime – across Europe and Asia overland to Australia. It took several months, and at the end – broke but inspired – they sat at their kitchen table writing and stapling together their first travel guide, *Across Asia on the Cheap*. Within a week they'd sold 1500 copies. Lonely Planet was born.

Today, Lonely Planet has offices in Tennessee, Dublin, Beijing and Delhi, with a network of over 2000 contributors in every corner of the globe. We share Tony's belief that 'a great guidebook should do three things: inform, educate and amuse'.

Our Writers

Amy C Balfour

Curator Amy practiced law in Virginia before moving to Los Angeles to try to break in as a screenwriter. If you listen carefully, you can still hear the horrified screams of her parents echoing through the space-time continuum. After a stint as a writer's assistant on *Law & Order*, she jumped into freelance writing, focusing on travel, food, and the outdoors.

Brett Atkinson

Big Sur Brett Atkinson is based in Auckland, New Zealand, but is frequently on the road for Lonely Planet. He's a full-time travel and food writer specialising in adventure travel, unusual destinations, and surprising angles on more well-known destinations. Craft beer and street food are Brett's favourite reasons to explore places, and he is featured regularly on the Lonely Planet website, and in newspapers, magazines and websites across New Zealand and Australia. Since becoming a Lonely Planet author in 2005, Brett has covered areas as diverse as Vietnam, Sri Lanka, the Czech Republic, New Zealand, Morocco, California and the South Pacific.

Andrew Bender

Orange County Award-winning travel and food writer Andrew Bender has written three dozen Lonely Planet guidebooks (from *Amsterdam* to *Los Angeles*, *Germany* to *Taiwan* and more than a dozen titles about Japan), plus numerous articles for lonelyplanet.com.

Alison Bing

Sonoma Valley; San Francisco Over 10 guidebooks and 20 years in San Francisco, Alison has spent more time on Alcatraz than some inmates, become an aficionado of drag and burritos, and willfully ignored Muni signs warning that safety requires avoiding unnecessary conversation.

→ More Writers →

STAY IN TOUCH LONELYPLANET.COM/CONTACT

IRELAND Digital Depot, Roe Lane (off Thomas St), Digital Hub, Dublin 8, D08 TCV4, Ireland

USA 230 Franklin Road, Building 2B, Franklin, TN 37064
📞 615 988 9713

 twitter.com/
lonelyplanet

 facebook.com/
lonelyplanet

 instagram.com/
lonelyplanet

 youtube.com/
lonelyplanet

 lonelyplanet.com/
newsletter